What's Good for Business

What's Good for Business

Business and American Politics since World War II

EDITED BY KIM PHILLIPS-FEIN

and

JULIAN E. ZELIZER

For Ira,

With Best Wishes,

OXFORD
UNIVERSITY PRESS

OXFORD
UNIVERSITY PRESS

Oxford University Press, Inc., publishes works that further
Oxford University's objective of excellence
in research, scholarship, and education.

Oxford   New York
Auckland   Cape Town   Dar es Salaam   Hong Kong   Karachi
Kuala Lumpur   Madrid   Melbourne   Mexico City   Nairobi
New Delhi   Shanghai   Taipei   Toronto

With offices in
Argentina   Austria   Brazil   Chile   Czech Republic   France   Greece
Guatemala   Hungary   Italy   Japan   Poland   Portugal   Singapore
South Korea   Switzerland   Thailand   Turkey   Ukraine   Vietnam

Published by Oxford University Press, Inc.
198 Madison Avenue, New York, New York 10016

www.oup.com

Oxford is a registered trademark of Oxford University Press

Library of Congress Cataloging-in-Publication Data
What's good for business : business and American politics since World War II / edited by
Kim Phillips-Fein and Julian E. Zelizer.
p.   cm.
Includes bibliographical references and index.
ISBN 978-0-19-975401-4 (hbk. : alk. paper) — ISBN 978-0-19-975400-7 (pbk. : alk. paper)
1. Business and politics—United States—History. 2. Industrial policy—United States—History.
3. United States—Economic policy—History. I. Phillips-Fein, Kim. II. Zelizer, Julian E.
JK467.W52   2012
322'.30973—dc23   2011029600

1 3 5 7 9 8 6 4 2

Printed in the United States of America
on acid-free paper

CONTENTS

ACKNOWLEDGMENTS

We would like to thank Susan Ferber and Oxford University Press for their outstanding work on this volume. Daniel Rodgers, Anthony Grafton, and William Jordan made possible the funding through the David Center, the Center for Collaborative History, and the Department of History at Princeton University for a conference that started this volume. Barbara Leavey did a wonderful job making sure that everything ran smoothly. Kim Phillips-Fein would like to thank Greg Vargo and Charlotte Phillips for their comments on the introduction and epilogue. All of the authors of this volume have been wonderful to work with. We would also like to thank Bruce Schulman and Anthony Badger, who along with Julian Zelizer, co-organized the Boston University-Cambridge University-Princeton University Annual Political History Conference at which the first draft of these chapters were presented.

CONTRIBUTORS

Anthony S. Chen is Associate Professor of Sociology at Northwestern University and Faculty Fellow at its Institute for Policy Research. His first book, *The Fifth Freedom*, tapped a wide assortment of evidence to reconsider the advent of affirmative action in employment. He is currently completing a book on the origins of affirmative action in college admissions (with Lisa M. Stulberg), and he is starting a new research project on business mobilization, economic risk, and the transformation of the regulatory state since the Nixon years.

N. D. B. Connolly is Assistant Professor of History at Johns Hopkins University. His work on Jim Crow segregation, urban redevelopment, and capitalism appear in the journals *Caribbean Studies* and *Urban History*, select edited volumes, and in the forthcoming book *A World More Concrete: Real Estate in the Remaking of Jim Crow South Florida*, to be published by the University of Chicago Press.

Darren Dochuk is Associate Professor of History at Purdue University. He is the author of *From Bible Belt to Sunbelt: Plain-folk Religion, Grassroots Politics, and the Rise of Evangelical Conservatism* (Norton, 2011) and co-editor of *Sunbelt Rising: The Politics of Space, Place, and Region* (University of Pennsylvania Press, 2011).

Shane Hamilton is Associate Professor of History at the University of Georgia. He is the author of *Trucking Country: The Road to America's Wal-Mart Economy* (Princeton, 2008) and is currently writing a book on the history of supermarkets.

Louis Hyman is Assistant Professor of Labor Relations, Law, and History at the ILR School of Cornell University. His book, *Debtor Nation: The History of America in Red Ink*, was published in 2011. He received his Ph.D. in U.S. history from Harvard University.

Meg Jacobs is Associate Professor at Massachusetts Institute of Technology. She is the author of *Pocketbook Politics: Economic Citizenship in Twentieth-Century*

America was published with Princeton University Press and won the Organization of American Historians' 2006 prize for the best book on modern politics. She is currently working on a book on the energy crisis of the 1970s.

Andrew Needham is Assistant Professor of History at New York University. His work examines the intersections of metropolitan growth, energy development, and environmental change in postwar America. He is the author of *Power Lines: Energy and the Making of the Modern Southwest*, forthcoming from Princeton University Press.

Kim Phillips-Fein is Assistant Professor at the Gallatin School of New York University, where she teaches courses in American political, business, and labor history. Her first book, *Invisible Hands: The Making of the Conservative Movement from the New Deal to Reagan*, was published in 2009 by W. W. Norton. Phillips-Fein has written widely for publications including *The Nation*, *Bookforum*, and *Dissent*, to which she has contributed articles and reviews. She is currently working writing a book New York City in the 1970s.

Elizabeth Tandy Shermer spent two years as the Paul Mellon Fellow of American History at the University of Cambridge before joining Loyola University of Chicago's Department of History. Her work has appeared in several edited collections and major journals, including the *Journal of American History*. Her monograph, *Creating the Sunbelt: Phoenix and the Political Economy of Metropolitan Growth*, is forthcoming from University of Pennsylvania Press.

Jason Scott Smith is the author of *Building New Deal Liberalism: The Political Economy of Public Works, 1933–1956*. After completing his Ph.D. at the University of California, Berkeley, he held postdoctoral fellowships at Harvard and Cornell before joining the faculty at the University of New Mexico.

Dominique A. Tobbell is Assistant Professor in the Program in the History of Science, Technology, and Medicine at the University of Minnesota and is author of *Pills, Power, and Policy: The Struggle for Drug Reform in Cold War America and its Consequences* (University of California Press/Milbank Series on Health and the Public, 2012).

Benjamin Waterhouse is Assistant Professor of History at the University of North Carolina at Chapel Hill. His research focuses on the political and economic history of the United States during the twentieth century, and he is currently at work on a book about the role of corporate lobbyists in American politics during the 1970s and 1980s.

Mark R. Wilson is Associate Professor of History at the University of North Carolina at Charlotte. He is the author of *The Business of Civil War* (2006). He is currently at work on a book about the business and politics of the U.S. industrial mobilization for World War II.

Julian E. Zelizer is Professor of History and Public Affairs at Princeton University. He is the award-winning author and editor of thirteen books on American political history. His most recent books are *Governing America: The Revival of Political History* (Princeton University Press), *Jimmy Carter* (Times Books), and *The Presidency of George W. Bush: A First Historical Assessment* (Princeton University Press). He writes a weekly column for CNN.Com and is a regular commentator in the media.

What's Good for Business

Introduction

What's Good for Business

KIM PHILLIPS-FEIN AND JULIAN E. ZELIZER

Early in 2010, the Supreme Court struck down legal century-old restrictions on corporate donations to political campaigns, finding that restricting business contributions to fund political advertisements during election campaign was a violation of the First Amendment. The ruling in *Citizens United vs. the Federal Election Commission*—which satisfied long-standing efforts to overturn such bans—caused many to warn of a new era of business dominance over national politics, and it brought questions about business influence in politics to the forefront of the country's attention. "With a single, disastrous 5-to-4 ruling, the Supreme Court has thrust politics back to the robber baron age of the nineteenth century," opined the *New York Times*.[1]

While there is no doubt that the *Citizens United* decision has affected the contemporary political landscape, this volume demonstrates that the Court's ruling was only one recent development in a long history of the political mobilization of business. This book examines the attempts of business to influence elections, shape legislation, determine regulations, and contribute to the creation of public opinion since the end of World War II. Rather than assuming the power of business in politics, the authors whose work appears in these pages try to unpack the evolution of this relationship. The history of business in political life that emerges from these pages is not a simple story of corporate power easily and unquestioningly exercised; instead, the stories told here show business actors organizing themselves to affect government in myriad different ways, resulting in an image of American politics that is more complex and contested than it often has been thought to be.

Few would argue with the idea that businesses have been profoundly affected by the labor, regulatory, and fiscal policies of government at the federal, state, and local level. Yet it has taken some time for historians to start to write about business and politics with the same fine-grained attention to archival detail and level of social analysis with which they have studied political parties, labor unions, and grass-roots social movements. A new generation of scholars who are attempting to reenergize the history of political economy, the authors whose work is collected here seek to show that the role of business in politics and the political efforts of economic elites need to be understood as historically specific and distinct, the subject of research and analysis instead of simply something to be taken for granted because business operates at a high level of social prestige, political access, and economic power.

The relationship between economic interests and political power is one of the oldest themes in U.S. historiography, just as it is in American politics more broadly. In 1913, the historian and political scientist Charles Beard created a great stir with the publication of *An Economic Interpretation of the Constitution of the United States*. Beard challenged historians such as George Bancroft who had focused on the intellectual foundations of the Constitution, arguing that the economic interests of the founding generation best explained the positions that were taken by the Federalists and Anti-Federalists. That highlighting that the founders' economic interests influenced the way that they approached the state was seen as scandalous suggests the strong emotions that have long surrounded the problems of economic interest and business power in a democracy.[2]

Historical scholarship on the twentieth century has been perennially concerned with this issue as well. Progressive historians such as Beard wrote grand narratives depicting an ongoing tension between business interests and the rest of American society, namely workers, farmers, and intellectuals, in a struggle that moved toward greater social equality. According to the progressive historians, "the people" struggled to gain power and expand government in order to tame the power of business and financial elites. The history of the United States was the story of the long fight to live up to its democratic promise—and the opposition of business was the central obstacle to be overcome. Historians such as Matthew Josephson advanced the argument that the business leaders of the late nineteenth century were "robber barons" who came by their wealth primarily through exploitation and plunder.[3] The progressive interpretation saw business as predatory, both toward its workers and toward the state. Businessmen subverted democratic ideals and sought to gain control over the political process.

During the 1940s and 1950s, liberal historians advanced a somewhat similar narrative, though they adopted a more pluralistic interpretation. According to scholars such as Arthur Schlesinger, Jr., the New Deal marked a transformative moment in which the federal government not only expanded to regulate destructive business power but also helped non-elite citizens to permanently organize for themselves. The government created a level playing field. Business became one interest among many competing for power.[4] At the same time, historians such as Richard Hofstadter rejected the idea that American history could be understood primarily as a struggle over wealth and power, arguing that this did not leave sufficient room for non-materialist factors in explaining political behavior. The older progressive interpretation also seemed to overstate the depth of disagreement about the basic principles of capitalism, which Hofstadter believed to be widely accepted by most of the populace. If there were conflicts, they were more likely to be between different interest groups, each seeking its own advantage in the market, than between a dominant business class and the rest of the people.[5] In a way, the mid-century work on business–government relations tended to echo the political faiths of liberalism at this point. It de-emphasized the political power of business and suggested that the expansion of the state in the New Deal had been able to tame whatever might have been destructive about private economic power in the early twentieth century.

Neither the "consensus" interpretation nor the pluralist one were convincing to the group of younger scholars in the 1960s that rejected the liberal understanding of the United States. Influenced by Marxian thinkers such as William Appleman Williams, as well as by the work of C. Wright Mills on the "power elite," they tapped back into some of the spirit from Beard's book on the Constitution to argue that in the twentieth century the expansion of government took place to protect, not tame, business power. The New Left claimed that many Progressive Era regulations were put into place because the emerging corporations of that period sought to stifle competition from small business and quell radical elements in society. Gabriel Kolko, Martin Sklar, James Weinstein, and others presented a story about "corporate liberalism" in which business interests played the central role in government expansion even when legislation seemed like a populist victory.[6] In this view, the Progressive Era marked the moment when the national ruling elite capable of using government power to augment its own status and position emerged in the United States. Social historians of this generation, who paid less attention to government and economic institutions, agreed with much of their analysis. They downplayed the ability of government to produce genuine reform given the power of business, focusing instead on grassroots efforts, from the shop floor to the saloons, to democratize America. (Subsequent historians, such as David Vogel, Kim McQuaid, Thomas Ferguson, Samuel Hays, and Colin Gordon, took a more critical attitude toward the idea of corporate liberalism, focusing on the deep divisions within the business community, as well as the continued opposition of many companies to almost any expansion of government regulation.)[7]

Also in the 1960s and 1970s, a group of historians began to advance what became known as the "organizational synthesis." This cohort of scholars—led by Robert Wiebe, Samuel Hays, Morton Keller, and Louis Galambos—was interested in cooperative efforts between government and business.[8] They argued that the central political narrative concerned the modernization of American society, which occurred between 1880 and 1920. The development of large-scale national institutions—both within the state and in industry—separated the nineteenth and twentieth century, and the rise of these massive institutions resulted in cooperative efforts between business and government to rationalize public policy and economic competition. While sharing many of the same themes as the arguments about corporate liberalism, they did not see business as the dominant member of this relationship nor did they frame their story in terms of class politics.

In the 1970s and 1980s, historians wrote much less about the relationship between business and government. In part, this had to do with the decline of political history, as many historians focused on social and cultural questions instead of legislative battles or the power of the state. Also in the 1970s, economic history began to be written primarily by economists, whose questions and methods were very different from those that interested most historians, focusing much more closely on the origins and dynamics of economic growth.[9] As a result, the literature on business and politics remained focused on the early part of the twentieth century. This unbalanced coverage meant a paucity of work on the more contemporary period when the level of government intervention in matters impacting business vastly expanded. The massive growth of the federal government and the labor movement in the New Deal and the war created new political, ideological, and economic problems—as well as new opportunities—for American business. The period between World War II and the end of the twentieth century raised vital questions: How did business groups seek to accomplish their political objectives in a landscape where they had to negotiate with a newly large and powerful federal state and interest groups, such as organized labor and the environmental movement, that were often in opposition to corporate goals? What was the dynamic between postwar liberalism and business? And how did business relate to the conservative movement that was developing over these years?

Finally, the subfield of business history itself has only intermittently dealt with questions about the state. Many of its leading practitioners have focused on questions about technological change, the development of markets, the structure of industries, and a wide range of more specifically economic matters, rather than politics. The work of Alfred D. Chandler, Jr. on the rise of vertical integration and its implications for the modern economy was itself crafted in part as a rejection of older interpretations that suggested there was no real economic motivation for the rise of large corporations. Chandler's classic 1977 work, *The Visible Hand*, which defined the field of business history for decades to come, downplayed the role of the state or politics more broadly. As Richard John wrote on the twentieth anniversary of its publication, *The Visible Hand* "pushed to the margins a host of other topics, including . . . government–business relations and the role of business in American life."[10] Even historians who challenged Chandler's central contentions about the efficiency of large corporations—such as Philip Scranton, in his work on the reasons for the tenacity of small businesses in the era of industrialization—often shared with him an emphasis on the history of the firm.[11] The relative absence of politics in much older business and economic history may be because scholars assumed that business people were not especially interested in politics, except in very narrow ways. Their actions with regard to government were only extensions of their market behavior, driven by economic self-interest instead of by ideas or by other considerations, and their political motivations are thought to be fairly constant across time and place. The political power of business might be merely an extension of its economic power: it exerts what influence it has simply through the promise of investment and the threat of disinvestment. If this is true, why look specifically at the relationship between business and the state at all?

But in recent years, political historians and business historians alike have started to return to the archives to examine the relationship between business and government, especially in the twentieth century. There are a number of reasons for this reinvigorated interest. First and foremost is just how central business and economic issues are to contemporary political life. We live, after all, in an era when levels of inequality of income and wealth have reached proportions unknown for a century. Business and lobbying groups seem to exert great power at all levels of government, shaping public policy in disproportionate ways. The recent financial crash and subsequent recession have generated concern throughout the country about how our economic institutions work and what to do when they fail. Tax cuts, deregulation, welfare, health insurance, Social Security, and the very idea of the free market all are fiercely contested. High-profile business scandals—from the Savings & Loan crisis of the 1980s to the market-frenzy fraud of Enron to Bernard L. Madoff's infamous Ponzi scheme—punctuate the headlines, although the popular books and articles that appear about them rarely take a long historical view. In a 2003 forum in the *Journal of American History*, David Hollinger called for a new focus on "political economy," arguing that these issues have been so important in our contemporary politics that historians need to do much more to account for them in the recent American past.[12]

At the same time—and perhaps because of the evident importance of business in politics and more generally in our social and cultural life today—there has been a broader resurgence of scholarship in the field of business history. Instead of focusing primarily on the questions of organizational structure, innovation, technology, and markets that had previously defined the field, there has been a strong push to analyze business as at once shaping and being shaped by

American politics, culture, and ideas. This has led historians to treat analyze many subjects that had not previously been seen as important. Scholars have written about the politics of advertising and of public relations.[13] They have explored the history of women entrepreneurs and the ways that the world of business opened up new roles for women, even as it remained a place that reproduced hierarchies of gender.[14] They have written about deindustrialization, capital flight, and the decline of the Keynesian economic order.[15] They have analyzed the history of the creation of an extensive set of employer-provided social benefits—especially health insurance—and its impact on public policy.[16] They have done important work on the politics of institutions such as the New York Stock Exchange and Wal-Mart, and the interplay between corporate identity and political culture.[17] They have looked at the political campaigns of business in postwar America.[18] They have worked on the ways that elite class identity is shaped at particular moments in history.[19] They have studied the impact of government policies on economic development.[20] Historians have even begun to describe the ways that business prerogatives shape the most personal cultural experiences—for example, the way that music is produced and heard.[21] Some scholars are suggesting that the old divisions between business, labor, and economic history should be dissolved, and that historians should instead write the "history of capitalism," taking as the starting point for research the idea that (as Sven Beckert puts it) "states and markets, politics and business" are mutually constitutive and cannot be understood independently of each other.[22] Property rights and economic relationships, these scholars argue, are created through state actions. Business people should not be seen as the profit-maximizing individuals of economic theory; they need to be understood within cultural, social, and political networks, as well as economic institutions. The work collected in this book is more narrowly focused on the relationship between business and government. But the larger revitalization of business history and the new "history of capitalism" has meant the incorporation of politics into the field in a new way and at a new level.

The recent revival of political history, too, has led scholars of American politics to business, just as business historians have come to politics.[23] While the "new political history" began with a focus on civil rights and public welfare, it has moved naturally to encompass the history of business in politics and the ways that government policies and institutional structures have influenced the marketplace. Many of the younger scholars who have focused on business and politics are people who might, in an earlier era, have approached these problems of political economy through the lens of labor history instead. But they came of age politically and intellectually at a time when it seemed clear that in order to understand the histories of working-class people, it was in fact necessary to start at the other side. Without analyzing the context in which workers lived and struggled, it was impossible to understand the power structures that surrounded them. The irony was that some labor historians, in seeking to give agency to workers and their organizations, had downplayed the structural hierarchies in which workers operated. In addition to looking at subaltern institutions, historians needed to pay attention to the role of elites—to see the ways that the actions of people with access to money and to political power were able to shape the terrain of political life.

In the earlier literature on business and politics, all too often, business actors remained skeletal, their motivations, ideas, and social worlds hardly sketched in. This is the central problem that the essays in this book seek to redress—to bring back to life the ways that business people thought about politics, and the manifold ways that they sought to act politically. For far from being concerned only with their individual firms and companies, business people consistently sought to shape political life throughout the post–World War II years. They tried to influence the creation of regulatory regimes, to shape public debate and ideas, to affect local politics, and to determine the nature of public investment. Instead of being insular, driven by a restricted vision of self-interest, they have been politically forceful, even when they were acting out of a sense of economic need: seeking to establish new ways of lobbying, developing new political identities, devising regulatory approaches, building broad popular campaigns, relocating their companies, creating new ways of thinking about the economy and politics. They have been active on issues ranging from the tax code and economic regulations to the adoption of greater investment in certain public services to seeking to find ways to fuse Christianity with free-market ideas. Their efforts often contributed to the development of a politics determined to undermine the regulatory welfare state, but they also helped to shape the content of what postwar liberalism was, what it could accomplish, and what its limits were.

In contrast to the image of the omnipotent "robber baron," the people whose stories are told in these essays met with significant obstacles. Nor were they typically unified: the chapters touch on the many divisions within the broader "business community," a phrase that suggests a more coherent common identity than has often existed. The contributors make the case that businesses become interested in finding ways to act collectively only in certain situations, under special conditions, and for particular periods of time. Sometimes the political influence of business is difficult to see. Certain companies have been able to avoid any proactive stance because they maintain so much influence within the political world. The mere threat of their action, or the threat of their willingness to leave a certain location, is enough to move politicians. But while there are many difficulties which business actors—like any others—face in taking political action, the essays collected in this volume indicate the tremendous interest that many business people historically have taken in political life, and the various ways in which businesses shaped the political world in which they needed to operate.

The contributors to this book cover a vast range of subjects, suggesting how diverse the category of "business" really is. Most deal with larger businesses, but some look at the political efforts of smaller or local companies. Not intended to be comprehensive, these essays illustrate the richness of the field, showing the way that doing this archival work can illuminate problems in both business and political history, and demonstrating the ways in which what one might call the "new business history" can garner insights into twentieth-century American politics and life. We have organized the book in a roughly chronological fashion, starting with World War II and ending with the political mobilization of business in the late 1970s and early 1980s. This might seem to mirror the story of the "rise and fall of the New Deal Order," which is often told about the period, in which the liberalism of the mid-twentieth-century disintegrates in the 1970s under the pressures of social upheaval and economic recession. But although the essays are arranged in this temporal frame, certain important themes run throughout the collection that cut against this familiar narrative of the postwar years.

The first has to do with the relationship between business and the ideas and policies of postwar liberalism. Business leaders and their organizations were cognizant of how American political culture had changed after the New Deal. The role of the state in the economy had vastly expanded and continued to do so through the 1970s. While business actors were often skeptical and even hostile toward the liberalism that emerged during and after the New Deal, they did not limit their politics to outright resistance. Many business leaders actively sought to shape the nature of the postwar state. The relationship was one of negotiation, also influenced by the ways that liberalism became less confrontational toward private industry. Sometimes business leaders tried to translate liberal political ideas into the economic sphere. At other times they attempted to improve their position within liberal governmental structures so as to have more influence on the implementation of regulatory policies. From early in the postwar period, the outright antagonism of some parts of the business world helped to foster the conservative critique of labor and government. Business was at once inside and outside the liberal order, both seeking to influence and seeking to oppose its growth.

Mark Wilson looks at the attempts of business during World War II—when some might imagine that the emergency and patriotism had tamed self-interested lobbying efforts—to create a sympathetic policy environment for the years of reconversion, with a focus on its efforts to shape the tax code in ways that would guarantee that the sacrifices of the war would not fall too heavily on corporations. Increasingly, political battles took place in technical areas of policy, outside the scrutiny of much of the public, where business hired experts and lobbyists to obtain favorable provisions in laws to increase profits. The sophistication of the business lobby, Wilson suggests, kept pace with the growth of the federal state. Jason Scott Smith's essay on the postwar career of David Lilienthal—who went from being a leading New Dealer and head of the Tennessee Valley Authority to having a prosperous career in international business in the postwar period— shows the ways that New Deal ideals about the use of the state for private development could be translated into the private sector. It also suggests how liberalism changed in the postwar period, becoming much less openly critical of business. Shane Hamilton addresses the rhetorical limitations of postwar liberalism when it came to addressing problems associated with "monopsony," or markets dominated by a single (or few) large buyer (or buyers). Policy makers remained trapped within the language of antimonopoly politics, inherited from the Populist campaigns of the late nineteenth century. Finally, Dominique Tobbell's piece on the attempts of the pharmaceutical industry to confront the debate over regulation of prescription drugs in the 1950s and 1960s—which formed a model for other industries, including tobacco—demonstrates that the drug companies pursued a wide array of strategies aimed at gaining greater control over the conditions of regulation. Ultimately, they participated in the creation of the regulatory regime, ensuring that it would develop in ways that they did not find too threatening.

A second major theme running throughout the collection addresses the role played by business in developing a conservative political mobilization that was openly opposed to state regulation. Darren Dochuk's essay about oil and evangelical religion treats the distinctive contributions of businessmen associated with the extractive industries to building conservative religious institutions in the postwar period. Dochuk challenges the tendency within the historiography to separate the "religious right," supposedly focused primarily on cultural issues, from economic conservatives and libertarians who advocate less government regulation, demonstrating, through the history of oil politics, how the two were interconnected. Andrew Needham's essay on debates over public power in Phoenix, Arizona, treats the attempts of private electrical utility companies to attack public utilities. He suggests that the political campaigns they crafted in the early 1960s helped to establish the rhetoric of "taxpayer" politics, helping to nurture an identity upon which the conservative movement would be able to build. Meg Jacobs's essay on business and environmental regulation treats the dramatic expansion of regulation in the 1970s—a shift in the legal landscape that the conservative movement was not able to fully undo in the 1980s or 1990s. In a decade considered a time of victory for free-market ideas, this highlights an example in which business opposition to regulation failed. It also explains the ferocity of the mobilization of the business community in an era that, according to conventional

accounts, should have been hospitable to their needs. Benjamin Waterhouse focuses on the end of the 1970s and the early 1980s, arguing that businesses were
able to overcome significant internal divisions to lobby against Big Business Day,
a 1980 attempt by Ralph Nader and the public interest movement to draw attention to corporate malfeasance. Waterhouse suggests that the challenges of the
public interest movement and of 1970s regulation spurred businesses to find
ways to build common organizations and work together politically. Louis
Hyman's piece looks at the changing idea of the corporation in the 1970s, and at
the ways that critiques of the conglomerate movement helped to stimulate a turn
toward "lean" corporations, away from the massive, vertically integrated firms of
the postwar years.

A third theme that appears in many of the essays focuses on the relationship
between business and government at the local level. While historians looking at
business and politics have often dealt primarily with national politics and corporate institutions that operate at the national level, for much of the business world
it was essential to influence state and local governments, over issues which might
in turn have national significance. Elizabeth Tandy Shermer's essay on postwar
Phoenix, Arizona, shows how the campaigns of local business leaders to remake
the city government and create a favorable climate for investment helped to
make the sunbelt metropolis a haven for manufacturing corporations eager to
flee the high-tax and heavily unionized states of the Northeast and Midwest.
These businessmen—the colleagues of Senator Barry Goldwater—understood
their local boosterism in deeply political terms, and they conceived of themselves as building an economic alternative to New Deal liberalism. They were
not, however, simple antistatists. On the contrary, they wanted to use public investment to woo business to Phoenix. Nathan Connolly's essay about the role of
black business in encouraging "law-and-order" politics in Miami, Florida, suggests that black entrepreneurs pressed the city to hire black police officers in the
1950s in order to fight illegal gaming. These essays indicate that the political activism of business at the local level can lead to an expansion of government, and
that business actors were often interested in using local government to win favorable conditions for themselves, even as they also advanced a broader political
criticism of liberalism. They also suggest the dialectical relationship between
local business activism and national politics. But, importantly, businesses often
accepted and adjusted to government only when they had no choice. This dynamic is carefully explored by Anthony Chen, who looks at the politics of municipal Fair Employment Practices ordinances, focusing on the role of employers.
His article examines battles that occurred in a number of cities, focusing on
Cleveland, where the local Chamber of Commerce abandoned its earlier resistance to mandatory ordinances after it was clear that this opposition had been
largely futile.

Together, the essays in this book show that business people have always tried to guide politics toward "what's good for business"—even as they argued amongst themselves about what this might be, and as they tried to insist that there should be no distinction between what was good for business and for the society as a whole. They sought to direct the state activity of the postwar years in ways that they felt would be favorable to the industries and groups they represented. At the same time, they helped to invest in campaigns to oppose regulation and labor. While they often acted alone, the political challenges they faced in postwar America frequently prompted collective action, both at the federal and at the local level.

Indeed, one of the themes to emerge in this collection is the continuity between business activism throughout the liberal and conservative periods in postwar history. Many of the features of business prominence that are thought to have emerged only after 1980 are in fact evident all throughout the postwar period. While the campaigns of labor unions, consumer groups, civil rights organizations, and other liberal and left grassroots groups helped to shape the postwar political landscape, so too did the organizing efforts of business. A complete understanding of the history of postwar America demands attention to the deep relationship among these groups and government.

Notes

1. "The Court's Blow to Democracy," *New York Times*, 22 January 2010, 30.
2. Charles A. Beard, *An Economic Interpretation of the Constitution of the United States* (New York: MacMillan, 1913).
3. Matthew Josephson, *The Robber Barons: The Great American Capitalists, 1861–1901* (New York: Harcourt, 1934).
4. See, for example, Arthur M. Schlesinger, Jr., *The Politics of Upheaval, 1935–1936*, rev. ed. (Boston: Houghton Mifflin, 1988).
5. Richard Hofstadter, *The American Political Tradition and the Men Who Made It* (New York: Knopf, 1948).
6. Gabriel Kolko, *The Triumph of Conservatism: A Reinterpretation of American History: 1900–1916* (New York: Free Press, 1963); Martin Sklar, *Corporate Reconstruction of Capitalism: 1890–1916: The Market, the Law, and Politics* (New York: Cambridge University Press, 1988); James Weinstein, *The Corporate Ideal in the Liberal State: 1900–1918* (Boston: Beacon, 1968). There has also been some important, more recent work on business and political organizing in the Progressive Era. For example, see Jeffrey Haydu, *Citizen Employers: Business Communities and Labor in Cincinnati and San Francisco, 1870–1916* (Ithaca, N.Y.: ILR Press, 2008); Chad Pearson, "'Organize and Fight': Communities, Employers and Open-Shop Movements, 1890–1920" (Ph.D. diss., State University of New York at Albany, 2008).
7. David Vogel, "Why Businessmen Distrust Their State: The Political Consciousness of American Corporate Executives," *British Journal of Political Science* 8 (1978): 45–78; David Vogel, *Fluctuating Fortunes: The Political Power of Business in America* (New York: Basic Books, 1989); David Vogel, *Kindred Strangers: The Uneasy Relationship between Politics and Business in America* (Princeton, N.J.: Princeton University Press, 1996); Kim McQuaid, *Big*

Business and Presidential Power from FDR to Reagan (New York: William Morrow, 1982); Kim McQuaid, *Uneasy Partners: Big Business in American Politics, 1945–1980* (Baltimore: Johns Hopkins University Press, 1994); Thomas Ferguson, "Industrial Conflict and the Coming of the New Deal: The Triumph of Multinational Liberalism in America," in *The Rise and Fall of the New Deal Order, 1930–1980*, ed. Steve Fraser and Gary Gerstle (Princeton, N.J.: Princeton University Press, 1989); Samuel P. Hays, *Beauty, Health and Permanence: Environmental Politics in the United States, 1955–1985* (New York: Cambridge, 1987); Colin Gordon, *New Deals: Business, Labor and Politics, 1920–1935* (Cambridge: Cambridge University Press, 1994).

8. Louis Galambos, "The Emerging Organizational Synthesis in Modern American History," *Business History Review* 44 (Autumn 1970): 279–90; Louis Galambos, "Technology, Political Economy, and Professionalization: Central Themes of the Organizational Synthesis," *Business History Review* 57 (Winter 1983): 471–93; Morton Keller, *The Life Insurance Enterprise, 1885–1910: A Study in the Limits of Corporate Power* (Cambridge, Mass.: Belknap Press, 1963); Samuel P. Hays, *The Response to Industrialism: 1885–1914*, 2d ed. (Chicago: University of Chicago Press, 1994); Robert H. Wiebe, *The Search for Order, 1877–1920* (New York: Hill and Wang, 1966).

9. William H. Sewell, Jr., "A Strange Career: The Historical Study of Economic Life," *History and Theory* 49 (December 2010): 146–66; Robert Whaples, "Is Economic History a Neglected Field of Study?" *Historically Speaking* 11 (April 2010): 17–20.

10. Alfred Chandler, Jr., *The Visible Hand: The Managerial Revolution in American Business* (Cambridge, Mass.: Belknap, 1977); Richard John, "Elaborations, Revisions, Dissents: Alfred J. Chandler, Jr.'s, 'The Visible Hand' After Twenty Years," *Business History Review* 71 (Summer 1997): 169. John's essay provides a thorough discussion of Chandler's historiographical impact, treating him as a contributor to the idea of the organizational synthesis. Also see Kenneth Lipartito, "The Future of Alfred Chandler," *Enterprise and Society* 9 (3 September 2008).

11. Philip Scranton, *Endless Novelty: Specialty Production and American Industrialization, 1865–1925* (Princeton, N.J.: Princeton University Press, 1997).

12. Interchange, "The Practice of History," *Journal of American History* 90 (September 2003): 576–611, especially 609–11.

13. Pamela Laird, *Advertising Progress: American Business and the Rise of Consumer Marketing* (Baltimore: Johns Hopkins University Press, 1998); Roland Marchand, *Creating the Corporate Soul: The Rise of Public Relations and Corporate Imagery in American Big Business* (Berkeley: University of California Press, 1998).

14. For example, see Kathy Peiss, *Hope in a Jar: The Making of America's Beauty Culture* (Philadelphia: University of Pennsylvania Press, 1998); Vicki Howard, *Brides, Inc.: American Weddings and the Business of Tradition* (Philadelphia: University of Pennsylvania Press, 1996); Angel Kwolek-Folland, *Incorporating Women: A History of Women in Business in the United States* (New York: Twayne, 1998); Mary Yeager, *Women and Business*, 3 vols., The International Library of Critical Writings in Business History, Elgar Reference Collection (Cheltenham, U.K. and Northampton, Mass.: Edward Elgar, 1999).

15. Jefferson Cowie, *Capital Moves: RCA's 70-Year Quest for Cheap Labor* (Ithaca, N.Y.: Cornell University Press, 1999); Tami Friedman, "Exploiting the North–South Differential: Corporate Power, Southern Politics and the Decline of Organized Labor," *Journal of American History* 92 (September 2008): 323–248; Judith Stein, *Pivotal Decade: How the United States Traded Factories for Finance* (New Haven, Conn.: Yale University Press, 2010).

16. Marie Gottschalk, *The Shadow Welfare State: Labor, Business and the Politics of Health Care in the United States* (Ithaca, N.Y.: Cornell University Press, 2000); Jennifer Klein, *For All These Rights: Business, Labor, and the Shaping of America's Public-Private Welfare State* (Princeton, N.J.: Princeton University Press, 2003).

17. For example, see Bethany Moreton, *To Serve God and Wal-Mart: The Making of Christian Free Enterprise* (Cambridge, Mass.: Harvard University Press, 2009); Julia Ott, *When Wall Street Met Main Street: The Quest for an Investors' Democracy* (Cambridge, Mass.: Harvard University Press, 2011); Kenneth Lipartido and David Sicilia, *Constructing Corporate America: History, Politics, Culture* (New York: Oxford University Press, 2004).

18. Howell John Harris, *The Right to Manage: Industrial Relations Policies of American Business in the 1940s* (Madison: University of Wisconsin Press, 1982); Robert Collins, *The Business Response to Keynes, 1929–1964* (New York: Columbia University Press, 1982); Elizabeth Fones-Wolf, *Selling Free Enterprise: The Business Assault against Labor and Liberalism, 1945–1960* (Urbana and Champaign: University of Illinois Press, 1994); Sanford Jacoby, *Modern Manors: Welfare Capitalism Since the New Deal* (Princeton, N.J.: Princeton University Press, 1997); Robert Collins, *More: The Politics of Economic Growth in Postwar America* (New York: Oxford, 2000); Wendy Wall, *Inventing the "American Way": The Politics of Consensus from the New Deal to the Civil Rights Movement* (New York: Oxford University Press, 2007); Kim Phillips-Fein, *Invisible Hands: The Making of the Conservative Movement from the New Deal to Reagan* (New York: W. W. Norton, 2009).

19. Sven Beckert, *The Moneyed Metropolis: New York City and the Consolidation of the American Bourgeoisie, 1850–1896* (Cambridge: Cambridge University Press, 2001); James Livingston, *Origins of the Federal Reserve System: Money, Class and Corporate Capitalism, 1890–1913* (Ithaca, N.Y.: Cornell University Press, 1986); Olivier Zunz, *Making America Corporate, 1870–1920* (Chicago: University of Chicago Press, 1990); Steve Fraser and Gary Gerstle, *Ruling America: A History of Wealth and Power in a Democracy* (Cambridge, Mass.: Harvard University Press, 2005).

20. Gerard Berk, *Alternative Tracks: The Constitution of American Industrial Order, 1865–1917* (Baltimore: Johns Hopkins University Press, 1994); Richard John, *Network Nation: Inventing American Telecommunications* (Cambridge, Mass.: Belknap Press of Harvard University Press, 2010); Richard White, *Railroaded: The Transcontinentals and the Making of Modern America* (New York: W. W. Norton, 2011).

21. David Suisman, *Selling Sounds: The Commercial Revolution in American Music* (Cambridge, Mass.: Harvard University Press, 2009).

22. Sven Beckert, "History of American Capitalism," in *American History Now*, ed. Eric Foner and Lisa McGirr (Philadelphia: Temple University Press, 2011), 319. There have also recently been two notable roundtables on the development of the history of capitalism as a subfield, one at the 2010 meeting of the Organization of American Historians in Washington, D.C., and the other at the 2011 New School University conference on "Power and the History of Capitalism," as well as a 2011 conference at Harvard University on "The New History of American Capitalism."

23. For a discussion of the revival of political history, see Julian Zelizer, *Governing America: The Revival of Political History* (Princeton: Princeton University Press, 2012); also see Meg Jacobs, William Novak, and Julian Zelizer, *The Democratic Experiment* (Princeton: Princeton University Press, 2003).

1

The Advantages of Obscurity

World War II Tax Carryback Provisions and the
Normalization of Corporate Welfare

MARK R. WILSON

As the year 1942 came to a close, Americans could sense that they were witnessing the opening of a new chapter in history. Recent Allied successes on the battlefield were matched by the increasingly impressive munitions production feats of the U.S. economy, which were turning the country's armed forces into a fearsomely destructive world power. This giant leap in American military capacity, which would continue to shape world events in the years to come, did not come cheap. The country's World War II bills would amount to $320 billion, about half of which the country borrowed by selling bonds to the public. But most of the rest of the huge war costs, about 43%, were covered by taxes. This was an impressive fraction, especially in comparison to past and future wars. To achieve this feat, the United States deployed impressive fiscal innovations. The most important of these, and the best remembered, was the mass income tax on individuals. This system was instituted by the Revenue Act of 1942, enacted ten months after Pearl Harbor, when the country had already spent tens of billions of dollars to support its global war effort. Before the war was over, the number of Americans paying individual federal income taxes had jumped from four million to over forty million people. There was nothing inevitable about this innovation, which the Roosevelt administration pushed in favor of alternative methods, such as a national sales tax. But it quickly became the centerpiece of the national government's revenue system, which it has remained to this day.[1]

No less important than the individual income taxes in the financing of World War II, if somewhat less revolutionary, were robust corporate income taxes. A key component of the new tax regime created during the Progressive Era,[2] corporate income taxes had been central to the country's revenue-raising efforts in World War I. These had included special excess profits and war profits taxes, along with regular corporate income taxes with higher rates. In the 1920s, business-friendly Congresses cancelled the excess profits tax, but corporate income taxes continued. In the mid-1930s, the Roosevelt administration pushed for higher taxes on corporations and wealthy individuals. It succeeded in convincing Congress to enact a new tax on undistributed corporate profits, but this controversial measure proved short-lived.[3] During World War II, despite the growing importance of individual income taxes, corporate income taxes again served as a critical component of the nation's war finances. Between 1940 and 1945, "normal" corporate income taxes (which included a hefty wartime surtax) raised $23.1 billion in revenue. The excess profits tax (EPT), the other main tax paid by corporations during the war, raised another $35.1 billion. The combined total, $58.2 billion, represented over 40% of the Treasury's wartime tax receipts. As business leaders were happy to point out, these taxes took a significant bite out of gross profits. From 1940 to 1945, U.S. corporations saw taxes take nearly 49% of their aggregate earnings.[4]

Given this impressive record of revenue collection, it may be tempting to understand the World War II years as a period in which American businesses and individuals proved to be remarkably compliant supporters of the burgeoning national state.[5] However, this was not quite the whole story, even when it came to corporate taxes. This becomes especially evident if we extend the boundaries of the war's fiscal history into 1946 and 1947, when many businesses were struggling to adjust to the end of military orders and to reconvert to civilian production. During those years, hundreds of American companies—and especially those most closely connected to the wartime military-industrial mobilization—enjoyed giant tax refunds that had the effect of erasing most of their reconversion losses. The most important sources of these tax refunds, which made 1946 different from any other year in American business history up to that time, were two "carryback" provisions, which had been written into the corporate income tax code in 1942.

The carryback provisions were remarkably helpful to many American businesses in the 1940s because they allowed companies to use reconversion losses— or even subpar earnings—to reduce their recent taxable wartime profits. To take a simple hypothetical example, a company that lost a million dollars in 1946 could "carry back" that loss to 1944, reducing its earnings for that year by the same amount. This downward revision of past profits was often highly significant, because most American companies had high pretax earnings during World War II and because wartime tax rates were so high—usually well above 50%. Thus, a million dollar loss in 1946 could easily translate, after profits and tax liabilities for 1944 were recalculated, into a half-million dollar tax refund. During the reconversion years of 1945–47, American corporations took full advantage of this accounting magic. They used two specific provisions written into the corporate tax code in

1942—one providing for the carryback of net operating losses, the other allowing the carryback of special wartime excess profit tax allowances—to collect hundreds of millions of dollars in tax refunds.[6] Especially for companies in the automobile, aircraft, transportation, and electrical equipment industries, along with more specialized military contractors, the tax refunds created by carrybacks were critical in erasing most of the losses in what would be their worst months of the decade.[7]

This chapter, which describes the origins of the carryback refund provisions in 1942 and the brief national controversy over them that broke out in early 1946, uses this single case to address some larger themes that deserve more attention from students of business and politics.[8] In the early twenty-first century, Americans are confronted with an enormously complex revenue system that is riddled with special exemptions, or tax benefits. These are so ubiquitous that nominal tax rates—especially for businesses—are often rendered almost meaningless. This fact is occasionally brought to public attention by the news media, as it was recently in stories about the "aggressive" accounting practices of General Electric (GE)—a single case of what is in fact a long-standing and widespread phenomenon.[9] But it is uncertain whether even the most dramatic journalistic accounts will allow prospective reformers to overhaul a revenue regime that features dozens of significant special benefits and allowances. As scholars of these "tax expenditures" have emphasized, the peculiar structure of the American tax system—as well as its overall scale and complexity—tends to discourage informed discussion and reasonable reform in the public interest.[10] But if we can better understand the origins and development of this tax system, Americans may be better able to conduct intelligent discussions and reforms.

Focusing on one small but significant piece of the corporate tax system developed in the 1940s, this chapter suggests that the benefit-ridden modern American tax system is not simply the result of decades of successful lobbying by special interests. Certainly, self-interested industries contributed to the carryback refund provisions of World War II, along with many other special allowances. However, the carryback story shows that business-friendly tax benefits owed a great deal to three other factors that were distinct from direct business lobbying, and more historically specific. First, many congressional representatives proved happy to assist business in using special provisions to chip away at high nominal rates. This was not simply because they were tied to business interests by naked economic incentives, but because they became increasingly concerned, in the era of the New Deal and World War II, about reining in the growing national bureaucratic state. One way to do so was to use public policy to benefit the private sector, sometimes in ways that were indirect and obscure. In the field of taxes, this congressional pushback was often expressed in a combative relationship with the Treasury. Congressional conservatives drew here upon the expertise of a second important set of actors:

business service professionals—especially lawyers and accountants—working in the private sector. As the story of the carryback refunds shows, it was sometimes these expert, semi-independent professionals, rather than business firms themselves, who served as the most important sources of specific tax innovations.[11] At least some of these business professionals regarded themselves as independent experts who were helping to create a fairer and more rational tax regime. But as developments in 1946 would suggest, the professionals' contributions, once put into practice, could easily become seen as unnecessary assistance to special private interests rather than enlightened public policy.

The involvement of expert professionals in shaping the tax system suggests the importance of a third, more abstract factor: the growing scale and complexity of legislation. By the 1940s, revenue legislation had become so lengthy and complicated that it baffled most members of Congress and the President, to say nothing of ordinary citizens. While some parts of proposed legislation were the subject of substantial reflection and debate, other provisions—especially those inserted into bills at a late stage—inevitably received much less attention. In this environment, only a handful of people with special interests and expert knowledge enjoyed disproportionate influence; even they, however, had little control of a process that was full of confusion and contingency. Thus, the history of the World War II carrybacks reminds us that although business may sometimes achieve important political victories through direct confrontation, overt capture of key seats or agencies, and strident ideological rhetoric, it has also benefitted from much more subtle developments, taking place with little or no public scrutiny.[12]

Without examining the many deliberate and accidental obscurities in the tax system, which historians have still done relatively little to document, it is difficult to understand how business has operated in the political field. Investigation of these more shadowy developments is especially important because they are so ubiquitous in the modern American political economy. The carrybacks of the 1940s are one small part of a much larger body of public policies, grown especially large since World War II, which have been designed and operated in ways that discourage public understanding. In this environment, businesses—and more specifically, business service professionals such as lawyers and accountants—found themselves in many ways newly empowered and enriched, despite their genuine frustrations with the growth of state regulation. In 1946, thanks to their accountants, many of the country's industrial giants enjoyed the new pleasure of receiving large checks from the Treasury. In subsequent years, as carryback and other tax relief provisions became more deeply institutionalized, such experiences would become more common. No less than business leaders' more direct and confrontational efforts to shape public policy, expert influence over complex legislation rewarded business with handsome dividends.

The foundations of the corporate side of the World War II tax system were established in the Second Revenue Act of 1940, which became law in October of that year. Although this was over a year before Pearl Harbor and several months before President Roosevelt proposed Lend-Lease, the American economy by the late summer of 1940 had already begun to make major strides toward industrial mobilization. Manufacturers were beginning to see large military contracts (from France and Britain, as well as the United States); some were building new war plants. At this time, popular memories of alleged Great War "profiteering" and "war millionaires" were strong, as were expert memories in Washington of the taxes enacted during that war. President Roosevelt and Treasury Secretary Henry Morgenthau, Jr. called for a new EPT as a matter of necessity and justice. In Washington and across the country, they had plenty of support. As one Treasury tax expert recalled a few years later, "[t]he primary reason for the excess profits tax was the public pressure for the limitations of wartime profits.... It was felt, at least in the democratic countries, that no one should make an inordinate profit out of a war in which conscripted men were risking their lives and in which many small businesses were being destroyed."[13]

The Second Revenue Act of 1940 created a new EPT that effectively combined the two special corporate taxes that had been used during World War I. The first of these, sometimes called a "high profits tax," had looked mainly to the ratio of a company's profits to its invested capital. Profits above a certain level (normally around 9% of invested capital) were taxed at graduated rates. The other, known as a "war profits" tax, was applied to amounts over and above the company's average earnings in the 1911–13 "base period."[14] In the 1940 legislation, Congress provided a single EPT that allowed corporations to choose either the "invested capital" or the "base period earnings" method. To calculate the amount of its earnings that would be exempt from the EPT (and thus taxed only at the "normal" rate), a corporation could either use 95% of its average annual earnings during a "base period" of 1936–39, or multiply its invested capital by 8%.[15] To the "excess" income over and above these allowances exempted from the EPT, the Second Revenue Act of 1940 applied an EPT with a graduated rate, ranging from 25% to 50%.[16]

For business, the Second Revenue Act of 1940 provided some sweetness along with the bitter. One benefit to business, which was the subject of considerable public discussion and some serious congressional debate,[17] was a provision allowing the "accelerated amortization" (depreciation for tax purposes) of war plant. Intended to encourage private investment in war plant at a time when the country was not at actually at war, this measure—which was supported by the White House and industrial mobilization officials—created a substantial tax deduction for some companies by allowing them to write off the entire cost of a certified war plant over five years (or the length of the war), instead of the normal ten or twenty.[18] No less significant, for many businesses, was the ability to choose the invested-capital or average-earnings method to determine EPT exemption allowances. This part of the law represented a victory by Congress—and in particular, by Colin Stam, the veteran chief of the staff at the Joint Committee on Internal Revenue Taxation—over the Treasury, which had wanted all corporations to be forced to use the invested-capital method.[19] The ability to choose meant that no corporation was worse off than it would have been under the Treasury plan; for those businesses that had managed to earn high profits in the late 1930s, the average-earnings option promised significantly lower taxes.

Although subsequent wartime revenue acts would introduce some important new measures, along with major rate hikes, the Second Revenue Act of 1940 established the basic approach to corporate income taxation that would continue throughout the war. In 1941, Congress raised the top EPT rate to 60%. With the Revenue Act of 1942, it created a flat EPT rate of 90% and set the normal (plus wartime surtax) rate at 40%. In early 1944, after passage of the Revenue Act of 1943, the EPT rate went to 95%. Meanwhile, Congress tightened the invested-capital rules, settling on a rate structure that exempted 8% of the first $5 million in capital, 6% of the next $5 million, and 5% of any capital above $10 million.[20] All of these increases in the potency of the EPT, combined with the war boom that brought many corporations record gross profits, made it a major tax measure. As noted above, the EPT would rank second, behind only the individual income tax, among the government's most important revenue sources during World War II. Significantly, the high wartime statutory rates were matched by high effective ones—i.e., the taxes actually paid by corporations, after accounting for depreciation and other deductions. In 1944, for example, a set of 2,500 leading American industrial corporations earned $3.9 billion after taxes, on pretax income of $10.1 billion. This translated into an effective corporate tax rate, for this large group, of 61%—a remarkably high figure, by any historical standard.[21]

Despite the impressive revenue-raising achievements of the EPT, it was less damaging to the fortunes of American corporations than it appeared on the surface.[22] As the pages that follow suggest, the high EPT rates were moderated by other, more business-friendly considerations. Several of these, including the carryback provisions that would prove so helpful to business during the reconversion period of 1945–47 (when they would briefly attract national attention), were introduced in the Revenue Act of 1942. The same law that created the mass individual income tax, this was the giant new revenue scheme that President Roosevelt dubbed "the greatest tax bill in American history."[23] As the record of the birth of the carrybacks suggests, they owed their existence in part to the bill's very "greatness," and in part to the professional accountants who best appreciated their utility.

One of the most complex pieces of legislation in American history to date, the Revenue Act of 1942 was the subject of extensive debate, especially in Washington but also across the nation. The House and Senate hearings on the bill, which stretched from March to August, filled 6,000 printed pages. The act itself ended up being squeezed into 208 printed pages of fine print, which detailed its 173 separate provisions, 43 of which were devoted to the EPT.[24] Of all of these provisions, the ones that received the least attention, relative to their significance, were the carrybacks. Barely mentioned in the hundreds of hours of hearings and written into the bill at a relatively late stage, they became part of the law with remarkably little discussion or controversy. Many business leaders and members of Congress, to say nothing of average Americans, appear to have remained ignorant of them for months or years after their creation. Even the Treasury and congressional staff experts who wrote them into the bill in late August in an effort to satisfy Senate conservatives had demonstrated little interest in them before that moment. Little known outside the accounting profession, the carryback mechanism at the beginning of World War II ranked as just one among many obscure forms of potential tax relief for business. This fact makes it all the more remarkable that it became so hotly debated in early 1946, and that by then it was being widely defended as an essential economic policy.

As its defenders occasionally noted, the carryback mechanism had some precedent in American law, because the Revenue Act of 1918 had allowed corporations with losses during the reconversion year of 1919 to carry them back and forward for one year to reduce tax liability for 1918 and 1920.[25] But it was the "carryover" (i.e., carryforward) of losses, and not carryback, that survived into the 1920s. In 1921, a Republican-controlled Congress, encouraged by the pro-business Treasury Secretary Andrew W. Mellon, repealed the EPT and instituted a two-year carryforward provision. Such a policy ostensibly encouraged entrepreneurialism, since a new company with early losses could look forward to reducing taxes on future profits. More generally, as accountants knew well, the policy prevented businesses with volatile earnings records from paying more taxes over a series of years (because of the graduated rate structure) than their counterparts whose earnings were more steady. Throughout the 1920s, Congress renewed the two-year carryforward in successive revenue bills. In 1933, as the New Deal was launched, the measure was abolished.[26] In 1939, the two-year carryforward was revived as part of an effort by Congress and the Treasury (resisted by President Roosevelt) to create a new "business recovery" tax code that would encourage business expansion in the wake of the recent recession.[27] And in 1941, Congress extended the two-year carryforward provision to apply to unused EPT exemption allowances, as well as net losses.[28]

This extension of carryforward to the EPT did not provide nearly enough relief, in the eyes of many business leaders, especially as they braced themselves after Pearl Harbor for a giant hike in normal and EPT rates. By early 1942, after two years of strong profits, it was becoming clear that like World War I, the new conflict would likely provide many American businesses with record levels of sales and pretax earnings, but that high tax rates would leave net margins (if not dollar earnings) rather low. This dynamic made it easy for business leaders to complain throughout the war of insufficient profits, even as their critics had no trouble providing statistics demonstrating that corporate profits were at record levels.[29]

As they retooled for war in early 1942, many companies contemplated the future expense of the postwar reconversion to civilian production. That summer, while the revenue bill was being debated, Andrew W. Robertson, the chairman of the formidable Westinghouse Electric & Manufacturing Co., wrote every member of Congress to say that he was deeply disturbed by the drop in after-tax earnings at his company, which had gone from $5.6 million in the fourth quarter of 1941 to $4.1 million (under 4% of sales) in the first quarter of 1942. Because Westinghouse during the 1936–39 base period had enjoyed average earnings of over $14 million a year, the company enjoyed a relatively high EPT credit. Nonetheless, Robertson was concerned that anything more would seriously threaten his company's ability to make the investments necessary to keep its high-tech electrical equipment business (now starting to produce top-secret radar systems) viable in the postwar era.[30]

Robertson soon received a favorable reply from Senator Walter F. George of Georgia, who had become chairman of the Senate Finance Committee in 1941. A conservative Democrat who had survived President Roosevelt's efforts against him in the 1938 elections, George now ranked as one of the most powerful members of Congress in the field of tax policy.[31] Wary of Roosevelt and hostile to many of the more progressive elements of the New Deal, George was exactly the sort of politician American business wanted to see as a congressional overseer of revenue legislation. In early 1942, George had discussed corporate tax policy with a top executive from General Motors (GM), who had suggested that it would be extremely helpful to allow companies to avoid paying taxes on the reconversion reserves that many of them were already setting aside. George agreed with GM. In the summer of 1942, in published reply to the recent open letter to Congress from Robertson of Westinghouse, he promoted the concept of reserves sheltered from taxes. Perhaps as much as 20% of corporate income might be made tax-exempt and used as a "nest egg for post war conversion and production," George suggested to Robertson. Above all, the senator hinted, it would be most effective for business to advocate for policies that would guarantee a more favorable environment in the immediate postwar period. "Private enterprise has lost its meaning for the duration," wrote George. "What should be your concern, my concern, everybody's concern, is the removal of these controls after the war."[32]

As George's reference to tax-exempt reserves suggests, carryback was not among the tax relief measures most discussed during the long evolution of the 1942 revenue bill. Given that carryback had been introduced briefly during World War I and that since that conflict carryforward had become a standard part of the tax code, it was not at all surprising that some interested parties would attempt to reintroduce carryback during World War II. The interest in doing so, however, was not at first particularly energetic or widespread. During the congressional hearings that preceded the creation of the Second Revenue Act of 1940, several expert witnesses did advise Congress to extend the two-year carryforward to unused EPT exemption allowances, which it would do the following year. These carryover proponents included Walter A. Cooper, chairman of the American Institute of Accountants's committee on federal taxation, and William J. Kelly, president of Machinery and Allied Products Institute, a Chicago-based association representing capital goods manufacturers.[33] During these summer 1940 hearings, only one witness asked Congress to allow carryback, as well as carryforward. This was Alger B. Chapman of the Controllers Institute of America, which represented the chief accounting officers of many large enterprises. Like other witnesses, Chapman also asked that companies in their EPT exemption allowance calculations be allowed to choose any three of four base period years and to exempt at least 8% of invested capital. In briefly making the case for carryback, Chapman pointed to the World War I precedent.[34]

Between the Second Revenue Act of 1940, which did end up allowing carryforward of the EPT exemption allowances, and the beginning of the debates over the bill that would become the Second Revenue Act of 1942, there seems to have been relatively little interest in the business community—or at the Treasury or in Congress—in creating carrybacks. Not long after the Second Revenue Act of 1940 became law, the Chamber of Commerce did issue a short pamphlet that endorsed Chapman's suggestions, including carryback and the option to choose three of four base years.[35] But in 1942, the big industrial associations did not use their time at the revenue hearings to make much of a case for carryback. The Chamber's main representative, Ellsworth C. Alvord (chairman of its committee on federal finance) mentioned it briefly, but treated it as one minor recommendation among many others. Spokesmen for the influential National Association of Manufacturers (NAM) never even mentioned it.[36]

This lack of interest in carryback came in part because the revenue bill was so comprehensive and ambitious. Its sheer size overwhelmed members of Congress, lobbyists, and probably even the Treasury experts as well. Among the many prospective provisions that overshadowed specific corporate tax relief provisions were the possibility of a federal sales tax; the basic rate structures for expanded corporate and individual income taxes; the question of whether to retain tax exemptions for municipal bonds; the fate of special "depletion allowance" benefits for the oil and mining industries; and the prospect of allowing married couples to file separate returns. The details overwhelmed even well-informed witnesses, such as Albert L. Hopkins, a member of the Chamber's committee on federal finance, who complained in his testimony before Congress that "[t]he bill is 320 pages long.... The committee report is 187 pages of fine print. I would like to lay a wager that no one person could name ten people who understand it.... Yet, millions of taxpayers are required to understand it and report accordingly under threat of great pains and penalties."[37] While Hopkins emphasized the bill's incomprehensibility to taxpayers, his remarks applied just as well to the creation of the legislation. Few groups or individuals understood all of it, nor could they successfully track every addition and modification as it developed.

To the extent that carryback was discussed at all in the 1942 hearings, it was emphasized not by business leaders or government experts, but by accountants and tax lawyers from the private sector. Treasury officials briefly referred to carryover in their testimony before the Senate in July 1942, but neither they nor the senators chose to discuss it.[38] Chapman, the Comptrollers' Institute spokesman who had been the lone champion of carryback in 1940, raised the issue again, emphasizing that the measure would properly smooth the tax burdens of corporations with uneven results from year to year. As a possible alternative, he suggested allowing the deduction of "reasonable reserves" for reconversion. M. L. Seidman, chairman of the taxation committee of the New York Board of Trade, also called for carryback and exemptions for reserves, among recommendations for many other measures, including the sales tax. Other witnesses who mentioned some sort of carryback in 1942, usually along with many other suggestions, were Cooper, of the American Institute of Accountants's committee on federal taxation; New York lawyer and accountant Joseph J. Klein, representing the Brooklyn Chamber of Commerce; and Paul D. Seghers, a New York tax lawyer associated with the Federal Tax Forum.[39] According to Seghers, a one-year net loss carryback, combined with some sort of automatic refund of a fraction of all EPT payments, "would give business far greater confidence, and it would offer a great cushion against a depression."[40]

Given that organized labor would end up complaining strenuously about carryback during the reconversion period, it is notable that the several labor representatives who testified at the 1942 hearings had nothing to say about any specific corporate tax relief measure, let alone carryback specifically. Given the scope of the bill, this was not surprising. But clearly, labor was overmatched in 1942 when it came to the details of the corporate tax code. Emphasizing the general point that the bill failed to achieve "equality of sacrifice," labor leaders, including CIO President Philip Murray, focused on supporting President Roosevelt's call for a cap of $25,000 for after-tax individual incomes, and backing the Treasury's opposition to the sales tax and its calls for a more progressive rate structure, including a 55% normal rate for corporations. Some labor witnesses, including Russ Nixon of the United Electrical, Radio, & Machine Workers of America, issued eloquent calls for Congress to create a tax bill that truly served the public interest, instead of the interests of the powerful. But when Nixon and other labor witnesses called for the abolition of tax "loopholes," they said little about what those might be or how they worked.[41] Understandably focused on the big picture, labor paid little attention to minor provisions like carryback.

Like organized labor, Treasury officials and Congress focused above all on EPT and normal corporate income tax rates, along with the size of the proposed automatic postwar EPT "credit" that would effectively reduce the nominal rate. Since Britain and Canada had already adopted a 100% EPT along with a 20% postwar credit (thereby creating an effective EPT rate of 80%), this was used as a common reference point. As they worked on the final bill in the late summer of 1942, Congress and the Treasury would settle with relatively little trouble on a 90% EPT rate and a 10% automatic postwar refund (amounting to an 81% effective EPT rate), along with a hard ceiling that insured that no corporation would be made to pay federal taxes that amounted to more than 80% of its profits. Far more controversial, as the Senate Finance Committee began to write amendments into the bill in late August, was the question of the proper "normal" corporate rate. (Applied to earnings exempt from the EPT, the "normal" rate technically consisted of a regular rate combined with a separate wartime surtax.) The House bill that emerged in July had set it at 45%, but Treasury officials wanted it to be 55%, especially if they were to agree on some mechanism for creating the sort of tax-exempt reserves that many businesses had suggested.[42] Colin Stam, the chief of the congressional tax staff, agreed with Senator George, Ways & Means Committee chairman Robert Doughton, and other members that the 55% figure was far too high; he also feared that the Treasury might structure the rules governing reserves in a way that would made it difficult for business to tap them at war's end.[43]

It was at this moment in late August 1942, as Congress wrangled with the Treasury over rates and relief provisions, that the carrybacks suddenly became part of the bill. There were actually two carryback mechanisms created. The simpler of the two, known as a "two-year carry back of net operating losses," allowed a company to apply a net operating loss to the company's accounts for one or both of the previous two years. The second type of carryback allowed a company to carry back to the previous two years any difference between its operating profits and its excess-profits tax exemption allowance, the measure of "normal" peacetime earnings that had been central to the calculation of corporate taxes since 1940. This second provision, which would prove important in 1946, was known as the carryback of an "unused excess profits credit." Both carryback mechanisms worked by reducing past profits and tax liabilities, thereby generating a refund of taxes paid during the war.[44] These provisions became a quick, manageable substitute for the more widely discussed proposals for tax-exempt reconversion reserves, which both Treasury and congressional experts had come to regard as too unwieldy to implement. The birth of carryback was covered to some extent by the press, perhaps best of all by the *Wall Street Journal*, which had an active Washington bureau and devoted hundreds of column inches throughout the year to tax news. According to the Treasury, the newspaper explained at the time, the purpose of the carrybacks, was to ease "extreme hardships on taxpayers with income later offset by losses."[45] More specifically, as Senator George explained to the paper, this addition to the bill "was designed to furnish a measure of relief for companies which have been forced to defer maintenance because of the war and for those who suffer inventory losses due to price conditions."[46]

Recollections by top Treasury officials more or less agree with this account of carryback's birth, just as they fail to note the role of private-sector accountants in bringing this policy option to the table. Toward the end of the war, Roy Blough, the economist who served as director of tax research for the Treasury, recalled that after the proposals for the reserve allowances were abandoned, members of the Senate Finance Committee asked "for another method to be developed which would correct the wartime income picture, or income figure, by allowing as a deduction against it those expenses and allowances which were due to the war, but not incurred until after the war." By looking back to the World War I precedent, Blough claimed, the Treasury was able to use carryback as a means of allowing corporations to properly account for costs associated with war mobilization that they did not formally incur until after the end of the military conflict. (They had the added benefit, Blough noted, of increasing a company's capacity, already allowed by the carryforward provisions, to average income for tax purposes.)[47] Another top Treasury official, general counsel Randolph E. Paul, agreed with the essence of Blough's account. The "major" purpose of adding the carrybacks in 1942, Paul wrote after the war, was "to provide a general method of offsetting reconversion costs and losses against wartime income."[48]

All of these accounts of the intended purposes of the carrybacks were technically accurate, but they tended to obscure the broader political and institutional context that prevailed at the moment of the birth of the provisions. As Blough recalled diplomatically, the carrybacks "grew out of the effort to resolve the conflict between considerations for and considerations against a high excess-profits tax."[49] More specifically, in fact, they had been drafted by the Treasury staffers only in an effort to provide enough tax relief to business—in whatever form—to preserve the 55% normal corporate income tax rate that they understood as critical to a successful revenue bill. Congress, intent on reasserting its power over the Treasury, was demanding additional corporate tax relief, along with dozens of other changes that were stretching Treasury capabilities and threatened to delay passage of the bill until after the 1942 elections. Senator George, who had long distanced himself from the Roosevelt administration on domestic issues and wanted to promote congressional authority over tax policy, had little interest in compromising with the Treasury.[50] Thus, while it would not be false to state that the Treasury was the source of the provisions, they were initially championed by a small group of corporate controllers, accountants, and tax lawyers; were reached for by the Treasury in an effort to appease congressional conservatives; and were introduced at a late stage into a giant bill, where they were soon lost in the forest of multiple complex provisions, many of which pertained not to corporate taxes but to the individual income tax.[51]

Days after their birth, the carryback provisions faded in the press coverage of the bill and probably also in the minds of many of those who created them. By the time the bill reached the Senate floor in early October, the carrybacks were certainly not given much notice. When Senator George presented the bill to his colleagues on 6 October, he spent less than a minute (roughly 2% of his overview) talking about the net loss carrybacks. Notably, the brief example he provided to illustrate how they might be used imagined a company with a net operating loss of $1,000. His treatment of the carryback of EPT credits amounted to a single sentence.[52] The first of his colleagues to respond was Senator McNary (R-OR), who admitted plainly that it was "a bill which it is almost impossible for one to understand, without sufficient time carefully to study it."[53] Over the next hour or so, the Senate approved nearly all of the 400 revisions that George's committee had proposed to the House bill, including the carrybacks, without any discussion or debate.[54]

No less than Senator McNary's comments about the bill's complexity, President Roosevelt's reaction to the bill was telling. When Roosevelt met with Treasury officials to discuss the bill before he signed it into law on 21 October, he reportedly complained to them, "The bill might as well have been written in a foreign language." Treasury undersecretary Daniel Bell paraphrased more of Roosevelt's comments at this meeting: "He did not understand it and did not think the Treasury understood it. . . . He was told he had to sign it that day in order to save some $60 million revenue, so that he was forced to sign it without reading it. He made quite a joke of the whole thing."[55] Although the wily Roosevelt likely exaggerated his own ignorance of the content of the legislation, these comments suggest that it is more than possible that the President had taken little notice, if any, of the carrybacks.

Once the act was passed, it was quickly understood to be a tax law that was unexpectedly friendly to business, despite the 90% EPT. George and his allies had succeeded in lowering the normal corporate rate to 40%, far below what the Treasury had wanted. The bite of the EPT was lessened by the automatic 10% postwar refund and the 80% overall ceiling. Some larger corporate entities that owned multiple subsidiaries could benefit considerably from the restoration of the privilege of filing consolidated returns (unavailable to nonrailroad corporations since 1934), which allowed some of them to use losses in one unit to reduce taxable profits in another.[56] Even for those critics of the bill who still took little notice of the carrybacks, its pro-business leanings were unmistakable. In the end, the Revenue Act of 1942 required corporations to pay only about half of the taxes they would have (and individuals twice as much as they would have), using the Treasury's recommendations or the original House bill. Despite the elevation of the EPT rate to 90%, Senator George had engineered a tax bill with an overall corporate tax burden that was remarkably close to the one sought at the outset by NAM and other conservative business interests.[57]

Well after the passage of the Revenue Act of 1942, few Americans, including many business leaders, seem to have grasped the implications of the carryback provisions. Some of the most thorough progressive critiques of the law, while emphasizing its generosity to business in general, did not even mention them.[58] As late as October 1943, top Treasury lawyer Randolph Paul told the American Institute of Accountants that "[t]he carry-back provision has received little attention," although it promised to perform many of the same functions as the more widely discussed mechanism of tax-deductible reconversion reserves.[59] But increasing numbers of people, especially in the legal and accounting professions, did take notice. According to one tax law expert who studied the entire act carefully in the weeks after its passage, the two-year carryback of net operating losses alone represented "a radical innovation in policy in our income tax law." Similarly, the carryback of the EPT exemption allowance stood as "an important new principle."[60] In the summer of 1943, one well-informed New York securities analyst published a magazine article calling attention to the provision. "Congress has done an important piece of postwar planning which nobody seems to have noticed," wrote Eugene Habas. Through carryback, he explained, "many (though not *all*) corporations can count on having 40 to 100 per cent of their *losses* in a postwar year covered by tax refunds, and that even if they show a small *profit* their tax refund will be sizable." Habas understood this as an important and useful reconversion policy, since it "should encourage many companies to spend money in ways which will maintain or increase employment."[61]

As the war went on and planning for reconversion increased, experts began to lavish more attention on the carrybacks. In January 1944, Bernard M. Joffe, an accountant, emphasized the merits of carryback in a lunchtime speech to a group of textile credit men in New York. "Unfortunately and peculiarly enough," Joffe claimed, carryback "has been given little publicity. . . . In many discussions with executives I have noted the scant attention paid to this provision." One reason the measure deserved more scrutiny by business leaders, Joffe explained, was that the law stated that a change in a firm's legal status, such as a shift from a corporation to a partnership, would cause it to lose access to the provision. Awareness of the carrybacks, in this case, might influence decisions about a company's future form.[62] More generally, accountants stressed the potential economic value of the carrybacks to any company anticipating losses during reconversion. According to a Summer 1944 article in a leading accountancy journal, professionals were by then well aware of their potential as "a valuable source of funds" for the postwar period.[63] Soon after the war ended, *Dun's Review*, a leading magazine for business executives, published a piece by leading accountant J. K. Lasser, who used a set of calculations applied to an imaginary firm to show how operating losses in 1946 might easily turn into after-tax profits. "Plan your current operations for 1946," Lasser urged business executives, "with the aid of your tax man."[64]

Accountants and business leaders stepped up their attention to carrybacks when they realized that the structure of the legislation meant that if the EPT was cancelled at war's end, the ability to carry back EPT exemption allowances would disappear along with it. As one economist observed in the fall of 1945, in this sense "the disposition of the carry-back presents a troublesome and somewhat embarrassing complication." Keeping the carryback of EPT exemption allowances while ending the EPT "is likely to give rise to charges of favoritism to business," he predicted, as well as concerns about abuses of the mechanism by firms who artificially crammed money-losing ventures into the postwar period. Even without such abuses, he noted, it would likely generate some huge refund checks to many corporations.[65] (Indeed, because the EPT exemption allowance was essentially the same as a company's average annual profits in the late 1930s, firms with high prewar base period earnings that simply broke even in the first postwar year would be able to claim millions of dollars in tax refunds, because they could subtract their whole allowance from earnings for a profitable war year.) Despite these potential difficulties, professional accountants—acting again, in effect, as auxiliaries to manufacturing corporations—argued that EPT itself should be ended right after the war, but the carrybacks continued, at least temporarily. Maurice Austin, a leading figure in the American Institute of Accountants, took this position in his talks about tax carryovers to the organization's annual meetings in 1943 and 1944. Admitting to this expert audience that carryovers "are one of those phases of the law which are surrounded by considerable complexity of language in statute and regulations," Austin praised them for their technical sophistication and promotion of equity. In essence, Austin explained, carryback amounted to "a recognition of the fact that wartime profits contain their own seeds of postwar losses." Naturally, then, they must be extended into the postwar period, preferably for at least two years. Furthermore, given their contribution to the legitimate goal of protecting firms in industries that tended to see volatile earnings records from year to year, they "might well find a permanent place in our post-war tax system." Although the question of their permanency was certainly debatable, Austin argued, the carrybacks must be available for reconversion, because they "formed so large a part of the postwar planning of business enterprises."[66] Similar arguments were made by parties on many sides of the growing debate in the business community on the future of the broader corporate tax code, including those who supported the maintenance of a high normal rate into the postwar era, as well as those who called for major cuts or a complete end to the tax.[67]

Legislators in Washington, giving little notice to the warnings about a potential political backlash, followed the advice of industry and the accountants. In the summer of 1945, the carryback refunds were endorsed in the Tax Adjustment Act, which Congress created to improve the cash position of business as it headed into reconversion.[68] Then, in the Revenue Act of 1945, passed at the end of the year, Congress cancelled the EPT itself but extended the EPT exemption allowance carryback for another year. (The carryback of net operating losses continued indefinitely; it would become a fixture in the tax code.) In the estimation of Carl Shoup, a Columbia University economics professor who was one of the nation's leading tax authorities, the 1945 law gave "corporations all, if not more than, they could have hoped for in a quick tax reduction bill."[69] While this did suggest Congress's interest in boosting the fortunes of business during the postwar years, it did not evidently indicate that legislators understood carrybacks much better than they had when they approved their creation three years before. In the summer of 1945, during some extended remarks he made on the House floor about the details of the Tax Adjustment Act that sped up the postwar refunds, Representative Thomas Jenkins, a conservative Republican from Ohio, implied that most of his colleagues had so little knowledge of the provisions that it would be impossible for him to broach the subject. "The subject of carry-overs and carry-backs," he told his fellow congressmen flatly, "is too complicated for me to discuss at this time."[70]

As Jenkins's words suggest, most congressmen knew little about the details of the corporate tax code, even though they were in some sense responsible for its content. In his 1945 remarks, he effectively suggested to his colleagues that he knew they did not share his knowledge, but that they should trust his expertise and sign off on the measures that would speed up the carryback refunds. Like the accounting experts in the private sector, whose authority he respected and perpetuated, Jenkins used his superior knowledge in ways that assisted business. Although he and his allies enjoyed remarkable success in the long run, it was not without enduring some substantial short-run blowback. This occurred in early 1946, in the midst of one of the biggest strike waves in American history.

Well before the winter and spring of 1945–46, when some three million American workers were out on strike, labor leaders had begun to call attention to the benefits that the tax code afforded corporations. Philip Murray, the leader of the steelworkers and president of the CIO, demonstrated a special interest in this subject. In March 1944, as Murray struggled to circumvent wartime wage caps and negotiate a pay increase for the steelworkers, a CIO report denounced "one of the most gigantic steals in U.S. tax history, engineered for the benefit of corporations by Congress." The two-year carryback provisions effectively guaranteed two years of postwar profits for business, the CIO explained; "why," it asked, "not some sort of guaranteed income for workers who may be laid off?" This new attention to carryback likely came in part from the efforts of Murray and his lieutenants to show that the steel industry could well afford to provide a raise. In addition, the CIO had recently come across a Prentice-Hall bulletin from January 1944, which advised businessmen of the uses of carryback. "Write your Congressman," the bulletin urged business leaders, to say "that expansion plans you are contemplating depend on carry-back and carry-forward. Remind him you are relying on their continuation."[71]

Labor's attention to the corporate tax code increased during the postwar strikes, when workers became especially interested in what corporate balance sheets suggested about their ability to grant wage increases. The major strikes began in November 1945 when Walter Reuther led the UAW's action against General Motors. From the beginning of the GM strike, it was understood that various aspects of the tax code, including the EPT itself, limited any losses the company might suffer from a walkout. "Never before," explained *Business Week*, "has a major employer had so little direct economic incentive to end a stoppage by making concessions to a union."[72] One of the most notable aspects of the GM strike was Reuther's insistence that GM open its books to reveal the details of its finances, so that anyone could assess its ability to pay the raise of 30 cents an hour that Reuther wanted. GM executives were outraged by these "capacity to pay" arguments, which they rejected out of hand as "an attack on American industry and free enterprise."[73] Given Reuther's interest in the details of corporate finances, and given that GM ended up receiving roughly $80 million in tax refunds in 1945 and 1946,[74] he might have logically become the leading critic of the carrybacks during the reconversion period. But it was Murray, far more than Reuther, who put the national spotlight on carryback.

In late January and early February 1946, when Murray's steelworkers were out on strike, the CIO president placed the carryback provisions at the very center of his critique of American industry's behavior during reconversion. According to Murray, the availability of the refunds did not merely add to the evidence that industry could easily afford to raise pay. The refunds themselves, by allowing companies to offset large fractions of their postwar nominal losses, actually encouraged business leaders to choose to endure strikes instead of settle. By insulating companies almost entirely from any dollar losses they suffered from strikes, the carrybacks limited the influence of labor. In a major speech on 21 January 1946, carried on the American Broadcasting System radio network, Murray referred explicitly to the ill effects of the "carry-back, carry-forward" parts of the tax laws. "American industry, fattened with war profits, guaranteed a high level of profits through special tax rebates under laws written at their behest," declared Murray, "have deliberately set out to destroy labor unions, to provoke strikes and economic chaos, and hijack the American people through uncontrolled profits and inflation."[75] Murray demanded that Treasury Secretary Vinson investigate industry's use of the tax benefits, which the CIO contended were significantly increasing companies' willingness to endure strikes.[76]

During the four weeks that the steelworkers were out on strike, before they settled on 15 February in an agreement that provided a raise of 18.5 cents an hour, the carryback issue was an obsession for the *CIO News*, the weekly newspaper published by Murray's organization. It was the tax provisions above all, according to the paper's editors, that explained why corporations seemed almost to encourage strikes during reconversion. "The secret of their audacity," the newspaper explained, "is that they are entering this fight with weighted gloves." Thanks to the relief measures created in the Revenue Act of 1942, including the 10% EPT credit and the carryback of EPT exemption allowances, the steel industry stood to receive $149 million in tax refunds if it broke even in 1946. In the electrical industry, GE and Westinghouse together stood to get $38 million in refunds if they recorded no profits. These "extraordinary" gifts, the *CIO News* argued, echoing language in Murray's speech and his letter to Vinson, had been "slipped through Congress at the behest of big business."[77]

Thanks to Murray's protests, carryback became, briefly, a subject of national political debate. "The general public hears the term 'carry-back' for the first time," declared the *United States News* magazine, "and deluges the Treasury for explanations."[78] The CIO's friends in Congress acted quickly to highlight the issue and call for reform. On the same day as Murray's speech, Congressman Cleveland Bailey (D-WV) introduced a bill to repeal the carrybacks completely. The corporate tax law, Bailey told the House, made the federal government a "silent partner" in "a conspiracy on the part of a few to destroy our economy in their frantic efforts to crush organized labor."[79] Other House members, including Charles LaFollette (R-IN) and Herman Eberharter (D-PA), introduced bills that would disallow carrybacks only in cases involving strikes.[80] Echoing the claims of the CIO, Eberharter told the House that because of "a little-understood provision of our wartime excess-profits tax provision," American taxpayers "will be called upon to guarantee the profits of the steel industry out of the public Treasury." By ending the EPT in 1945 but continuing the EPT credit carryback, Eberharter explained, "we said to these corporations, 'It's heads you win, tails we lose.'"[81]

The challenges to carryback by the CIO and pro-labor congressmen were quickly denounced by business associations, accountants, conservative politicians, and the business press. They argued that the refunds were the result of the democratic legislative process, as well as sound modern accounting and tax principles, and must not be rolled back. Outraged by Murray's challenge to the refund provisions, the *Wall Street Journal* devoted two editorials in late January to exposing what it regarded as his tricks. After explaining that Murray was ignorant of the details of U.S. Steel's actual EPT payments record and eligibility for refunds, the newspaper emphasized that Murray was wrong to claim that the carryback measures had been slipped into the law back in 1942. In truth, "these and all other provisions of the war revenue acts were discussed at great length in open committee hearings before their enactment and the discussions were elaborately reported in the press. He is only amusing when he says that there was something furtive about this legislation."[82] Six days later, another editorial added that Murray's claim "that the taxpayer is in effect financing the companies against strikes," was wrong because only some fraction of a dollar lost in 1946 would be recoverable through carrybacks, so business executives still had an incentive to limit losses. This piece, too, focused on explaining the origins of the provision. Back in 1942, "corporations, well aware that war production costs would involve the rehabilitation and reconversion of plants after the conflict, asked that they be permitted to set up non-taxable reserves for these purposes. The Treasury opposed this and evolved instead the carry-back provisions which were designed to afford business just relief. The proposal was debated in Congress and in the public press for months before enactment."[83]

By early 1946, these editorials show, there was a considerable interest, on both sides of the debate over the carrybacks, to misunderstand the history of their origins. For Murray, it made sense to make the leap from the real lack of publicity surrounding their introduction to the claim that they had been slipped in secretly. For the *Journal* and its allies it was convenient to overstate the amount and quality of conversation about the measures during the long evolution of the 1942 bill. If Murray exaggerated the underhandedness of the process, he also did more than the *Journal* to suggest the extent to which the carrybacks became part of the law with remarkably little open discussion.

The *Journal* was far from the only defender of business interests to denounce Murray's radical claims about the carryback provisions and their origins. The measures "were placed in the tax laws upon the recommendation of Treasury officials," a spokesman for the NAM explained, "and were approved by Congress. They were designed by the Treasury to permit corporations to charge off deferred war costs that could not be determined until war production was complete."[84] Maurice Austin of the American Institute of Accountants, long a leading expert on the provisions and a champion of them, warned that a repeal would be "calamitous." Even strike costs, Austin argued, qualified as regular reconversion expenses.[85] This hard-boiled position was echoed by Senator George, the Finance Committee chairman, who defended the laws he had written, declaring that strike expenses were "legitimate losses."[86] These views were repeated a few weeks later in the House by Congressman Jenkins of Ohio, who used an extended dissertation on taxes in March 1946 to explain that the carrybacks had been created "upon the express recommendations of the Treasury Department and the staff of the Joint Committee on Internal Revenue Taxation." While acknowledging that carryback had become the most controversial of the corporate tax relief mechanisms because it could be manipulated and abused, Jenkins maintained that the refunds "cannot be regarded as an unwarranted postwar gift" to business. Condemning the efforts by Murray and others "to mislead and confuse the public," Jenkins counseled his fellow congressmen to remember that the "basic truth" about carryback provisions was "that they guarantee adherence to sound and long-accepted principles of taxation."[87] Thanks to the decidedly non-radical sensibilities of Perkins, George, Ways & Means Committee chairman Doughton, and their colleagues, none of the several bills calling for the reform of carryback made it out of committee.[88]

Outside Congress, as well as inside it, the furor over carryback proved shortlived and was soon eclipsed by other concerns. Despite Murray's serious interest in the issue, the settlement of the steel strike removed the most immediate cause of his complaint. It also allowed the steel industry to return quickly to profitability (thanks to a $5 a ton government-authorized price increase, as well as the resumption of production), which reduced the impact of carrybacks in the industry that concerned Murray the most. The spring and summer of 1946 brought new struggles, including fights against new "right to work" initiatives and for continuation of government price controls.[89] Although Murray and Reuther both continued to speak about the injustice of the carryback refunds through the end of the year, by then they had become secondary concerns.[90] Labor's de-emphasis of the issue, however, stemmed more from the press of other issues and the settlement of the strikes than from any correction of the larger problems that labor leaders alleged were manifested by the carryback provisions. The strategic decision of Murray and Reuther to downgrade the issue effectively returned it to political obscurity, where business was able to dominate policymaking.

Although 1946 turned out to be an unexpectedly good year for many American businesses, most of which became too profitable to claim the carrybacks, some companies recorded big losses that made carryback highly relevant. Those most affected tended to be those in the industries that had been most heavily involved in the war effort, including the automotive, aircraft, and electrical equipment sectors. In the months that followed the public blowup over the carrybacks in early 1946, these corporations and their accountants began to tally up the size of the refunds. They would amount to about $1.1 billion for 1946 alone; in 1945–47 all together, they totaled $1.8 billion.[91] Expert observers regarded the carryback refunds as one of the most important parts of the broader reconversion tax-cut initiative, passed by Congress in 1945, that helped push aggregate U.S. corporate profits up from about $9 billion in 1945 to $13 billion in 1946.[92]

For some of the country's leading industrial corporations, the carrybacks meant that most of their reconversion losses could be written off. In many cases, this allowed companies to avoid dipping into large stores of wartime profits that had been set aside to assist with reconversion. One striking example was the case of the United Aircraft Corp., whose Pratt & Whitney division, a top producer of aircraft engines, put it at the heart of the American military-industrial juggernaut. In 1946, as many of its big war contracts ran out, United Aircraft suffered a net operating loss of $5 million. However, thanks to income tax refunds of nearly $11 million, the company was able to report a respectable $6 million in financial net income for the year. And it did so without diminishing the giant reconversion reserves it had created during the war, $24 million of which it now declared to be pure profit.[93] This was a welcome gift to United Aircraft executives, who, at the outset of World War II, had wondered whether they would come out of the war and reconversion experience with any profit at all.[94] At dozens of other companies, the results were similar. General Motors actually made a bit of money in 1946, despite the trials of reconversion. But because its $88 million in profits for the year were lower than its EPT exemption allowance, General Motors was able to use carryback to generate a $60 million tax credit. This allowed GM to declare a "special income credit" of $30 million, taken from a reconversion reserves fund that was now unneeded.[95] At the smaller Packard Motor Car Co., a $4 million net loss in 1946 was more than offset by tax credits of $6 million and the transfer of $3 million in reconversion reserves to the earned surplus account.[96]

Although the provision allowing the carryback of EPT exemption allowances expired after 1946, the carryback of net losses continued; it was used widely in 1947 by companies in the aircraft industry, which were still suffering from the downturn in military orders.[97] For instance, North American Aviation, one of the big wartime airframe makers, used carryback to offset nearly all of its $12 million operating loss for 1947, over $8 million of which was attached to its failed effort to secure large orders of its "Navion" four-passenger personal airplane.[98] During the Korean War, as it created another temporary EPT, Congress altered the permanent carryover provisions, substituting a one-year carryback, along with a five-year carryforward, of net operating losses.[99] Although they have been altered frequently since their installation in 1942, the carryback and carryforward combination has endured long in U.S. tax law. By the early twenty-first century, the tax code provided a two-year carryback of net operating losses, along with a twenty-year carryforward.

Now taken for granted, these carryovers continue to be well known to accountants, economists, and finance experts, who have developed sophisticated models of their effects on business investment decisions. These provisions are one reason that for many corporations, a nominal dollar in operating losses translates into considerably less than a dollar in after-tax losses. Conversely, they—along with many other tax benefits—help to insure that the Treasury sees revenues far lower than those that would be required if tax accounting stopped with a simple application of nominal rates. At the end of the twentieth century, the carryback and carryover together reduced federal revenues from corporate income taxes by about 15%.[100]

For the generations of Americans who came of age in the United States after World War II, many of the political and economic dynamics that manifested themselves in the birth of carryback and its controversial implementation would come to seem normal. To a considerable extent, however, this reflects the triumph of the private-sector experts, who fed their authorized policy provisions to a Congress predisposed to lend business a helping hand. It was also promoted by the continued growth in the scope and complexity of legislation, which soon made the big bills that so impressed observers in the 1940s look puny. For business, this remarkable growth of the state and the law could be genuinely frightening. But for some companies, and for the business service professionals who served them, complexity and obscurity had considerable compensations.

Notes

I thank Steve Bank and Ajay Mehrotra for their generous suggestions along the way as I composed this chapter.

1. W. Elliot Brownlee, "Tax Regimes, National Crisis, and State-Building in America," in *Funding the Modern American State, 1941–1995: The Rise and Fall of the Era of Easy Finance*, ed. W. Elliot Brownlee (New York: Cambridge University Press, 1996), 91; Bartholomew H. Sparrow, *From the Outside In: World War II and the American State* (Princeton, N.J.: Princeton University Press, 1996), 97–160; Carolyn C. Jones, "Mass-based Income Taxation: Creating a Taxpaying Culture, 1940–1952," in *Funding the Modern American State*, ed. Brownlee, 107–47; Joseph Jacobs Thorndike, III, "The Price of Civilization: Taxation for Depression and War, 1932–1945" (Ph.D. diss., University of Virginia, 2005), esp. 425–42; James T. Sparrow, "Buying Our Boys Back," *Journal of Policy History* 20 (2008): 263–86.
2. Ajay K. Mehrotra, "American Economic Development, Managerial Corporate Capitalism, and the Institutional Foundations of the Modern Income Tax," *Law and Contemporary Problems* 73 (Winter 2010): 25–61.
3. Joseph J. Thorndike, "'The Unfair Advantage of the Few': The New Deal Origins of 'Soak the Rich' Taxation," in *The New Fiscal Sociology: Taxation in Comparative and Historical Perspective*, ed. Isaac William Martin, Ajay K. Mehrotra, and Monica Prasad (New York: Cambridge University Press, 2009), 29–47; Steven A. Bank, *From Sword to Shield: The*

Transformation of the Corporate Income Tax, 1861 to Present (New York: Oxford University Press, 2010), 153–87.

4. Alfred G. Buehler, "The Problem of the Excess Profits Tax," in *Excess Profits Taxation* (Princeton, N.J.: Tax Institute, 1953), 7.

5. See James T. Sparrow, *Warfare State: World War II Americans and the Age of Big Government* (New York: Oxford University Press, 2011).

6. E. Cary Brown and Richard Eckhaus, "Operation of the Carrybacks of World War II during the Reconversion Period," *National Tax Journal* 5 (September 1952): 196–97.

7. Kenneth S. Reames, "The Place of Carry-Back and Carry-Over in Excess Profits Taxation," in *Excess Profits Taxation*, 68.

8. Many historians of the era, while well informed about the titanic struggles over the end of price controls, the Full Employment Bill of 1946, and the Taft-Hartley Act of 1947, have demonstrated little interest in this smaller piece of the larger story of postwar political economy. See, for example, Michael J. Lacey, ed., *The Truman Presidency* (New York: Cambridge University Press, 1989); Meg Jacobs, *Pocketbook Politics: Economic Citizenship in Twentieth-Century America* (Princeton, N.J.: Princeton University Press, 2005). Even historians of the massive postwar strikes, many of whom mention the role of corporate tax provisions in those struggles, fail to do enough to suggest their significance. Barton J. Bernstein, "Walter Reuther and the General Motors Strike of 1945–1946," *Michigan History* 49 (1965): 262; Bernstein, "The Truman Administration and the Steel Strike of 1946," *Journal of American History* 52 (March 1966): 795–96; Nelson Lichtenstein, *Labor's War at Home: The CIO in World War II* (New York: Cambridge University Press, 1982), 216. For a masterful account of the strikes, see Nelson Lichtenstein, *The Most Dangerous Man in Detroit: Walter Reuther and the Fate of American Labor* (New York: Basic Books, 1995), 233–46.

9. David Kocieniewski, "G.E.'s Strategies Let It Avoid Taxes Altogether," *New York Times*, 24 March 2011, A1.

10. Christopher Howard, *The Hidden Welfare State: Tax Expenditures and Social Policy in the United States* (Princeton, N.J.: Princeton University Press, 1997). See also Stanley S. Surrey, *Pathways to Tax Reform: The Concept of Tax Expenditures* (Cambridge, Mass.: Harvard University Press, 1973); Stanley S. Surrey and Paul R. McDaniel, *Tax Expenditures* (Cambridge, Mass.: Harvard University Press, 1985). Even the tax expenditure literature seems to understand carrybacks and carryforwards as normal accounting measures, rather than tax expenditures. See Surrey, *Pathways to Tax Reform*, 72–81. For a valuable study that emphasizes "incrementalism" in the formation of an excessively complex tax system, see John F. Witte, *The Politics and Development of the Federal Income Tax* (Madison: University Press of Wisconsin, 1985). Among the studies of corporate tax policy by political scientists that focus on public and private interest groups and lobbying, see Cathie J. Martin, *Shifting the Burden: The Struggle over Growth and Corporate Taxation* (Chicago: University of Chicago Press, 1991); Carla Inclán, Dennis P. Quinn, and Robert Y. Shapiro, "Origins and Consequences of Changes in U.S. Corporate Taxation, 1981–1998," *American Journal of Political Science* 45 (January 2001): 179–201; Brian Kelleher Richter, Krislert Samphantharak, and Jeffrey F. Timmons, "Lobbying and Taxes," *American Journal of Political Science* 53 (October 2009): 893–909.

11. Here I emphasize the role of business service professionals in the private sector, rather than those working on the government side. For studies that demonstrate the importance of the latter, see Herbert Stein, *The Fiscal Revolution in America* (Chicago: University of Chicago Press, 1969), 180–86; Julian E. Zelizer, *Taxing America: Wilbur D. Mills, Congress, and the State, 1945–1975* (New York: Cambridge University Press, 1998), esp. 43–54; Ajay K. Mehrotra, "Lawyers, Guns, and Public Moneys: The U.S. Treasury, World War I, and the Administration of the Modern Fiscal State," *Law and History Review* 28 (February 2010): 173–225; and Mehrotra, "American Economic Development, Managerial Corporate Capitalism, and the Institutional Foundations of the Modern Income Tax." For brief but suggestive discussions of accountants' influence on tax policy before World War II, see Paul J. Miranti, Jr., *Accountancy Comes of Age: The Development of an American Profession, 1886–1940* (Chapel Hill: University of North Carolina Press, 1990), 96–98, 130–32, 164–66.

12. Here the carryback story helps us to appreciate some important deficiencies in the historiography of American business in the era of World War II. This literature has said a great deal about the wartime growth of alliances between corporations and the national state, but it has done so most often by tracing the displacement of New Dealers in Washington by business conservatives, who settled into key posts in the Pentagon and war mobilization agencies including the War Production Board. See, for example, Paul A. C. Koistinen, *Arsenal of World War II: The Political Economy of American Warfare, 1940–1945* (Lawrence: University Press of Kansas, 2004); Brian Waddell, *The War Against the New Deal: World War II and American Democracy* (DeKalb: Northern Illinois University Press, 2001). Another important dimension of the subject has been illuminated by a growing literature on the highly ideological and well-funded campaign, led by the members of peak business associations like the National Association of Manufacturers (NAM), to ensure that the New Deal order would be succeeded by a postwar political economy that promoted "free enterprise." Mark Leff, "The Politics of Sacrifice on the American Home Front in World War II," *Journal of American History* 77 (1991): 1296–1318; Andrew A. Workman, "Manufacturing Power: The Organizational Revival of the National Association of Manufacturers, 1941–1945," *Business History Review* 72 (1998): 279–317. Howell John Harris, *The Right to Manage: Industrial Relations Policies of American Business in the 1940s* (Madison: University of Wisconsin Press, 1982); Elizabeth Fones-Wolf, *Selling Free Enterprise: The Business Assault on Labor and Liberalism, 1945–1960* (Urbana: University of Illinois Press, 1994); Cynthia Lee Henthorn, *From Submarines to Suburbs: Selling a Better America, 1939–1959* (Athens: Ohio University Press, 2006); Kim Phillips-Fein, *Invisible Hands: The Making of the Conservative Movement from the New Deal to Reagan* (New York: W. W. Norton, 2009); Mark R. Wilson, "'Taking a Nickel Out of the Cash Register': Statutory Renegotiation of Military Contracts and the Politics of Profit Control in the United States during World War II," *Law and History Review* 28 (May 2010): 343–83.

13. Roy Blough, "Problems of Corporate Taxation in Time of War," *Law and Contemporary Problems* 10 (Winter 1943): 114–16; Thorndike, "Price of Civilization," 453–69.

14. George E. Lent, "Excess-Profits Taxation in the United States," *Journal of Political Economy* 59 (December 1951): 481–83; Steven A. Bank, Kirk J. Stark, and Joseph J. Thorndike, *War and Taxes* (Washington, D.C.: Urban Institute Press, 2008), 63–81; Mehrotra, "Lawyers, Guns, and Public Moneys."

15. In the end, about 35% of the 68,000 corporations subjected to the EPT during World War II chose the average-earnings method. But these made up 54% of the total EPT tax yield. Dan Throop Smith, "The Role of Invested Capital in Excess Profits Taxation," in *Excess Profits Taxation*, 104–6.

16. Roy G. Blakey and Gladys C. Blakey, "The Two Federal Revenue Acts of 1940," *American Economic Review* 40 (December 1940): 724–35; E. Gordon Keith, "Excess Profits Taxation and Profit Limitation," *Accounting Review* 18 (April 1943): 103–10; C. Rudolph Peterson, "The Statutory Evolution of the Excess Profits Tax," *Law and Contemporary Problems* 10 (Winter 1943): 3–27.

17. Senator LaFollette of Wisconsin led the opposition to accelerated amortization in the Senate. His amendment to eliminate it was defeated in a 41–20 vote. See Witte, *Politics and Development of the Federal Income Tax*, 112.

18. On FDR's support for the measure, see John Morton Blum, *From the Morgenthau Diaries: Years of Urgency, 1938–1941* (Boston: Houghton Mifflin, 1965), 289–96. By the time the war was over, industry had applied accelerated amortization to $8.6 billion worth of new plant. See Koistinen, *Arsenal of World War II*, 300.

19. Lent, "Excess-Profits Taxation," 483–84; Thorndike, "Price of Civilization," 462–63. For more on the evolution of the JCIRT (established in 1927) and the Division of Tax Research at the Treasury (created in 1938), and the importance of Stam and Treasury tax experts such as Roy Blough and Randolph Paul, see Peterson, "Statutory Evolution of the Excess Profits Tax"; Thorndike, "Price of Civilization," 441–52.

20. Buehler, "Problem of the Excess Profits Tax," 7.

21. Office of Price Administration, *Corporate Profits, 1936–1946, Part I: Profits Growth to Wartime Peak, 2,500 Leading Industrial Corporations* (Washington, D.C., 1947), 2.

22. Indeed, the EPT should be given much more consideration by those who are interested in the most important wartime public policies in favor of "big business." Because of the way the credits were designed, the EPT favored companies that either enjoyed uncommonly good earnings in the late 1930s or started the war with very large amounts of invested capital. As one tax expert observed at the end of World War II, the tax tended to "favor the mature, well-established, heavily capitalized concerns over the young, growing, risky ventures." Buehler, "Problem of the Excess Profits Tax," 12. According to World War II tax policy celebrity Beardsley Ruml, the EPT was "a veritable engine of concentration." See Norris Darrell, "How Long Should the Accounting Period Be for Corporate Income Tax Purposes?" in *How Should Corporations be Taxed?* (New York: Tax Institute, Inc., 1947), 144. During the hearings that preceded the Second Revenue Act of 1940, there were numerous protests about the proposed EPT from newer, smaller, growing businesses. These included the Pepsi-Cola Co. and the small companies associated with the Los Angeles-based Aircraft Parts Manufacturers' Association, among many others. One of the companies that would benefit most from the invested-capital option, many agreed, was U.S. Steel, which in 1940 was capitalized at about $1.3 billion. *Second Revenue Act of 1940: Hearings before the Committee on Finance, Seventy-Sixth Congress, Third Session* (Washington, D.C.: GPO, 1940), 111, 201, 232. Many histories that describe World War II as promoting industrial concentration tend to blame the concentration (wrongly, I believe) on military procurement policies. See, for example, John Morton Blum, *V Was for Victory: Politics and American Culture during World War II* (New York: Harcourt Brace & Co, 1976), 121–24; Alan Brinkley, *The End of Reform: New Deal Liberalism in Recession and War* (New York: Alfred A. Knopf, 1995), 192–93.

23. Bank, Stark, and Thorndike, *War and Taxes*, 96.

24. Peterson, "Statutory Evolution of the Excess Profits Tax," 3; Witte, *Politics and Development of the Federal Income Tax*, 118–19.

25. Darrell, "How Long Should the Accounting Period Be for Corporate Income Tax Purposes?" 141; J. K. Lasser, "Loss Carryovers under the Internal Revenue Law," *Cornell Law Quarterly* 33 (1947): 51. The history of the use and impact of this carryback provision remains obscure. During World War II, it was understood to be a model for the new version that was created in 1942, but there was little sense, even among experts, if it had made any difference in 1919. As one leading tax economist ventured in early 1945, the 1919 measure "probably was not of substantial importance, because the year 1919 was generally a very good year." Roy Blough, "Averaging Income for Tax Purposes," *Accounting Review* 20 (January 1945): 90.

26. *Second Revenue Act of 1940*, 324.

27. Turner Catledge, "Senate Will Act on Taxes, Harrison Tells Roosevelt," *New York Times*, 16 May 1939, 1; "Bill to Ease Taxes Passed by Senate," *New York Times*, 23 June 1939, 1; William J. Enright, "Losses Provision in Tax Bill Hailed," *New York Times*, 25 June 1939, F1; Blum, *From the Morgenthau Diaries: Years of Urgency, 1938–1941*, 13–31; Leff, *Limits of Symbolic Reform*, 264–75.

28. Peterson, "Statutory Evolution of the Excess Profits Tax," 20; Kenneth S. Reames, "The Place of Carry-Back and Carry-Over in Excess Profits Taxation," in *Excess Profits Taxation*, 65. Because the overwhelming majority of firms saw considerable gains in pretax profits during World War II, these carryforward provisions did not become especially significant.

29. For a discussion of how the debate played out at the local level, see Richard L. Pifer, *A City at War: Milwaukee Labor during World War II* (Madison: Wisconsin Historical Society Press, 2003), 68–70.

30. A. W. Robertson, "Dear Mr. Congressman," *Nation's Business* 30 (July 1942): 25–26.

31. "George of Georgia: Senate's Undisputed Leader on Taxes," *Wall Street Journal*, 6 October 1942, 1, 8.

32. Report on "Conversation between Mr. Donaldson Brown and Senator Walter F. George," 6 March 1942, Folder 33b, Box 837, Papers of Walter S. Carpenter, Jr., Ser. II, Part 2, Records of E. I. Du Pont de Nemours & Co., Hagley Museum & Library, Wilmington, Del.; Walter F. George, "Dear Mr. Businessman," *Nation's Business* 30 (August 1942): 18.

33. *Second Revenue Act of 1940,* 47, 309. The companies Kelly represented were particularly interested in increasing their tax-averaging options, since they belonged to industries that tended to see particularly uneven results from year to year. In the 1940 hearings, Treasury officials expressed interest in extending the carryovers, but explained that they had decided not to recommend them because doing so would reduce revenues. *Excess Profits Taxation, 1940: Joint Hearings before the Committee on Ways and Means, House of Representatives, and the Committee on Finance, United States Senate* (Washington, D.C.: GPO, 1940), 90.

34. *Second Revenue Act of 1940,* 394; *Excess Profits Taxation: Joint Hearings,* 380.

35. Finance Dept., Chamber of Commerce of the U.S., "Immediate Amendments to the Excess Profits Tax Act" [pamphlet] (December 1940), Box 15, Ser. II, accession 1960, Hagley Museum & Library.

36. *Revenue Act of 1942: Hearings before the Committee on Finance, United States Senate, 77th Congress, 2nd Session* (Washington, D.C.: GPO, 1942), 2:1777–91.

37. *Revenue Act of 1942,* 2:1755.

38. Ibid., 1:39–105.

39. Ibid., 1:151, 1175; 2:1530, 1601, 2080, 2087.

40. Ibid., 1:694–95.

41. Ibid., 1:312–35.

42. "Hearings on Tax Bill May End on Thursday," *Wall Street Journal,* 10 August 1942, 2; "Tax Report," *Wall Street Journal,* 26 August 1942, 1; "Senate Committee Expected to Settle Major Points of 1942 Tax Measure This Week," *Wall Street Journal,* 31 August 1942, 5.

43. "House Adds $160 Million to Corporate Tax Burden by Boosting Excess Profits Levy," *Wall Street Journal,* 21 July 1942, 2. "Tax Report," *Wall Street Journal,* 23 September 1942, 1; "Treasury Renews Plan for Stiff Corporation Tax Rates, Suggests Measures to Ease Impact," *Wall Street Journal,* 26 August 1942, 5; "Senate Committee Rejects Ruml Tax Plan," *Wall Street Journal,* 27 August 1942, 3; "Corporation Tax Compromise Is Discussed," *Wall Street Journal,* 28 August 1942, 3; "Senate Group Approves Provisions Easing Excess Profits Tax Impact on Corporations," *Wall Street Journal,* 29 August 1942, 3.

44. Arthur H. Kent, "The Revenue Act of 1942," *Columbia Law Review* 43 (January 1943): 17, 28. For detailed contemporary explanations of how the carrybacks worked, see J. K. Lasser, "How the New Tax Law Affects Company Operations," *Dun's Review* (March 1946): 15–22; J. H. Landman, "Tax Reduction by Carry-Backs and Carry-Overs," *Journal of Accountancy* 81 (April 1946): 284.

45. "Treasury Renews Plan for Stiff Corporation Tax Rates, Suggests Measures to Ease Impact," *Wall Street Journal,* 26 August 1942, 5; "Senate Committee Rejects Ruml Tax Plan," *Wall Street Journal,* 27 August 1942, 3; "Corporation Tax Compromise Is Discussed," *Wall Street Journal,* 28 August 1942, 3; "Senate Group Approves Provisions Easing Excess Profits Tax Impact on Corporations," *Wall Street Journal,* 29 August 1942, 3.

46. "Senate Group Votes Normal-Surtax of 45%, 90% Excess-Profits Levy, 10% Post-War Credit," *Wall Street Journal,* 1 September 1942, 3.

47. Roy Blough, "History, Intent and Significance of the Tax Refund Provisions," in *Conference Board Reports: Carry-Back, Carry-Over and Refund Provisions* (New York: National Industrial Conference Board, 1945), 2–3.

48. Randolph E. Paul, *Taxation for Prosperity* (Indianapolis: Bobbs-Merrill, 1947), 109.

49. Blough, "Problems of Corporate Taxation in Time of War," 117.

50. George B. Bryant, Jr., "War Tax Bill No. 1: Congress in Driver's Seat on Revenue Policy and Intends to Stay There," *Wall Street Journal,* 12 October 1942, 1.

51. See the detailed discussion of the making of the Revenue Act of 1942 in John Morton Blum, *From the Morgenthau Diaries: Years of War, 1941–1945* (Boston: Houghton Mifflin, 1967), 33–52.

52. *Congressional Record,* 77th Cong., 2d. sess., 1942, 88, pt. 6: 7793–95.

53. Ibid., 7798.

54. Ibid., 7813, 7831; "Senate Approves Higher Individual Taxes: Battle Looms Over Victory, Corporate Levies," *Wall Street Journal,* 7 October 1942, 2. Senator LaFollette (Prog.-WI), one of the few to question the final bill, did not address the carrybacks but did argue for a 50% normal plus surtax rate. "The Finance Committee is a very conservative committee of

the Senate," he complained. LaFollette's amendment lost 75–79. See *Congressional Record,* 77th Cong., 2d sess., 1942, 88, pt. 6: 7880–88.

55. Blum, *From the Morgenthau Diaries: Years of War,* 51.

56. Kent, "Revenue Act of 1942," 25; Bank, *From Sword to Shield,* 152.

57. "New Hope for Business," *Time,* 26 October 1942, 88–90; Joseph G. Rayback, "Strange Story of the Tax Bill," *Current History* 3 (December 1942): 302–11; Keith Hutchison, "Everybody's Business: A Tax Victory for Business," *Nation* 155 (31 October 1942): 450–51. For an attack on the law, see T.R.B., "Washington Notes: The New Reaction," *New Republic* 107 (26 October 1942): 543. For a characterization of the bill that does more to stress its progressive elements (and says relatively little about the corporate tax side), see Thorndike, "Price of Civilization," 516. For a subtle suggestion of the law's generosity to corporations, Roy G. Blakey and Gladys C. Blakey, "The Federal Revenue Act of 1942," *American Political Science Review* 36 (December 1942): 1079.

58. Rayback, "Strange Story of the Tax Bill."

59. Randolph E. Paul, "Business Reserves for Reconversion," in *Accounting Problems in War Contract Termination, Taxes, and Postwar Planning, 1943* (New York: American Institute of Accountants, 1943), 70.

60. Kent, "Revenue Act of 1942," 17, 28. See also Peterson, "Statutory Evolution of the Excess Profits Tax," 19.

61. Eugene Habas, "Congress *Has* a Postwar Plan," *Harper's Magazine* 187 (September 1943): 311–13.

62. "Tax Act Carryback Called 'Insurance,'" *New York Times,* 20 January 1944, 25.

63. Charles Melvoin, "Wartime Taxes as a Source of Postwar Funds," *Journal of Accountancy* 78 (August 1944): 108.

64. J. K. Lasser [CPA], "How the New Tax Law Affects Company Operations," *Dun's Review* (March 1946): 15–22.

65. B. U. Ratchford, "The Excess Profits Tax, Part Two: Some Economic and Political Implications," *Southern Economic Journal* 12 (October 1945): 105; see also a summary of objections in *Post-War Tax Plans for the Federal Government,* Senate Committee Print No. 7, 79th Cong., 1st sess. (Washington, D.C.: GPO, 1945), 44–45.

66. Maurice Austin, "Carry-back and Carry-forward of Net Operating Losses," in *Accounting Problems in War Contract Termination, Taxes, and Postwar Planning* (New York: American Institute of Accountants, 1943), 89, 95; Maurice Austin, "Implications of the Carry-back and Carry-forward Provisions," in *Termination and Taxes* (New York: American Institute of Accountants, 1944), 82–83.

67. For a discussion of this broader debate, see Bank, *From Sword to Shield,* 191–203.

68. The law allowed companies to use current estimates, instead of final year-end accounts, so that they could receive tax refunds—including refunds from carryback—much more quickly than they would have done under normal circumstances. "Tax Adjustment Bill of 1945," House Report 849, 79th Cong., 1st sess. (1945); "Tax Adjustment Bill of 1945," Senate Report 458, 79th Cong., 1st sess. (1945); Landman, "Tax Reduction by Carry-Backs and Carry-Overs," 284.

69. Carl S. Shoup, "The Revenue Act of 1945," *Political Science Quarterly* 60 (December 1945): 487.

70. *Congressional Record,* 79th Cong., 1st sess., 1945, 91, pt. 6: 7323.

71. "Steel Firms Guaranteed Gravy in Tax Return Plot," *CIO News,* 27 March 1944, 2; "Tax Laws Guarantee Corp. Profits after War," *CIO News,* 3 April 1944, n.p. See also "CIO Ends Steel Wage Evidence; Murray Assails Tax 'Carry-Back,'" *New York Times,* 30 March 1944, 11.

72. John Barnard, *American Vanguard: The United Auto Workers during the Reuther Years, 1935–1970* (Detroit: Wayne State University Press, 2004), 215.

73. Lichtenstein, *Most Dangerous Man in Detroit,* 230, 239.

74. "GM Sales Drop—But Not Those Profits," *CIO News,* 29 April 1946, 10; "Profits from Strikes," *New Republic* 114 (20 May 1946): 717; General Motors Corp., *Annual Report,* 1946.

75. Fred d'Avila, "Murray Charges Plot to Wreck All Unions," *CIO News,* 21 January 1946, 3.

76. "CIO Asks Tax Inquiry," *New York Times*, 14 January 1946, 10.

77. "Industry's Gimmick," *CIO News*, 28 January 1946, 4.

78. "Tax Refunds as Strike Issue," *United States News*, 1 February 1946, 13.

79. *Congressional Record*, 79th Cong., 2d. sess., 1946, 92, pt. 1: 169.

80. Landman, "Tax Reduction by Carry-Backs and Carry-Overs," 285.

81. *Congressional Record*, 79th Cong., 2d sess., 1946, 92, pt. 1: 372–73.

82. "Philip Murray Errs," *Wall Street Journal*, 24 January 1946, 6.

83. "Union Red Herrings," *Wall Street Journal*, 30 January 1946, 6.

84. "Hits Murray Total on Tax Carry-Back," *New York Times*, 24 January 1946, 14. See also Godfrey N. Nelson, "Carry-Back Action of Taxes Cleared," *New York Times*, 10 February 1946, 59.

85. "Warns on Abuses of Tax Carryback," *New York Times*, 27 January 1946, F1.

86. "End of 'Carry-Back' Sought by Bailey," *New York Times*, 22 January 1946, 21.

87. *Congressional Record*, 79th Cong., 2d sess., 1946, 92, appendix: A1582.

88. This is also pointed out in Bernstein, "Truman Administration and the Steel Strike of 1946," 796.

89. One of these concerned the Case bill, which foreshadowed the efforts in Congress to roll back state support for unions that would culminate in the Taft-Hartley Act the following year. Senator Guffey's introduction of a carryback reform bill in May 1946 very similar to the ones proposed by his House colleagues in January was interpreted by some as a tactical effort to derail the antilabor legislation, more than a serious effort. See *Congressional Record*, 79th Cong., 2d sess., 1946, 92, pt. 4: 5416; C. P. Trussell, "Pepper Plan Upset," *New York Times*, 23 May 1946, 15. On the OPA fight, see Henry C. Fleisher, "Halt the Profiteers: CIO Meets, Hits Wage Freeze while Prices Run Wild," *CIO News*, 19 August 1946, 3; Jacobs, *Pocketbook Politics*, 221–31; Lizabeth Cohen, *A Consumers' Republic: The Politics of Mass Consumption in Postwar America* (New York: Alfred A. Knopf, 2003), 102–7.

90. "Conflicting Opinions Wreck Labor–Management Meeting," *New York Times*, 4 August 1946, 65–66; Walter W. Ruch, "Mead Auto Inquiry Asked by Reuther," *New York Times*, 4 August 1946, 48; "The 79th Congress—'Neglect,'" *CIO News*, 18 November 1946, 8.

91. Brown and Eckhaus, "Operation of the Carry-backs of World War II," 196–97.

92. "Data on Wages and Profits," Senate Doc. 21, 80th Cong., 1st sess. (Washington, D.C.: GPO, 1947), 1–3, 14–15; "How the Income-Tax Carryback Is Working," *Newsweek*, 19 August 1946, 68; Harlowe D. Osborne and Joseph B. Epstein, "Corporate Profits since World War II," *Survey of Current Business* 36 (January 1956): 9; Robert Higgs, "From Central Planning to the Market: The American Transition, 1945–1947," *Journal of Economic History* 59 (September 1999): 609–10.

93. United Aircraft Corporation, *Annual Report*, 1946; *Moody's Manual of Investments: Industrial Securities* (New York: Moody's, 1947), 1596.

94. E. E. Wilson to Robert E. Gross, 2 December 1941, Box 7, Robert E. Gross Papers, Library of Congress.

95. General Motors Corp, *Annual Report*, 1946, 32.

96. Packard Motor Car Co., *Forty-Third Annual Report*, 1946, 4–8.

97. To take just one example, the Glenn L. Martin Co. had a $21 million operating loss in 1947 and declared an additional $19 million in losses, but cut these in half thanks to a $20 million carryback refund. *Moody's Manual of Investments: Industrial Securities, 1948* (New York, 1948), 2938. See also William L. Cary, "Government Financing of Essential Contractors: The Reorganization of the Glenn L. Martin Company," *Harvard Law Review* 66 (March 1953): 835–36.

98. North American Aviation, Inc., *Annual Report*, 1947, copy in North American Aviation Inc. Board Minutes, 1946–1948, unboxed volume, Boeing Historical Archives, Bellevue, Wash.

99. John D. Morris, "Tax Framers Seek to Avoid Inequity," *New York Times*, 24 December 1950, 29; Clayton Knowles, "Excess Profit Tax Voted by Congress," *New York Times*, 2 January 1951, 10; Godfrey N. Nelson, "Loss Carrybacks Put on New Basis," *New York Times*, 1 October 1950; Randolph Paul, *Taxation in the United States* (Boston: Little, Brown & Co., 1954), 568.

100. Michael G. Cooper and Matthew J. Knittel, "The Implications of Tax Asymmetry for U.S. Corporations," *National Tax Journal* 63 (March 2010): 34–36; Alan J. Auerbach, "The Dynamic Effects of Tax Law Asymmetries," *Review of Economic Studies* 53 (1986): 205–25; Jack M. Mintz, "An Empirical Estimate of Corporate Tax Refundability and Effective Tax Rates," *Quarterly Journal of Economics* 103 (February 1988): 225–31; Rosanne Altshuler and Alan J. Auerbach, "The Significance of Tax Law Asymmetries: An Empirical Investigation," *Quarterly Journal of Economics* 105 (February 1990): 61–86.

2

Virtue, Necessity, and Irony in the Politics of Civil Rights

Organized Business and Fair Employment Practices in Postwar Cleveland

ANTHONY S. CHEN

In 1950, Cleveland's city council voted overwhelmingly to pass an enforceable fair employment practice (FEP) ordinance. The new law prohibited discrimination on account of race, religion, color, national origin, or ancestry, covering not only private-sector jobs but also municipal employment and contracting.[1]

For those who had yearned for the protection and symbolism that such a law would offer, it was a "history-making" occasion. A large crowd had assembled at city hall on the January day that the ordinance passed, breaking into loud applause after the last vote was cast. Henry Jaffe (R-Ward 25) and Charles V. Carr (D-Ward 17), cosponsors of the bill, lauded the ordinance as a "tremendous step forward" that represented a "victory for decency and justice." The *Cleveland Call and Post*, the city's largest black newspaper, announced that it was now time for Cleveland to "proudly take its accustomed position as one of the nation's most liberal and progressive cities." When the law took effect in March, more than 1,500 people attended a celebratory rally at Cory Methodist Church in Glenville, a neighborhood in northeastern Cleveland that was home to thousands of black and Jewish residents who had demanded the passage of a law.[2]

The hullabaloo and fanfare were understandable, but there was nothing unprecedented at the time about a large, northern city passing a law billed as promoting "fair employment practices." In the late 1940s, before the storied movement to dismantle racial apartheid in the South began to dominate the national headlines, it was arguably the issue of FEP legislation that was at the center of the struggle over civil rights in the United States. The major theater of conflict was not the South, as it would later become, but rather the states and localities of the North, Midwest, and West. In fact, state legislatures and city halls outside the South had become the venues of choice for liberally minded men and women who believed that government could and should regulate job discrimination—especially since it had become clear that the coalition of southern Democrats and conservative Republicans that was blocking the passage of an FEP law on Capitol Hill would not yield until greater political pressure was brought to bear. This interracial, interfaith collection of liberals believed that the passage of state and municipal laws could help to generate momentum for national legislation. By 1950, their strategy of exploiting the policymaking potential of the federal system had begun to bear tangible fruit. More than half a dozen states had enacted enforceable FEP legislation, and Cleveland's new law made it the fifth major American city to pass a robust FEP ordinance, following Chicago, Milwaukee, Minneapolis, and Philadelphia.[3]

What distinguished Cleveland's experience from that of other cities was the unexpected backing that the law publicly received from leaders of the local business community. In their histories of race and inequality in the postwar urban North, Thomas J. Sugrue, Martha Biondi, and Matthew Countryman have rightly highlighted the strong and widespread opposition of many business groups to FEP discrimination legislation. Little else, it seemed, sparked the ire of company owners and management more readily than the prospect of having to run a competitive business under the burdensome yoke of "compulsory" FEP legislation. When invited to testify before legislative bodies, spokesmen for employer associations, chambers of commerce, and trade groups seldom hesitated to denounce "mandatory" laws at every level of government, often in the harshest terms. Government regulation of discrimination would only backfire, they contended. Real and lasting change could only come through voluntary efforts.[4]

This, indeed, was one of the arguments advanced by Cleveland's most powerful group of companies, the Cleveland Chamber of Commerce (CCC), shortly before it launched a year-long, voluntary program to incorporate African Americans and other minorities into the city's private-sector workforce. The CCC spent a substantial amount of money running the program, known as the Cooperative Employment Practices Program (CEPP). During the 1949–50 fiscal year, CEPP cost the chamber $24,000 to operate—roughly six times the cost of publishing the *Clevelander*, its monthly membership magazine, and roughly five times the budget of the Junior Chamber of Commerce. One of the most visible manifestations of the initiative was a massive, fifty-foot-wide sign posted in the outfield of Cleveland Municipal Stadium. It featured a straightforward proclamation: "Cleveland Says: Ability Counts . . . Not Nationality, Creed, or Color."[5]

Yet the CCC joined with liberal groups in 1950 to endorse the passage of an enforceable ordinance. Reporters and editorialists at the local newspapers noted the significance of the move right away. Even the *Cleveland Press* sang the praises of the business community, which it had regarded skeptically until then. Unlike the "investment bankers," who "blindly" fought legislation and found themselves with an "inflexible and hostile law," Cleveland employers took a more "intelligent approach." They invested their resources in carrying out a skillful educational campaign and then "convinced their members of the soundness and apparent inevitability of such legislation." The result was an FEP law that was passed "with" business rather than "in spite of" business, and it was a fine example of business "helping to regulate itself."[6]

The reversal was also widely observed around the country. It was featured in the monthly newsletter of the American Council on Race Relations, and it was mentioned prominently in legislative battles from Harrisburg to Capitol Hill. The men who led Cleveland's biggest and most successful companies had broken from the historic tendency of organized business to oppose enforceable FEP legislation, and nearly everyone who paid attention to civil rights at the time took notice. Compared to their intransigent peers elsewhere, Cleveland businessmen seemed almost virtuous.[7]

Cleveland was neither the first nor the biggest city to pass an FEP ordinance, but the nationwide struggle over the Fair Employment Practices Commission (FEPC) peaked in intensity during the late 1940s, and Ohio was arguably at the center of the political maelstrom. Ohio's senior U.S. Senator Robert A. Taft was a central player in the national politics of the FEPC, where he set the pace for the conservative wing of the Republican Party, and he would be standing for reelection in 1950. In the meantime, there was a chance that Ohio—where the Democrats held the governor's office and narrowly controlled the legislature in 1949—might actually pass an FEPC law, which would place Taft under enormous pressure. For its part, Cleveland was a decisive battleground where a liberal victory could conceivably set off a chain reaction resulting in the passage of state and federal legislation. The stakes were unusually heightened and the politics unusually contested in Cleveland and Ohio in the late 1940s.

How should the role of Cleveland business be interpreted at this clarifying moment? In what sense might it be seen as a "source of social progress" in the struggle for the racial integration of the U.S. workplace?[8]

A close look at the historical record suggests that Cleveland business was far less exceptional than it might at first seem. While individual executives and even the chamber itself clearly endorsed the principle of racial equality—at times out of genuine conviction—the actions they took to realize fair employment practices were guided overwhelmingly by political and strategic considerations. Few businessmen—and certainly not the chamber—expressed strong interest in or took significant voluntary action to promote fair employment practices until after the introduction of an FEPC bill that stood a serious chance of passing. Fewer still supported the actual bill, and most accepted legislation only when it seemed they had little other choice. In point of fact, Cleveland business became involved in the question of fair employment practices not out of social enlightenment but primarily out of a desire to stave off any legislation that threatened to encroach on their prerogative to hire, promote, or fire their employees. When the chamber eventually decided to endorse the 1950 ordinance, it did so knowing full well that the recent election of a pro-FEPC majority to the city council in the previous year made the passage of a mandatory bill nearly inevitable. Its stance was almost certainly a calculated attempt to turn a sure loss on policy into a definite gain on public relations. Even then, it tried as best it could to minimize the punitive and regulatory features of the law. All in all, it seems doubtful that organized business in Cleveland would have done as much to promote fair employment practices if the threat of strong legislative action had not been so credible. The initiatives undertaken by the chamber should be seen less as a source of social progress than as a sign of the times.[9]

The irony is that the chamber may have been forced to make a virtue out of necessity because its voluntary program had done so much to raise awareness of job discrimination. While the program had been largely ineffective at breaking down many of the most deep-seated patterns of racial and religious exclusion in the labor market, it legitimated public concern about the problem and may have thereby stoked electoral demands for reform—demands that it ultimately proved incapable of meeting. And so despite its intent, organized business may have inadvertently facilitated the passage of legislation, something that most Cleveland businessmen probably never really wanted or expected.

On the June day in 1947 when Republican councilman Harry Jaffe (Ward 25) introduced a bill prohibiting job discrimination, Cleveland was in the middle of a big comeback. Its economy had been laid low by the Great Depression, but a massive injection of wartime spending had begun to revive it. Industry and manufacturing were recovering their footing, and Clevelanders were finally starting to find jobs. By 1946, total employment in Cuyahoga County was at 560,000, with 66,000 workers employed in machinery, 50,000 in iron and steel, 34,000 in transportation equipment, and 26,000 in electrical machinery. Four thousand workers manned the Cleveland Union Stockyards, and more than a thousand worked at one of the nine breweries in the area. The city was even growing again, albeit slowly. It was nowhere near as populous as Chicago or Detroit, but it was bigger than all of its competitors in the Midwest. Things were beginning to look up, and city boosters minted a new catchphrase to attract yet more people and dollars. Cleveland was the "best location in the nation": It was easy and cheap to ship raw materials there, and much of the population of the United States and Canada lived within a close radius. The economic resurgence would prove only momentary, but Clevelanders could be forgiven for their confidence and optimism.[10]

The resumption of growth led to growing pains. Among the most visible growing pains were those associated with the shifting demographic geography of the metropolis. In 1940, nearly nine hundred thousand people lived in center-city Cleveland, and roughly 10% of them were African American. The number of African Americans in center-city Cleveland would nearly double over the next ten years, while the number of whites would fall slightly. White families were choosing instead to live in Cleveland's surrounding suburbs, whose population rose by well over a hundred thousand from 1940 to 1950. Many new residents of the suburbs were leaving the ethnic enclaves where they had initially settled or had been reared, and the "conveyor belts" of their exodus continued to be the major thoroughfares that ran out of the city in every direction save north. The white population was growing less centralized over time, while the black population grew more centralized.[11]

Residential segregation was nothing new to Cleveland. It had been a prominent feature of life in the city since African Americans began moving there in large numbers in search of work. By 1950, African Americans were concentrated along a belt of neighborhoods that ran southeastwardly from downtown, including Central-West, Central, Central-East, and Kinsman. Glenville, Mount Pleasant, and Lee-Miles were other neighborhoods with a substantial proportion of African Americans. Residential segregation was a burden and annoyance to black Clevelanders in obvious ways, but it also meant that they constituted a relatively powerful voting bloc in number of city wards. The two councilmen who would lend their names to Cleveland's ordinance, Harry Jaffe (Ward 25) and Charles V. Carr (Ward 17), each represented districts with a significant black population. Jaffe's ward overlapped partially with Glenville, which at the time was still home to many Jewish Clevelanders as well. Originally born in Russia, Jaffe himself was Jewish, as were Joseph Horwitz (Ward 10) and Herman Finkle (Ward 12), both of whom represented wards with numerous black and Jewish residents. Residential segregation excluded both blacks and Jews from the main currents of Cleveland life, but it also concentrated their electoral power.[12]

The deepening residential segregation of African Americans was paralleled by a clear pattern of occupational segregation, which was partially (though not wholly) the consequence of job discrimination. Indeed, occupational segregation in Cleveland was just as severe as it was in other Midwestern cities like Detroit. Job discrimination was perhaps most rampant in the aftermath of the war, but it remained prevalent for years thereafter. In 1950, black Clevelanders would still remain heavily concentrated in semi-skilled and unskilled occupations, and they would continue to be severely underrepresented in professional, managerial, clerical, and sales positions (table 2.1).

Jaffe's bill addressed racial and religious exclusion head on by expressly prohibiting discrimination in public and private employment because of "race, creed, color, national origin or ancestry." Enforcement of the law was made the responsibility of

Table 2.1. **Index of Relative Occupational Concentration for Black Males in Cleveland, 1950**

Occupational category	Score
Professional	26
Manager, proprietor, or official	24
Clerical worker	37
Sales worker	26
Craftsman	49
Operative	121
Service worker	288
Laborer	396

Note: Scores on the index are calculated by dividing the percentage of black workers who belong to a given occupational category by the percentage of white workers who belong to the same category, and then multiplying the quotient by 100. A score of 100 indicates that an occupational category contains the same percentage distribution of black workers as white workers. A score above 100 indicates black overrepresentation, while a score below 100 indicates black underrepresentation.

Methodological Note: This table is calculated using the method reported in Thomas J. Sugrue, *The Origins of the Urban Crisis: Race and Inequality in Postwar Detroit* (Princeton, N.J.: Princeton University Press, 1996), 277.

Source: Roger Mitton, *The Negro in Cleveland, 1950–1963* (Cleveland, Ohio: Cleveland Urban League, 1964), table 9, 33. Mitton's data is originally taken from the U.S. Census.

the Community Relations Board (CRB), which had been established during the war to promote racial and religious tolerance. The CRB's most notable action to date was calling for the passage of a law prohibiting municipal amusement parks from discriminating in their admissions, in response to the exclusion of African Americans from Euclid Beach Park. Under Jaffe's proposal, the board would be authorized to receive complaints of job discrimination, look into their merits, and recommend valid complaints for prosecution in city court. The courts, in turn, could find defendants guilty of a misdemeanor, fine them as much as $50, order their imprisonment up to three months, and revoke any city licenses.[13]

Jaffe explained his reasons for introducing the bill in the Republican-leaning *Cleveland News*, which featured the question of a municipal FEPC in its weekly debate on public issues. Jaffe argued that nothing was "closer to our hearts as Americans" than the principle enshrined in the Declaration of Independence that "all men are created equal." FEP laws took aim at violations of this principle. Employment discrimination not only constituted an abridgement of equal rights but also compromised the "right to work," undermined the development of "individual initiative," and interfered with "freedom of enterprise." Legislating tolerance was admittedly not possible, but Jaffe insisted that "you CAN legislate against discrimination." The concerns raised by critics of the law were exaggerated and misplaced. In jurisdictions where FEP legislation had been passed, most cases had been "amicably adjusted." Indeed, some businessmen had become "staunch supporters" of the law, "just as they have in the case of health and welfare legislation which many of them opposed." Of course, education, persuasion, and other voluntary methods were valuable and could do a "large part of the job," but they could not get the whole job done without the backing of a law. Major cities like Chicago, Minneapolis, and Milwaukee had all recently recognized this, and Cleveland could not afford to "lag behind."[14]

Charles Hollman took the other side of the issue. President of Interstate Business Exchange and a major figure among private employment agencies, Hollman argued that it was not equality but "liberty and freedom" that were the most fundamental values of the United States. Liberty and freedom were the basis of the free enterprise system and indeed the whole way of American life, which would be jeopardized by the passage of a municipal FEP law. Hollman saw only unmitigated disaster in Cleveland's future if it took legislative action. The law would discriminate "against" employers "in favor of" employees. It would "reduce the efficiency and destroy the morale" of private enterprise. Employers would be forced to "re-employ dismissed employees" or "employ rejected applicants who were incapable and unfit." If racial and religious discrimination actually existed in Cleveland, it was a "moral issue" and not a political one, and "morals cannot be legislated into the hearts and lives of our people." The proper remedy was not the passage of a new law but education and "voluntary co-operation."[15]

Jaffe's opinions enjoyed more traction among the 140,000 readers of the *News* than Hollman's. Seventy-three percent of those responding to an editorial poll indicated that they sided with the councilman. A resident of University Heights, Mrs. R. Glazer, said she endorsed the proposed law because she believed that employers discriminated in private even though they denied it in public. Writing from near Mount Pleasant in southeast Cleveland, Arnold M. Edelman argued that the FEPC was simply the "modern application of the Bill of Rights." A resident of the Fairfax neighborhood, Lloyd E. Squarer, reported his recent unsuccessful experience looking for a job. He had spent the entire morning answering job ads that he had clipped from the newspaper. No employers expressed any interest in him. It was infuriating because he was left wondering why they rejected him, even though he could guess. "If I had been told politely and firmly by these several companies that they did not hire Negroes, I would not be so bitter," he wrote. Another black resident of Fairfax, Joseph L. Boatner, explained that he was a veteran and then asked a pointed question about the meaning of the sacrifice that he and his brothers-in-arms had made. "I was a solider and served in this last war, hoping to prove myself and other members of my race worthy of full citizenship," he wrote. "Tell me, gentlemen, did we sweat, shed our blood and die for democracy, in vain?" If these letters to the editor were any indication of public sentiment, Jaffe could count on more than a few allies if he decided to push the issue.[16]

Individual anecdotes of discrimination were plentiful. But stronger evidence emerged at a series of hearings convened by the CRB. Arnold Walker reported that the Cleveland Urban League (CUL) had contacted hundreds of employers in the hopes of working with them to integrate their workforce, but none responded favorably. Sidney Levine of the Jewish Vocational Service explained that the falloff in federal employment after the end of the war left many Jews unable to find work in the private sector, where employers refused to hire them. But perhaps the most systematic piece of evidence was reported by Paul C. Seiple, head of a local office of the Ohio State Employment Service, who had collected data indicating that 23% of the job orders placed by Ohio employers from 1 February to 31 October 1946 were restricted to "white only."[17]

When it came time for them to share their views, business groups refused to cede any ground. Chester Nikodym of the Associated Industries of Cleveland (AIC), an industrial relations organization with a membership of several hundred local companies, thought that Jaffe's proposal was a terrible idea. An FEPC ordinance would put the "honest employer at the mercy of the shiftless and the incompetent," who would use it to elbow their way into jobs they were not qualified to hold. A law could also make the labor movement vulnerable to Communist infiltration. Most of all, it would "cause and aggravate the evils its sponsors say its absence creates." Race consciousness would become heightened rather than lessened. Not surprisingly, J. W. Vanden Bosch of the CCC expressed similar sentiments, albeit in more measured tones. The chamber had "grave misgivings about the legislative approach," he said. Tolerance and understanding "cannot be effectively legislated." The chamber had felt the same way in 1945, when it opposed the Norton bill in the U.S. House of Representatives and two other FEPC bills that were pending in the Ohio legislature. Its message could not have been any clearer: FEPC had no place in public policy at any level of government.[18]

Editors at the *Press* implored employers to abandon their "negative attitude" and reminded them that their failure to take significant action could perversely strengthen the case for legislation. What was needed was a bona fide effort on the part of the private sector to create jobs for black Clevelanders where and when it was possible. Legislation was admittedly not the "best way" forward, but attempts to pass it would only multiply if "employers and employers' organizations won't get together and deal positively and constructively with the discrimination problem."[19]

The warning fell on deaf ears. A serious threat had not yet materialized in 1947, and few, if any, Cleveland employers made a constructive effort to address job discrimination. Perhaps they hoped that further action would be unnecessary. How deep did support for the bill run? Were its backers organized and serious? Was a municipal ordinance merely a device for keeping interest in the FEPC alive until prospects of national or state legislation improved? Would the bill fall prey to partisan wrangling?

Any hopes that the campaign for a municipal FEPC would disappear quietly were dashed in 1948, when the CRB announced that it would endorse a slightly amended version of Jaffe's bill. It was then that it became clear to all sides that "one of the most controversial issues in race relations today" (in the words of the *Press*) would receive a thorough look by the city council. The 1947 hearings had merely been a dress rehearsal.[20]

When an interfaith, interracial coalition of liberal Clevelanders showed up in Room 217 of City Hall on 7 April to demonstrate their support for Jaffe's bill and civil rights, it was a scene reminiscent of ones that had already played out in Albany, Boston, and even Los Angeles. The massive turnout in Cleveland, as elsewhere, was far from spontaneous. The groups responsible for it, operating under the banner of the prosaically named Organization for a Cleveland FEPC (OCFEPC), had been organizing for weeks. Dozens of groups were affiliated with the OCFEPC, but the organizational nucleus of the operation consisted of the Jewish Community Council (JCC), the NAACP, and the CRB. Its "inner circle" of leadership included the JCC's Sidney Vincent, the NAACP's Charles Lucas, the CRB's Roosevelt Dickey, and Dr. D. R. Sharpe of the Cleveland Baptist Association. The "grand strategy" and legislative tactics of the coalition were set by the leadership of the OCFEPC, while ordinary Clevelanders served as the foot soldiers, bombarding council members with letters, mobilizing voter delegations, distributing educational literature, attending neighborhood meetings, participating in phone trees to get the word out about important events, staffing fundraising activities, and going to legislative hearings en masse. The room was jam-packed with supporters when Sharpe, Lucas, and Arnold Walker of the Cleveland Urban League (CUL) rose to make a case for a municipal FEPC before the legislation committee of city council. Hundreds of Clevelanders heard Sharpe argue that it was the responsibility of government to tackle discrimination through legislation and then highlight the surprising support that the FEPC idea had garnered from forward-looking businessmen like Charles E. Wilson of General Electric and Charles Luckman of Lever Brothers.[21]

The first hearing was only the opening salvo. The next few months witnessed a remarkable burst of political energy on the part of liberal groups. More than a thousand people gathered at Antioch Baptist Church to hear Elmer L. Carter of the New York State Commission Against Discrimination explain why "FEPC works." Other speakers at the hearing included academics, Catholic and Protestant leaders, labor representatives, and individual businessmen such as Joseph Homchis of the Acme Pie Company, Joseph Newman of retailer Newman Stern Company, and Joseph McKenna of the insurer Truman Cummings. Perhaps the most emotional moment of the day came when veteran John Price told the gathered audience that soldiers belonging to a segregated, black division saved his life decades earlier in Cuba. Anyone who put on the uniform to fight overseas deserved a fair shake on a job opportunity at home. "If they're good enough to fight, they're good enough to return home and get jobs."[22]

The momentum seemed irresistible. Jaffe was even featured in a *Call and Post* article predicting the unopposed passage of his bill. But liberal fantasies of a quick and decisive victory were rudely scotched by the results of a straw poll that was taken in early May. Only twelve of the thirty-three councilmen pledged to vote for the bill. Five were undecided, and sixteen declined to take a public position. Seventeen votes were usually needed to form the slimmest majority, so liberals were five votes shy of victory—precisely the number of councilmen who were undecided. What made the situation even more challenging was that many of the councilmen who remained silent or undecided had said that they were waiting to hear the testimony of opponents before speaking out or making up their minds. The passage of a bill was far from a foregone conclusion, and the views of employers would count.[23]

Organized business did not squander its opportunity. Chester Nikodym brazenly reprised many of his arguments from the previous year, arguing that an FEPC would put the "honest employer at the mercy of the shiftless and incompetent." Nikodym went on to claim that evidence of discrimination against blacks and Jews was thin and unconvincing. "There is absolutely no need for an FEPC here." FEPC backers were "stirring race feelings" and injecting racial questions into industrial relations. A law was a dreadful idea, but if the passage of a law was absolutely necessary, he concluded, then it should be done by popular vote. "If we are going to go about this in a truly democratic fashion," he said, "the decision should be determined by the people of the City of Cleveland."[24]

Nikodym was no doubt aware that FEPC had already been plunged into the crucible of a plebiscite elsewhere in the country—and failed the test. At the same hearing, Charles Hollman, who insisted that it was "impossible to legislate brotherly love," pointed out that the "great state of California defeated FEPC by an overwhelming majority in referendum." Neither man mentioned the costly and intensive campaign that the California Chamber of Commerce had waged against Proposition 11, perhaps because it ran counter to their point, but it was true that Californians voting in the 1946 general election had rejected a ballot initiative that would have created a statewide FEPC by more than a 2–1 margin. The implication was hard to miss: Representative democracy was an imperfect form of government, and there were times that it failed to properly translate the will of the people. In this instance, city council could not be trusted to resist the concerted pleading of pressure groups, and a legitimate outcome could only be reached letting the people decide for themselves, as they had in the Golden State.[25]

Nikodym and Hollman may have expressed the most extreme views, but similar points were made in more restrained language by others. The chamber representative, Spencer D. Corlett, conceded that the objective of the ordinance was laudable, but argued that a law was no way to achieve it. "The similarity between this legislation and the attempt to attain temperance by the national prohibition amendment is striking." Like others before him, Corlett claimed that passage of the ordinance would actually lead to "greater race consciousness and greater discriminatory practices." Indeed, it might stymie the "remarkable progress" that "minority groups" had been making in the way of "economic advancement" and "equal opportunity." Things were getting better on their own. A compulsory law would make things worse. Employers and their allies took a second, public crack at the bill at another overflow hearing a few weeks later, when, in the words of the *Call and Post*, they "splattered testimony with Communist scares and race baiting." Max Gustin, a representative of a merchant group based in southeast Cleveland, argued that the bill would "set Negroes back twenty-five years." Opposition to the bill, he said, was actually widespread among African Americans themselves, but they were afraid to attack FEPC in public. Besides, there was nothing wrong with discrimination per se. If he wanted to exclude a Catholic or a Jew from his company—not that he did—it was his "inalienable right" to do so. "A gentleman has a right to prefer a blonde if he wants to." Harry Vaughn of the Employers' Counselors' Association claimed that he was in possession of the "secret minutes" of a group that was pushing the bill to create racial discord. "Stalin backed the bill," he reportedly said.[26]

Employer broadsides took a toll. The heady optimism of the early spring gave way to genuine uncertainty by late June. To be sure, Jaffe's bill managed to make it out of committee. A key break came when Democratic mayor Thomas A. Burke spoke out in favor of the bill. But it was difficult for vote counters on either side of the issue to discern how Jaffe's bill would fare before the full council. Employers had raised worries with their aggressive testimony. At the same time, there were suggestions that a few more council members were now willing to support an FEPC law.[27]

A roll-call vote on 28 June revealed a sharply divided city council, which, at a packed meeting that adjourned only at 1:00 A.M., decided to refer the bill back to committee by a razor-thin margin of 17–16. Employers had eked out a win, but the vote also gave them fresh reasons to doubt the long-term tenability of their position. It seemed increasingly clear that city council was dominated by a Democratic majority that wanted to pass a municipal FEPC bill but was understandably loathe to see the GOP receive credit for it. A faction of the Democratic leadership, moreover, had been dissatisfied with the large role that Jaffe's bill contemplated for the CRB. If the Democratic majority could find a way to resolve both issues, it would have the votes to pass the bill. Worse still for employers, Democrats had a strong electoral incentive to try. As one reporter warned, "Negroes are going to flock to the GOP banner" unless Democrats passed a strong FEPC bill.[29]

Employer fears were realized in early August, when Jaffe teamed up with a black Democrat, Charles V. Carr (D-Ward 17), to introduce a new bill. The new bill retained the CRB as the primary enforcement agency, but Carr's participation meant bipartisan backing, and the move injected "new enthusiasm" into the campaign. "Passage of the jointly sponsored legislation is almost assured," said one close observer. The prediction seemed overconfident, but a major partisan obstacle had suddenly been swept aside.[30]

Leaders of the chamber were sufficiently concerned about the developing situation that they convened a special meeting at downtown-Cleveland's prestigious Union Club, a stately and august setting that city elders had long used to deliberate privately on the major issues that confronted the city and region. At lunchtime on 11 August, it played host to a concerned group of businessmen who were trying to work out a response to the unprecedented grassroots demand for legislative protection from racial and religious discrimination. Among those in attendance were William I. Ong of American Steel and Wire (a subsidiary of U.S. Steel), E. J. Westerlund of General Electric, Carl H. Metz, Jr. of Standard Oil, Stanley Kuhns of Aluminum Company of America, Edgar H. Gustafson of Ohio Bell Telephone, John Danforth of Higbee's, W. A. Harmon of National City Bank, and several of the chamber's top staff members.[31]

The chamber's executive vice president, Walter I. Beam, opened up the meeting by explaining that the gathering had been convened to "explore possible alternatives to the proposed fair employment practices ordinances[,] which are generally objectionable to business and industry of the community." Beam observed that "it was not at all certain" that the proposals would be "defeated." In his view, there were three options for the chamber. It could "(1) simply oppose legislation; (2) propose modified legislation; or (3) propose a non-legislative approach to the problem."[32]

One of the men—left unidentified by name in the minutes—had a special interest in the topic and was invited to share his thoughts. He began by conceding that Cleveland had been doing more than other cities to give minorities a fair shake in the job market. But much more could and should be done, and the main problem was how to do it. Legislation was "highly objectionable," but how was it possible to accomplish "'something' with 'nothing'"? There was also a more "immediate problem at hand": "Business is faced with legislation unless something is done." A referendum was tempting, but "bringing the subject to a head" in such a manner could lead to a "sharpening in the lines of conflict" and may yield "many lasting detrimental effects." There was perhaps a better idea: "If industry, through a representative group, proposed a voluntary, self-policed code of employment, supplemented by an appropriate education program, it might be possible to avert legislation." It would take at least a year to see any results, but a voluntary code would benefit the community far more than a municipal ordinance. What was more, business and industry stood to "gain a great deal of prestige in the eyes of the community and nation."[33]

The suggestion elicited a lengthy commentary from the men gathered. A year might not be long enough to yield favorable results. "Quotas" should be "scrupulously avoided," and minorities should be hired "only where their qualifications are equal to or better than other applicants." The public should hear more about stories of employers were who already practicing merit employment. A voluntary program could not be a "one-shot affair." Both employers and employees were responsible for discrimination. The severity of the problem varied from one area (e.g., office work) to another (e.g., mechanical). Taking a voluntary approach would make it possible for "[l]eft wing groups" to claim credit for pushing business to admit and address the problem, but these groups might be a greater annoyance if nothing at all is done. Perhaps the FEPC idea was better implemented on a statewide level.[34]

The group concluded by considering the value of a "two-pronged approach" in which the chamber made a "strong effort" to "defeat the ordinance" and simultaneously made a detailed, positive statement of what it was doing—"Here is our program." It then agreed to draft a set of recommendations to the board of directors for approval.[35]

Representatives of the Cleveland Urban League (CUL) picked up on the strategic shift almost right away. The CUL had arranged a September meeting with the chamber in the hopes of launching a voluntary program to expand "job opportunities for qualified Negro workers in the professional, skilled, and clerical occupations," and chamber officials proved a highly receptive audience. It seemed obvious to the head of the CUL's industrial relations department, Clifford E. Minton, that the "FEPC legislation pending before the City Council, which the C of C opposes, played a great part in stimulating more than passive interest in 'racial employment.'" The legislative situation had created a "very favorable climate for the conference and commitments made by C of C officials." Minton felt that it was clearly "evident that the Chamber would like to take advantage of intensive voluntary action at this late date and the UL program to obstruct enactment of FEPC legislation."[36]

Minton's intuitions were borne out in subsequent weeks. Shortly after Truman's stunning upset of Dewey in November, which further strengthened pro-FEPC forces, the chamber dispatched two top officials to a meeting of the council's legislation committee to set the two-track strategy into motion. The first official to speak, President Elmer L. Lindseth, told the audience that the chamber had studied the Jaffe–Carr proposal and opposed it. A law would only backfire and make employees more rather than less conscious of race. Lindseth's argument was nothing new, but he then conceded that racial and religious discrimination was a problem in Cleveland. Something should be done.[37]

Lindseth then turned over the floor to a CCC director, Clifford F. Hood, who made a surprise announcement. The chamber was establishing a new voluntary program to help Cleveland business fulfill the "principle of equivalent economic opportunity for all." Under the "Co-operative Employment Practices Plan" (CEPP), as it was dubbed, all 4,400 chamber members would be advised to adopt concrete measures to extend equal job opportunity—educating employees on their "obligation to work harmoniously" with one another, declaring an adherence to the principle of merit employment, and upgrading employees according to ability. Judged by the outcome of the meeting, Lindseth and Hood turned in a virtuoso performance. The legislation committee declined to take action on either FEPC bill.[38]

The chamber proposal elicited a mixed reaction in the wider community. Newspapers opposed to an ordinance leapt to applaud it. "We believe this plan can work," wrote the Plain Dealer. It signified "frank recognition by socially enlightened employers of the existence of unfair employment practices rooted in bigotry and ignorance," and it deserved a chance before "compulsion." The News praised the "non-compulsory, non-legislative" plan and offered that it deserved a "year's trial." Liberals were instantly wary. The CUL was forced to explain awkwardly that it had approached the chamber earlier but did not consider the voluntary program a substitute for legislation. D. R. Sharpe noted that business had made similar promises earlier without any follow-through. A spokesman for the OCFEPC condemned the chamber, which it accused of offering up an "eleventh hour scheme dreamed up as a further delaying device." The timing was not coincidental. "Why hasn't the Chamber done something to correct this evil before now?" Both the NAACP's Charles P. Lucas and the Call and Post's W. O. Walker suspected that the real goal of the chamber was to kill the ordinance.[39]

It would have been difficult for the chamber to dispute the charge that it was hoping to avert legislation. This possibility was indeed uppermost on the minds of the men who arranged the August meeting at the Union Club, and it was how chamber officials would subsequently describe the program to their membership. The only real question, it seemed, was whether the chamber would operate CEPP in good faith, or if the committee was solely a delaying device.[40]

The council, amidst signs that the public preferred an educational approach, shelved Jaffe–Carr and agreed to a request by Mayor Burke to give the plan a trial run. Cleveland's business community would get a chance to prove itself. "If the voluntary plan does not work," said Burke, "we have no other choice [except to pass a law], but if a record of accomplishment can be achieved then it is preferable." A steering committee known as the Cleveland Committee on Employment Practices (CCEP) was appointed. It adopted the can-do slogan, "Fair Employment through Voluntary Cooperation," and William I. Ong of American Steel and Wire was made chairman. After a year and a half of uncertainty, it now seemed that the fate of a municipal FEPC in Cleveland rested with the performance of Ong's committee.[41]

The CCEP set an ambitious agenda for itself, and few would ultimately question whether it was serious about trying to educate employers, employees, and the public. Almost everyone was impressed with the scale of the resources it had put behind the campaign and how hard it had tried. A whirlwind of activity issued forth from its downtown headquarters in the Union Commerce Building on Euclid Avenue. The committee asked Cleveland employers to remove discriminatory references from their job ads. It encouraged the Cleveland Newspaper Publishers' Association to ban discriminatory references from help-wanted ads. It launched a massive advertising blitz that included print, radio, and film. It held dozens of meetings in churches, companies, and college campuses. It compiled lengthy mailing lists of local employers and sent them a detailed array of original, educational materials, including a monthly news bulletin. It eventually distributed more than 100,000 pieces of literature.[42]

The most important item in CCEP's educational arsenal was a three-piece kit that introduced employers to the program and provided specific advice about how to revise job application forms and help-wanted ads. The centerpiece of the kit was a manual entitled, "How to Apply Cooperative Employment Practices." It offered twenty-seven specific "suggestions" to employers, stressing among other things the importance of formulating a clear fair employment practices policy, taking the time to explain it to everyone at the company, placing non-white workers where they could be seen by the public, maintaining performance and behavior standards, avoiding any kind of segregation, and reminding everyone involved to be patient. The kit was distributed to 8,000 employers in metropolitan Cleveland, and 2,000 copies were circulated in Ohio and elsewhere throughout the country.[43]

The committee also pursued an ambitious program to reach and educate the general public. Through the creative programming of its Public Relations Committee, led by powerhouse advertising executive Allen L. Billingsly, CCEP made use of almost every conceivable means of communication available at the time. CCEP catchphrases were printed on the mailing envelopes of fourteen large companies. Cleveland-area libraries distributed 100,000 specially designed bookmarks. The committee developed an eight-week radio program that ran on seven AM stations in the area. The first four weeks involved airing "recorded musical jingles emphasizing the over-all importance of tolerance and understanding," and the selection of tunes included "The Brown-Skinned Cow," "It Could Be a Wonderful World," and "I'm Proud To Be Me"—all of which had never before been aired in Cleveland. The next two weeks involved Cleveland radio personalities reading aloud announcements, while the final two weeks were rounded out by panel discussions and dramatizations.[44]

CCEP signs appeared in venues all over the city. Display boards measuring 4 x 6 feet were installed in several downtown buildings. The boards featured a boosterish message: "Fair Employment Practices Through Voluntary Cooperation—A Heads Up Program for a Heads Up City!—Cleveland Committee onEmployment Practices." Streetcar cards were posted and rotated monthly in 1,000 vehicles that were operated by the Cleveland Transportation System and Shaker Rapid Transit. One such card read, "Fellow Employees Say: Nationality, Creed, or Color Doesn't Matter! Ability Is The Job Qualification That Counts" Another read, "Let's Weigh The Man Against The Job . . . Not Against Our Prejudices." The chamber claimed that the cards had been "seen daily by 1,000,000 Clevelanders in 1000 transit vehicles during the last eight months."[45]

Perhaps the most original CCEP production was a thirty-minute, sound-slide film entitled "Challenge for Cleveland." Written by the author of a popular local radio program, narrated by two well-known Cleveland announcers, and featuring photographs of scenes around the city, it discussed the challenges and importance of equal treatment and addressed "common objections" to the employment of black workers. Dozens of local groups screened the film, including churches, colleges, civic and educational organizations, and the management of several companies. It was well received, winning the endorsement of a writer in the *Plain Dealer*: "It is my hope that this film will be show in our schools as well as in our business places because it is necessary for our young people to understand how contrary employment prejudices are to the practice of good Americanism."[46]

A statistics-filled pamphlet with the title "Let's Face It!" was developed to accompany the film, and it was subsequently repurposed for general distribution. The pamphlet asserted that "Clevelanders realize that minority group members are not getting even 'breaks' in employment opportunity," and it went on to cite survey results showing that Clevelanders did not want job discrimination to remain a problem. The solution to discrimination, it maintained, was for employers, employment agencies, and labor unions to eliminate racial and religious requirements from help-wanted ads and to employ people on the basis of merit. But everyone had a part to play. Ordinary people could do their part by accepting and working with their fellow employees no matter their racial or religious background. "It's everybody's job" to fight discrimination, exhorted the pamphlet. "It's up to you too!"[47]

The volume and quality of materials produced and distributed by the voluntary program over the course of the year were impressive by any standard. The only remaining doubt revolved around the question of effectiveness. The CCEP, of course, knew that it would be judged on results. From the start it claimed success using a variety of yardsticks. Its first report to the mayor was completed in April and unabashedly titled "The Cooperative Employment Practices Plan...is working." The report had argued that "results cannot be measured statistically" in a short period and submitted instead that a "real indication of progress is the amount of constructive interest" that the program generated. It noted that more than 150 companies had pledged to follow the program, and it related anecdotes of employers opening up jobs previously off limits to nonwhites. In a supplemental report filed in September, more concrete figures were offered to support the case that employers were changing their behavior. A summer survey of employers found that 82% of respondents had decided to adopt a formal policy of nondiscrimination. Fifty-nine percent had eliminated discriminatory references from their job application forms, while 69% had deleted discriminatory references from their help-wanted ads. Sixty-nine percent had reviewed their company policies and practices in light of the suggestions made by CCEP in its manual. CCEP used the battery of statistics to argue that it had made significant progress in "cultivating proper attitudes in the community," as well as "obtaining employment consideration for minorities on merit."[48]

Critics disputed the CCEP's claims of progress. Rey L. Gillespie wrote in the *Plain Dealer* that the committee had helped to cultivate a citywide atmosphere of goodwill and cooperation, and he recognized that "some progress was made." But he argued that "not enough progress was made to justify any further opposition" to legislation. The CUL's Shelton B. Granger was similarly evenhanded. The educational campaign had "some merit," but it was simply not making much of a difference in changing long-standing employment patterns. Many employers felt that if they simply participated in the educational campaign they did not have to do "anything constructive toward implementing fair practices." Even the CCEP's own survey was open to legitimate criticism. Only 12% of the surveys (540 out of 4,500) had been filled out and returned to the committee, making the CCEP an easy target. As one critic said of the nonresponders, "The 88% who failed to answer did so because they were not interested or because they were opposed."[49]

By September, liberals decided to revive the legislative campaign. Carr and Jaffe announced that they would push for the release of their bill from the legislation committee. In their view, it was time for the city to take action, especially since state legislation had recently failed by single vote. A new umbrella organization—the Citizens' Committee for Cleveland Fair Employment Practices (CCCFEP)—was formed to replace the now-moribund OCFEPC.[50]

The new group's case against the CCEP was most fully expressed in a lengthy letter it sent to members of city council. The voluntary program alone, argued the CCCFEP, could not eliminate discrimination; it needed the authority only a law could provide. CEPP was not properly equipped to address individual complaints of maltreatment. It could do nothing to change the behavior of individual employers who decided not to cooperate. It had little, if any, power to eliminate patterns of discrimination that prevailed in entire industries. It had no ability to stop the continuing flow of discriminatory job orders to employment agencies. It was powerless to address discrimination that originated with labor unions, not employers. It was incapable of verifying whether employers were indeed placing new minority workers at their companies, and it had even been unable to present data that demonstrated the reduction of discrimination. What was more, legislation had few downsides. The educational campaign of the voluntary program would not be compromised with the passage of a law; it could actually be enhanced. And there was a strong chance that the opposition of business groups would melt away, as it had almost everywhere else in the country that legislation had been enacted. "It would therefore seem wise," CCCFEP concluded, "to combine both approaches."[51]

Nothing exemplified CEPP's limits as clearly as the employment practices of Cleveland department stores. Despite repeated efforts by the Cleveland Urban League since 1945, most stores continued to maintain a nearly all-white workforce. In 1948, the CUL had tried to arrange meetings with the heads of Cleveland's nine department stores to discuss the issue. Executives were promised in advance that the meetings would be small and unpublicized, yet the committee met largely with silence. CCEP's voluntary program fared no better. At the end of the year, the head of the CUL's retail committee correctly observed that "no progress WHATSOEVER has been made in the retail stores' field." As he noted wryly, CCEP "failed in the retail stores' field as completely as we did."[52]

The intransigence of the department stores proved a liability for the chamber, leading the mayor to promise Jaffe, Carr, and the CCCFEP that he would back a law if black workers were not hired before Christmas. But the mayoral ultimatum was the least of the chamber's political problems. The results of the 1949 councilman elections in November posed a far bigger problem. Responding no doubt to the sentiment of the voters in their districts, thirty-eight of the sixty-six candidates who were running for office had indicated they would support Jaffe–Carr, and many of these candidates had won their races. In fact, anyone who had bothered to collect information from readily available public sources could have easily ascertained that a seven-vote, pro-FEPC majority would likely be sitting on the 1950 city council. Of the thirty-three members comprising the council, at least fifteen had publicly pledged to support FEP legislation during the 1949 election. Of the members who had declined to make a pledge when they were polled, five had been incumbents who had voted for the 1948 bill. The election had given liberals a definite majority.[53]

Ironically, the CCEP itself may have been partly—if indirectly—responsible for creating the new majority on city council. The voluntary program had failed to breach the color line at department stores and certain other Cleveland employers, but it nevertheless succeeded in raising public awareness about the existence and prevalence of job discrimination. The establishment of the voluntary program, moreover, had the effect of legitimating job discrimination as a matter of public concern. If organized business had denied there was a problem in the past or tried to minimize its scope or severity, it was now conceding implicitly and explicitly that job discrimination was a real and widespread problem that required action. The new stance surely fueled demands for change that the voluntary program was incapable of fully addressing, playing into the hands of liberal, pro-FEPC candidates who were only too glad to argue that stronger medicine than the voluntary program was necessary.[54]

Whatever the reasons behind the rise of the clear majority on city council, FEPC legislation seemed highly likely. The establishment of a strong Cleveland FEPC was probably only a matter of time, and the chamber could do basically nothing to prevent it. The only remaining question was how the chamber should position itself strategically in anticipation. Theoretically, it was possible for the chamber to adopt a stance of hard-line opposition, which, if it did not yield an unexpected, last-minute victory, might at least prepare the chamber to launch a subsequent campaign to repeal the new law. But the costs of such a choice were enormously high. It would have contradicted the cooperative image that the chamber had been trying to project, and it would have risked squandering whatever goodwill they had succeeded in cultivating. The main question, it seemed, was whether and how the chamber might use a promise of legislative support to broker a compromise that would minimize the regulatory burden on its membership while permitting it to claim some of the credit for passing a popular new law.[55]

Many of these considerations were surely foremost in Ong's mind when he addressed a gathering of the chamber board at the Union Club on 30 January. Over the previous weekend, Ong had met for hours with Carr, Jaffe, and community leaders to hammer out a potentially acceptable compromise bill, and he was now appearing before the board to request its approval of the result. The board had declined to reverse its opposition to "compulsory" FEPC as recently as the previous September, so its approval was not exactly a foregone conclusion.[56]

The surviving minutes reveal a thoughtful, engaged board that was fully informed about the strategic context of the decision it was preparing to make.

Lindseth had rotated out of the presidency, and the new president, John K. Thompson, asked Ong for a summary of the situation. Ong noted first of all that the voluntary program was widely lauded as a success. Even the "sharpest critics" of the chamber credited it with having done the "finest educational job in the country" over the last year. The program had "resulted in the Chamber's being in better grace with many more people than ever before." But the political winds had shifted dramatically last November, and "quite a number of the members of the new City Council had been elected because they favored an F.E.P.C. ordinance." The implication hung in the air: Categorical opposition to FEPC legislation was no longer politically viable, and compromise was the only option. Ong said that he "did not like to compromise, but that it was sometimes necessary."[57]

To that end, he had been working closely with leaders of the CCCFEP to amend Jaffe–Carr in ways that "would not harass industry." The proposed modifications involved the enforcement procedure. While the CRB would still be authorized to receive and adjust complaints, it could refer insoluble cases to the mayor, who would make an attempt to resolve the complaint. If the mayor failed, the CRB would then hold a public hearing to determine whether the complaint was valid. If a positive determination was made, the CRB would order the respondent to cease the commission of any ongoing discriminatory behavior. Only if the respondent refused or failed to comply with the order could the complaint be referred to the city attorney for prosecution.[58]

Thompson wanted to know whether the city council really would pass a "compulsory F.E.P.C. ordinance." Ong said yes. The point should have been obvious to everyone at the meeting. Cleveland was going to get an FEP law whether the chamber wanted one or not. A lone dissenter nevertheless objected. More time for study was needed, especially since FEP laws were so "contrary to American principles." Did the chamber have to take action right away? One board member argued that it did. It was "important to take an affirmative action and thereby help good administration." And if it did not approve the amendments, the "Chamber's influence would go down." The remainder of the board concurred with the analysis. Only one member voted in the negative, and the rest approved the package. This was a time when compromise did indeed seem necessary.[59]

Right after the meeting, Ong rushed over to city hall. There he joined with Lucas to present the amended proposal to city council, which voted to approve it by a margin of 27–5. After more than two years, Cleveland finally had a municipal FEPC.[60]

The chamber sought to claim a share of the credit for the victory, and Thompson shrewdly portrayed the CCC as a long-time supporter of equal employment opportunity. It had initiated a voluntary program that had cultivated a "proper atmosphere" for making progress, and the amended legislation simply created a "workable means of carrying forward the educational program" that it had started. The editorial board of the *Cleveland Plain Dealer* agreed. It claimed that the 1950 law was a "vast improvement" over early versions of Jaffe–Carr, and the passage of a "more enlightened version" could be credited to the "educational campaign" sponsored by the Chamber of Commerce.[61]

Anyone with a clear memory of 1947 or 1948 might have wondered whether the chamber and its allies were exaggerating how interested it had been in promoting fair employment practices and whether its support for the new law was a straightforward extension of its educational program. The most perceptive observers might have wondered whether there was a grain of truth in Thompson's claim that the voluntary program of the chamber had created a "proper atmosphere" for addressing discrimination. Had the voluntary program raised concerns about discrimination that it proved incapable of satisfying, leading ironically to demands for government action? But backers of municipal FEPC were happy to let such concerns slide, at least for the moment. In a celebratory photograph taken days after the law went into effect, Ong took his place alongside Jaffe, Carr, and the NAACP's Lucas as one of the four men responsible for "another Cleveland first." The swift inclusion of the chamber's representative in a photo-op would certainly send a signal to other chambers of commerce that credit would be shared if credit was due. But only time would tell whether what had happened in Cleveland was a fleeting aberration or harbinger of things to come.[62]

Scarcely a year after backing a municipal law, chamber directors once again met at the Union Club. The legislative committee had recently learned that a campaign for a state FEP law would soon get underway, and the committee had prepared a recommendation for consideration. The recommendation was short and unconflicted. While the committee still supported "equal economy opportunity for all persons regardless of race, color, creed, national origin or ancestry," this principle could not be fulfilled through "legislative compulsion." It could only be realized through "local educational work based on a desire by employers and employees to avoid discrimination." Accordingly, the committee recommended that the chamber, which had opposed statewide legislation in 1945, continue to "oppose all attempts to legislate on the subject." The board approved the recommendation without any record of discussion. All of the glowing rhetoric from the year earlier and all of the praise showered on Ong's program seemed to have been forgotten. There was no talk of building on previous successes or taking other affirmative actions. The political arm of Cleveland business had reverted to form in one quick vote. Although the example of the chamber's stance on the Cleveland ordinance would be brought up repeatedly thereafter, often by liberals hoping to win over skeptics, how the chamber voted to handle FEP legislation in the 1951 Ohio legislature made it clear that the

about-face from the previous year did not represent the beginnings of a permanent change. Its surprising position in 1950 had been a momentary reversal born
out of political motivations.[63]

The way that organized business approached civil rights politics and civil
rights policymaking in Cleveland was not exceptional. How it spoke and acted—
and why it spoke and acted—reflected a common pattern in business politics,
one that was evident as well during the struggle over Title VII of the Civil Rights
Act of 1964 and the subsequent fight to strengthen the Equal Employment Opportunity Commission. The playbook involved a simple strategy: Oppose legislation from start to finish on the grounds that legislation was unnecessary,
unworkable, and possibly even harmful. Express or demonstrate a willingness to
take voluntary action against the problem for which legislation was proposed as
a solution. However, if legislation of some kind seemed highly likely no matter
what, then trade the promise of eventual acquiescence for influence over the
particulars of regulatory design, working to minimize the cost and burden of the
new regulations on business. Organized business followed this playbook faith-
fully several decades into the postwar period. It consistently and resolutely opposed antidiscrimination legislation, determined to remain as free from regulation
as possible. Its deep core of pragmatism, its sense of realpolitik, was triggered
only when it believed with a high degree of confidence that there was no realistic
alternative to legislation. In the vast majority of instances, organized business
was happy to do whatever it could to obstruct or delay the passage of antidiscrimination legislation. In the rare instances when organized business participated openly and constructively in opening up postwar labor market—such as it
did in Cleveland through a combination of voluntary and legislative action—it
did not boldly lead from the front so much as involuntarily follow from behind,
out of the conviction that it had no better options. There, as elsewhere, necessity
proved not only the wellspring of invention but also a catalyst of virtue.

Notes

1. Ordinance 1579–48 (passed 30 January 1950); City of Cleveland, *The City Record*, 1 February 1950, 17; ibid., 8 February 1950.
2. *Cleveland Plain Dealer* (hereinafter *CPD*), 31 January 1950, 1, 5; "An Editorial," *Cleveland
   Call and Post* (hereinafter *CCP*), 4 February 1950; "1,600 Hail City's New F.E.P. Law,"
   CPD, 13 March 1950.
3. On the centrality of state and municipal battles over fair employment practices and fair
   housing to the postwar struggle for civil rights in the urban North, see Thomas J. Sugrue,
   Sweet Land of Liberty: The Forgotten Struggle for Civil Rights in the North (New York: Random
   House, 2008), 111–21; as well as Martha Biondi, *To Stand and Fight: The Struggle for Civil
   Rights in Postwar New York City* (Cambridge, Mass.: Harvard University Press, 2003); Mat-
   thew J. Countryman, *Up South: Civil Rights and Black Power in Philadelphia* (Philadelphia:

University of Pennsylvania Press, 2006); and Shana Bernstein, *Bridges of Reform: Interracial Civil Rights Activism in Twentieth-Century Los Angeles* (New York: Oxford University Press, 2011), 164–71. The starting point for any investigation of the politics behind the passage of state and local laws against discrimination is Duane Lockard, *Toward Equal Opportunity: A Study of State and Local Antidiscrimination Laws* (New York: Macmillen, 1968). On the politics of FEP legislation in Congress, see Paul Moreno, *From Direct Action to Affirmative Action: Fair Employment Law and Policy in America, 1933–1972* (Baton Rouge: Louisiana State University Press, 1997) and Louis Ruchames, *Race, Jobs, and Politics: The Story of the FEPC* (New York: Columbia University Press, 1953). See also W. Brooke Graves, *Fair Employment Practice Legislation in the United States, Federal—State—Local*, Public Affairs Bulletin No. 93 (Washington, D.C.: Library of Congress Legislative Reference Service, 1951). A new and important contribution to the history of fair employment practices and civil rights is David Freeman Engstrom, "The Lost Origins of American Fair Employment Law: Regulatory Choice and the Making of Modern Civil Rights, 1943–1972," *Stanford Law Review* 63 (May 2011): 1071–1143. On the importance of states and localities to American political history, see Thomas J. Sugrue, "All Politics Is Local: The Persistence of Localism in Twentieth-Century America," in *The Democratic Experiment: New Directions in Political History*, ed. Meg Jacobs, William J. Novak, and Julian Zelizer (Princeton, N.J.: Princeton University Press, 2003), 301–26.

4. Sugrue, *Sweet Land of Liberty*; Thomas J. Sugrue, *The Origins of the Urban Crisis: Race and Inequality in Postwar Detroit* (Princeton, N.J.: Princeton University Press, 1996); Biondi, *To Stand and Fight*; Countryman, *Up South*. See also Sidney A. Fine, *"Expanding the Frontier of Civil Rights": Michigan, 1948–1968* (Detroit: Wayne State University Press, 2000); Nancy MacLean, *Freedom Is Not Enough: The Opening of the American Workplace* (New York and Cambridge, Mass.: Russell Sage Foundation and Harvard University Press, 2006), 31; and Anthony S. Chen, *The Fifth Freedom: Jobs, Politics, and Civil Rights, 1941–1972* (Princeton, N.J.: Princeton University Press, 2009), 74–76, 131–47. For a new and important look at organized business and FEPC policy at the state level, see Alexander Gourse, "'Such Power Spells Tyranny': Organized Business, The Administrative State, and the Transformation of Fair Employment Policy in Illinois, 1945–1964," in *The American Right and U.S. Labor: Politics, Ideology, and Imagination*, ed. Elizabeth Tandy Shermer and Nelson Lichtenstein (Philadelphia: University of Pennsylvania Press, forthcoming).

5. "Council Hears Industry Hit Proposed F.E.P.C. Plan," *CPD*, 13 May 1948 and "FEPC Opponents Argue Bill Would Cause Racial Strife, Job Troubles," *CCP*, 22 May 1948; Supplemental Report of the Cleveland Committee on Employment Practices, Folder 1, Box 40, Urban League of Cleveland Records (hereinafter ULCR), Western Reserve Historical Society (hereinafter WRHS). The financial figures are taken from the income and expenditures statement on 12 April 1950. See the Board of Directors Minutes, Box 62, Greater Cleveland Growth Association Records (hereinafter GCGA Records), WRHS.

6. Excerpt from *CP*, 7 February 1950, Folder 1, Box 40, ULCR, WRHS.

7 American Council on Race Relations, "Cleveland FEPC," *Report*, Vol. 5, No. 2 (February 1950), 3; State Council for a Pennsylvania FEPC, Press Release, 15 April 1951, Folder 42, Box 3, Ohio Committee for Fair Employment Practice Legislation Records (hereinafter OCFEPL Records), WRHS; Mildred H. Mahoney to Sidney Z. Vincent, 8 February 1950, Folder 61, Box 4, Jewish Community Federation of Cleveland Records (hereinafter JCFC Records), WRHS; Wilfred J. Leland, Jr., to Sidney Z. Vincent, 9 February 1950, ibid.; U.S. Senate, Hearing before the Subcommittee on Labor–Management Relations, 82nd Cong., 2d sess., *Discrimination and Full Utilization of Manpower Resources* (Washington, D.C.: U.S. Government Printing office, 1952), 198. On the broader orientation of American business toward economic regulation in the postwar period, see Elizabeth Fones-Wolf, *Selling Free Enterprise: The Business Assault on Labor and Liberalism, 1945–1960* (Urbana and Chicago: University of Illinois Press, 1994); Howell John Harris, *The Right to Manage: Industrial Relations Policies of American Business in the 1940s* (Madison: University of Wisconsin Press, 1982); and Kim Phillips-Fein, *Invisible Hands: The Making of the Conservative Movement from the New Deal to Reagan* (New York: Norton, 2009).

8. Based on her research in the internal records of several large companies with varying reputations for racial inclusivity, Jennifer Delton makes the case that it is "time to recognize corporations as a source of social progress." Chronicling the efforts of men and women such as Inland Steel's William G. Caples, International Harvester's Ivan Willis, Fowler McCormick, and Sarah E. Southall, and Pitney-Bowes' Walter Wheeler and Joseph I. Morrow, Delton concludes in her important study that "there were executives and managers at large corporations who promoted fair employment, equal opportunity, and, later, affirmative action." See Jennifer Delton, *Racial Integration in Corporate America, 1940–1990* (New York: Cambridge University Press, 2009), 4, 7, 65, 42–71, 283.

9. Delton notes that "executives who promoted fair employment and equal opportunity often did so to avert government legislation," citing the example of Willis, Caples, and the National Association of Manufacturers. See Delton, *Racial Integration in Corporate America*, 61. My history of the Cleveland ordinance builds upon her work by showing just how closely business initiatives on fair employment practices in mid-century Cleveland were driven by the political prospects of legislative action. In doing so, it raises questions about how to interpret the role of American companies and organized business in the politics of civil rights.

10. "OK Terms for Browns' Stadium Use," *CPD*, 10 June 1947; Cleveland Community Relations Board, *To Promote Amicable Relations* (Cleveland, 1949), 23, Cleveland Public Library (hereinafter CPL); *Cleveland Jewish News* (hereinafter CJN), 9 July 1999, 46; Carol Poh Miller and Robert Wheeler, *Cleveland: A Concise History, 1796–1990* (Bloomington and Indianapolis: Indiana University Press, 1990), 146–55, especially 149 and 150 for the employment figures. For "best location in the nation," see various issues of the Cleveland Chamber of Commerce's newsletter, *Headlines from Cleveland*, Periodical Center, CPL.

11. Roger Mitton, *The Negro in Cleveland, 1950–1963* (Cleveland, Ohio: Cleveland Urban League, 1964), 25; Edward M. Miggins, "Between Spires and Stacks: The Peoples and Neighborhoods of Cleveland," in *Cleveland: A Metropolitan Reader*, ed. W. Dennis Keating, Norman Krumholz, and David C. Perry (Kent, Ohio: Kent State University Press, 1995), 194. For a very important account and analysis of racial transition in southeastern Cleveland, see Todd M. Michney, "Changing Neighborhoods: Race and Upward Mobility in Southeast Cleveland" (Ph.D. diss., Department of History, University of Minnesota, 2004).

12. Kenneth Kusmer, "Black Cleveland and the Central-Woodland Community, 1865–1930," *Cleveland*, 265–92; Fred McGunagle, *Accepting the Challenge: The Cleveland Community Relations Board, 1945–1995* (Cleveland, Ohio: Community Relations Board, 1995), 5, General Collection, CPL; Eleanor K. Caplan, *Non-White Residential Patterns*, (Cleveland, Ohio: Community Relations Board, 1959), 11; Mitton, *The Negro in Cleveland, 1950–1963*, 15, 18; CJN, 9 July 1999, 46; CJN, 5 March 1999, 46; various entries in the David D. Van Tassel and John Grabowski, eds., *Encyclopedia of Cleveland History* (Bloomington: Indiana University Press, 1987). See also Kenneth L. Kusmer, *A Ghetto Takes Shape: Black Cleveland, 1870–1930* (Urbana: University of Illinois Press, 1976) and Kimberley L. Phillips, *AlabamaNorth: African-American Migrants, Community, and Working-Class Activism in Cleveland, 1915–45* (Urbana: University of Illinois Press, 1999).

13. *The City Record*, 11 June 1947, quoted in Associated Industries, "Bulletin to Members," 13 August 1947, Folder, 1945–1947, Periodical Department, CPL; McGunagle, *Accepting the Challenge*, 9; Cleveland Community Relations Board, *To Promote Amicable Relations*, 16–20.

14. Harry Jaffe, "Saturday Town Meeting," *Cleveland News* (hereinafter CN), 9 August 1947.

15. Charles Hollman, ibid.

16. "Reader Response to Town Meeting," CN, circa August 1947. Boatner was one of thousands of black veterans in the United States who played a crucial role in the struggle for civil rights. See Christopher S. Parker, *Fighting for Democracy: Black Veterans and the Struggle against White Supremacy in the Postwar South* (Princeton, N.J.: Princeton University Press, 2009).

17. "Racial Body Asks FEPC Ordinance," *CPD*, 9 July 1947; Cleveland Community Relations Board, *To Promote Amicable Relations*; "Initial FEPC Hearings Show Job Bias on Increase in City, *CCP*, 2 August 1947.

18. Associated Industries, "Bulletin to Members," 13 August 1947, Folder, 1945–1947, Periodical Department, CPL; "Fair Hiring Measure Called Red Balm by Industry Voices," *CPD*, 9 August 1947; "Continue Hearings on Anti-Bias Plan," *CN*, 9 August 1947; Committee on National Legislation to Board of Directors, 23 May 1945, in Cleveland Chamber of Commerce, Board of Director Minutes, Vol. 1, 1945–6, 31 May 1945, 10–18, Box 59, GCGA Records, WRHS. Local college officials expressed a similar skepticism about the value of legislation "I'm just not in favor of the law," said Harold E. Adams, placement director at Western Reserve University. "You can't change attitudes by passing a law." What was more effective, Adams suggested, was "moral suasion" behind the scenes. A law could potentially "drive discrimination underground," said Ralph Knapp, a placement director at Cleveland College. See "Experts Doubtful on Law against Job Discrimination," *CPD*, 2 August 1947.

19. "Against Job Discrimination," *CP*, 29 October 1947.

20. "Amity Board Readies for FEP Action in 1948," *CCP*, 3 January 1948; "Board to Act on FEPC Bill Friday," *CCP*, 31 January 1948; "Backs Proposal for FEPC in City," *CPD*, 7 February 1948; "Council Faces Explosive Fair Employment Issue," *CP*, 7 February 1948.

21. Biondi, *To Stand and Fight*, 18–19; Leon Mayhew, *Law and Equal Opportunity: A Study of the Massachusetts Commission against Discrimination* (Cambridge, Mass.: Harvard University Press, 1968), 77–91; Bernstein, *Bridges of Reform*, 164–71; Sidney Vincent, *Personal and Professional: Memoirs of a Life in Community Service* (Cleveland: Jewish Community Federation, 1982), 74–75; Mrs. Frances Williams to Dear Friend, 21 December 1949, Folder 61, Box 4, JCFCR, WRHS; Minna Sharp to Telephone Committee, n.d. (probably June 1948), ibid.; Letter from Henry M. Busch et al. to Gentlemen, 25 June 1948, ibid.; Max E. Epstein to Dear Mr. Kane, 19 April 1948, ibid.; Glenville Bulletin, May 1948, Folder 46, Box 3, OCFEPL Records, WRHS; Glenville Area Community Council, Pamphlet, n.d. (probably June 1948), ibid.; Glenville Area Community Council, Glenville Bulletin, July 1948, ibid.; OCFEPC, Campaign Bulletin No. 1, 5 April 1948, ibid.; OCFEPC, Campaign Bulletin No. 2, 9 April 1948, ibid.; OCFEPC, Campaign Bulletin No. 3, 4 May 1948, ibid.; OCFEPC, Campaign Bulletin No. 4, 7 May 1948, ibid.; OCFEPC, Campaign Bulletin No. 5, 20 May 1948, ibid.; OCFEPC, Campaign Bulletin No. 6, 4 June 1948, Folder 61, Box 4, JCFCR, WRHS; OCFEPC, "URGENT," 23 November 1948, ibid., WRHS; "One out of Four Clevelanders Locked Out!" ibid.; "Council Committee to Hold FEPC Hearings on Wednesday," *CCP*, 3 April 1948; "Supporters of FEPC Jam Council Chambers," *CCP*, 10 April 1948; "Sharpe Urges 'Fair-Hiring' OK by Council," *CN*, 7 April 1948; "Council Group to Hear Foes of FEPC April 21," *CP*, 8 April 1948; "Many Urge Fair Employment Bill," *CPD*, 8 April 1948. Other groups with representatives who spoke out strongly for the measure included B'nai B'rith, the American Jewish Congress, the Mount Pleasant Community Council, the Glenville Community Council, the Central Areas Community Council, and the Communist Party.

22. "'FEPC Works'—Carter; Backers of Cleveland Law Urge Community Aid," *CCP*, 24 April 1948; "FEPC Seems Sure to Reach Council Vote," *CCP*, 28 April 1948; "Civic Leaders Urge FEP Law Before Council Hearings," *CPD*, 22 April 1948; "Job Equality Is Carter's Topic for Mass Meet," *CCP*, 10 April 1948; "Cleveland Citizens Turn Out in Support of FEPC in Second Hearing," *CCP*, 1 May 1948.

23. "Jaffe Optimistic as Measure Heads for Council Vote," *CCP*, 1 May 1948; "Poll Reveals Cleveland's FEPC Lacks Support," *CCP*, 8 May 1948.

24. "Council Hears Industry Hit Proposed F.E.P.C. Plan," *CPD*, 13 May 1948; "FEPC Opponents Argue Bill Would Cause Racial Strife, Job Troubles," *CCP*, 22 May 1948; "Postpone Action on FEP in City," *CN*, 13 May 1948; "Referendum Considered on Heated FEPC Issue," *CP*, 13 May 1948; "Two Experts at FEPC Hearings," *CCP*, 15 May 1948.

25. Ibid.; "Changes Fade for City FEP Law," *CPD*, 27 May 1948. On the fight over California's Proposition 11 in 1946, see Kevin Allen Leonard, *The Battle for Los Angeles: Racial Ideology and World War II* (Albuquerque: University of New Mexico Press, 2006), 279–92; Anthony S. Chen, Robert Mickey, and Robert P. Van Houweling, "Explaining the Contemporary Alignment of Race and Party: Evidence from California's 1946 Ballot Initiative on Fair Employment," *Studies in American Political Development* 22 (Fall 2008): 204–28; Chen, *The Fifth Freedom*, 126–31.

26. "Council Hears Industry Hit Proposed City F.E.P.C. Plan," *CPD*, 13 May 1948. "FEPC Critics Launch Dramatic Campaign to Torpedo Legislation," *CCP*, 5 June 1948; "Chances Fade for City FEPC Law," *CPD*, 27 May 1948.

27. "Fair Job Measure Clears Council Committee, 6–1," *CPD*, 10 June 1948; "Vote on City FEPC Due in Two Weeks," *CPD*, 15 June 1948; "Anti-Bias Bill Is Clear for Council Vote," *CN*, 10 June 1948; "Council Expects Full House for FEPC Show Tonight," *CPD*, 28 June 1948; "Clear Up Two Objections Before Creating City FEPC," *CN*, 28 June 1948; Fact Sheet on FEPC, n.d. (probably June 1948), Folder 46, Box 3, OCFEPL Records, WRHS; "Mayor Burke Makes Plea for Strong Measure" *CCP*, June 1948 (possibly 19 June).

28. "The Judicious Course," *CPD*, 27 June 1948; "City FEPC Put on Shelf by 17–16 Vote," *CPD*, 29 June 1948; "Democrats Hold Key for FEPC," *CCP*, 10 July 1948. See also "Backers of Two Local FEPC Measures Split," *CCP*, 14 July 1948.

29. "Council Gets New FEP Proposal," *CPD*, 3 August 1948; "Council Gets New FEPC Bill," *CCP*, 7 August 1948; "So We're Gonna Get FEPC Law," *CCP*, 14 August 1948.

30. Minutes, Special Meeting on Employment Problems of Minority Groups, 11 August 1948, Box 61, GCGA Records, WRHS.

31. Ibid.

32. Ibid.

33. Ibid.

34. Ibid.

35. Field Report made by Clifford E. Minton, Director, Department of Industrial Relations, 27 September 1948, Folder 7, Box 39, ULCR Records, WRHS.

36. "FEPC 'Bottled' in Committee: Carr–Jaffe Bill Runs into Stiff C of C Opposition," *CCP*, 4 December 1948; "Blocked in Council Committee," *CPD*, 2 December 1948.

37. Cleveland Chamber of Commerce Statement on Employment Practices, n.d. (probably 1 December 1948), Folder 1, Box 40, ULCR Records, WRHS; "Blocked in Council Committee," *CPD*, 2 December 1948.

38. "Worth Trying, Certainly," *CPD*, n.d. (probably December 1948); "Voluntary FEPC Deserves Trial for a Year," *CN*, 2 December 1948; "C of C Accused of Attempting to Stall FEPC," *CP*, 3 December 1948; "Urban League Affirms Strong Support of City FEPC Ordinance," *CCP*, 11 December 1948; "FEPC 'Bottled' in Committee," *CCP*, 4 December 1948; "19th Ward Councilman 'Fathers' Plan Advanced by Chamber of Commerce as Substitute for Carr–Jaffe Bill," *CCP*, 11 December 1948; "Down the Big Road," *CCP*, 8 January 1949.

39. Parker Hill to Chamber of Commerce Executives, 15 February 1950, Folder 1, Box 40, ULCR, WRHS.

40. "Survey on Discrimination," *CPD*, 15 December 1948; "Poll Data on Discrimination to Be Used in FEPC Hearing," *CPD*, 15 December 1948; Statement by Mayor Thomas Burke at FEPC Hearing before the Legislative Committee of City Council on December 15, 1948, Folder 61, Box 4, JCFCR, WRHS; Cleveland Committee on Employment Practices, "The Cooperative Employment Practices Plan . . . is working!" 11 April 1949, Folder 1, Box 40, ULCR, WRHS; Shelton B. Granger to Charles T. Steele, 23 December 1949, Folder 1, Box 40, ULCR, WRHS. See also CCEP, Report, 11 April 1949, 4–5, Folder 1, Box 40, ULCR, WRHS; Supplemental Report of the Cleveland Committee on Employment Practices, 22 September 1949, ibid.

41. CCEP, "The Cooperative Employment Practices Plan . . . is working!" 11 April 1949, Folder 1, Box 40, ULCR, WRHS; News Bulletin, December 1949, Folder 7, Box 39, ULCR, WRHS.

42. CCEP, "The Cooperative Employment Practices Plan . . . is working!" 11 April 1949, Folder 1, Box 40, ULCR, WRHS; CCEP, "How to Apply Cooperative Employment Practices," February 1949, ibid.

43. Supplemental Report of the Cleveland Committee on Employment Practices, 22 September 1949, Folder 1, Box 40, ULCR, WRHS; CCEP, News Bulletin, October 1949, Folder 1, Box 40, ULCR, WRHS; "Fuller & Smith & Ross," *Advertising Age*, 15 September 2003. For more background on the songs used in the CCEP program, see Brendan Gill and Rex Gardner, "Birri, Birri," *New Yorker*, 16 July 1949, 11; Douglas Martin, "Hy Zaret, Tin Pan Alley Lyricist, Dies at 99," *New York Times*, 3 July 2007.

44. CCEP, News Bulletin, November 1949, Folder 7, Box 39, ULCR, WRHS; CCEP, News Bulletin, December 1949, Folder 1, Box 40, ULCR, WRHS; Supplemental Report of the Cleveland Committee on Employment Practices, 22 September 1949, Folder 1, Box 40, ULCR, WRHS. The promotional materials, which include photos of the signs and publications, are located in Box 40, ULCR, WRHS.

45. CCEP, News Bulletin, November 1949, Folder 7, Box 39, ULCR, WRHS; CCEP, News Bulletin, December 1949, Folder 1, Box 40, ULCR, WRHS. The writer for the *Plain Dealer* is quoted in News Bulletin, November 1949.

46. Attached to CCEP, News Bulletin, December 1949, Folder 1, Box 40, ULCR, WRHS.

47. CCEP, "The Cooperative Employment Practices Plan . . . is working!" 11 April 1949, 15–16, Folder 1, Box 40, ULCR, WRHS; Supplemental Report of the Cleveland Committee on Employment Practices, 22 September 1949, 10, ibid.

48. "Community Relations," *CPD*, 17 April 1949; Shelton B. Granger to Charles T. Steele, 23 December 1949, Folder 1, Box 40, ULCR, WRHS; "Voluntary F.E.P. Extended 90 Days," *CPD*, 23 September 1949.

49. Minutes of Organization Meeting for a Citizens Committee for Cleveland Fair Employment Practices Legislation, 8 September 1949, Folder 61, Box 4, JCFCR, WRHS; "Revives Fight for FEPC Ordinance in City Council," *CPD*, 13 September 1949.

50. CCCFEP to Members of City Council, n.d. (probably January 1950), Folder 61, Box 4, JCFCR, WRHS.

51. Statement by the Chairman of the Retail Stores committee, n.d. (circa late 1949), Folder 61, Box 4, JCFCR, WRHS.

52. Memorandum on meeting with Mayor Thomas Burke, Wednesday, November 23 at 9:30 am in the Tapestry Room of City Hall, Folder 61, Box 4, JCFCR, WRHS; *CPD*, 29 June 1948; Citizens' Committee for Cleveland Fair Employment Practices Legislation, Press Release, 31 October 1949, Folder 61, Box 4, JCFCR, WRHS; *The City Record*, 30 June 1948; ibid., 1 February 1950.

53. Thanks to Bonnie Honig for suggesting to me that the voluntary program of the chamber may have inadvertently contributed to electoral success of pro-FEPC candidates in 1949—and hence the passage of the 1950 law.

54. Thanks to Len Rubinowitz for pushing me to think more fully about the strategic dimensions of the chamber's calculations.

55. Minutes, Board of Directors Meeting, 30 September 1949, Box 62, GCGA Records, WRHS; Minutes, Board of Directors Meeting, 30 January 1950, 33, ibid.; "Council Approves FEP Measure," *CPD*, 31 January 1950.

56. Minutes, Board of Directors Meeting, 30 January 1950, 33, Box 62, GCGA Records, WRHS.

57. Ibid.

58. Ibid., 34.

59. "Council Approves FEP Measure," *CPD*, 31 January 1950.

60. A Statement by John K. Thompson, President of the Cleveland Chamber of Commerce, Upon Passage of Cleveland's Fair Employment Practices Ordinance, Folder 1, Box 40, ULCR, WRHS; *CPD*, 31 January 1950, 1, 5; "The FEP Ordinance," *CPD*, 1 February 1950.

61. *CPD*, 14 March 1950.

62. Minutes, Board of Directors Meeting, 5 February 1951, Box 62, GCGA Records, WRHS.

3

Moving Mountains

The Business of Evangelicalism and Extraction in a Liberal Age

DARREN DOCHUK

Mounted on the wall of a museum of a Christian engineering college in Longview, Texas, is a black-and-white picture that captures the essence of oil-patch political culture in the mid-twentieth century. Framed in this image is George H. W. Bush clasping hands with Robert (R. G.) LeTourneau, Protestant industrialist extraordinaire. The year is 1954, the occasion a visit by Bush, president of the Zapata Off-Shore Company, to purchase the first mobile offshore drilling platform from LeTourneau, Inc. By signing this contract LeTourneau pledged to revolutionize oil-drilling technology. He delivered on this promise. In December of the same year, he unveiled a 4,000-ton platform, whose three electro-mechanically-operated legs allowed it to move between drill sites in open waters. In late 1955, near Vicksburg, Mississippi, the platform "walked" on its 140-foot steel legs into the Mississippi River, where it was then fitted with state-of-the-art drilling equipment. Three months later, at a public ceremony full of pomp, LeTourneau handed over control of the platform to Bush, pocketed his million-dollar payment and 38,000 shares of Zapata-Off-Shore stock, then watched as his creation entered service for Standard Oil in the Gulf of Mexico. Barely two years after having promised to do so, this self-trained engineer and self-professed evangelical had found a way to deliver black gold on demand with a reduction in costs, an increase in efficiency, and the capacity for maximum profit.[1]

If a first glance at the photo captures an intriguing moment in modern oil's development, further inspection reveals a historical trend of even greater significance: the marriage of modern evangelicalism to the business of extraction and oil. More ample proof of this phenomenon lies just beyond the photo. Although set off on its own, the snapshot of Bush and LeTourneau rests within a circular glass full of images of other power players—men like Sun Oil (Sunoco) chief executive J. Howard Pew and evangelist Billy Graham. The case itself occupies a wing of the new student center at LeTourneau University, which sits across the street from LeTourneau Inc.'s bustling factory and testing grounds, where some of the world's largest land-moving equipment is calibrated before being shipped to some of the world's largest mines and oil fields. Illustrative as they are, these hints of influence pale in comparison to the fuller record that emerges from the religious and corporate enterprises of R. G. LeTourneau himself. In rich detail, this record—correspondence, newspaper clippings, contracts, and sermons—casts fresh light on the confluence of Christ and commerce and opens up new ways of thinking about evangelicalism's investment in modern American political culture.

LeTourneau's extensive dossier reveals the ways in which an emerging evangelical theology of the mid-twentieth century compelled its most prominent devotees—Christian businessmen like LeTourneau—to think and act on a range of issues that transcend the "culture wars." Historians still often highlight battles over social issues when tracking evangelical politicization from the 1920s to the present day, and for good reason, since home and hearth have always been central to this process. Yet by emphasizing matters of morality at the cost of other concerns, and by drawing rigid lines between social and fiscal conservatism (or Main Street and Wall Street conservatives), these scholars essentially cordon evangelicalism off as a parochial entity rather than appreciate it as a multivalent, sprawling influence with global impact. Indeed, LeTourneau and his cohort saw something more expansive at stake than narrow notions of the culture wars suggest. Theirs was a quest for "moral geography"—the right for Christian citizens to claim dominion over earth and its resources in ways that conform to Scripture.[2] In LeTourneau's case, this meant literally designing and building the most innovative, high-tech machinery possible and monitoring political trends that aided or hindered this cause. Hardly the staunch traditionalists or "anti-moderns" usually associated with evangelical culture-war activism, Christians of LeTourneau's ilk manipulated the modern in order to advance their gospel. They also sought to advance the machinations of corporate capitalism. Indeed, LeTourneau's vocational commitments came wrapped in a particular view of political economy. Amid the political tumult of the 1940s, and in opposition to the New Deal liberal state, Christian businessmen like LeTourneau became the driving force behind a new evangelical movement epitomized by the founding of the National Association of Evangelicals. While internally they looked for ways to reinforce Christian capitalist teachings in the workplace, as activists they helped set in motion a postwar conservative insurgency. Toward this end, they looked for greater political leverage and found it in the rising cold war Sunbelt. Striving to amass influence, LeTourneau and his brethren forged propitious ties with the Sunbelt's economic "power base" of defense, electronics, agribusiness, and especially oil.[3] Through their financial investments in the petroleum sector, and with the help of government largesse, they found the means to expand their ministries and, in LeTourneau's own words, "move men and mountains" for Christ.

LeTourneau's ardor for Christ and capitalism stemmed from the lessons of his youth. Growing up in a middle-class, Midwestern family, he absorbed the faith of his parents who adhered to the teachings of the Plymouth Brethren Church, the small church-movement that sprang up in Britain before moving across the Atlantic in the last years of the nineteenth century. Inspired by its founder, John Nelson Darby and his premillennialist eschatology, which called for personal Christian commitment to evangelism in anticipation of the apocalypse, the Brethren church formed the intellectual backbone of the fundamentalist movement that would sweep this continent after the turn of the century. For the young convert, oblivious at the time to his church's broader cultural significance, Brethren doctrine offered several theologies that were critical to his personal development. As a result of his immersion in common-sense Biblicism, the Baconian precept that every individual had access to Scripture's truths by way of close reading, LeTourneau grew certain in his ability to attack any intellectual problem through self-taught methods of induction. Learning rules of engineering as much as biblical exegesis fell under this application. By gleaning his community's principles of stewardship, LeTourneau also learned to conflate the worth of a person with the value of his or her production. What one did with his beliefs was every bit as important as how one conceptualized them. A third Brethren teaching was just as weighty: because Christ's return was imminent, Christians needed to work feverishly to rescue "lost souls." These directives converged in LeTourneau's worldview to create a self-identity that melded spiritual calling with professional ambition and one's vocation with an unquenchable desire to win the world for Christ, regardless of the method or cost.

LeTourneau internalized this vocational outlook as a young man while setting up his own construction business, initially in Stockton, California, then Peoria, Illinois. As a rookie entrepreneur LeTourneau grew weary of his competition and frustrated with the inadequacies of his equipment. By this point in the 1910s, Stockton had already become the headquarters for earth-moving equipment firms like Caterpillar, which took advantage of the city's proximity to an expanding metropolis (San Francisco) and flourishing rural agribusiness to market its graders and tractors. LeTourneau wanted a piece of the road-building business and achieved it by creating a mechanical scraper that outclassed the mule-pulled scrapers of the day. For him, driving the machine was existential: "When I was in dry going, the track type treads . . . threw sand and dust in my face. When I was down in the bottoms, they threw mud, and I loved it. I wanted to move dirt. Lots of dirt."[4] Even while seeing his company achieve new heights with government contract work on the Boulder Dam during the 1920s, LeTourneau realized that his satisfaction came from manufacturing his equipment. Built initially to help him get ahead as a contractor, the machines themselves became the endgame. After shifting his business strategy, LeTourneau relocated his main plant to Peoria and transformed it into an epicenter of inventive engineering. Several of his breakthroughs deeply impacted the field. Though ridiculed at first by the competition, LeTourneau's employment of the rubber tire on his largest land-movers soon generated praise for the way it "reduced the angle of climb and . . . amount of pull needed" for large machinery. Scorn then commendation followed another LeTourneau creation: the Tournapull. Introduced in 1937, the Tournapull revolutionized land-moving equipment by combining tractor and carrier into one carryall machine that could clip along with a full load at fifteen miles per hour. Powering this machine were four large wheels, each containing their own electrical power sources. One of LeTourneau's least appreciated inventions at the time (but now one of his most heralded) the electric wheel provided a smooth, consistent application of energy to the machine without the necessity of a complex system of brakes, clutches, and transmission.

It was the pursuit of another power, however, that animated LeTourneau's enterprise. Since his youth he had seen his passion for technology as an extension of his theology; to move mountains for Christ was a goal he had always envisioned in spiritual, as well as literal terms. So, with business booming, he established the LeTourneau Foundation as a way to channel his profits into several evangelistic ministries. The first was a chaplaincy program that featured daily Christian "shop talks." With an estimated one thousand employees, LeTourneau had a large, captive audience, and he took full advantage, using the allotted time to share the New Testament. The engineer was unrelenting in his routine. "I make no apologies for the gospel meetings we hold in our plants. Their purpose is to promote the honor of our Lord Jesus Christ. Christianity is the essence of fair and square dealing."[5] Bringing faith into the workplace was the philosophy behind the creation of a technical institute, whereby he educated his workers in the basics of engineering and Christian devotion. Nothing thrilled LeTourneau more than to illustrate Scripture through laws of mechanics, or to expound on an engineering marvel by way of biblical metaphor. His third ministry—*NOW*, a magazine that soon claimed 600,000 readers worldwide—gave him an outlet for this delight. From its pages readers gained insight into technology and the human condition, for instance, how the laws of traction and torque applied to evangelism, or how different grades of steel represented stages of Christian growth.[6]

Outside his factory, LeTourneau began speaking out for fundamental Protestantism and free enterprise, and it is in this context that his designs for a Christian moral geography dovetailed with others'. For him, the 1930s marked a period of tribulation whose cause he attributed to society's lax spirituality, a condition he believed had grown exponentially worse since Tennessee's Scopes Trial in 1925. In the wake of Scopes, when critics proclaimed victory for "modernists" over a defeated William Jennings Bryan and his fundamentalism, LeTourneau traveled the country, championing the vision Bryan had died defending. He did so usually on behalf of the Christian Business Men's Committee International (CBMCI), a Rotary Club for evangelical industrialists. Within its ranks, managers, small businessmen, and chief executives funneled their energy into the cause of practical Christianity. As historian Sarah Hammond observes, these corporate leaders believed that functional faith was a necessary corrective to the over-intellectualized version preachers offered that had driven evangelicals into irrelevance.[7] LeTourneau himself best articulated CBMCI's mission when, in a speech to Peoria's business community, he stated, "The preachers can tell us that Christianity works. . . . They are God's salesmen, selling salvation and the Christian way of life. But unless we businessmen . . . testify that Christianity is the driving power of our business, you'll always have doubters claiming that religion is all talk and no production."[8] Stated another way, LeTourneau and his colleagues had decided that it was time to offer a form of Christianity with the "shirt sleeves rolled up."[9] Clerics cloaked in tidy garb could no longer be counted on to defend the gospel; evangelicalism had to get down and dirty and busy among the masses of laborers, managers, and rank-and-file citizens that shouldered the weight of society's hard times.

With their sleeves rolled up, Christian industrialists in LeTourneau's world worked overtime to sell this message. During the late 1930s, the CBMCI, along with parallel ministries like the Business Men's Evangelistic Clubs (BMEC) and the Gideons, widened their efforts to offset spiritual declension by sponsoring revivals, distributing Bibles, creating radio programs, and setting up youth outreach centers. Herbert J. Taylor, a former executive with Sinclair Oil and one of LeTourneau's contemporaries, had a hand in these programs. President of Club Aluminum, in Chicago, Taylor funded Christian business foundations and established his own, the Christian Workers Foundation (CWF).[10] Through its various subsidiaries, the CWF echoed Taylor's evangelical message to America: repent as individuals or continue to see society face God's wrath, reform or prepare for worse to come. Together, Taylor and LeTourneau echoed corporate evangelicals' hardening anti–New Deal message. As concerned as they had become during the 1920s with the modernist teachings of evolution, it was Roosevelt's experiments in economic policy that drove them to political outspokenness, not that cultural and economic politics were ever separate in their imagination. In Roosevelt's support for expanded government, industrial unionism, and social welfare, evangelical entrepreneurs identified a dangerous leviathan that touched the home, church, schoolroom, and workplace, and allowed several dark "isms" (collectivism, internationalism, secularism) access to each sphere.[11] Strip bare the union of capitalism and Christianity in the corporate sector, they believed, and one was sure to see the dismantling of an entire social ethic based on individual responsibility, family values, and moral community. Financiers thus left plenty of room in their logic for sweeping cultural criticism of the sort fundamentalist pastor Louis Bauman declared: "Russia has her Stalin, Germany has her Hitler; and impossible as it may seem, the United States of America has her Roosevelt!"[12]

Still, the bottom line for evangelical entrepreneurs was fiscal in kind: in their eyes, Roosevelt's New Deal was first and foremost an affront to sound Christian economics, and as such it required a sound economic response. Very naturally, then, the ministries they had erected assumed a more conspicuously political tenor. Taylor and others spoke in this tone, but LeTourneau did it especially well. In the pages of *NOW*, he blended news about his factories and evangelistic activities with opinion pieces on Roosevelt's administration, few of which needed any heavy interpretive work for their political messages to shine through. While on one occasion *NOW* sounded off against labor leaders in Peoria who questioned LeTourneau's shop talks, on another it repeated Republican Party boilerplate by condemning Roosevelt's efforts to pack the Court with Democrats, expand government bureaucracy, and legitimate labor unions.[13] LeTourneau's shop-room maneuvers matched his media work. In his devotions on engineering and Christian living LeTourneau propagated a politicized message that suggested loyalty to Christ and the company was synonymous.[14] In his social programming, he used welfare capitalism as a weapon, supplying bonuses, family benefits, and recreation through the LeTourneau Employees' Union to subdue workers' solidarity.[15] Above all, he expanded his educational offerings. Locking arms with other conservatives in the National Association of Manufacturing (NAM), he saw private vocational training as the necessary counterweight to a system of higher education he believed had grown increasingly more liberal and secular under Roosevelt's watch.[16] With ever-increasing determination, he used his industrial training program to mold workers in a bootstrap ethic of self-help, an ethic he saw threatened by New Deal labor's collectivist dreams. Political victory, in his estimation, depended on Christian capitalism's ability to convince the mind—not just capture the heart—of America's rank-and-file.

As Depression turned to war, evangelical businessmen banded together in their religious associations to counter the New Deal as one united, political force. Thriving in the 1930s as venues for talk about better evangelism in the corporate world, organizations like the CBMCI entered the 1940s teeming with anxious members who wanted to talk about better politics for the nation. And so they started another organization that could take such discourse to a new level: the National Association of Evangelicals (NAE). Created in 1943 to counter the Federal Council of Churches (FCC), the NAE quickly became the flagship agency of a new evangelicalism that sought distance from old-time fundamentalism by avowing an irenic, cooperative, and culturally engaged orthodoxy. Its impetus came from two men: J. Elwin Wright, a New England real estate agent turned church activist, and Harold Ockenga, pastor of Park Street Church in Boston, whose charge that evangelicals had "suffered . . . defeats for decades" because of the "terrible octopus of liberalism" encapsulated his constituency's feelings.[17] Ockenga initiated the NAE with a vision of political crisis, saying the NAE "is the only hopeful sign on the horizon of Christian history today."[18] With such grand eloquence pulsating through NAE's founding ceremonies, it must have been easy for critics to ignore this agency's political substance. Historians themselves, in fact, have downplayed this dimension, emphasizing instead the NAE's role as a clearinghouse for evangelism.[19] It performed this role, certainly, but the NAE was also a political federation, the culmination of evangelical entrepreneurs' 1930s spadework to undermine the New Deal.

The business-mindedness behind NAE operations was obvious from the very beginning. Its mouthpiece, United Evangelical Action, offered members regular advice on current events, monitored government policy, and disseminated complaints about Congress's acquiescence to liberal interests. The NAE's field office in Washington, D.C., researched and filed grievances against bills that seemed questionable in intent. In one statement, printed in the late 1940s, the paper highlighted several proposed laws deemed dangerous for employers:

> There are bills classified under the high-sounding phrase, "Fair Employment Practice Commission." F.E.P.C. bills . . . would open the way for large numbers of bureaucrats, "Investigators," to pry into one's personal business. It is class legislation of the worst kind. . . . If this bill passes you can anticipate the arrival of that day when the government will tell you with whom you must work, with whom your children must attend school, whom you must hire.[20]

In this same report, NAE director R. L. Decker declared that in order to fight conspiring foes, the NAE needed to "sponsor a nationwide, evangelical 'Secret Service'" comprised of "trusted, loyal, evangelical people in every city and region of America who is [sic] in a place of any importance or influence, in public life or education or business circles."[21] Behind the scenes, meanwhile, businessmen dictated the NAE's organizational priorities of rigorous fundraising, marketing, and pocketbook politicking, and ensured that it sought out recruits in the corporate world. They located them in organizations like the NAM. Besides employing an official liaison to the NAM, the NAE also courted elite executives who bridged these worlds, men like J. Howard Pew, head of Sun Oil.[22] As an elite executive, Pew feared Roosevelt's encroachment on corporate freedom; as a conservative Presbyterian with evangelical sensibilities, he feared liberal, ecumenical Protestantism's encroachment on congregational sovereignty and the traditional gospel. Both concerns made him a patron of the NAE. NAE officials thanked him by including him in their "inner circle"—the "Secret Service" Decker envisioned.[23]

World War II provided evangelical businessmen, enlivened by the NAE's founding, yet further opportunity to advance their vision. Sensing the birth of a new political order at home and abroad, they dreamed of breaking through as the vanguard of an empowered Christian Americanism. NAE actions in Washington, D.C., and burgeoning defense communities around the country spoke to this confidence. Under the leadership of Wright and Taylor, the latter of whom assumed a Pentagon post on the Price Adjustment Board, the NAE first adopted an aggressive posture on media matters.[24] Irate that the FCC enjoyed official sanction over the nation's radio airwaves, Wright and Taylor helped form the National Religious Broadcasters (NRB), which would henceforth lobby successfully for evangelical airtime.[25] While the NRB allowed the new evangelical message to penetrate communities across the country, in many of these same towns a second NAE venture had equally significant impact. Evangelical businessmen looked for ways to guarantee American capitalism's escape from the Depression. Wary that organized labor might derail them, they formed the Commission on Industrial Chaplaincies to propagate an "applied Christianity" that could solve "employees' personal work problems, and . . . improve labor-management relations."[26] In essence, the Commission channeled 1930s evangelical welfare capitalism into a focused wartime program designed to offset labor demands with pleas for Christian cooperation, service, and patriotism.

R. G. LeTourneau led these crusades. Besides heavily investing in the NRB's mission, his own chaplaincy program served as the model for the NAE's. Yet his contribution to evangelicalism's wartime renaissance did not end there. Through *NOW* he inspired his workers and a wider public with his patriotic vision: "Wherever our armed forces [and] our allies go, picture LeTourneau equipment. . . . Because it's wartime around the world, it's wartime around the clock . . . at LeTourneau's."[27] *NOW* backed these proclamations with statistics that proved LeTourneau's wartime commitment to ministry and the military. The numbers were impressive. In the first years of World War II, the LeTourneau Foundation distributed 20,000 Bibles to schools, 50,000 Scripture calendars to subscribers, and 25,000,000 tracts to churches and citizens.[28] LeTourneau's dedication to America's military was no less pronounced. Early in his career, when working on the Boulder Dam, he had recognized the benefits accrued through government contracts. With no sense of compunction, the anti–New Dealer once again partnered with Washington, legitimating government aid in this case as a short-term necessity for the protection of Christian democracy. Between 1942 and 1945, with Pentagon orders for equipment rolling in, he turned out 78 new inventions, machinery that carried men ashore at Normandy, and carved roads out of jungles in the South Pacific, desert in North Africa, and frozen tundra in Alaska. *NOW* provided readers weekly accounts of how LeTourneau's technology was turning the tide for the Allies. Such bold declarations were warranted: by war's end 70% of all heavy earthmoving equipment used by the allies had been built in his plants.[29]

LeTourneau drew satisfaction from his wartime accomplishments but also a measure of anxiety: Could capitalism and Christianity's wartime momentum be sustained? Confronting doubt, he and many of his allies contemplated migration to the New South—the Sunbelt South. By the early 1940s, amid ongoing battles with unionists in his plants and disillusionment with the secularism he considered rampant in the North, LeTourneau was convinced that his goals necessitated a different environment. He came to this realization in successive stages, the first of which began transpiring in the late 1930s when the president of a Bible school in Toccoa, Georgia, convinced him that his state was ripe for business. For years LeTourneau had wanted virgin land—preferably of a hilly and forested kind—to test his equipment, and northeastern Georgia offered this in spades. Toccoa's human resources struck him as favorable too. Surely the town's unskilled but earnest laborers could easily be trained in his methods of production and models of citizenship, beyond the specter of union politicos.

Local boosters bought LeTourneau's plan. In July 1939 the *Atlanta Constitution* hailed LeTourneau's arrival: "Toccoa factory is dedicated to principles of Christianity—guidance of God is implored for a $2,000,000 plant; Big gathering of friends and employees cheer dedication in revival-like atmosphere."[30] The caption barely conveyed the scale of LeTourneau's welcoming. Five thousand citizens greeted the industrialist on the first day of a weeklong festival that featured evening revival meetings and testimonials from their new boss. LeTourneau also fed the multitudes by providing "twenty hogs, thirty sheep, fourteen hundred pounds of beef, and thousands of bottles of soft drinks" for a "regulation Southern Barbecue."[31] Several businessmen and politicians partook in the festivities, including U.S. Senator Richard B. Russell, Georgia Governor E. D. Rivers, and Preston Arkwright, President of the Georgia Power Company. One esteemed guest put the gathering in religious perspective when he greeted LeTourneau as "a man of God" who knew how to cure society's ailments. "What America needs so desperately is thousands of business men who will really consecrate themselves and their businesses to God. Peace and brotherly love would naturally follow and there would be no strife between capital and labor."[32] Arkwright portrayed LeTourneau's business venture in sharper political light.

There is no kinder philanthropy than . . . enterprise of this type. This man is not starting a sweatshop. He pays better wages than the average employer. He works his laborers reasonable hours. His employees need not protection. He came to our State with this magnificent industry of his own accord. No chamber of commerce inveigled him into building his plant in Georgia. Not a railroad ticket was spent to lure him into coming here. He received no land grant. He selected this property and bought it himself. He received no Reconstruction Finance Corporation loan. He received no PWA grant. All we see here today is individual enterprise. This is brand new wealth, adding to the wealth of our State.[33]

Historians have highlighted the way wartime mobilization, defense monies, and southern boosterism turned states like Georgia into the Sunbelt. In tiny Toccoa, early evidence of such regional transformation rose up around LeTourneau and his new neighbors.[34]

Even still, in LeTourneau's mind, the decision to relocate south stemmed from something more personal than macroeconomics: Christian vocation. In the Sunbelt he saw fresh soil to till and souls to stir for God, and so he pursued this goal with unceasing verve, next on the shores of the Mississippi River, where he bought land for testing new amphibious equipment and shipping access to the Gulf. It was farther to the west, however, where LeTourneau found his paradise. He found it from the air. LeTourneau had long wished for a plant that could produce its own steel with which he could forge his machinery. Invited by a local booster to check out Longview, he immediately identified potential in the failed Lone Star Steel Company, which at least had proved East Texas's rusty soil was loaded with iron. While flying into the community to evaluate the abandoned mill, LeTourneau discovered another hidden gem below: a government-owned hospital that had housed convalescent patients during war but now was up for sale. Things moved quickly after these two finds. At the same time he secured Lone Star's property and began building a plant, LeTourneau presented plans to Washington to turn Harmon Hospital into LeTourneau Technical Institute, "with special attention being paid to veterans desiring a technical education under the G.I. Bill of Rights." The pitch worked. For property valued at $870,000, LeTourneau paid a token one-dollar, then set out to build his empire.[35]

Over the next decade, as cold war tensions escalated, LeTourneau's empire reached heights of influence that its creator never imagined. The industrialist's ascent reflected the new evangelicalism's ascent; success on both counts was predicated on what had come before but also on something distinctively empowering about the emerging Sunbelt economy: the pursuit of oil. To be sure, the South's postwar economy was primed for a wider "power base" built on other sectors, but oil was the pivot around which this base turned, and evangelicals were aware of it. This did not necessitate any epiphany on their part; evangelicalism and oil had always worked well together. Since the 1850s, the independent-minded wildcatters who had dredged oil's frontiers had readily appealed to the sacred assurances of the evangelical tradition. John D. Rockefeller spoke for his contemporaries when, as a young entrepreneur, he announced that America's untapped oil reserves "were the bountiful gifts of the great Creator," a "blessing... to mankind." Finding spiritual inspiration in the way oil was extracted and refined ("the whole process seems a miracle," he said) he reciprocated by using this evidence of divine blessing to anoint an entire industry.[36] Such was the providential view of petroleum that fused Christianity and capitalism into union and fused evangelicalism and oil's manifest destiny in the modern age.

Nowhere was this bond stronger than in southern oil-producing states like Texas and Oklahoma, and in California. Even in their nascent stage during the early twentieth century, these states' petroleum sectors found an ally in the impassioned evangelicalism that enjoyed hegemonic status there. A number of factors contributed to this effect, beginning with loose governance. As Roger Olien and Diana Davids Hinton explain, with weak governments unable to curtail the "freewheeling" nature of frontier oil exploration, individuals enjoyed the freedom to skip legalities, make deals with handshakes, and join the rush for black gold "with very little capital" and only a few necessary tools.[37] This hands-off approach to business matched evangelicals' hands-off approach to religion, which encouraged low-church denominations (Baptist, Methodist, Pentecostal, Church of Christ) and the folks who filled their pews to strike out against top-down ecclesiastical control, build churches to their liking, worship as they preferred, witness to "the lost" with an eye on local needs, and ultimately graft their wildcat religiosity onto the region's corporate culture. Such shared confidence in the independent and speculative side of capitalism only grew stronger through the first half of the century as southwestern oilmen and evangelicals (often one in the same) constructed an interlocking system of business, educational, ecclesiastical, and political institutions, reifying in the process an ideology of bootstraps, cowboy conservatism, as well as a new sense of regional identity. With the dawn of the automobile age driving the demand for Texas, California, and Oklahoma crude to unprecedented heights, and with it the dreams of a consuming citizenry, and amid the rising tides of industrial unionism and New Deal liberalism in the North, which seemed to suppress the individual in favor of the collective, southwestern oil assumed import as "America's lifeblood" and the symbolic link to a pristine, democratic, capitalist past.[38] Armed with this assumption, the Southwest's oil-patch Protestants carved out their identity as guardians of the nation's elemental life source.

This rich history notwithstanding, the ties forged between evangelicalism and oil would become especially tight in the cold war Sunbelt, in part because the two constituencies needed each other like never before. In the wake of the Scopes Trial of 1925, which forced them to the cultural margins of American society, and throughout the financial difficulties of the 1930s, which further undermined their churches and schools, evangelicals in the South felt embattled and overwhelmed. As difficult as the Depression had been for evangelicalism, petroleum had borne an even heavier burden. Amid years of boom-bust cycles brought on by new oil finds in East Texas, America's oilmen faced multivalent challenges. Within their cohort, they debated the type of regulation that should be imposed to conserve petroleum reserves and quell pricing fluctuations.[39] Oil's external challenges proved just as difficult. Following the Teapot Dome scandal of the 1920s, oil sunk to its nadir in public perception; always questioned for its "Hobbesian" excesses, it became lodged in America's imagination as a "gigantic system of wrong."[40] In the 1930s, when citizens sought to pin complaints about capitalism on something conspicuous and concrete, oil and oilmen easily fit the bill. Already viewed as problems in American society, they now acquired added meaning as an impediment to society's reform.

Together, then, oil and evangelicalism were ready to be revitalized in the cold war era, and the Sunbelt's ability to bring these two overlapping constituencies into communion paid resounding dividends. Thanks to evangelicals' deft use of popular media, cultural influence, and political mobilization, the relationship between God and black gold flourished again. The first payout came in the popular realm with the new evangelicalism's capacity to recast petroleum's life story as a redemptive narrative of Christian American exceptionalism. Tellingly, in this formative moment, NAE spokesman Billy Graham counseled famous oilmen like Sid Richardson into conversion experiences, then produced two movies that told these individuals' salvation stories, one called "Mr. Texas" (1951) and the other "Oiltown, U.S.A." (1953). Both were released to mainstream fanfare that evangelicals in the 1930s could not have thought possible. Other evangelists like Oral Roberts and Charles Fuller helped redeem oil by becoming oilmen themselves and using profits from their companies to fund independent ministries. In Fuller's case, this meant building a seminary in California, which opened its doors in 1947. With Harold Ockenga as its president, Graham on its Board, and the backing of a who's who of evangelical businessmen, Fuller Seminary instantly became the intellectual hub of the new evangelical movement. As if to announce this dawn, Fuller called his company Providential Oil.[41]

Sunbelt evangelicalism's knack for accentuating the positives in this industry— especially its throwback values of individual initiative and capitalist drive— proved invaluable in the battle for public opinion, yet this style was also backed by substantive gains in two other cold war spheres: philanthropy and politics. As much as Christian businessmen like LeTourneau seized on opportunities during the 1930s and 1940s to build an apparatus of nonprofit agencies that could channel capital into Christian ministry, these opportunities remained fairly limited. Thanks to government largesse, corporate executives who held strong evangelical convictions found the cold war milieu much more amenable to their philanthropic designs.

Government monies came through various channels, most obviously by way of business deals. As the cold war state expanded, making way for a military-industrial complex that commanded policy decisions in myriad sectors—from housing and education to transportation—the Sunbelt's evangelical boosters found new ways of funding their business projects, hence faith-based initiatives. LeTourneau's ability to secure government contracts (some via the Federal Highway Act of 1956), which called for his machines to clear land for roads and residential communities, and funnel profits into the LeTourneau Foundation, illustrates the breadth of evangelical investments in and benefits from the cold war state. In terms of scale, though, evangelical boosterism received its biggest lift from oil-generated munificence. Sun Oil executive J. Howard Pew saw his company's fortunes spike in the 1940s as it serviced the American navy. By the early 1950s, he was redirecting corporate gains through the Pew Foundation into countless charitable causes. An earnest evangelical, Pew ensured that these causes stayed true to his faith. Other oilmen like "Tex" Thornton may not have worn their religious convictions in such overt fashion, but they used monies accrued through government contracts to support Christian institutions whose philosophy was the same as their own. As the multimillionaire owner of Litton Industries, Thornton combined profits from his oil ventures and high-tech communications firm, which built guidance systems for the military, to fund the Church of Christ–based Pepperdine University in Los Angeles. Thornton not only helped Pepperdine stay afloat in difficult times but also guaranteed that the school's blend of conservative pedagogy and politics would secure it a national reputation. Thornton and Pepperdine's was a formula repeated multiple times across the Sunbelt.[42]

There was more to Sunbelt oil and evangelicalism's cold war prosperity, however, and it had as much to do with the state's increasingly flexible handling of the nonprofit sector as its loosened purse strings. Historian Axel Schäfer has demonstrated how American policy makers encouraged "subsidiarity" or an "allocative" state during the 1950s, in which "nongovernmental actors" played a critical role in government "revenue gathering and distribution" and "policy implementation."[43] Unlike the 1930s, when Roosevelt's interventionist liberalism sharply distinguished between government and voluntary welfare programs, Eisenhower's associative liberalism married private and public sectors in "mutual construction of the Cold War State." "Combining national security and welfarist components, massive federal funding was made available to private businesses and nonprofit organizations in order to shore up services in areas such as higher education, defense-related and medical research, hospital building, social services, foreign aid, urban renewal, and community development."[44] Despite their purported anti-government stand, evangelicals reaped the greatest rewards of the new federal system.[45] Now willing to engage the state and mainstream culture, the new evangelicals who followed LeTourneau's lead by supporting the NAE captured disproportionately large pieces of Washington's pie. Whether directing them into relief efforts and missionary enterprises around the world, or into educational and social services on American soil, evangelicals used government funds to build their own welfare system, even as they, in exchange, helped build a larger, more diffuse, and ultimately stronger state.[46] Considering their preponderance in the nation's emerging southern rim, it is no surprise that petroleum-friendly foundations like LeTourneau's and the Pews' flourished under this new dispensation.

And it is little wonder that such success encouraged Sunbelt petro-capitalists and petro-Christians to adopt a potent form of politics. Despite their claims to the contrary, cold war evangelicals revitalized rather than resisted a role in formal politics. Again, as Schäfer notes, anti-government rhetoric notwithstanding, evangelicals in fact played a "key role in constructing the ideological underpinnings of the Cold War state, which combined the image of limited government and sanctification of liberal capitalism with the massive expansion of the state's military and welfare components."[47] They also became the self-proclaimed custodians of a spirit and policy of containment, which sanctioned America's role as global protector of freedom. And so, as the cold war heated up in Asia and South America, Sunbelt evangelicals, whose presence along the nation's southern and western edges gave them special access to (and a special sense of responsibility for) these geopolitical hot-zones, redoubled their efforts to champion corporate capitalism, a strong military and foreign policy, and easy access to the world's natural resources. Oil's global interests henceforth became inseparable from theirs. While lesser-known evangelicals supported campaigns to open up the America's tidelands for drilling and the Amazon for exploration, petro-patriarchs like Pew, H. L. Hunt, Sid Richardson, and Clint Murchison funded right-wing political candidates with the same fervor they funded churches, evangelistic ministries, and Christian schools. Their efforts would culminate in Barry Goldwater's GOP candidacy in 1964, Ronald Reagan's gubernatorial win in 1966, and Richard Nixon's ascent to the White House in 1968, campaigns that would cause liberal critics to speak out against the extremist, conspiratorial intentions of God and black gold.[48] Yet already much earlier, in the 1950s, evangelicalism and oil had emerged as a dynamic political couple linked not by conspiracy but by long-standing institutional and ideological compatibilities.

LeTourneau may not have been able to match Pew, Hunt, or Richardson's clout, but as illustrated by three of his boldest cold war ventures, he operated above the rest when it came to fusing evangelicalism and oil's imperatives into one quest for Christian dominion. At his new home base in Longview, located on the edge of East Texas' oil boom, he spent the late 1940s and early 1950s building an international reputation in oil technology. In his 88,000 square-foot mill, workers produced 25 tons of molten steel every 3–4 hours, then transported it to the machinery plant where some of the largest earth-moving equipment could be built and then shipped for use on oil patches around the world.[49] Northern Alberta was one such landscape reshaped by LeTourneau's vision. The industrialist first visited Edmonton in the late 1940s to address the city's evangelicals. Alberta premier Ernest Manning helped ensure a warm, friendly welcome. Because of shared religious convictions and evangelical business associations Manning and LeTourneau easily struck up a relationship that would last for the rest of their lives. The friendship changed Alberta's economy. In the late 1950s Manning and another ally—J. Howard Pew—worked a deal allowing Sun Oil to begin extracting crude from the Athabasca oil sands. Backed by Pew's money and Manning's political capital, LeTourneau's largest-scale machinery began churning up the northern Alberta soil in 1967. A corporate bulletin announced the project to shareholders, with no small measure of hyperbole:

> This venture combines drama (man against nature), daring (the risk of large financial resources), and science (the technology of the operation is itself a fascinating story). It is a pioneering undertaking in a frontier area in more than one respect. Success can bring a direct pecuniary return to Sun as the principal supplier of funds and talent, but even the attempt contains an indirect gain through burnishing the image of the Company as a progressive and venturesome organization in the eyes of the Canadian and American . . . public.[50]

The operation was impressive in business terms, but all three of the Great Canadian Oil Sand's players measured their labor prophetically as well.[51] LeTourneau spoke to this at a World Trade Conference in the 1950s. In his mind, his work was God's work; "God gave us the raw materials to work with for nothing, and there is plenty to be had if we go to work and produce the things we want."[52]

LeTourneau sought to fulfill this potential in a second way. Like many businessmen, he saw the new American South as a vital launch for missions and commerce in the new global South, and so, from his Sunbelt base, he moved into Peru. Through partnership with Cameron Townsend, founder of North Carolina–based, Southern California–headquartered Wycliffe Bible Translators, LeTourneau reached agreement with Peruvian President Manuel Odria, whereby he would complete thirty-one miles of the Trans-Andean Highway, linking the Amazonian hinterland with the Pacific, in exchange for a million acres of uncultivated land on which he could build an evangelical mission. By opening up the hinterland, Odria hoped Mobil Oil and Gulf Oil's Peruvian subsidiaries would gain access to the country's reserves, paving the way for his country's economic expansion. With land secured, the engineer-evangelist began leveling forests. Aiding him was his "jungle crusher," which, at 74 feet long, 22 feet wide, 19 feet high, and 280,000 pounds, attacked walls of trees at a rate of four acres an hour. The end result of this demolition was Tournavista, a community of natives and missionaries, which, throughout the cold war era, carried out LeTourneau's plan to establish a "free," self-sustaining economy that might be used as a model of capitalism for third-world societies and a beachhead for retrieval and exportation of natural resources by first-world nations.[53]

In order to staff his factories and missions, LeTourneau needed young people trained in his methods and values. Through LeTourneau Technical Institute, he met this challenge. No longer satisfied with educating just his workers, LeTourneau spent the early 1950s transforming his industrial program into an accredited college whose curriculum would meet the "spiritual requirements of the modern age; the educational demands of a scholastic aid; the practical needs of a technical age."[54] Courses offered in construction, electrical, industrial, mechanical, and welding engineering accentuated the schools commitment to "a technical age," while those in theology and missions reminded students that they were being called to a different sort of career, one whose threefold emphasis on "head, heart, and hand" stressed the priorities of Christian service.[55] Although not the only new Sunbelt evangelical to promote this philosophy, LeTourneau's ambitions exceeded most. By the early 1960s, with an enrollment of four hundred, LeTourneau College was sending graduates around the globe to engineer a Christian future. While some stayed to help LeTourneau Incorporated design machinery for the world's mines and oil fields, others moved into the private and public sectors to ensure similar progress in related fields. And many began their careers on the mission field. One of the most popular programs at LeTourneau College was missionary aviation. Drawn from churches all over North America, young Christian men underwent intense training in Longview then began flying for Wycliffe and evangelical mission organizations worldwide.

Despite their international range, it is in the Sunbelt where LeTourneau's achievements would leave their profoundest legacy. Offered the opportunity by this region to explore the extent of his vocational aspirations, LeTourneau returned the favor by helping give it economic, cultural, and political form. It was a decidedly conservative form, constructed out of evangelicalism's decades-long quest to build a New Right. LeTourneau would die before seeing this project achieve its ultimate partisan expression in Ronald Reagan's Sunbelt-bolstered victory in 1980. Yet, the conservative revolution that transpired after LeTourneau's 1967 passing was hardly sudden. Forged in the crucible of Depression and

war, it was the product of Roosevelt's time, not Reagan's.[56] LeTourneau's illus-
trious business practices bear witness to this. By synchronizing faith in God with
faith in the machine, a theology of production with a passion for earthmoving,
LeTourneau helped fasten evangelicalism to a Republican program premised on
entrepreneurialism, venture capitalism, and easy access to land and its resources.
And by infusing his corporation with sacred meaning, he and his Bible-believing,
business-minded allies encouraged a fledgling new evangelicalism to fold matters of faith and culture into matters of money and commerce. So it is that evangelicals since LeTourneau's time have continued to advance an undifferentiating
politics that deems land-use policies and untapped oil reserves just as vital to the
Christian conscience as Court rulings on prayer and the unborn child. For them,
the political fight has always been about something more than "culture wars"; it
has been about protecting the right to extract the "bountiful gifts of the great
Creator" in ways that conform to an expansive gospel of Christ, capitalism, and
dominion over the earth.

Notes

1. "R.G. Talks," *NOW*, 15 September 1961, 2; "The Wildcat and the Black Dog," *NOW*, 15
   September 1961, 2–3. *NOW* was accessed at the LeTourneau University Archives (LUA),
   Longview, Texas.
2. On "moral geography": Simon Schama, *The Embarrassment of Riches* (Berkeley: University
   of California Press, 1988), 35.
3. On Sunbelt economy: Kirkpatrick Sale, *Power Shift: The Rise of the Southern Rim and Its
   Challenge to the Eastern Establishment* (New York: Random House, 1975).
4. R. G. LeTourneau, *The Autobiography of R. G. LeTourneau* (Chicago: Moody Press, 1967),
   97.
5. Quoted in Albert W. Lorimer, *God Runs My Business: The Story of R. G. LeTourneau* (New
   York: Fleming H. Revell Company, 1941), 102, 158–59.
6. "Shifting of Load from Traction," *NOW*, 1 February 1962, 1; "Steel to Illustrate a Spiritual
   Truth," reprinted in *NOW*, September 1971, 1.
7. Here I am drawing from Sarah Hammond's first-rate study of evangelical entrepreneurialism in the 1930s and 1940s, "'God's Business Men': Entrepreneurial Evangelicals in Depression and War" (Ph.D. diss., Yale University, 2010).
8. *Mover of Men and Mountains: The Autobiography of R. G. LeTourneau* (Chicago: Moody
   Press, 1967), 203.
9. R. G. LeTourneau, "The Industrial Chaplain" and "Novel On-Job Bible Class Big Hit with
   D-X Workers," *Tulsa Daily World*, 22 August 1952, 1, Industrial Chaplaincy—Background
   Material, NAE Files, 1960s, Box 38, National Association of Evangelical Records (NAE),
   Wheaton College, Wheaton, Illinois.
10. Hammond, "God's Business Men," 158–60; 182.
11. Donald Critchlow, *Phyllis Schlafly and Grassroots Conservatism* (Princeton, N.J.: Princeton
    University Press, 2005), 34–35.
12. Louis S. Bauman, "Present-Day Fulfillment of Prophecy," *The King's Business*, June 1933,
    181.
13. "President's Proposal Resemble Jethro's," *NOW*, 29 January 1937, 3; "Questions Preach-
    ing at LeTourneau Plant," *NOW*, 5 February 1937, 3; "Union Pledges Loyalty to
    R. G. LeTourneau," *NOW*, 7 June 1937, 3; "President's Popularity Sliding, Says Writer,"

NOW, 24 September 1937, 3; "Coal Mine Fire Burning 51 Years," *NOW*, 23 October 1936, 2; "President's Voice Used to 'Prove Broken Pledge,'" *NOW*, 23 October 1936, 3.

14. "R. G. LeTourneau Talks on Status of Employees," *NOW*, 26 February 1937, 2–3.

15. On welfare capitalism: Elizabeth Fones-Wolf, *Selling Free Enterprise: The Business Assault on Labor and Liberalism, 1945–1960* (Champaign: University of Illinois Press, 1994), 189–92; Lisabeth Cohen, *Making a New Deal: Industrial Workers in Chicago, 1919–1939* (New York: Cambridge University Press, 1990), 160–83.

16. On Depression Era evangelical education and corporate politics: Darren Dochuk, *From Bible Belt to Sunbelt: Plain-folk Religion, Grassroots Politics, and the Rise of Evangelical Conservatism* (New York: W. W. Norton, 2011), ch. 3.

17. Quoted in Garth Rosell, *The Surprising Work of God: Harold Ockenga, Billy Graham, and the Rebirth of Evangelicalism* (Grand Rapids, Mich.: Baker Academic, 2008), 97–98.

18. Ibid.., 101–2.

19. Illustrative, in this regard, is Joel Carpenter, *Revive Us Again: The Reawakening of American Fundamentalism* (New York: Oxford University Press, 1997).

20. "Report of the Directors of Information," Original Minutes, 1963–1964, National Association of Evangelical Minutes, 63–69, 74–88, Box 32, NAE.

21. "Annual Report of the 'Committee on Christian Liberty,'" Minutes of the Meeting of the Board of Administration, National Association of Evangelicals, Tuesday, April 19, 1949, Chicago, Illinois, National Association of Evangelicals Master Minutes 1940s–50s, Box 30, NAE.

22. Hammond, "God's Business Men," ch. 4.

23. J. Howard Pew to Howard Kershner, 8 March 1950, Christian Freedom Foundation: Founding Documents Folder, Box 180, J. Howard Pew Papers (JHP), Hagley Museum and Library, Wilmington, Del. J. Elwin Wright's designation of Pew as "inner circle": J. Elwin Wright to J. Howard Pew, 4 February 1958, National Association of Evangelicals Folder, Box 61, JHP.

24. Hammond, "God's Business Men," 221.

25. Dochuk, *From Bible Belt to Sunbelt*, 119; Tona Hangen, *Redeeming the Dial: Radio, Religion, and Popular Culture in America* (Chapel Hill: University of North Carolina Press, 2002), 22–26, 105–17, 122–27.

26. R. G. LeTourneau, "The Industrial Chaplain" and "Novel On-Job Bible Class Big Hit with D-X Workers," *Tulsa Daily World*, 22 August 1952, 1, Industrial Chaplaincy—Background Material, NAE Files, 1960s, Box 38, NAE.

27. "Around the Clock around the Calendar and around the World," *NOW*, 17 April 1942, 1–3.

28. Lorimer, *God Runs My Business*, 190–91.

29. "Invasion," *NOW*, 8 December 1944, 1; "Chaplains Distribute NOW," *NOW*, 9 July 1943, 1–3; "Cancellation Committee Works on First Contract," *NOW*, 17 March 1944, 1–3. The tally included 10,000 Carryalls, 14 bulldozers, 1,600 sheepfoot rollers, 1,200 rooters, and 1,800 Tournapulls.

30. Quoted in LeTourneau, *Mover of Men and Mountains*, 222, 239.

31. Lorimer, *God Runs My Business*, 88–89.

32. Quoted in ibid., 91.

33. Quoted in ibid., 98–99.

34. See Bruce Schulman, *From Cotton Belt to Sunbelt: Federal Policy, Economic Development, and the Transformation of the South, 1938–1980* (New York: Oxford University Press, 1991).

35. "Vicksburg Dedication Day," *NOW*, 13 October 1944, 1–3; LeTourneau, *Mover of Men and Mountains*, 241–42.

36. Quoted in Ron Chernow, *Titan: The Life of John D. Rockefeller, Sr.* (New York: Vintage [Paperback Edition], 2004), 76, 153.

37. Roger M. Olien and Diana Davids Hinton, *The Wildcatters: Texas Independent Oilmen* (College Station: Texas A&M University Press, 2007), 14.

38. Carl Coke Rister, *OIL! Titan of the Southwest* (Norman: University of Oklahoma Press, 1949), pp. vii, 392.

39. Olien and Davids Hinton, *Wildcatters*, 43–45, 64.

40. Ibid., 23, 36, 171.

41. My insight on Fuller draws on Philip Goff's unpublished book manuscript, "By Radio Every Sunday: Charles E. Fuller, Religious Radio, and the Rise of Modern American Religion."

42. On Pew, Thornton, and oil funding in Sunbelt evangelicalism: Dochuk, *From Bible Belt to Sunbelt*, esp. chs. 6–9.

43. Axel R. Schäfer, "The Cold War State and the Resurgence of Evangelicalism: A Study of the Public Funding of Religion since 1945," *Radical History Review* 99 (Fall 2007): 22. Also, Lester H. Salamon, *Partners in Public Service: Government–Nonprofit Relations in the Modern Welfare State* (Baltimore: Johns Hopkins University Press, 1995); Peter Dobkin Hall, "The Welfare State and the Careers of Public and Private Institutions since 1945," in *Charity, Philanthropy, and Civility in American History*, ed. Lawrence J. Friedman and Mard D. McGarvie (Cambridge: Cambridge University Press, 2003), 363–83.

44. Schäfer, "The Cold War State and the Resurgence of Evangelicalism," 22.

45. Stephen V. Monsma, *When Sacred and Secular Mix: Religious Nonprofit Organizations and Public Money* (Lanham, Md.: Rowman and Littlefield, 1996), 70.

46. Schäfer, "The Cold War State and the Resurgence of Evangelicalism," 24, 27–28, 29, 37.

47. Ibid., 20.

48. For an illustrative critique of oil, evangelicalism, and the "radical right," see Benjamin R. Epstein and Arnold Forster, *The Radical Right: Report on the John Birch Society and Its Allies* (New York: Random House, 1967), 208; Sale, *Power Shift*, 5–7, 15.

49. LeTourneau, *Mover of Men and Mountains*, 242; "Building the Alcan Highway," *NOW*, 14 January 1944, 1–3.

50. "Athabasca Press Conference Proposal," Athabasca Tar Sands Project Great Canadian Oil Sands, 1963–1964 Folder, Box 35, Sun Oil Papers, Hagley Museum and Library.

51. Lloyd Mackey, *Like Father, Like Son: Ernest Manning and Preston Manning* (Toronto, Ontario: ECW Press, 1997), 126.

52. LeTourneau, *Mover of Men and Mountains*, 245.

53. James C. LeTourneau to Mr. M. C. Gleter, 24 August 1961, Mobile Oil Company Del Peru, 1961 Folder, Box JFE; Roy LeTourneau to Mr. R. G. LeTourneau, 21 December 1959, Letters from Roy LeTourneau—1959 Folder, Box B5G; Roy LeTourneau to Sterling Stephens, 1 July 1960, Letters from Peru—1960 Folder, Box B5G, LUA; also "Jungle Disappears," *NOW*, 1 May 1959, 1–3; "Peru," *NOW*, 1 February 1962, 3.

54. "LeTourneau College," *NOW*, 1 May 1962, 1.

55. Rick Ostrander, *Head, Heart, and Hand: John Brown University and Modern Evangelical Higher Education* (Fayetteville: University of Arkansas Press, 2003).

56. Recent, fresh scholarship on corporate and evangelical conservatism's pre-1970s origins includes Bethany Moreton, *To Serve God and Wal-Mart: The Making of Christian Free Enterprise* (Cambridge, Mass.: Harvard University Press, 2009); Kim Phillips-Fein, *Invisible Hands: The Making of the Conservative Movement from the New Deal to Reagan* (New York: W. W. Norton, 2009); Steven Miller, *Billy Graham and the Rise of the Republican South* (Philadelphia: University of Pennsylvania Press, 2009); Darren Grem, "The Blessings of Business: Corporate America and Conservative Evangelicalism in the Sunbelt Age, 1945–2000" (Ph.D. diss., University of Georgia, 2010).

4

"Take Government out of Business by Putting Business into Government"

Local Boosters, National CEOs, Experts, and the Politics of Midcentury Capital Mobility

ELIZABETH TANDY SHERMER

Capital mobility was, and remains, a fundamentally political project. Purely academic considerations never fully dictated plant closures or factory openings, which suggests that movement is best analyzed as a dimension of a long-running labor–management conflict but also a broader assault on New Deal promises of security, stability, and economic growth. Itinerant executives and investment-hungry boosters endeavored to weaken the trade union movement, to reduce taxes on corporate enterprise, and to limit the reach of the liberal, regulatory state. Their actions were well documented and publicized, which underscores that the visibility of capital's movement enhanced the ideological, even the theatrical, quality of this political work.[1]

The Sunbelt phenomenon, well represented by Phoenix, Arizona's growth, exemplified such midcentury industrial investment politics. Capital's internal migration rested on a much-discussed, seemingly benign concept: the favorable "business climate." This free-enterprise ethos proved anything but apolitical. The term, which acquired near-universal familiarity in the early postwar years, signified and calibrated the desirability of a particular area for outside investment. Its characteristics varied by industry, region, and city but generally featured lower taxes, fewer business regulations, enterprise-oriented infrastructure projects, and state-level laws designed to retard unionization. As mushrooming Sunbelt cities and declining Rustbelt communities fought to acquire or keep investment, executives played one locale off against another, generating a spiral of demands and counteroffers that distorted American politics, as well as the geographical distribution of economic activity.

Hence, the very idea of the "business climate," and the corporate welfare state that it required, represented a challenge to midcentury liberalism. Both liberals and business conservatives embraced new state powers and projects but their ultimate intentions, to provide protections for the citizenry or business, put them in conflict. Competition to generate the most favorable conditions for industry inspired an entrepreneurial faith in the corporate capacity to generate employment opportunities, which simultaneously marginalized local needs for tax revenue, social investment, or assurance that new jobs would be good and permanent.

The Rustbelt/Sunbelt dynamic highlighted the extent to which such New Deal Era assurances of stability and security were always contested. Emerging markets, lower operating costs, and the regulatory state's long-term burdens motivated many executives to shift production out of the old Boston–Chicago industrial heartland. Profits and politics, postwar surveys revealed, figured heavily in relocation decisions. "Property taxes are important," one Northeastern business owner reported, "but greater importance is given to Massachusetts politicians['] desire to initiate and implement legislation which will get them votes from the labor unions. . . . The legislators must be made to realize that they cannot kill the 'Goose that lays the golden egg.'"[2]

Early corporate migrants stood out in the business world. They were more likely to be among that subset of businessmen at war with the New Deal. They often resisted conducting business where liberalism seemed well entrenched, even if this proved economically unwise. General Electric, for example, seemed poised to become a computing giant in the mid-1950s. The firm's small Palo Alto lab built one of the first machines able to keep up with the demands of modern consumer banking. Bank of America, which contracted with GE, wanted the machines built outside of the progressively taxed, well-organized, and well-regulated Golden State to avoid $1.2 million in sales taxes, a large figure in the 1950s, but nonetheless small in relation to the bank's profits. GE President Ralph Cordiner, a key business conservative, was also eager to move operations outside of California. He shifted operations to Phoenix over his staff's objections to leaving the nascent Silicon Valley. Phoenix was an aeronautics outpost, not a computing wellspring. GE's isolated, remote Computer Division withered and never had a substantive impact on this vital postindustrial sector.[3]

Experts, academics, and relocation firms endeavored to help CEOs avoid such costly mistakes by providing the data and rationale for moves and, in the process, delineating the broad business-climate ideal. Analysts had begun to see, and celebrate, antiunion regulations, tax incentives, and other guarantees as a part of a desirable business environment by the mid-1950s. Key economist John D. Strasma asserted tax levels were decisive in constructing a kind of "climate," which industrial scouts, including the well-known Fantus Factory Location Service, calculated, compared, and advertised. Similar studies asserted that location decisions were equally influenced by low levels of taxation and unionization, as well as good public services, which were necessary for a firm to both function and attract the desired workforce. Experts began to see this "business-friendly" ethos as both a material advantage and representative of an antiliberal mindset, which top executives, local boosters, and researchers often shared. A North Carolina economist, for example, trumpeted aggressively pro-business, antitax policies to redeem the South. He theorized that private investment and a firm commitment to free enterprise policies would raise Southerners' wages and thus transform the region without extensive state welfare programs or union protections.[4]

Mobility experts proved invaluable. Fantus provided a full range of services, including studies of land prices, transportation costs, labor force statistics, and tax codes. Many executives admitted to monitoring current and potential plant sites. Business journalist Thomas Kenny reported, in a 1959 survey of 107 businesses, that a third annually analyzed their current locations based on "shifts in markets, changes in raw materials and product mix, deterioration of labor relations, and many other factors [that] may have changed the situation entirely." Larger outfits routinized in-house relocation surveys and procedures and even designated a vice president in charge of plant location or expansion. Kenny also noted that while unions and taxes remained important to manufacturers, "Several are now more concerned with finding locations which provide good schools and a cultural environment that attracts high-level technical people." He discerned "a much keener awareness today of the importance of the 'business climate,'" which he defined as "the community attitude toward business."[5]

These forecasts publicized the contemporaneous refashioning of the South and Southwest's political economy. Local trade groups spearheaded municipal reforms through nonpartisan slating groups, which utilized an antiliberal rhetoric to attack the New Deal regulatory state and the empowered labor movement. The majority of votes, nonpartisan slates, and elected officials came from affluent, Anglo neighborhoods in these racially and economically diverse cities because at-large voting arrangements largely stopped poor, working-class, or minority communities from sending representatives to city hall. Thus, between 1931 and 1971, 157 of 182 Dallas City Council members had the Citizens' Charter Association's endorsement; between 1955 and 1971, San Antonio Good Government League candidates only lost four City Council races; the Albuquerque Citizens' Committee never lost a race between 1954 and 1966. Southern municipal politics underwent a simultaneous revolution but white businessmen found themselves with less power and control. The Supreme Court frustrated these booster regimes when justices consistently ruled against white-only primaries in the mid-1940s.

These decisions triggered registration drives in the urban South. After a ruling pertaining to a Georgia case, Atlanta activists tripled the number of black Fulton County registrants in three weeks. By decade's end, Atlanta's white political elite had to respond to these constituents' demands, particularly the most affluent and influential. Similar biracial coalitions ruled the industrializing South. Such political arrangements, some of which continued into the early 1960s, still left African Americans, for all intents and purposes, as junior partners and second-class citizens but white Southern businessmen-politicians still had less overall control over their cities than their Southwestern counterparts, whose machinations occurred outside the national spotlight on Southern race relations.[6]

Corporate welfare state architects also waged their fights at the state level. Legislatures were critical venues for pro-growth, anti–New Deal politics because city and county governments could not fully control tax and labor policies. Proto-Sunbelt state governments were often bitterly divided between commodity-beholden, liberal, and booster politicians. Factionalism prompted investment-focused elected officials and bureaucrats to work in concert. Sympathetic legislators sponsored and promoted business-climate legislation and even turned controversial measures, those likely to be buried in committee or vetoed, into ballot propositions. Governor Luther Hodges, a self-described "businessman in the statehouse," worked with such North Carolina assemblymen throughout the 1950s to overhaul the state's tax code and budget. He also circumvented hostile representatives by expanding the executive bureaucracy. His Department of Conservation and Development appointees dedicated themselves to scouting for investment, monitoring the state's recruitment potential, and fine-tuning North Carolina's business climate, bureaucratic practices that became standard across the emerging Sunbelt and rusting Steelbelt throughout the postwar period.[7]

Booster governments relied on a variety of initiatives but revenue policy was universally important to investment statecraft. A wave of pro-business tax legislation, often introduced by business interests but supported by members of both parties, resulted. Revised tax codes included: industrial property and sales tax exemptions, tax "freezes" for new businesses, and guaranteed write-offs. Boosters often copied existing laws to compete. The Reno Chamber of Commerce, for example, pushed a "free-port" bill through the legislature in 1949, which permitted manufacturers to avoid property taxes on stored goods deemed "in transit" from or en route to California ports. The Nevada-California border subsequently became a warehouse and wholesaling center, which in turn prompted Arizonans to lobby for a similar loophole.[8]

"Right-to-Work" laws, like taxes, were symbolic of, and endemic to, business climates. These antiunion statutes, passable by individual states under section 14b of the 1947 Taft-Hartley Act and most often enacted through ballot initiatives, prohibited unions from making membership a requirement for work in an organized shop. The earliest referenda were in the South and Southwest. By 1960, substantial majorities in most Sunbelt states had enacted such restrictions. Only Colorado, California, and New Mexico did not have a broad right-to-work law, though roughly 40% of voters had approved of such a measure in at least one election. These statutes hamstrung the proto-Sunbelt labor movement. Union ranks increased but their percentage of the workforce decreased markedly within a decade of passage.[9]

Fierce, national competition for investment and constant reports on a locale's desirability forced Sunbelt boosters to expand the business climate's scope and scale. State spending reflected this trend. In the 1960s state-level disbursements rose almost 10% per year nationwide, even as pressure to cut taxes on industry slowed revenue growth and shifted the tax burden onto homeowners and consumers. Chamber men eager to attract firms with a well-educated, highly skilled workforce spent public and private funds on cultural and recreational opportunities, such as tennis courts, museums, and sports teams. Education emerged as one of the highest ticket items in industrial recruitment packages. Good schools and advanced educational opportunities were requirements for light electronics, aerospace, and high-tech industries, which needed a research university as a part of their local R&D nexus and their hiring pool. Direct state and local expenditures for education rose dramatically: between 1957 and 1964 the national per capita average soared from $82.47 to $137.38. Few Steelbelt states, where private and public schools were more developed, spent more than the national average in this period. Southern states devoted far less per student but the region's leaders, Florida, Georgia, South Carolina, and North Carolina, disbursed just a few dollars more or less per student than New Hampshire, Massachusetts, Rhode Island, and Pennsylvania. The industrializing West expended more than the national average. California, Nevada, Utah, Colorado, New Mexico, and Arizona each spent between 16% and 30% above the mean in this era.[10]

Arizona earmarks indicated how the state and its capital exemplified the broad, multifaceted, political dynamics of midcentury American capitalism. The town emerged as a force in light electronics and aerospace during the 1950s and 1960s and took its place among the ten largest U.S. cities by 1980. A young cohort of businessmen revitalized the Chamber of Commerce after the commodity-based economy collapsed during the Depression. Stalwarts came from the city's most profitable businesses, particularly its banks, law firms, newspapers, and major stores. Each cohort played a particular role in the broad movement to transform Phoenix into a manufacturing metropolis. Newsmen, such as Eugene Pulliam, had a monopoly on information, which allowed them to set the parameters of debate over Phoenix's future. Lawyers, most notably Frank Snell, drafted new legislation, including the state's right-to-work statutes, and defended them in the courts. Bankers, including Carl and Walter Bimson, financed the Chamber's industrial recruitment campaigns and political initiatives. Retailers, whose eponymous stores, such as *Goldwater's*, were well known, served as the face of the Chamber's industrialization initiative and its political work.[11]

Department store heir Barry Goldwater enjoyed the most renown. His prominence grew during the Depression when he made a name for himself as a guest editorialist for the *Phoenix Gazette*. He denounced businessmen for not challenging the "minority groups who are causing the tax increases" in "Scaredee-Cat" (1939). The "American businessman," "the biggest man in this country . . . afraid of his own shadow," Goldwater complained, "condemns . . . the politician over his luncheon tables and his desks . . . but never in the open where his thoughts and arguments would do some good toward correcting the evils to which he refers in private."[12]

Goldwater and his compatriots committed themselves to Phoenix's industrial and political overhaul. Arizona's Democratic Party seemed unchallengeable at the time; there were four registered Democrats for every Republican. Many Democrats were quite conservative—Jeffersonian Democrats they called themselves—and uncomfortable with the expansion of federal power, liberalism, and unionism. Many began to vote for the Phoenix Republicans, most often drafted into running by Goldwater, who promised an antiliberal prosperity driven by individual initiative, opportunity, and freedom. GOP membership rose steadily during the 1950s while the number of Democrats increased at a much slower rate. By 1960, the margin had slipped to two registered Democrats per Republican, while the Democratic edge had all but vanished in election returns.[13]

Boosters also transformed city governance. Leaders formed the Charter Government Committee (CGC) in order to overturn recent progressive tax statutes and labor protections that had established Steelbelt business conditions in postwar Phoenix. The 1949 election swept the first slate into office and inaugurated the CGC's twenty-five year reign over Phoenix, which made this Sunbelt booster political machine one of the most powerful and entrenched. The Selection Committee, which had roughly the same twenty-person roster throughout CGC rule, sought to mask the overwhelming influence of the Republican Party and the Chamber of Commerce. All candidates ran without a party affiliation and the CGC always picked a few well-known Democrats, often conservatives, on the ticket. The CGC encountered little serious opposition until the early 1960s when challenges arose both on the left, among progressives critical of the CGC's lip service to civil rights, and on the right, from Anglo homeowners frustrated with rising personal property taxes, opposed to metropolitan growth, and discontent with public funds going to both the social and corporate welfare states.[14]

The CGC always championed politics within the emergent business-climate ideal. The first slate pledged that their policies would give Phoenix a "sound business basis." The four CGC-endorsed ballot initiatives of 1949 encapsulated this promise. The first three proposals focused on increasing the city council's power and efficiency over municipal affairs, thus strengthening business control over the city. The fourth Chamber-drafted measure eliminated taxes on inventory, both for raw goods used in manufacturing, as well as finished products ready to be shipped, and also scaled back the tax on equipment used in these industries. This proposal had no other purpose but to attract industrialists and wholesalers, whom the Chamber had identified as central to their plans for Phoenix. The CGC deemed these levies bad for the economy because "these two taxes have been keeping many manufacturers out of Phoenix, thereby robbing us of jobs for people and of increased prosperity."[15]

The CGC's resounding 1949 victory enhanced the Chamber's investment efforts, formally inaugurated in March 1948. A well-organized, highly effective Industrial Development Committee compiled information for specific firms, promoted the Phoenix Valley nationally, and raised funds for recruitment packages offered to prospective investors. The Committee prioritized light electronics and aerospace manufacturing and research and development. Such enterprises were lucrative, high profile, and, relative to heavy industry, modest in their water and power needs. The Chamber "did not want dirty industries," Snell remembered. "There was talk of a refinery in this area," he recalled, "we did our best to kill it." This concern for "clean industry," as he called it, also went to the heart of the Chamber elite's vision for an Anglo-led industrial Phoenix with little dependence on agriculture and mining. These firms, Snell explained, were "inclined to bring . . . engineers and people who had somewhat higher income than you might otherwise have."[16]

Boosters also crafted specific policies to maintain their area's competitiveness with other emerging Sunbelt metropolises, chiefly the defense-dependent "fortress" cities of California and the later Texas and Mountain West boomtowns. "Industry must have the assurance it will receive a fair deal from the locality in which it locates," declared the Industrial Development Committee's first chairman. CGC policies included local initiatives to change the tax code, amend labor statutes, and overturn municipal zoning ordinances that restricted businesses. Arizonans had already passed the first Southwestern right-to-work law in 1946 and the Chamber leadership defended and enforced the statute. Boosters also lobbied for and often managed to push through impressive state-level tax breaks for aerospace, electronics, and computer manufacturers. Legislators signed off, for example, on a repeal of the tax on sales made to the federal government, an exemption on inventory, and a loophole that permitted businesses to subtract the amount firms paid to the federal government when figuring what they owed Arizona. Firms paid 32.7% of the state tax burden in 1957, just 0.5% higher than the South's overall average and much lower than the tax burden for New England, the Mid-Atlantic, and Great Lakes regions. Business property

taxes accounted for 4.9% of Arizona's tax revenue in 1962, just above the tradi-
tionally low-tax southern states.[17]

The Chamber also pioneered widely employed industrial recruitment techniques. The Industrial Development Committee moved beyond tried-and-true
tactics, such as mass mailings, trips to the coasts, and hosting individual executives. Boosters, for example, experimented with a five-day tour of the Valley for
plant location services, which cost approximately $20,000, a huge sum for 1958.
"Scouts" toured different industrial sites and sampled local recreational opportunities. The Chamber streamlined industrial recruitment further over the next
few years: boosters made frequent pilgrimages to the Northeast, the upper Midwest, and California to visit firms that Chamber researchers had identified as
"likely to be interested in Phoenix in the future." Members considered these pre-
emptive calls imperative: "The location for a new facility may be determined
before we even hear about the company looking for a new area."[18]

Phoenicians also formed their own consulting firm, Western Business Consultants, later Western Management Consultants, in order to better equip themselves to fight for industry. With support from the local government, as well as
various businesses, the company probed various aspects of the Salt River Valley's
economy and speculated on its potential. Competitiveness with cities such as
Houston, San Diego, and Las Vegas was a major concern. Even in 1960, when
the CGC was at the height of its power, the Phoenix elite feared that mimicry
decreased potential investment. "There are other areas in the West and South,"
analysts warned, "which offer the same basic locational advantages to people and
industry as does the Phoenix Area and Maricopa County."[19]

Consultants based recommendations on national reports on corporate relocation and the company's interviews with local manufacturers. Advisors found
that labor supply and markets, climate and community life, state and local labor
codes, as well as freight and wage rates weighed heavily on executives' minds.
They noted that high-tech manufacturers "place relatively high value upon educational, cultural, and scientific resources as locational attractions" and concluded, "Maricopa County should preserve and enhance these resources."
Analysts culled information specific to the defense industries as well. They
warned that aerospace firms surveyed election results because they wanted representatives who had the power and prestige to aid them with government
contracts.[20]

Advisors saw potential trouble ahead. Western Management Consultants
found that more than half of the larger firms already in Phoenix considered the
area to have "better labor relations" and "more favorable wage scales" than other
areas. Yet aerospace and electrical equipment manufacturers, whose companies
were largely responsible for Phoenix's growth, worried about the city's educational infrastructure. Almost a third reported problems attracting skilled workers,

scientists, and engineers and demanded: "More vocational training in local schools," "Improve educational facilities for advanced study," and "Expand technical education and campus laboratory facilities to better support the over-all requirements of industry."[21]

Higher education became a cornerstone of the Chamber-constructed business climate. In 1945, Arizona's largest post-secondary schools were in Flagstaff, Tempe, and Tucson. The latter housed the state's only university, the land grant, agriculturally oriented University of Arizona. But Phoenix, not Tucson, swelled in population. After the war, the American Legion, the Chamber, and the Farm Bureau, which wanted a closer agricultural research station, formed a coalition to transform the nearby state teacher's college in Tempe into a full-fledged university. The Chamber considered the local education of engineers and scientists at a top-notch research school essential to its industrial recruitment campaign. Overcoming objections from the Tucson-based University of Arizona, the Board of Regents, upon which a couple of Chamber men now sat, expanded Arizona State College's curriculum in 1954, which made it, because of the new emphasis on graduate and undergraduate education in the hard sciences and engineering, a college in name only. After the official name change in 1958, ASU grew into one of the largest single-campus universities in the nation.

The ASU founding coincided with Clark Kerr's celebrated overhaul of California higher education. Science research and engineering education were part of both ASU and the University of California's core missions. Yet there were clear distinctions between the mission and intent behind these two endeavors. Kerr was a New Deal liberal who assumed that, in a knowledge-based economy, corporate capitalism could and should be transformed to help build a social-democratic polity. His UC was a system that invested heavily in the humanities and social sciences and served as the final rung in an educational ladder that provided all Californians with an opportunity to receive a post-secondary school degree. Phoenix boosters, in contrast, championed a university specifically tailored to meet the personnel demands of a set of industries that were already present in Phoenix or that could be enticed to invest in the Valley. ASU, then, had a highly instrumental character, which sustained industry-oriented curricular needs but starved the liberal arts. For example, Phoenix manufacturers started a private organization, the ASU Foundation, which prioritized science and engineering by supplementing state funds for expensive equipment, quality lab space, and faculty wages in selected fields (so as to better woo respected researchers from out-of-state schools). Contributions were made solely on the guarantee that this investment would benefit Phoenix firms, existing and potential. Hence, ASU's growth, unlike UC's enlargement, occurred without proper funding for the arts, humanities, and social sciences or a larger mission to improve educational opportunities throughout the state.[22]

Education policy and other facets of Phoenix industrial recruitment transformed this small city into a boomtown. Over 700 firms moved to or opened
branch plants in Phoenix between 1948 and 1964. The Sperry Rand aviation
electronics division deal exemplified the relocation mechanics behind this investment. Executives had demanded: elongation of a local airport's runways to
accommodate Sperry's B-47s, financial backing for a new manufacturing facility,
and a repeal of the sales tax on products made in Arizona but sold to the federal
government. Negotiations took place mainly between the Chamber and the
corporation. Private fundraising, for instance, hinged on settling the lease
between the firm and the city but the council had little involvement in the agreement's finer points. During "informal discussion" of the Chamber's progress, a
booster warned that this issue needed to be settled: "It gets harder and harder to
raise money as we go into the Summer." A councilman motioned for immediate
approval. Brief discussion included updates on the Chamber's investigations
into the necessary bonds, zoning classifications, and insurance policies. Council
approval was, nonetheless, swift.[23]

Most deal making occurred outside city hall. Days before Sperry Rand vice-
president Percy Halpert arrived in Phoenix to visit the potential site, Chamber
members scraped together $650,000 in just 72 hours to meet demands. Boosters
feted Halpert at the Camelback Inn, where he golfed, rode horses, and sun-
bathed while Chamber men promised that the sales tax repeal would pass
because they held sway over many legislators. The Bimsons took a direct role in
pressuring representatives. Carl, also serving as the Chamber's president, sent a
staff attorney on the Arizona Bankers Association's behalf. Bimson even convinced several financiers to lobby for passage during committee meetings. Executives announced the move from their New York headquarters one day after the
legislature approved the changes. The board had unanimously chosen Phoenix
because of "enthusiastic and cooperative spirit displayed by the community and
its leaders," "growing opportunities for higher education in the physical sciences,
electrical engineering and other technical fields," and "proximity to many major
aerospace equipment markets."[24]

Sperry prospered in Phoenix. It completed three plant expansions in just six
years, employing about 1,600 by 1963. An executive reported, "Both the commercial and military aspects of our business have done well here." This investment also created a ripple effect throughout the Arizona economy, particularly
among small supplier firms that Sperry and other high-tech firms utilized.[25]

Yet, Chamber men had almost failed. Although Phoenix boosters controlled
their city, the state government, unlike the CGC-controlled city council, was not
a rubberstamp. Democrats still held a majority in the legislature, where a liberal
faction, joined by rural representatives less enthusiastic about Phoenix-style industrialization, opposed yet another investment-focused change to the tax code.

Representatives were deadlocked on the issue in the fall of 1955. Governor Ernest McFarland, a liberal most famous for his work on the GI Bill, called lawmakers back into session to settle the matter. He embraced industrialization but remained wary of additional tax cuts for manufacturers and the subsequent loss of revenue. "We should encourage industry to come to the State of Arizona," he explained, "Our population is growing by leaps and bounds, and we must have additional and new employment" but "real property tax payers should not be required to carry this burden alone." He called for a excise tax, which he deemed "an equalization of taxes," which "serve[d] a double purpose: the protection of industry in our state and the raising of revenue to take the place of that lost by the repeal of the tax on sales to the federal government."[26]

Phoenix boosters disdained this compromise. Chamber-Republicans ran a 1958 gubernatorial candidate who dedicated himself to advancing their political, industrial ambitions on a statewide level. Propane magnate Paul Fannin had been an active, eager chairman of the Industrial Development Committee. Like his childhood friend Goldwater, who Arizonans reelected in 1958, an otherwise good year for Democrats elsewhere, Fannin held that businessmen had a responsibility to be active in governmental affairs. "Take Government out of business by putting business into government," he decreed, "If businessmen do not take a part in government, government will take business apart." His gubernatorial campaign promised investment throughout the state, not just its capital, asserting that job growth and a higher standard of living lay "in the establishment of new plants and factories compatible with Arizona's unique climate and scenic advantages."[27]

The Fannin administration centralized and expanded executive power in order to create a statewide business climate favorable to the kind of growth pioneered by Phoenix businessmen. His efforts fit within Hodges' and other Sunbelt governors' use of executive bureaucracies to circumvent legislatures. Fannin created two industry advisory groups. The Arizona Community Development Advisory Committee, which Fannin described as "made up of industrial development specialists from several of the banks, utilities and transportation companies, for the purpose of pooling the member organizations' resources," gave leading entrepreneurs and high-tech firms easy access to the governor's mansion. More oriented toward Chamber-style public relations was the Governor's Committee for Industrial Arizona, which Fannin called a "group of 40 industrialists many of whom retired from the leading corporations in the country, who act as Ambassadors for Arizona" in cooperation with state officials paid for such work. Fannin used both brain trusts to link the state government and the business community, mirroring the dense web of Chamber men, city council members, consultants, and manufacturing executives who continued to oversee Phoenix's business climate.[28]

Fannin also restructured the executive branch. His administration was mar-
bled with numerous McFarland appointees, who served staggered, three-year
terms (governors had two-year terms) and were therefore in a position, so
Fannin asserted, to subvert his industrial recruitment program. Fannin increased
the executive bureaucracy's size and power in order to bypass liberal Democrats'
objections, appointees, and the state constitutional provisions that gave office-
holders' statutory autonomy. He claimed the governor's staff was "too small and
too lacking in both variety and extent of experience" for the proper "review and
evaluation of existing state programs, the development of new ideas, the study
and research necessary for intelligent action, and the initiation of new policies
and programs." He demanded greater power to build "a cooperative group of
state officials," who would "provide executive leadership."[29]

Fannin created the Assistant for Industrial Development, which embodied
his, and his contemporaries', industrial and political frustrations and aspirations.
The appointee reported only to Fannin and served as secretary for both business-
advisory groups. Chamber man Boyd H. Gibbons, Jr. was an easy choice for this
post. He was an energetic, conservative Republican who prioritized "maintaining a good business climate and more particularly a receptive community attitude" for business groups and their political spokesmen. Part of his work entailed
mobilizing Arizona's sixty-three Chambers of Commerce along the lines of the
Phoenix group. He spent his first four months traveling the state to meet with
local Chambers, convincing boosters that the governor's plans had merit, and
acting as a liaison between Fannin and locals.[30]

Gibbons's trips outside Arizona were equally important. He realized that
broad, aggressive promotion was vital during a 1959 Los Angeles expedition,
when he met with a Telecomputing Corporation executive intrigued by Arizona's favorable tax and labor laws. The executive, Gibbons recounted, "bemoaned
the fact that only recently they had purchased high-priced land in nearby Re-
seda, California, to build a large plant wherein they were going to consolidate
three plants under one roof as an economy move." "If he had known the full story
of Arizona," Gibbons lamented, "he intimated that they might have put this operation in Arizona."[31]

This setback invigorated Gibbons, who went on to broker an impressive deal
with Unidynamics, a Universal Match Company division. He laid the ground-
work for this investment in 1959, when he contacted the Avondale–Goodyear–
Litchfield Park Chamber of Commerce. He stressed the need for a carefully
managed industrial campaign and followed up with letters beseeching Chamber
members to create an organization "that will devote its entire activities toward
attracting and inviting new businesses." He offered them "any assistance to you in
regard to a new industrial concern." Two years later, after careful consideration of
the town's ability to attract and sustain investment, its president asked Gibbons

to present a plan for the area's development to the membership. The representative asked pointed questions that signaled an embrace of manufacturing, including "How does one go about securing a diversified industry? . . . How can we [the] Cahmber [*sic*] of Commerce best participate in an Industrial Development Program?"[32]

Gibbons's deal making, though started with open proclamations of industry mindedness and concluded with public celebrations of plant openings, were covert in the interim. His negotiations with Unidynamics fit this general clandestine–public pattern. In 1962, UMC's head in Ferguson, Missouri, called the governor personally to ask him to meet with an industrial scout, "Ben 'X'" of the "'X' Company," already scheduled to arrive that evening. The next morning, the surveyor had a two-hour breakfast meeting with Gibbons, who gave the visitor "a detailed report on the availability of labor, the Arizona State University engineering graduate school program and a summary of economic advantages that Arizona could offer to this particular company. Immediately thereafter, he was given a 3-hour tour of four potential sites; spent two hours at [ASU] interviewing the Dean of the Engineering College and met with President [G. Homer] Durham of the University." The deal came together rapidly. "Five days later, a team of three men, all unidentified except for first names, came to Phoenix and specifically surveyed in detail the original four sites and spent several hours with [a colleague of Gibbons] concerning recruitment of skilled labor and other facts involved with employment," Gibbons recorded. "Ten days later, Mr. [Carl] Gottlieb [a top UMC executive] himself appeared on the scene and a tentative decision was made to narrow down the site selections to two." "At this time, in a meeting with the Governor," Gibbons noted, "Mr. Gottlieb identified himself and his company and asked that this be maintained in strictest confidence until a meeting could be held with their board of directors which he hoped would be within the next 90 days, at which time a decision might be made." Fannin met with Unidynamics executives and board members in the interim. Six months after the preliminary meeting, UMC announced its Unidynamics division would establish a plant in Litchfield.[33]

UMC and the other 275 investments made under Fannin's watch thrilled the governor. He celebrated that Arizona was "experiencing the rebirth of capitalism within the framework of constitutional provisions that literally guarantee industry against discriminatory state taxes." "We cannot overemphasize," he proclaimed, "that state and local governments have a duty to impress upon our citizens that the United States is a business nation and that only private enterprise and profit motive can truly supply productive jobs for the people." He summed up his administration when he declared that Arizona's "business-minded" citizens, moratoriums on "discriminatory State taxes" against industry, flexible labor codes, and advanced educational programs were "assurances that industry in our State is WELCOME, WANTED AND NEEDED." "This rapidly growing, pioneering frontier Western State," he crowed, "is setting an example for other states and governments to follow."[34]

Fannin's proclamation was not hyperbolic. This desert miracle and the entire Sunbelt arose out of open, systematic, subversive political work by a phalanx of local boosters, national manufacturers, and industrial relations experts who endeavored to undercut, delegitimize, and dismantle the New Deal. Even their policies, such as increased opportunities for higher education, which seemed within the general expansion of economic citizenship, were, in fact, injurious to the trade union movement and liberal statecraft. The broad competition for the best business climate, which CEOs encouraged, boosters engaged in, and scholars studied, stood as a total affront to security and stability, both within the larger dynamics of American and global capitalism and for the citizenry, whose welfare was left not to the state or labor but increasingly transient corporations.

Notes

1. Jefferson Cowie, *Capital Moves: RCA's 70-Year Quest for Cheap Labor* (New York: New Press, 2001).
2. Quoted in John D. Strasma, *State and Local Taxation of Industry: Some Comparisons* (Boston: Federal Reserve Bank of Boston, 1959), unpaginated index; Elizabeth Tandy Shermer, "Creating the Sunbelt: The Political and Economic Transformation of Phoenix, Arizona" (Ph.D. diss., University of California, Santa Barbara, 2009), chs. 6–8.
3. Ibid., ch. 8; Kim Phillips-Fein, *Invisible Hands: The Making of the Conservative Movement from the New Deal to Reagan* (New York: W. W. Norton & Co., 2009).
4. John F. Due, "Studies of State-Local Tax Influences on Location of Industry," *National Tax Journal* 14 (June 1961): 163–73; Strasma, *State and Local Taxation of Industry*, 13–16, esp. 16; Joe Summers Floyd, Jr., *Effects of Taxation on Industrial Location* (Chapel Hill: University of North Carolina Press, 1952).
5. Thomas Kenny, "Planning Tomorrow's Plants: New Light on Site Seeking," *Dun's Review and Modern Industry* 73 (March 1959): 90–91 and 104–11, esp. 90, quoted on 104, esp. 106.
6. Amy Bridges, *Morning Glories: Municipal Reform in the Southwest* (Princeton, N.J.: Princeton University Press, 1997), 52–174; Shermer, "Creating the Sunbelt," ch. 5.
7. Ibid., ch. 8; James C. Cobb, *The Selling of the South: The Southern Crusade for Industrial Development, 1936–1990* (Urbana: University of Illinois Press, 1993); Luther H. Hodges, *Businessman in the Statehouse: Six Years as Governor of North Carolina* (Chapel Hill: University of North Carolina Press, 1962).
8. Shermer, "Creating the Sunbelt," ch. 6.
9. Elizabeth Tandy Shermer, "Counter-Organizing the Sunbelt: Right to Work Campaigns and Anti-Union Conservatism, 1943–1958," *Pacific Historical Review* (February 2009): 81–118, esp. 105.
10. Shermer, "Creating the Sunbelt," chs. 5–6.
11. Ibid., ch. 3.
12. Ibid.; Barry M. Goldwater, "Scaredee-Cat," *Phoenix Gazette*, 23 June 1939, page number missing from clipping, frame 79, Scrapbook CD 1, Personal and Political Papers of Senator Barry M. Goldwater, Arizona Historical Foundation, Tempe.
13. Shermer, "Creating the Sunbelt," chs. 3–6; Nancy Anderson Guber, "The Development of Two-Party Competition in Arizona" (M.A. thesis, University of Illinois, 1961).

14. Shermer, "Creating the Sunbelt," chs. 5 and 10.

15. Ibid., ch. 5; "Be Sure You Vote in the City Primary Tomorrow" postcard, frame 15, Scrapbook CD 5, Goldwater Papers.

16. Shermer, "Creating the Sunbelt," chs. 3–4, 6–8; Frank Snell interview by G. Wesley Johnson, 7 December 1978, 6, Phoenix History Project, Arizona Historical Society, Tempe.

17. Shermer, "Creating the Sunbelt," chs. 6–8; Gerald Whitney Stone, "A Study of Business Tax Burdens in the Southwest" (M.A. thesis, Arizona State University, 1969), 1–2, 36–50; Advisory Commission on Intergovernmental Relations, *State-Local Taxation and Industrial Location: A Commission Report* (Washington, D.C.: Government Printing Office, 1967), 31–48.

18. Shermer, "Creating the Sunbelt," chs. 3 and 8; "Visit by Plant Locators Is Another First for Phoenix," *Phoenix Action!* 13 (November 1958): 3; "Headquarter Visits," *A Special Report for . . .* [Chamber newsletter] 1 (June 1968): 2, Folder 2, Box 1, Orme Lewis & Paul M. Roca and Phoenix Chamber of Commerce Collection, Arizona Historical Society, Tempe; Board of Directors, Minutes of Meeting, 17 June 1958, 1–2, volume labeled "1957–1958," Board of Directors Records, Greater Phoenix Chamber of Commerce, Phoenix.

19. Meeting Minutes enclosed with V. O. Allen to [Boyd] Gibbons, 5 August 1959, 2, Folder 4, Box 8, Paul Fannin Papers, Arizona State Library, Archives, and Public Records, Phoenix; Western Business Consultants, Inc., *Economic Analysis and Projection for Phoenix and Maricopa County* (Phoenix: Maricopa County Planning and Zoning Department, 1960); Western Management Consultants, Inc., *The Economy of Maricopa County 1965 to 1980* (Phoenix: Western Management Consultants, Inc., 1965), esp. 9.

20. Western Management Consultants, Inc., *The Economy of Maricopa County 1965 to 1980,* 1–15, 109–13, esp. 9.

21. Ibid., 113–26, quoted on 124; Western Business Consultants, *Economic Analysis and Projection for Phoenix and Maricopa County,* 72–75.

22. Ernest J. Hopkins and Alfred Thomas, Jr., *The Arizona State University Story* (Phoenix: Southwest Publishing Co., Inc., 1960), 245–94; Shermer, "Creating the Sunbelt," chs. 7 and 8; Paddy Riley, "Clark Kerr: From the Industrial to the Knowledge Economy," in *American Capitalism: Social Thought and Political Economy in the Twentieth Century,* ed. Nelson Lichtenstein (Philadelphia: University of Pennsylvania Press, 2006), 71–87.

23. Shermer, "Creating the Sunbelt," ch. 8; *Record of Commission,* Vol. 35: January 1, 1956–December 31, 1956, 356–57, City Clerk Official Records, Phoenix City Hall, Phoenix.

24. Shermer, "Creating the Sunbelt," ch. 8; F. S. Hodgman to Frank A. Murphy and Wm. P. Reilly, [month and day missing] 1955, Board of Directors, Minutes of Special Meeting, 8 September 1955, volume labeled "1955–1956," Board of Directors Records; Western Management Consultants, *The Economy of Maricopa County 1965 to 1980,* 94–101; Robert Roe to Paul Fannin, 9 December 1963, 1–2, Folder 2, Box 4, Fannin Papers.

25. Robert Roe to Paul Fannin, 9 December 1963, 2, Folder 2, Box 4, Fannin Papers; W. Cullen Moore, "Arizona Industry in the Missile and Space Program," 8 June 1962, 6, Folder 1, Box 4, Fannin Papers.

26. Shermer, "Creating the Sunbelt," ch. 2; Ernest McFarland, [untitled message to the legislature], 24 October 1955, 1–2, Folder "Governor's Legislative Message File. 1955–1957," Box 96, Governor's Office Subject Files, Arizona State Library, Archives, and Public Records, Phoenix; Ross R. Rice, "The 1958 Election in Arizona," *Western Political Quarterly* 12 (January 1959): 266–75; Guber, "The Development of Two-Party Competition in Arizona," 35.

27. Shermer, "Creating the Sunbelt," chs. 3 and 8; Paul Fannin, "Remarks of Governor Fannin at the National Sand and Gravel Association and National Ready Mixed Concrete Association Meeting in Chicago, Illinois," 27 February 1964, 6, Folder 2, Box 21, Fannin Papers; Quoted in Matthew Gann McCoy, "Desert Metropolis: Image Building and the Growth of Phoenix, 1940–1965" (Ph.D. diss., Arizona State University, 2000), 228.

28. Ibid., 5–7.

29. Paul Fannin, "The Governor's Office in Arizona," n.d., 1, 3, 6, Folder 1, Box 1, Fannin Papers.

30. Paul Fannin, "The Governor's Office in Arizona," n.d., 5–6, Folder 1, Box 1, Fannin Papers; McCoy, "Desert Metropolis," 236–37; Boyd H. Gibbons, Jr. to Lawrence Mehren, 4 June

1964, 1, Folder 2, Box 21, Fannin Papers; Boyd H. Gibbons, Jr. to Bill Rhodes, 5 November 1963, Folder 4, Box 8, ibid.; Lewis E. Haas to Boyd Gibbons, [n.d.], Folder 6, Box 5, ibid.

31. Boyd H. Gibbons, "Report to Governor Paul Fannin on 'Prospecting' Tour to Los Angeles, December 2–5, 1959," [n.d.], 2, Folder 11, Box 11, ibid.; McCoy, "Desert Metropolis," 230–38.

32. Ed Hazelton to Boyd Gibbons, 16 January 1961, Folder 4, Box 8, Fannin Papers; Meeting Minutes enclosed with V. O. Allen to [Boyd] Gibbons, 5 August 1959, 2, Folder 4, Box 8, ibid.; Boyd H. Gibbons, Jr. to Kenneth McGeorge, 22 July 1959, Folder 4, Box 8, ibid.

33. Boyd Gibbons, "UNIDYNAMICS (Division of Universal Match Corporation) (Universal Match Corporation, St. Louis, Missouri): Litchfield Park (Goodyear), Arizona," [n.d.], Folder 2, Box 11, ibid.

34. Paul Fannin, "Governor Paul Fannin's Remarks at Unidynamics Division Dedication, Litchfield Park, Arizona," 1 November 1963, 1–3, Folder 2, Box 21, ibid.; Boyd H. Gibbons, Jr. to Lawrence Mehren, 4 June 1964, 2, Folder 2, Box 21, Fannin Papers; Paul Fannin, "Arizona . . . An Invitation to Industry," [n.d.], 1–2, Folder: "'ARIZONA . . . An Invitation to Industry' (Rep. & Gaz. Ind. Dev. Project)," Box 314, Governor's Files, Arizona State Library, Archives, and Public Records, Phoenix.

5

The Liberal Invention of the Multinational Corporation

David Lilienthal and Postwar Capitalism

JASON SCOTT SMITH

People on both sides of the political spectrum have long believed that American liberalism has constrained free-market capitalism. On the Right, economists inspired by the work of Milton Friedman have argued that the increased regulations and welfare state created by Franklin Roosevelt's New Deal—and by American liberalism, more generally—served only to weaken the power of the market to improve people's lives. On the Left, economists who identify with the work of John Kenneth Galbraith have asserted that government must provide a necessary check on the excesses of laissez-faire capitalism, arguing that the core of twentieth-century liberalism can be found in the ability of government to serve as a "countervailing power" in a society dominated by large corporations. Closer historical study, however, reveals that liberalism and capitalism have not always existed in opposition to one another. Indeed, instead of fading away after the Great Depression, New Deal–style liberalism actually played a vital role in helping to create the ideas and institutions that allowed American capitalism and influence to travel overseas after 1945.

This symbiotic relationship between liberalism and capitalism can be seen in the activities of a prominent New Deal reformer—David E. Lilienthal—whose career put him on each side of the relationship between business and government. During the 1930s and 1940s, Lilienthal helped run the Tennessee Valley Authority (TVA), serving as the TVA's chairman between 1941 and 1946. Appointed by Franklin Roosevelt, Lilienthal was on the front lines of the New Deal's battles with big business, leading the TVA in its fight against private power companies to provide low-cost electricity to the people of the Tennessee Valley. Lilienthal amassed a great deal of political and administrative experience while defending the TVA as a worthwhile public investment, countering attacks made by conservative politicians and corporate leaders.[1] In 1955, however, Lilienthal drew on the experience of running the TVA to start his own business. Lilienthal's Development and Resources Corporation, or D&R, as it was commonly called, provided a wide range of services around the world for nations interested in developing their natural resources, working in such countries as Iran, Afghanistan, Brazil, Colombia, and Vietnam.

While helping to create the field of international development, Lilienthal invented a new terminology in order to accurately describe all of D&R's cross-border activities, ultimately coining the phrase "the multinational corporation" in 1960. This phrase reflects Lilienthal's deep experience in both the public and private sectors: as a New Dealer, and then as a businessman. Lilienthal's career thus illuminates the changing relationship between American liberalism and market capitalism, as well as the growing engagement of American institutions (the public state and the private multinational firm) with the problem of economic development in the postwar world.

After World War II, Lilienthal was one of a number of prominent liberals who became more active in the business world. This network included the Chair of the Democratic Party in the 1930s and a member of FDR's Cabinet, James Farley, who served as the Chairman of the Coca-Cola Export Corporation from 1940 to 1973. Adolf Berle, who along with Gardiner Means had written the canonical work on the dangers of corporate power to society, *The Corporation and Private Property* (1932), had proudly served as an early member of FDR's brain trust during the Great Depression. Ambassador to Brazil during the 1940s, Berle, during the postwar years, became an important figure in Latin American business, helping to broker loans from U.S. banks to nations like Haiti and serving on the board of directors of the American Molasses Company, a significant player in the Caribbean sugar industry. Berle wanted to see Latin American and Caribbean nations become part of a common market with the United States, in order to keep communism at bay and to help develop Latin American economies. Notable lawyers, such as Thomas Corcoran, parlayed their public service to President Roosevelt into lucrative private practices, consulting with a range of corporations and business organizations, including United Fruit, Lever Brothers, and the Pharmaceuticals Manufacturing Association. "When you're charging fees [to clients], charge them high," Corcoran boasted. "The world takes you at your own valuation. You decide whether you're Tiffany or Woolworth." In leaving behind public service and entering the private sector, these liberals found that business presented a chance make money, as well as the opportunity to test one's ideas without the restrictions of government service. As Berle advised Lilienthal, in business "one grows in experience, [and] ideas seem more causative than the day-to-day work in the front lines, in which no one in public life is really a free agent."[2]

The postwar activities of these and other New Dealers signal a shift within American liberalism more generally. During the 1930s, the collapse of capitalism, along with massive and sustained unemployment, had driven the fractious politics of the New Deal years. Mobilization for World War II transformed this contentious political economy, replacing it with an unprecedented run of economic growth and, in so doing, altering American politics. Between 1940 and 1973, the United States experienced an amazing run of prosperity, as each year the nation's GDP grew at a rate of 3% per capita. For liberals, as a result, statecraft soon became less a forum for conducting an adversarial relationship with business and more a venue for using Keynesian management of the economy to tame the oscillating business cycle. The growing cold war with the USSR shaped this change in liberalism, too. Policy alternatives on the Left were soon repressed or rendered impotent by the imperatives of anticommunism and national security. For liberals like Lilienthal, the shift in the nation's political economy and in its politics meant that government was becoming a less welcoming and less interesting place to work, and that the private sector was simultaneously becoming less threatening and more intriguing.[3]

While a small number of conservative businessmen, such as General Electric's Lemuel Boulware, put their energy and finances into important attempts to roll back the New Deal order, many businessmen made their peace with the social safety net crafted by the New Deal, and some prominent members of the business community even embraced the liberal achievements of the 1930s. The head of IBM, longtime Democratic Party supporter Tom Watson, capitalized on the growth of the federal government during the Great Depression, particularly on the government's need for data processing equipment with the creation of social security. IBM quickly became the program's main contractor, supplying the punch card equipment necessary for tracking the employment history of 26 million workers by their social security numbers. During the depths of the Great Depression, IBM was one of the few companies to prosper and grow. This strong position in an expanding market brought IBM further contracts and orders for equipment from other parts of the federal government. For IBM, the welfare state was big business.[4] Henry Kaiser, the prominent industrialist and contractor, took pride in the generally good relationship he forged with organized labor during the 1930s and 1940s. The health care schemes that Kaiser created while building public works projects during the Great Depression would grow, after the war, into Kaiser Permanente, one of the largest health management organizations in the United States. Republican Nelson Rockefeller, after working for FDR's State Department on Latin American development issues, helped to implement Truman's Point Four program to transfer U.S. technical know-how to developing nations. Rockefeller's International Basic Economy Corporation (IBEC) similarly reflected his strong interest in overseas development issues, as well as his general satisfaction with FDR's New Deal.[5]

Against this changing political and economic landscape Lilienthal made a sustained case for the use of public authority in pursuit of economic development, wherein governments relied on private companies for the technical expertise, institutional networks, and access to capital necessary for realizing the potential of river valleys around the world to provide electrical power and other resources for impoverished nations. Although Lilienthal faced major obstacles in fully realizing this vision overseas, the history of private multinational firms like D&R provides an important window into understanding how American liberalism—and its attitudes toward market capitalism and the global economy—shifted and changed between 1933 and the late 1970s.

During the 1930s, Lilienthal helped the TVA become the largest public utility in the nation. By 1941, the TVA stood as one of the New Deal's most successful programs, both in terms of its results (the cost curve of electricity produced by the TVA would slope downwards, uninterrupted, for the next three decades) and in serving as a kind of laboratory for New Deal liberals. Lilienthal gained invaluable experience running a huge organization (the TVA had over 42,000 employees by 1941) and had become an expert in the politics of selling his program to a range of audiences: ordinary citizens, politicians at the state and federal levels of government, and business people.[6] Lilienthal elaborated on his postwar vision for the TVA to Supreme Court Justice Felix Frankfurter, who had been one of Lilienthal's professors at Harvard Law School. Internationally, Lilienthal informed Frankfurter, "There is the keenest interest in our innovations and experiments in management methods, as applied to the new problems that are emerging in foreign countries. China, the Danube River Valley, India, Africa, Latin America, and so on are among the parts of the world from which observers have studied the TVA from this point of view."[7]

Lilienthal aimed to publicize this story, with all of its implications, in book form. The TVA could be a "pattern for the New World," he wrote, serving as a "resource development germ, if not indeed readily adaptable working model, of post war world."[8] In *TVA: Democracy on the March* (1944), he created an enormously popular portrait of the inhabitants of the Tennessee Valley, "the 'dreamers with shovels' who have built tomorrow out of yesterday."[9] A partisan celebration of the TVA and its accomplishments, *Democracy on the March* portrayed the TVA as an example of a new kind of relationship between government and the economy. "My purpose," Lilienthal argued, "is to show, by authentic experience in one American region, that to get ... new jobs and factories and fertile farms our choice need not be between extremes of 'right' and 'left,' between overcentralized

Big-government and a do-nothing social policy, between 'private enterprise' and 'socialism,' between an arrogant red-tape-ridden bureaucracy and domination by a few private monopolies." Rather, Lilienthal declared, the TVA demonstrated that a democratic polity could, through a combination of science, technology, and pragmatic administration, create economic growth where it previously did not exist. Furthermore, this model of development could be exported abroad:

> I write of the Tennessee Valley, but all this could have happened in almost any of a thousand other valleys where rivers run from the hills to the sea. . . . In Missouri and in Arkansas, in Brazil and in the Argentine, in China and in India there are just such rivers . . . waiting to be controlled by men—the Yangtze, the Ganges, the Ob, the Parana, the Amazon, the Nile. In a thousand valleys in America and the world over there are fields that need to be made strong and productive, land steep and rugged, land flat as a man's hand; on the slopes, forests—and in the hills, minerals—that can be made to yield a better living for people.[10]

Democracy on the March was, for its author, literally a declaration of his "faith" in the power of technocratic liberalism to do the seemingly impossible. Indeed, for all that the New Deal is properly remembered today for creating a social welfare safety net, many of its achievements were rooted in an embrace of technology and efficiency. The New Deal's public works programs, along with the TVA, helped bring into the American state a host of engineers, construction experts, and technically savvy planners, all of whom served to redefine what was possible for government to accomplish. As Lilienthal put it, "Impossible things can be done, are being done in this mid-twentieth century" by the federal government.[11]

Lilienthal's vision not only served to commemorate the achievements of the 1930s, it also became a touchstone for cold war liberalism. Drawing on the social scientific framework of modernization theory, many postwar policy makers would simply assume, as historian Nils Gilman has observed, that the United States demonstrated "an apparently universalizable American model of development." Economists, in particular, fresh from their success in guiding the nation's mobilization during World War II, reinforced this assumption. This intellectual scaffolding, when joined to the accomplishments of the TVA, presented a potent and heady combination for many liberals. As Arthur Schlesinger, Jr. argued in his cold war manifesto, *The Vital Center*, "Our engineers can transform arid plains or poverty-stricken river valleys into wonderlands of vegetation and power. . . . The Tennessee Valley Authority is a weapon which, if properly employed, might outbid all the social ruthlessness of the Communists for support of the people of Asia." Pointing to a range of American firms that were already ramping up their involvement in overseas development projects, Lilienthal declared that these companies "realize that it's good business all around to do anything that will improve the living conditions of a people," concluding, "I believe the TVA shows us one way to postwar prosperity."[12]

Lilienthal's emphasis on melding practical considerations with the promise of liberalism carried him from the TVA into his service as chairman of the Atomic Energy Commission from 1946 to 1950. As the cold war with the Soviet Union began to take shape, Lilienthal was forced to grapple with a range of issues connected with nuclear energy. In so doing, he was distressed to find that his management talents, administrative skills, and speechmaking abilities did not seem to translate from his experience running the TVA. While Lilienthal stressed the importance of organizational transparency and public outreach about the potentials of atomic energy to improve civilian life, political and institutional rivalries thwarted his efforts to control the AEC. Congressional concerns about communist espionage, nuclear security, and the military uses of the atom meant that Lilienthal was often on the defensive, unable to realize his agenda for the Commission. Suffering from years of bureaucratic and political conflicts, Lilienthal stepped down from the AEC, exhausted. In his next position, he was determined to avoid the bureaucratic constraints of public service, as well as to make a lot of money.[13]

When Lilienthal began considering entering the private sector, he had a number of possible opportunities to pursue. By May 1950, he framed his choice as one between returning to the practice of law or entering consulting, with his friend Joseph Davies counseling Lilienthal that he thought highly of Lazard Frères & Company, the well-known investment banking firm.[14] Lilienthal thus arranged to meet with Lazard's managing partner, André Meyer. After discussing the history of Lazard and its business activities, Meyer offered Lilienthal a starting retainer of $25,000, with the understanding that, even though he did not have specific duties defined, Lilienthal would bring his knowledge of economic development and his network of political contacts (at home and abroad) to Lazard. As one Lazard partner instructed Lilienthal, just "keep yourself uncomplicated, 'floating,'" since Lilienthal had served in "a great position of trust, [had] done two huge jobs, [and could capitalize on his] brilliant name."[15]

In choosing to join Lazard, Lilienthal was setting out on a journey that would reveal the intertwined nature of his two worlds—a past career where he mastered the world of politics, and a new transition into the relatively unfamiliar world of industry and finance, where power operated in a different register. After returning from a trip to Europe, where he discussed international development issues with a range of public and private leaders, Lilienthal reconvened in New York with Pierre David-Weill, the chairman of Lazard Frères. David-Weill cautioned Lilienthal that if he wanted to be effective in business he would have to curtail his public speaking and writing in order to win the trust of business people. Lilienthal recorded David-Weill's advice, that "businessmen don't associate writing, etc., with businessmen." Instead, they "believe things should be effected by 'quiet methods,' contact and the right places, persuading those who have the political power of decision, etc." Lilienthal paused to add to his notes of the meeting the question, "Is this why businessmen are so inarticulate?" Lilienthal made his conditions known to the Lazard partners: "I was interested in developing (a) third career, i.e., one in business; (b) one that I would enjoy and would not be contrary to the things I believed in; and (c) a *must*, it would have to have good prospects of enabling me to accumulate a substantial sum of money in the next ten years."[16] To put it mildly, Lilienthal was not particularly enthused about becoming a businessman. "I may find all this terribly boring, in time," wrote Lilienthal, "and actually, the added money may not begin to compensate for the sense of doing something rather inconsequential or even contrary to my whole life and purpose." However, ever the pragmatist and interested in the dynamics of organizations, Lilienthal continued, "there is only one way to find out" if the business world was for him, and that was by entering into it.[17]

Lilienthal's correspondence and papers from the early 1950s reflect the tensions between his budding career in the private sector and in his interests in the use of public authority and private capital to facilitate economic development. Lilienthal continued his consulting work for Lazard and for other clients, leveraging his network of connections and considerable expertise. "The actual work involved in my role as 'consultant to management,'" he was soon surprised to realize, "has been less active, less burdensome, than I'd wanted or expected." The main drawback, Lilienthal thought, was that "it is hard to get used to receiving large checks regularly, and performing only intermittent and advisory service for this, after long, long years of taking responsibility and *receiving* advice."[18]

Business was indeed very good to Lilienthal. By 1955 his yearly income exceeded $110,000, and his compensation included options for Lazard stock worth nearly $1.5 million. As he noted, "What counts in acquiring a business reputation is not sitting on boards but making money. . . . I'm no longer David Lilienthal, the 'controversial' public servant, but . . . someone who succeeds in *their* own game, and so an almost respectable and possibly even respected individual."[19] Lilienthal channeled his interest in business and his enthusiasm over his financial success into a brief book hailing the achievements of capitalism, publishing *Big Business: A New Era* in 1953.[20] Large firms, Lilienthal argued, could provide society with innovation, competition, and high productivity, thus enhancing national security. Most reviewers were skeptical of Lilienthal's claims, and Lilienthal's embrace of bigness put him at odds with the sophisticated critique of capitalism offered by John Kenneth Galbraith in his *American Capitalism: The Concept of Countervailing Power*, which called for government to empower labor and consumers in order to counter the influence of big business. Lilienthal's view of business, however, flowed from the liberalism he practiced during the New Deal. As Richard Hofstadter has noted, Lilienthal's embrace of business signaled less "a conversion to a new philosophy" than it underscored his "ability to find in private organization many of the same virtues that as TVA administrator he found in public enterprise."[21]

While Lilienthal had made a good showing from his transition into the business world, he found many of his daily activities boring and soon desired to do something that held greater significance. He hit on the idea of launching a new firm of his own, even though it would be a risky and difficult undertaking. Lilienthal was ambitious: he wanted to see if he could take the expertise he developed at the TVA and bring it, via private enterprise, to the rest of the world. With financial backing from André Meyer and Lazard, he conceived of this new venture in a deeply personal way, initially referring to it with his own initials, as DEL, Inc. "Can I manage to do the things about rivers, land, people, that I have demonstrated I can in a public or *pro bono* setting," wondered Lilienthal, "but get them done through a combination of private money-making techniques and public activity?" This was the core of the challenge that appealed to Lilienthal.[22]

With his longtime TVA colleague, Gordon Clapp, serving as president, and with a pledge from Lazard to cover operating losses for three years, Lilienthal took on the role as chairman of his new company, now named Development and Resources Corporation (D&R). D&R finished its first four months of existence with two major contracts in hand, one with the Cauca Valley Corporation of Colombia, the other with the Water Resources Authority of Puerto Rico. To drum up more business, Lilienthal and Clapp planned foreign trips to Turkey, Italy, Iran, and Venezuela, as well as to Egypt and other parts of Africa. For all that Lilienthal, in his public pronouncements about the TVA, touted the universality of economic development, privately, he was aware that the reality was far more complicated than his rhetoric might have indicated. "It will undoubtedly be tough, especially for the first year or two," Lilienthal wrote to André Meyer. "The distances involved, the utter dis-similarity of the situations in Italy, say, and Colombia or Iran, the complex and sensitive political situations in all countries. Factors like these don't make the problem any easier."[23]

Fortunately for Lilienthal and D&R, an institutional infrastructure to facilitate international development was emerging by the late 1950s. American government and business, with a commitment to increasing productivity, strove to bring economic stability to the marketplace, muting class conflict via economic growth. Many segments of organized labor worked with business and government to achieve these ends, purging radicals from their membership and otherwise accommodating the growing imperative of anticommunism at home and abroad. International programs like the Marshall Plan, along with such institutions as the

World Bank, the International Monetary Fund, the International Finance Corporation, and the Inter-American Development Bank, helped create foreign markets for American goods and made capital available for development projects in
other nations, albeit often under stringent terms.[24] Against this background,
D&R set to work applying its organizational knowledge of economic development around the world, in Europe, Latin America, the Middle East, and Asia,
throughout the late 1950s, the 1960s, and the 1970s. As it grew and prospered,
Lilienthal's company took the development expertise first deployed in the Tennessee River Valley and exported it abroad. As the years passed, D&R also reim-
ported this expertise back to the United States, consulting for a range of state and
federal bodies on a number of domestic issues.

   D&R undertook a range of activities in Italy in 1956 and 1957, in consulting
work it performed for Cassa per Opere Straordinarie di Pubblico Interesse
Nell'Italia Meridonale, a public body created by the Italian government to help
develop the southern region of Italy. Lilienthal's team consulted with Cassa to
help improve the use of the Flumendosa River in Sardinia for irrigation and agriculture. D&R also assisted Cassa staff and Italian officials in creating ways to leverage private capital in order to spur industrial development in southern Italy.[25]
Cornell University political scientist Mario Einaudi worked with D&R and
assisted Lilienthal and his colleagues in their dealings with Italian officials. In
addition to writing letters of introduction for Lilienthal to various Italian elites,
Einaudi evaluated the Italian government's plans for Cassa. Government proposals to appropriate the equivalent of $200 million for development efforts
perplexed Einaudi. Given this relatively small amount of public funding, as well
as uncertainty surrounding the possibilities for private investment in the region,
he warned D&R officials that further involvement in Italian development might
not repay the investment of their time and energy. As a result, when the head of
Cassa informed D&R that their services were no longer required, Lilienthal
readily refocused D&R's energies on other opportunities. He understood that
D&R stood a better chance of success when the company was working with
partners who understood that profitable development ventures depended on
both public and private economic investment.[26]

   D&R's involvement in Latin America spanned a number of nations, but it
began in Colombia's Cauca River Valley. Building on the survey conducted in
Colombia for the World Bank by Lauchlin Currie and Albert Hirschman, D&R
looked to encourage the Colombians to embrace their vision of economic development. Lilienthal recommended to the World Bank that Colombia be encouraged to set up a governmental body to coordinate development, with guidance
and counsel to be provided by Lilienthal and D&R. Once the Colombians had
gathered sufficient information to proceed, Lilienthal would encourage them to
make a project loan application to the World Bank.[27] In a nutshell, Lilienthal was

proposing to export to Colombia the same methodology that the New Deal had used within the United States. Technocratic expertise, combined with the pragmatic techniques of management, could transform the landscape and remake the relationships between the individual, the state, and the market.

In its first five years of operation, D&R expanded rapidly. Employing a range of personnel, including many who had previously worked for the TVA, by 1958 D&R had some 64 workers in the United States, along with over 400 local staff in different nations. By the late 1960s, D&R had grown to over 200 core employees. Lilienthal continued to serve as chairman, relying on the prudent and cautious Gordon Clapp, the firm's president, to handle organizational matters. Between 1955 and 1969, D&R consistently reported a small profit each year, somewhere between $40,000 and $180,000, on annual revenues that generally ranged between $2 and $4 million. Lilienthal personally spent approximately three months each year, between 1955 and 1960, traveling abroad to drum up business. Trips to Latin America, Iran, Italy, Africa, and Asia filled his itinerary. Given this exotic travel schedule, perhaps the least likely place for Lilienthal to journey in 1960 might have been the city of Pittsburgh.[28]

An invitation from the Carnegie Institute of Technology brought Lilienthal together with a group of notable academics, public servants, and businessmen, including Adolf Berle, Friedrich Hayek, Robert Hutchins, Theodore Houser (the former CEO of Sears, Roebuck), and Ralph Paine (the publisher of *Fortune*), to discuss how management and corporations might look twenty-five years in the future. Hayek presented one point of view of capitalism—that corporations "serve the public interest best by devoting their resources to the single aim of securing the largest return in terms of long-run profits." Lilienthal made a strikingly different argument, one that looked across national borders and emphasized a vision of the corporation that accomplished social good while doing business.[29]

Influenced by his years of foreign travel and his experience running a global business, Lilienthal reflected upon the concrete accomplishments of his firm. "Many large and even medium-sized American corporations," Lilienthal boldly declared, "are already operating in other countries, in one way or another." By this, Lilienthal meant not that these firms had taken a financial stake in a different organization abroad, either via a joint venture or through portfolio investment in foreign firms, but rather that American firms themselves were engaging in "industrial or commercial operations abroad which directly involve corporate managerial responsibility." These firms, "which have their home in one country but which operate and live under the laws and customs of other countries as well—I would like to define here as *multinational corporations*."[30] Lilienthal was on to something important. While American companies had operated across borders for a very long time, following World War II they had undertaken operations abroad far more intensely and extensively.[31]

Lilienthal, in his typical mixture of enthusiasm, big thinking, and liberal idealism, became the first person to label this overseas activity by businesses. In his conception this phrase meant more than simply firms undertaking direct managerial responsibility across national borders. The multinational corporation was also a vehicle for extending his vision of the New Deal overseas. Elaborating on the phrase's meaning, he aimed "to present the practical notions which I have developed in the course of my responsibility for managing large-scale enterprises, more specifically as the head of a multinational Western corporation working in Asia, South America, and Africa."[32]

The main challenge facing any manager of a multinational corporation was, Lilienthal thought, business–government relations. A firm might not only engage in direct operations abroad, it might also create entirely new organizations in partnership with firms hailing from several different governments. Lilienthal cited as an example Industrial and Mining Development Bank of Iran as "so to speak, a multi-multinational corporation, managed as a private institution responsible to shareholders of several countries and to creditors who are government agencies," in this case, Lazard Frères, Chase International, and their banking counterparts in England, France, and Italy, as well as private Iranian investors.[33] New supranational regional associations, such as the European Common Market and the United Arab Republic, similarly created new lines of authority. "Accommodating to these conflicts will become a part of the multinational corporate manager's daily tasks," Lilienthal predicted. A multinational executive "will be, in a sense, an economic citizen of this new federal government, and he has, or should have, a sense of the federal system, for it is in such a system that he has been raised."[34]

Above all, Lilienthal argued, the multinational manager would have to cope with politics, which shape and determine the policies which, in turn, govern the competitive environment—from taxes to antitrust laws to regional federations. Stockholders would become more international, organized labor would look to organize across borders, and managers and technicians would become cross-cultural, Lilienthal predicted. Optimistically, he declared that "the simple demands of efficiency in the setting of the multinational corporation will help to destroy the fatuous assumption of nineteenth-century colonialism that men of one color or origin are made of stuff inferior to those of another."[35] American business would need better communications and language skills to bridge national differences and perfect the "art of overseamanship," as Lilienthal referred to it.[36]

Where Hayek had stressed the maximization of long-run profits, Lilienthal argued instead for a more capacious vision: "The Western manager, fully as much as the diplomat, may be able to convey graphically the West's outlook, culture, and ethics, and its adherence to a plural and open society." In so doing, Lilienthal proposed, the multinational corporation could stand as "another facet of internationalization . . .[wherein] the ultimate prize is peace—and not a merely sterile coexistence—in which the peoples of the world may devote themselves wholly to useful arts and not the destructive, in the interests of the betterment of man and his lot."[37] Lilienthal thought his presentation "a pretty solid piece of work" that "contributes some ideas on a surprisingly wide range of subjects, showing that 'management' can be the focus or nucleus for *general* thinking, as well as mere craftsmanship."[38] He happily recorded at the close of the symposium at Carnegie Tech, "I was the only one today who gave Friedrich von Hayek, the *Road to Serfdom* gloomy gus, a scornful kidding about how he has mellowed since the predicted serfdom failed to show up."[39] Hayek, an intellectual forefather of the modern conservative movement, had articulated in *The Road to Serfdom* his fear that top-down centralized planning schemes would ultimately extinguish individual liberty, a prospect that seemed unlikely during the prosperous postwar years.[40]

Lilienthal's vision of the multinational corporation, like D&R, appeared to be in good shape in the early 1960s. Lilienthal imagined his firm and his ideas about international development to be at the leading edge of history, itself. The viability of his corporatist idea and D&R's fortunes, however, were not only tied to the ascendancy of postwar liberalism but also to Lilienthal's place among the nation's political elite. As liberalism and members of the cold war establishment encountered a range of challenges in the late 1960s and 1970s, Lilienthal's vision of the multinational corporation and D&R also experienced hard times.[41] Within the United States, the Tennessee Valley Authority—the program Lilienthal ran for years, and the model for D&R—remained a controversial example of large-scale economic development. In 1964, Ronald Reagan regularly attacked the TVA during his rousing "time for choosing" speech, which he gave several times to raise money for the Republican Party presidential nominee, Barry Goldwater. Beyond the United States' borders, two of D&R's most visible development undertakings gradually fell apart, destroyed by a combination of foreign policy blunders, national differences, and politics. For a time, D&R made an effort to refocus its activities within the United States, consulting for state governments on hydroelectric projects, providing manpower training for the staff of the Office of Economic Opportunity's Community Action Program and for the Peace Corps, and working for the Environmental Protection Agency on issues such as water pollution.[42]

In the early 1960s, Lilienthal's long-standing fascination with the notion of replicating the TVA in Vietnam's Mekong Delta had been reawakened by the United States' increasing involvement in Southeast Asia. In 1966, Lyndon Johnson and his aides pressed Lilienthal to lead what the White House termed "a nongovernmental team to work with Vietnamese experts on long-range planning for the Vietnamese economy."[43] Lilienthal made four trips to South Vietnam between 1967 and 1969, and, after the first, declared he was greatly impressed with Vietnam's people and the country's "fantastically productive resources," describing the Mekong Delta as "like Texas with a lot of water and no oil," adding, "And there may be oil too, for all we know."[44] The Tet Offensive in early 1968, though, helped to signal to many that the prospects for New Deal–style economic development to somehow stabilize South Vietnam were, to put it mildly, severely limited.

Despite this, the final report of Lilienthal's team—confidently detailing plans for the economic development of South Vietnam while the war continued to rage—served as a 600-page "monument to unfounded assumptions and exaggerated optimism," in the words of Lilienthal's biographer.[45] While Lilienthal continued to make big plans, the limitations of multinational firms like D&R to remake other parts of the world were becoming apparent to many other policy makers and business people. Eugene Black, the president of the World Bank, understood that the Vietnam War had seriously crippled the brand of liberalism that had been forged during the Great Depression and exported abroad after World War II. State-sponsored economic development by multinational firms in the Third World was not a panacea. "Nothing," Black realized, "marks the end of the New Deal era more certainly than our incipient awareness that there is no substitute for diplomacy in the affairs of nations and that development is not the same thing as economic growth."[46]

By the 1970s, D&R found itself in serious financial difficulties. The company's revenues depended mainly on its work on hydroelectric development in the Khuzistan region of Iran. Lazard ended its relationship with D&R in 1970, forcing Lilienthal, who at points had to rely on his own wealth to make D&R's payroll, to enter into a partnership with the International Basic Economy Corporation (IBEC), run by Nelson Rockefeller's son, Rodman. Lilienthal had long been proud of D&R's work for the Shah of Iran, dating back to the 1950s, but his friendship with the monarch prevented him from recognizing the rise of militant Islam in Iranian society and the growing unpopularity of the Shah's rule, which was increasingly dependent on the ability of the Shah's secret police to crush dissent. By 1977, Iranian society was seething and its government was falling apart. Iran owed D&R over $1.5 million in unpaid fees, a direct consequence of the Shah's corrupt rule. By the end of 1978, Iran voided its contracts with D&R, leaving the company with almost $2 million in unrecoverable assets within its borders. The Shah went into exile in January 1979. After revolutionary forces took over Iran, IBEC liquidated the remaining assets of D&R. Lilienthal refused to acknowledge the true nature of the Shah's regime, blaming his fall instead on radical Islam and the problematic Iranian bureaucracy. In his final months of life, Lilienthal, in his capacity as a trustee of the Princeton Theological Seminary's Center for Theological Inquiry, pushed the Center to work to "throw some light

on the practical problem facing the world, how to understand Islam and the misuse—as I saw it—of the political and military power of the Islamic religious
leaders."[47]

The 1970s thus marked not only the final years of David Lilienthal's life but
also the end of his vision for the multinational corporation to serve as a vehicle
for exporting New Deal–style economic development projects overseas.
Between the 1930s and the 1970s, however, Lilienthal, like many of his liberal
colleagues who entered the business world, looked to use market capitalism to
bring about positive social outcomes. With the TVA, Lilienthal demonstrated
that government authority could effectively transform the political economy of
a region deeply marked by entrenched inequality and poverty. With D&R, Lilienthal demonstrated his faith that governments and businesses, working together, could cross national borders and replicate the New Deal's achievements
outside the United States. By the late 1970s, though, events in Vietnam and Iran
vividly demonstrated the limits of Lilienthal's multinational corporation to
improve foreign societies. At the end of his life, Lilienthal's faith in large organizations remained the same, but the multinational corporation he had first
described turned out to be better at fulfilling the prediction that Friedrich Hayek
made in Pittsburgh in 1960. Maximizing profits around the world, rather than
solving the global problem of underdevelopment, would be the central legacy of
the multinational corporation.

Notes

1. Erwin C. Hargrove, *Prisoners of Myth: The Leadership of the Tennessee Valley Authority, 1933–
   1990* (Princeton, N.J.: Princeton University Press, 1994); Steven M. Neuse, *David E. Lilienthal: The Journey of an American Liberal* (Knoxville: University of Tennessee Press, 1996).
2. Daniel Scroop, *Mr. Democrat: Jim Farley, the New Deal and the Making of Modern Politics*
   (Ann Arbor: University of Michigan Press, 2006); Jordan A. Schwarz, *Liberal: Adolf A.
   Berle and the Vision of an American Era* (New York: Free Press, 1987), 281; Allan J. Licht-
   man, "Corcoran, Thomas G.," in *The Yale Biographical Dictionary of American Law*, ed.
   Roger K. Newman (New Haven, Conn.: Yale University Press, 2009), 129–30.
3. Thomas K. McCraw, "The New Deal and the Mixed Economy," in *Fifty Years Later: The New
   Deal Evaluated*, ed. Harvard Sitkoff (New York: Alfred A. Knopf, 1985), 37–67; Thomas K.
   McCraw, *American Business Since 1920: How It Worked*, 2d ed. (Wheeling, Ill.: Harlan
   Davidson, Inc., 2009), 88; Robert M. Collins, *More: The Politics of Economic Growth in Postwar America* (New York: Oxford University Press, 2000); Campbell Craig and Fredrik
   Logevall, *America's Cold War: The Politics of Insecurity* (Cambridge, Mass.: Harvard University Press, 2009).
4. Kim Phillips-Fein, *Invisible Hands: The Making of the Conservative Movement from the New
   Deal to Reagan* (New York: W. W. Norton & Company, 2009); Rowena Olegario, "IBM and
   the Two Thomas J. Watsons," in *Creating Modern Capitalism: How Entrepreneurs, Companies, and Countries Triumphed in Three Industrial Revolutions*, ed. Thomas K. McCraw
   (Cambridge, Mass.: Harvard University Press, 1995), 351–95.
5. Elizabeth A. Cobbs, *The Rich Neighbor Policy: Rockefeller and Kaiser in Brazil* (New Haven,
   Conn.: Yale University Press, 1992).

6. Thomas K. McCraw, *TVA and the Power Fight: 1933–1939* (Philadelphia: J. B. Lippincott Company, 1971); Bruce Schulman, *From Cotton Belt to Sunbelt: Federal Policy, Economic Development, and the Transformation of the South, 1938–1980* (New York: Oxford University Press, 1991); and Jordan A. Schwarz, *The New Dealers: Power Politics in the Age of Roosevelt* (New York: Alfred A. Knopf, 1993).

7. David E. Lilienthal to Felix Frankfurter, 1 September 1942, in "Frankfurter, Felix 1942" Folder, Box 100, David E. Lilienthal Papers (hereinafter DEL Papers), MC 148, Seely G. Mudd Manuscript Library, Princeton University.

8. David E. Lilienthal journals, 14 November 1942, Box 198, DEL Papers; David E. Lilienthal, *The Journals of David E. Lilienthal* (New York: Harper & Row, 1964), 1:554–56.

9. David E. Lilienthal, *TVA: Democracy on the March* (New York: Pocket Books, Inc., 1945 [1944]), back flap.

10. Ibid., 2.

11. Ibid., 3. For more on technocratic liberalism, see Jason Scott Smith, *Building New Deal Liberalism: The Political Economy of Public Works, 1933–1956* (New York: Cambridge University Press, 2006).

12. Nils Gilman, *Mandarins of the Future: Modernization Theory in Cold War America* (Baltimore: Johns Hopkins University Press, 2003), 39; Arthur M. Schlesinger, Jr., *The Vital Center: The Politics of Freedom* (Boston: Houghton Mifflin Company, 1949), 233; Michael A. Bernstein, *A Perilous Progress: Economists and Public Purpose in Twentieth-Century America* (Princeton, N.J.: Princeton University Press, 2001); and David Ekbladh, *The Great American Mission: Modernization and the Construction of an American World Order, 1914 to the Present* (Princeton, N.J.: Princeton University Press, 2010).

13. Neuse, *David E. Lilienthal*, 199–244.

14. DEL journals, 18 April 1950; 22 April 1950; 2 May 1950, all in Box 198, DEL Papers; Lilienthal, *Journals*, 3:4–5; and Cary Reich, *Financier: The Biography of André Meyer: A Story of Money, Power, and the Reshaping of American Business* (New York: William Morrow & Co., 1983).

15. Neuse, *David E. Lilienthal*, 247.

16. Lilienthal, *Journals*, 3:24.

17. DEL journals, 19 July 1950, Box 198, DEL Papers.

18. Lilienthal, *Journals*, 3:45, emphasis in original.

19. Neuse, *David E. Lilienthal*, 251.

20. David E. Lilienthal, *Big Business: A New Era* (New York: Harper & Brothers, 1953).

21. Neuse, *David E. Lilienthal*, 251–56; Richard Hofstadter, *The Age of Reform: From Bryan to FDR* (New York: Vintage Books, 1955), n. 8, 324–25.

22. Lilienthal, *Journals*, 3:629.

23. DEL to André Meyer, 1 January 1956, in "Development and Resources Corporation 1956" Folder, Box 403, DEL Papers.

24. Charles S. Maier, *In Search of Stability: Explorations in Historical Political Economy* (New York: Cambridge University Press, 1987); Mira Wilkins, *The Maturing of Multinational Enterprise: American Business Abroad from 1914 to 1970* (Cambridge, Mass.: Harvard University Press, 1974), 332–33; Nelson Lichtenstein, "Labor in the Truman Era: Origins of the 'Private Welfare State,'" in *The Truman Presidency*, ed. Michael Lacey (New York: Cambridge University Press, 1989), 128–55; Michele Alacevich, *The Political Economy of the World Bank: The Early Years* (Stanford, Calif.: Stanford University Press and The World Bank, 2009); and Amy L. S. Staples, *The Birth of Development: How the World Bank, Food and Agriculture Organization, and World Health Organization Changed the World, 1945–1965* (Kent, Ohio: Kent State University Press, 2006).

25. DEL to Eugene R. Black, 4 March 1957, in "Black, Eugene R. 1957" Folder, Box 405, DEL Papers.

26. Mario Einaudi, "Comments by Mario Einaudi on Review of Reports, etc., on South of Italy," 28 January 1957, in "Italy—Einaudi, Mario, 1956–1957" Folder, Box 272, Development and Resources Corporation Papers, MC 014, Seely G. Mudd Manuscript Library, Princeton University. Gabriele Pescatore to DEL, 24 July 1957; and DEL to André Meyer, 7 August 1957; both in "RE Italy 1957" Folder, Box 406, DEL Papers.

27. Memo for Robert Garner, Vice-President of the International Bank for Reconstruction and Development, from DEL, 27 August 1954, in "CVC-World Bank-General, 1954–1956" Folder, Box 240, DEL Papers. See also Alacevich, *Political Economy of the World Bank*, 11–63; and Staples, *Birth of Development*, 22–45.

28. Neuse, *David E. Lilienthal*, 265–66; 290.

29. Friedrich A. Hayek, "The Corporation in a Democratic Society: In Whose Interest Ought It and Will It Be Run?" in *Management and Corporations 1985: A Symposium Held on the Occasion of the Tenth Anniversary of the Graduate School of Industrial Administration, Carnegie Institute of Technology*, ed. Melvin Anshen and George Leland Bach (New York: McGraw-Hill Book Company, Inc., 1960), 116–17.

30. David Lilienthal, "The Multinational Corporation," in Anshen and Bach, eds., *Management and Corporations 1985*, 119.

31. See, for example, Mira Wilkins, *The Emergence of Multinational Enterprise: American Business Abroad from the Colonial Era to 1914* (Cambridge, Mass.: Harvard University Press, 1970); Wilkins, *Maturing of Multinational Enterprise*; and Geoffrey Jones, *The Evolution of International Business: An Introduction* (New York: Routledge, 1996).

32. Lilienthal, "Multinational Corporation," 121.

33. Ibid., 122–23.

34. Ibid., 124–25.

35. Ibid., 146.

36. Ibid., 148.

37. Ibid., 158.

38. David Lilienthal, *The Journals of David E. Lilienthal* (New York: Harper & Row, 1971), 5:86.

39. Ibid., 5:87.

40. George Nash, *The Conservative Intellectual Movement in America Since 1945* (New York: Basic Books, 1976).

41. Alan Brinkley, "Icons of the American Establishment," in Brinkley, *Liberalism and Its Discontents* (Cambridge, Mass.: Harvard University Press, 1998), 164–209.

42. For example, see the project files in Box 348, 354, 382 and 383, D&R Papers.

43. White House press release, 16 December 1966, quoted in Neuse, *David E. Lilienthal*, 276.

44. Neuse, *David E. Lilienthal*, 277.

45. Ibid., 281.

46. Eugene R. Black, *Alternative in Southeast Asia* (New York: Frederick A. Praeger, 1969), 153. For more on business–government relations in Southeast Asia, see James M. Carter, *Inventing Vietnam: The United States and State Building, 1954–1968* (New York: Cambridge University Press, 2008).

47. Neuse, *David E. Lilienthal*, 292–315 (DEL quoted on 315); David Farber, *Taken Hostage: The Iran Hostage Crisis and America's First Encounter with Radical Islam* (Princeton, N.J.: Princeton University Press, 2006); for D&R's financial difficulties in the 1970s, see the material in Box 55, International Basic Economy Corporation Papers, The Rockefeller Archive Center.

6

Pharmaceutical Politics and Regulatory Reform in Postwar America

DOMINIQUE A. TOBBELL

In February 1962, Merck's chief executive officer, John Connor, offered a warning to the company's researchers: "[T]he industry has to be prepared to accept more Government regulation . . . irrespective of how we feel about stronger control from Washington I think that the pharmaceutical industry has in a way asked for greater Government control."[1] As the CEO of a leading pharmaceutical firm and a prominent figure in the national business community (Connor was vice chairman of the Business Council), Connor's comments are unusual. When he made them, conservative business leaders were engaged in a political campaign to discredit New Deal liberalism and reduce the federal government's involvement in the American economy.[2] Moreover, Connor made his comments in the midst of a pharmaceutical reform movement, which had as its goal the passage of legislation that would increase the government's control over drug development, distribution, and therapeutic practice, and reduce prescription drug prices.[3]

This reform movement emerged in the late 1950s amidst growing concerns about rising health care costs and consisted of two decades' worth of congressional hearings into the structure, operation, and regulation of the American pharmaceutical industry. It brought together congressional Democrats committed to protecting the economic interests of consumers and organizations dedicated to increasing Americans' access to affordable health care. Most notable among the congressional reformers were Senators Estes Kefauver (D-TN), Gaylord Nelson (D-WI), and Edward Kennedy (D-MA). The movement's most prominent organizations included the American Association of Retired Persons, the American Federation of Labor—Congress of Industrial Organizations, Consumers Union, and Public Citizen. The membership of the pharmaceutical reform movement thus overlapped with the public interest movement of the 1970s and mirrored that of the broader reform effort to secure national health insurance for the elderly, an effort that escalated during the early 1960s and culminated in passage of Medicare and Medicaid in 1965. The pharmaceutical reform movement also included state welfare agencies and hospital groups struggling to balance their budgets amidst rising costs, and a growing number of physicians who accused pharmaceutical firms of spending far more on misleading and excessive marketing than on research and needlessly driving up the costs of prescription drugs.

That pharmaceutical executives embraced a certain degree of regulation in the early 1960s is reflective of the industry's response to this reform movement. In the 1950s, the drug industry had adopted a hands-off approach toward political affairs. Enjoying favorable public opinion and good relations with Food and Drug Administration (FDA) officials, the industry remained on the political "sidelines."[4] In the early 1960s, however, as reformers criticized its research, marketing, and pricing practices, the industry mobilized into a politically activist industry. In doing so, it adopted a proactive approach to regulatory reform, promoting those reforms that would further their economic interests, while opposing those that would undermine them.[5] Pharmaceutical executives thus held a very specific vision of the government's role in their industry. While it was appropriate for the government to ensure that manufacturers meet safety and efficacy standards for their products and maintain truth-in-advertising (thereby promoting product safety and raising barriers of entry into the market), pharmaceutical executives were hostile to any regulations that threatened the economic underpinnings of the industry. This included reform efforts to restrict the use of pharmaceutical patents and trademarks, and to dictate to physicians the types of drugs they could prescribe. Pharmaceutical executives saw it as their task to set the limits of regulatory reform and "keep the government from seeking to do too much, from intruding still further into our business."[6]

Critical to the industry's collaborative approach to regulation was its mobilization of scientific elites—researchers and physicians in their employ and on their rosters of consultants and directors—who possessed regulatory knowledge, pharmaceutical expertise, and credibility with government officials. By forging political alliances with these experts—and the politically powerful American Medical Association (AMA)—the industry challenged the scientific rationale on which economic reform was predicated and advocated regulations that preserved the industry's and medical profession's interests.

The pharmaceutical industry's mobilization served as a model for the broader business community as it politicized in response to the environmental and consumer protection regulations of the 1970s.[7] The nature of the pharmaceutical industry's approach to regulatory reform was distinctive. Although part of the postwar business assault on New Deal liberalism, the pharmaceutical industry held neither a conservative view of government nor was it singularly focused on undermining trade unionism. Pharmaceutical executives instead regarded a certain degree of regulation—cooperatively constructed—as a necessary part of doing business.

In the 1950s, the American pharmaceutical industry was a diverse and highly competitive industry, with worldwide sales of $2.7 billion in 1959. The industry was composed of more than 1,300 firms of varying size, degrees of research, marketing, and manufacturing capacity, and extent of vertical integration and product diversification.[8] The most innovative sector of the industry consisted of large research-based drug firms. These firms developed extensive industrial research laboratories and marketing activities. They discovered, developed, and marketed the majority of new drugs that constituted the so-called therapeutic revolution, and as such were the industry's most economically important firms. Many of these new drugs were patented and thus marketed under a brand name, conferring upon the innovator firm a commercial monopoly. These included cortical steroids such as Merck's Cortone, broad-spectrum antibiotics like Parke, Davis & Co.'s Terramycin, Merck's anti-hypertensive drug Diuril, and tranquilizers such as Smith, Kline & French's Thorazine and Wyeth's Equanil.[9] In recognition of this, research-based drug firms are often referred to as brand name manufacturers. In 1955, eleven such firms accounted for half of all sales of prescription drugs in the United States.[10] The majority of pharmaceutical firms, however, did little if any research, conducted minimal promotion, and focused on the packaging and distribution of unpatented or off-patent generic drugs. These firms were typically referred to as generic drug manufacturers, though brand name manufacturers were also responsible for marketing a vast array of generic drugs, and some generic manufacturers marketed brand name drugs.

The pharmaceutical industry rode a wave of public and political support in the postwar decade. Stories of death-bed ridden, crippled, and suffering patients saved by the growing cadre of "wonder drugs" could frequently be found in the pages of the *New York Times, Washington Post, Reader's Digest, Fortune,* and *Newsweek.*[11] By the end of the 1950s, however, as health care costs mounted, congressional Democrats, consumer groups, and the press accused the industry of exploiting the American patient for the sake of high profits. In 1959, for example, Senator George Smathers (D-FL) expressed his frustration at "the extremely high cost of antibiotics and other medicines and drugs which must be borne by every American family" and committed to discovering "the extent to which pharmaceutical houses are ballooning drugs costs."[12]

The problem, as Smathers described it, rested in part with the seemingly high price of prescription drugs. In November 1958, *Consumer Reports* lamented the "precipitous rise in the cost of medicines since World War II," reporting that the "average price per prescription has jumped from $1.51 in the 1947–49 period to $2.62 in 1956—a 73% increase," while the "overall cost of living rose only about 18% over the same span."[13] The prices patients paid for prescription drugs had increased since the end of the war. Yet relative to other health care and consumer goods, prescription drug prices had actually remained fairly stable.[14] In spite of this, government and public concern about health care costs focused disproportionately on prescription drugs.

Consumer groups railed in particular against the apparent discrepancy in the prices paid for generic and brand name drugs. In 1958, the Citizens' Committee for Children of New York City found that patients suffering from arthritis, rheumatism, cancer, heart disease, and tuberculosis "often have great difficulty meeting the cost of medicines essential to survival or alleviation of pain." It was the cost, specifically, of brand name drugs that presented the "real hardship" to low- and middle-income families. The Committee argued that patients would be able to buy drugs "at a fraction of the cost" if physicians used a drug's generic name when writing a prescription.[15]

The focus on prescription drugs was borne of a consumer culture in which new innovations begat competitor products, which in turn begat a reduction in the prices paid for those innovations. Seeing little difference between the pharmaceutical economy and the consumer goods economy, the American consumer expected the typical laws of the marketplace to apply also to drugs, so that every time a new drug was joined by a succession of similar drugs, they expected a marked reduction in the drug's price.[16] The frustration over drug prices was also a reaction to the massive postwar growth of the American drug industry. For Representative Chet Holifield (D-CA), it was difficult to reconcile rising prescription drug prices with the high profits of the industry. As he noted in May 1958, the "[a]mounts paid by consumers for drugs have increased tremendously in recent years." Citing a *Business Week* survey, Holifield stated that drug manufacturers "made an average return after taxes of more than 20 percent on their net assets . . . [and] more than 10 percent of sales . . . double the average for all industry groups and the highest return of any reporting group."[17] For Holifield, these figures made clear that American drug firms were profiteering off the pain and suffering of America's ill.

The burgeoning congressional and public critique of prescription drug prices also stemmed from two government investigations into allegations of price-fixing among vaccine and antibiotics manufacturers in the mid-1950s, one of which led to the indictment of five of the country's leading pharmaceutical firms.[18] These investigations were part of a postwar antimonopoly movement led by economic New Dealers seeking to curb inflation, prevent underconsumption, and secure the country's economic prosperity. As part of this effort, these economic reformers sought to eliminate oligopoly formation, the practice by which a small number of large firms dominated a market by arranging prices and controlling product supply.[19] Leading this antimonopolist charge was Senator Estes Kefauver (D-TN) who between 1956 and 1959, as chair of the Senate Subcommittee on Antitrust and Monopoly, investigated economic concentration in the automobile, bread, and steel industries. Although Kefauver's investigation revealed evidence of administered pricing, the hearings generated no new legislation and little in the way of publicity.[20] At the end of 1959, Kefauver turned his attention to the drug industry. The price-fixing investigations had disclosed that government agencies had "received literally hundreds of bids [for the polio vaccine] which were identical to the fraction of a cent," raising concerns that vaccine manufacturers were violating antitrust laws.[21] While all manufacturing industries operated at average annual profits of 4.8%, the pharmaceutical industry was operating at average annual profits of 10.3%, the majority of which, Kefauver charged, were concentrated among only a handful of manufacturers.[22]

After two years of investigative hearings, Kefauver called for significant economic reform of the pharmaceutical industry. From the testimonies of representatives from pharmaceutical manufacturers, state welfare agencies, consumer groups, hospital pharmacists, clinicians, researchers, and various government officials, Kefauver concluded that brand name manufacturers did in fact hold unfair monopolies in the pharmaceutical marketplace. They controlled the pharmaceutical market, Kefauver contended, through three major mechanisms. The first was through the government's granting of product patents with seventeen years of market exclusivity to the developers of new drugs. The second was the expense and intensity of firms' marketing efforts to physicians. The third mechanism, Kefauver claimed, was the propensity of physicians to prescribe using brand names rather than generic names.[23]

For Kefauver, the key to increasing competition in the pharmaceutical market and reducing the price of prescription drugs was to limit the power of drug patents and the pharmaceutical brand. In April 1961, Kefauver introduced to the Subcommittee on Antitrust and Monopoly a bill proposing significant economic reform of the pharmaceutical industry. The bill's provisions were comprehensive in scope and taken together promised the federal government greater authority over each aspect of the pharmaceutical enterprise: development, marketing, and therapeutic practice. In particular, Kefauver's bill employed two strategies for increasing competition. The first called for a revision of the patent law such that drug patents would confer only three years of market exclusivity instead of the standard seventeen and would only be awarded to drugs that had a significantly different molecular structure and significantly greater therapeutic effect than other drugs already on the market. The second strategy was to mandate physicians to prescribe by generic name rather than by brand name.[24]

Kefauver's hearings on the pharmaceutical industry represent a critical moment in the political history of prescription drugs. On the one hand, they signaled the emergence of a pharmaceutical reform movement, committed to securing through legislation a reduction in prescription drug prices and Americans' universal access to prescription drugs. On the other hand, the hearings marked the transformation of American pharmaceutical firms into a politically activist industry.

In the early 1950s, American drug manufacturers had taken their public relations for granted. Physicians regarded advertising by drug companies directly to consumers as a dangerous incursion into the doctor–patient relationship. As such, drug firms felt they "had little duty—in fact, little right—to speak directly to the public." Drug firms instead assumed their therapeutic achievements were enough to guarantee the public's high regard.[25] The congressional attention on the pharmaceutical industry in the mid-1950s, however, prompted the industry to reevaluate this position. As the *Saturday Evening Post*'s executive editor, Robert Fuoss, warned the industry at the December 1957 meeting of the American Pharmaceutical Manufacturers Association (APMA), "The very fact that millions of people can identify their personal interest with a flu shot, a polio vaccine, a tranquilizer, a possible chemical solution to the cancer problem means only that, henceforth, there is an entirely new dimension to your corporate enterprises," that of public relations.[26]

The presence of Fuoss at the APMA meeting reflected the industry's efforts to build closer relationships with the press. In 1956, the industry's two trade associations—the APMA and the American Drug Manufacturers Association (ADMA)—had created the Health News Institute (HNI). Headed by a former *Newsweek* editor, the HNI was a public relations organization charged with educating the public on the role of the health care team in distributing to consumers the drugs developed by pharmaceutical companies. It organized symposia for newspaper editors and science writers at which the "facts of the drug industry" could be relayed and discussed; published a booklet titled *Facts about Pharmacy and Pharmaceuticals*, distributed to the press, schools, and community organizations; and distributed speaker's kits containing facts, statistics, and "quotable quotes" for ready reference for representatives to use when preparing speeches on the drug industry.[27]

The industry also merged the two trade associations representing drug companies: the APMA and ADMA. The groups had initiated informal discussion of a merger in 1956 at the height of the government's price-fixing investigations. Their leaders were particularly concerned that having "two legislative or legal groups speaking for our industry," which often failed to present a united front, was having a detrimental impact on the industry.[28] Although the merger took two years, the establishment of the Pharmaceutical Manufacturers Association

(PMA) in July 1958 created "a single voice for the pharmaceutical industry," which would act as a united front "in its relations with the medical profession, pharmacy, and related professions, with other scientific organizations, with government agencies, and with the public." The unification also brought consolidation of the industry's finances, with the new trade association owning about $400,000 of assets and with a potential annual income of more than $350,000.[29] The following spring, the PMA hired its first full-time president to serve as "a spokesman for the industry." Reflecting—and institutionalizing—the industry's commitment to building supportive relationships with the medical profession, the PMA Board elected the editor of the *Journal of the American Medical Association*, Austin Smith, to the post.[30]

The merger signaled the beginning of the pharmaceutical industry's transformation from a disparate collection of manufacturers with similar political and economic interests into a unified and activist trade association. A clear distinction was drawn between those firms that engaged in innovative research and marketed patented and thus, brand name prescription drugs (eligible for membership), and those firms that lacked any commitment to original research (excluded from membership) and marketed only unpatented drugs or generic versions of off-patent brand name drugs. In 1960, of the more than 1,300 firms that made up the U.S. drug industry, just 140 of them belonged to the PMA. The PMA's member firms, however, produced approximately 95% of all prescription drug sales in the United States, with twenty of those member firms accounting for 80% of those sales.[31]

As Kefauver prepared to launch his investigation of the drug industry, the PMA coordinated the industry's defense. The PMA leadership believed the congressional focus was based on a fundamental lack of understanding among the public, Congress, and the federal government about the industry's work. As Merck's John Connor lamented in 1959, the public "knows little about the long road between the research laboratory and the prescription counter." It was time, Connor argued, for the "industry to account to the public for what we do."[32] To aid in this task, the PMA retained the services of one of the largest public relations firms, Hill & Knowlton.[33]

The PMA's defense strategy centered on telling "the drug industry story," the key elements of which explained the high level of risk and research expense involved in drug development, the health care savings made possible by new drug developments, and the therapeutic gains already achieved by the American public thanks to the industry's innovations. It presented its therapeutic achievements as powerful evidence of the superiority of a capitalist mode of pharmaceutical production (especially when compared to the lackluster performance of the Soviet pharmaceutical industry). And it argued that greater government involvement in drug development threatened both the public's health and the nation's

technological superiority, inviting socialism—in the form of socialized medicine—into the domestic economy. In doing so, the industry tied the economic—
and thus regulatory—fate of the drug industry to the fate of the nation's health
and the free enterprise system in America. As Hill & Knowlton president Bert C.
Goss explained, the "story of the enterprise system, and its advantages to the
public is a great asset in the campaign you face." After all, Goss warned, if the drug
industry were to "suffer the dire consequences" of economic reform, "then all
private enterprise should quiver in its boots."[34] The industry thus extended the
postwar "business assault" beyond the political machinations of business and
organized labor, connecting the interests of business with those of physicians,
researchers, and patients everywhere. The result was to bring home to all Americans—irrespective of their stance on business and labor—the seemingly very
real dangers of letting socialism get a grip on the American political economy.[35]

The PMA disseminated "the drug industry story" in a series of advertisements published throughout the 1960s in national magazines such as *Reader's
Digest*, *The Saturday Evening Post*, and *Look*.[36] *Medicine at Work*, the PMA's
monthly magazine that circulated among "14,000 opinion leaders," showcased
the industry's work with other members of the health care team to "solve community health problems on a voluntary cooperative basis without government
interference."[37] The PMA also published pamphlets, distributed to physicians'
offices, pharmacists, and hospitals, aimed at educating readers on specific issues
of concern to pharmaceutical consumers.[38] It organized Speakers Bureaus, in
which industry representatives told the "drug industry story" to community
groups like the Kiwanis and Rotary Clubs. In 1961, the PMA reported that "well
over 500 field representatives" had "reached more than 2,500 groups—more
than 100,000 community leaders."[39]

At the same time, the PMA initiated a public affairs program. In addition to
hiring a cadre of lobbyists to promote the industry's interests in Washington,
D.C., firms worked to get "business-oriented, free-enterprise philosophy individuals" elected in congressional district elections instead of those congressional
members who pushed for "Fabian-socialist type of government controls." The
industry also embedded itself in state and local politics. Eli Lilly & Co., for example, encouraged their employees to run for elective office in the Indianapolis
community, seeking "such spots as precinct committee man, ward chairman,
state representative, city council members, members of town boards and
trustees, board of education members."[40]

The PMA mobilized two further strategies to defend against Kefauver's legislative reforms. The first, as PMA president Austin Smith announced in 1959, was
for the industry to use "the help of its friends, present and acquired, to pursue
objectives in which there is a mutuality of interest."[41] Smith referred, in particular,
to industry's "friends in medicine," and specifically their shared concern over the

increasing role of government in medicine. The AMA was already a powerful lobby in health care politics, having defeated the Truman administration's efforts to pass a national health insurance plan at the end of the 1940s. It had continued its vociferous opposition to health policy reform throughout the 1950s.[42]

Against this backdrop, the AMA regarded Kefauver's efforts to introduce pharmaceutical reform as a dangerous trend in health care policy at a time when reformers were pushing for nationalized health insurance for the elderly. As far as the AMA leadership was concerned, the medical profession and the drug industry were "involved in a large scale war" against "what must be viewed as a broad-scale attempt to make health care a government responsibility."[43] In particular, Kefauver's attempt to mandate generic prescribing threatened the sanctity of physicians' prescribing autonomy. In June 1961, the AMA's House of Delegates unanimously approved a resolution that put the AMA "[i]n opposition to legislative and administrative mandates which would compel physicians to prescribe drugs, or require pharmaceuticals to be sold, by generic name only."[44]

The PMA's second legislative strategy was to build upon its existing networks with leading academic physicians to challenge the scientific rationale that underpinned Kefauver's legislative agenda. On the issue of mandatory generic prescribing, academic physicians joined with brand name manufacturers in arguing that generic drugs were not necessarily therapeutically equivalent to their brand name counterparts. As PMA chairman Eugene Beesley testified, advocates of generic prescribing "overlook the fact that there can be important variations between drugs with the same generic therapeutic agent."[45] While a generic drug might be chemically equivalent (and thus contain similar quantities of active ingredient) to its brand name counterpart, as Walter Modell, a clinical pharmacologist at the Medical College of Cornell University, explained,

> There are slight differences in fabrication of fixed forms. I don't mean the drug itself, but the vehicle and the incipients and the other materials that make up a solution or a mixture or a tablet or a capsule. . . . In addition to that, some of the materials other than the drug itself which are contained in medical systems are capable of causing reactions, certain oils and certain other materials.[46]

Because physicians could "identify these important variations by the manufacturer's brand name," the PMA's Beesley argued it was "most desirable that the physician know exactly what his patient has taken so that he can assess its value and chart his future treatment of the patient."[47]

The patent provisions of Kefauver's bill also raised scientific concerns for academic physicians involved in developing new drugs. For Dr. Philip S. Hench, a Nobel Laureate and collaborator of Merck & Co. in the development of cortisone, the proposed patent reforms were "astonishing." Hench questioned the rationale behind the "sharp limitation of patent rights and other restraints in this bill which tend to reduce incentive [sic] and impose psychological handicaps" on the industry's continued investment in drug research. After all, he reminded the committee, only the drug industry had the financial resources to "compulsively sustain the pursuit of almost hopeless investigations" that would lead to the discovery of new drugs.[48]

In the end, Kefauver's efforts to institute economic reform of the drug industry failed. Without the support of the Kennedy administration, which having barely scraped through the 1960 election had no interest in pursuing such controversial legislation, Kefauver's bill was dead until the summer of 1962 when news broke of the thalidomide tragedy. Reports that thousands of babies had been born in Europe with severely shortened limbs because their mothers had taken the drug thalidomide to reduce morning sickness during pregnancy brought home to Americans the dangers of taking potent pharmaceutical agents and the potential limits of the regulatory system in the United States. Although the FDA had denied marketing approval to the manufacturers of thalidomide, some 20,000 Americans (including 624 pregnant women) had taken the experimental drug, leading to the birth of seventeen thalidomide babies in the United States (compared to the approximately 10,000 born elsewhere). The tragedy renewed support for pharmaceutical reform in Congress and a significantly revised version of Kefauver's bill passed unanimously on both floors of Congress in October 1962.[49] The reforms embedded in the 1962 Drug Amendments, however, reflected nothing of Kefauver's commitment to making prescription drugs more affordable and instead focused on protecting research subjects and patients from potentially dangerous drugs. The Drug Amendments were thus reflective of a broader transformation in the American political economy from a politics of production to a politics of consumption.[50]

Although the Drug Amendments improved the safety of prescription drugs, they also strengthened the economic position of PMA member companies—brand name manufacturers. They tightened restrictions on pharmaceutical advertising by—among other measures—mandating that all advertisements contain information about a drug's side effects and by transferring the regulatory authority over drug advertising from the Federal Trade Commission to the FDA. But as Merck's CEO John Connor noted, the advertising provisions could prove beneficial to companies like Merck. The hearings, after all, had made "clear that there is a large amount of dissatisfaction with the advertising and promotion practice of some of the companies." As industry leaders saw it, it was no longer "practical to think in terms of continuing the status quo because there's been attracted to the pharmaceutical industry many fringe operators." Rather, Connor continued, "From the point of view of protecting the honest firms and the firms that have some scientific practices and try to do a good job on the commercial side I think its absolutely necessary that we have stronger Government regulations and this view is now rather generally accepted in the industry."[51]

The Drug Amendments also required that manufacturers submit to the FDA evidence not only of the safety but also of the "substantial efficacy" of their drug before the FDA would grant them marketing approval. The efficacy requirement, however, merely codified what the FDA had been doing for the previous decade and, together with the increased factory inspections mandated by the new regulations, raised the barrier of entry into the pharmaceutical marketplace. The result was to reduce competition from the smaller companies unable to afford the costs entailed by these new requirements.[52] In many ways then, the pharmaceutical industry gained more than it lost from passage of the Drug Amendments. Three months after the bill was signed into law, Merck's Connor announced to a group of Texas physicians, "the new law—on the whole—is sound." Connor recalled that of the provisions included in the final bill, "many grew out of proposals that had either been advanced or advocated by the drug industry itself."[53]

To be sure, passage of the Drug Amendments raised profound concerns for pharmaceutical executives who questioned the FDA's ability to handle its new regulatory authority and its tendency to "probe the outer limits" of that authority. In reaction to the Kefauver hearings though, the pharmaceutical industry changed its approach to the government and to regulatory reform. As Connor noted, it was no longer willing to "roll over and play dead" while reformers or the FDA challenged the regulatory status quo.[54] Instead, the recent reform effort had taught the industry "that it's absolutely essential for those of us who will be affected by governmental action to get right down in the arena and to grapple with the problems." It was time for the industry to "pla[y] a constructive as well as an active role" in shaping pharmaceutical regulation and policy.[55] Key to this was the institutionalization of its political alliance with academic physicians.

For several years academic physicians had been concerned about the FDA's ability to fulfill its regulatory responsibilities. In 1959, Johns Hopkins clinical pharmacologist Louis Lasagna had lamented the FDA's perennially inadequate budget, noting that it hampered the agency's "ability to attract top-drawer men in sufficient quantity." To resolve the FDA's intellectual and workforce shortfalls, Lasagna had proposed "universities and the pharmaceutical industry join forces in providing reasonable advice to government." Such a solution, Lasagna suggested, would strengthen the FDA and "preven[t] unwise participation of the government in drug development."[56] During the Kefauver hearings, several leading academic physicians had voiced similar concerns and urged the FDA to appoint "a council of leading scientists, who would advise it regarding overall policies."[57]

In the summer of 1962, in reaction to the thalidomide disaster, the PMA responded to these concerns and established an ad hoc advisory body composed of pharmaceutical experts from industry and medicine. The Commission on Drug Safety, which provided guidance to industry and the government on how to deal with issues of drug safety, was in operation for eighteen months, funded entirely by the PMA. At the end of its tenure, the Commission recommended the establishment of a permanent advisory body, independent of both industry and government financing.[58] In late 1963, the Commission transferred its operations to a new entity, the Drug Research Board (DRB), to be operated under the aegis of the National Academy of Science–National Research Council and funded by the National Institutes of Health. Composed of high-ranking industry and academic physicians, many of whom had affiliations with industry, the DRB institutionalized the political alliances that the industry had forged with academic physicians during the Kefauver hearings. Although never a straightforward proxy for the industry, the shared interests of the two groups were deeply ingrained in the policy work of the DRB.[59]

In August 1966, for example, the FDA introduced new regulations to ensure the informed consent of human research subjects enrolled in clinical trials. Prior to the 1962 Drug Amendments, human research subjects voluntarily consented to participating in clinical research. The FDA, however, required no formal documentation of voluntary consent, nor did it require that patients be fully informed about the nature of the research they were participating in. After 20,000 Americans took thalidomide as an experimental drug without knowing it had yet to receive FDA approval, Congress and the FDA realized voluntary consent did not offer sufficient protection to human research subjects. Although the Drug Amendments had included an informed consent provision, the FDA did not formalize that provision into enforceable informed consent regulations until August 1966. These new regulations mandated that clinical investigators include a signed statement from all human subjects participating in a trial, acknowledging that they had been fully informed of the risks and were willing to accept them and participate in the trial.[60]

The FDA's 1966 ruling unleashed a storm of protest among clinical researchers. The PMA and numerous researchers urged the DRB to intervene and convince the FDA to revise the informed consent regulations so as to allow "the scientist to exercise his best judgment in carrying out his studies with individual patients."[61] Between the fall of 1966 and the spring of 1967, the DRB met with FDA officials on several occasions. In recommending revision of the informed consent regulations, the DRB suggested the FDA remove any "attempts to dictate the substance of the physician's communication with his patient" and reaffirm the clinical investigators' authority to determine when informed consent should be given and exactly how much information should be shared with each patient.[62] The FDA responded favorably. When the agency published final revisions of the informed consent regulations in March 1967, the DRB was satisfied that the FDA had "incorporated substantially all of the amendments that [had been] agreed upon."[63] The DRB thus played an instrumental role in moderating the FDA's authority over clinical research and producing informed consent regulations that everyone—researchers, drug firms, and the FDA—could live with.[64]

Through the 1970s, the DRB enabled the drug industry and academic physicians to play a cooperative role in the shaping of pharmaceutical policy and regulations. In the process, they tempered the expanded regulatory authority granted to the FDA by the Drug Amendments. At the same time, the PMA continued its public relations campaign, mobilizing "the drug industry story" against pharmaceutical reformers' persistent efforts to introduce economic reform. During the late 1960s, for example, Senator Gaylord Nelson (D-WI) sought passage of a mandatory generic prescribing bill. The DRB, however, challenged the scientific and regulatory rationale of the bill, while the PMA distributed pamphlets in physicians' offices and pharmacies and to congressional members warning of the dangers of making generic prescribing mandatory. They also campaigned against Nelson's reelection bid. In the end, the PMA's political activism and the work of the DRB helped defeat Nelson's reform bill.[65]

The effectiveness with which the pharmaceutical industry undermined regulatory reform led other industries to model their political strategies on those of the PMA. The tobacco industry was one such industry. From the mid-1960s, it confronted increasing government efforts to regulate the production and consumption of cigarettes. In response, the industry trade group, the Tobacco Institute (TI) expanded its public relations activities, hiring William Kloepfer as its vice president for public relations. Kloepfer had been instrumental in the pharmaceutical industry's politicization, serving as the PMA's public relations director from 1959 to 1967. Kloepfer thus brought to the TI "a particular appreciation for both the opportunities and limitations of research and scientific literature, as well as a knowledge of the Washington scene."[66]

During the 1960s and 1970s, the TI employed several strategies from the PMA playbook, including "a counterpart cigarette industry activity" to the PMA's Speakers Bureau program. It also mobilized prominent academic researchers as allies in undermining the scientific rationale for regulatory reform. For decades, the tobacco industry had funded academic researchers who questioned the scientific link between smoking and lung cancer. From the 1960s onward, they also funded researchers who provided "expert evidence" of the health benefits of smoking.[67] That the tobacco industry explicitly modeled its research and political strategies on those of the pharmaceutical industry is suggestive of the influence that the pharmaceutical industry's politicization had on other corporations, particularly those that operated in the health and science fields. Indeed, the TI looked to the pharmaceutical industry as a model "[b] ecause of their heavy involvement with the FDA" and success at preventing the enactment of tighter government regulation of its products and practices.[68] Like the pharmaceutical industry, the tobacco industry had much to gain from nurturing the support of physicians and pharmacists as it attempted to sell the public on the beneficial health effects of its products.[69]

In the space of a decade, then, the American pharmaceutical industry had built politically important alliances with academic physicians and the AMA, all of whom were politically and scientifically invested in maintaining the status quo in pharmaceutical policy. These alliances helped transform the industry from a collection of individual pharmaceutical firms into a well-organized industry, one possessing an extensive public relations and political affairs machinery, which it used to influence public opinion and shape pharmaceutical reform. This transformation thus reflected the increasingly pivotal and highly professionalized practices of corporate public affairs and public relations that emerged during the postwar decades. Although there were divisions and tensions within the industry and between it and the medical profession, by the mid-1960s the pharmaceutical industry was a politically astute institution. In the decades that followed, it proved to be a highly robust and adaptive institution that played a significant role in the development of American health care policy.

Notes

Many thanks go to Julian Zelizer, Kim Phillips-Fein, Margot Canady, Corinna Schlombs, and the participants of the Johns Hopkins University History Department Seminar who provided me with insightful feedback on earlier versions of this chapter.

1. John T. Connor, "State of the Company: MS&D—West Point—February 21, 1962," Merck Archives, Whitehouse Station, N.J. (hereinafter Merck Archives).
2. Elizabeth A. Fones-Wolf, *Selling Free Enterprise: The Business Assault on Labor and Liberalism, 1945–1960* (Urbana: University of Illinois Press, 1994); Kim Phillips-Fein, *Invisible Hands: The Businessmen's Crusade Against the New Deal* (New York: W. W. Norton, 2009).
3. This chapter draws from material presented in my book, *Pills, Power, and Policy: The Struggle for Drug Reform in Cold War America and its Consequences* (Berkeley: University of California Press/Milbank Series on Health and the Public, 2012).
4. Connor, "State of the Company."
5. John Connor, "Government and Industry Relationships: Their New Impact on Medicine," presented at the Texas Medical Association, Austin, Texas, 19 January 1963, Merck Archives.
6. Henry W. Gadsden, "Merck in 1966: The Rationale for Growth," presented to the Financial Analysts of Philadelphia, Philadelphia, March 3, 1966, Merck Archives.
7. David Vogel, *Fluctuating Fortunes: The Political Power of Business in America* (New York: Basic Books, 1989).
8. Jules Backman, "Economics of the Drug Industry," in *PMA Year Book, 1960–1961* (Washington, D.C.: PMA, 1961), 52–65.

9. On pharmaceutical innovation and the therapeutic revolution, see Andrea Tone and Elizabeth Watkins, eds., *Medicating Modern America: Prescription Drugs in History* (New York: New York University Press, 2007).

10. *FDC Reports*, 14 April 1958, 8.

11. For example, William L. Laurence, "Victory Predicted in Arthritis Fight," *New York Times*, 4 May 1949, 34; William L. Laurence, "More Relief Found in Arthritis Cases," *New York Times*, 1 June 1949, 33.

12. "Study and Investigation of Present Prices of Drugs," *Congressional Record*, 1959, 105, pt. 15: 19053–54.

13. "The High Cost of Rx Drugs," *Consumer Reports*, November 1958, 597.

14. Between 1955 and 1960, the consumer price index for medical care services (which included hospital and professional fees) changed 4.4%, while the CPI for prescription drugs changed 2%. U.S. Department of Health, Education and Welfare, *Health United States 1975*, DHEW Publication No. (HRA) 76–1232, 11–16, 72–73.

15. "The High Cost of Rx Drugs," 598.

16. Nancy Tomes, "Merchants of Health: Medicine and Consumer Culture in the United States, 1900–1940," *Journal of American History* 88 (2001): 519–47.

17. "Price Fixing and Profiteering on Polio Vaccine," *Congressional Record*, 1958, 104, pt. 13: 16751–55.

18. Robert Bud, "Antibiotics, Big Business, and Consumers: The Context of Government Investigations into the Postwar American Drug Industry," *Technology and Culture* 46 (2005): 329–49.

19. Meg Jacobs, *Pocketbook Politics: Economic Citizenship in Twentieth Century America* (Princeton, N.J.: Princeton University Press, 2005), esp. 246–61.

20. Estes Kefauver with Irene Till, *In a Few Hands: Monopoly Power in America* (Baltimore: Penguin Books, 1965); Bud, "Antibiotics, Big Business, and Consumers"; Daniel Scroop, "A Faded Passion? Estes Kefauver and the Senate Subcommittee on Antitrust and Monopoly," *Business and Economic History On-Line*, 2007 <http://www.thebhc.org/publications/BEHonline/2007/scroop.pdf>.

21. "The Salk Vaccine," *Congressional Record*, 1955, 101, pt. 6: 7115–19.

22. Profits measured as percentage of sales based on FTC-SEC reports. Richard McFadyen, "Estes Kefauver and the Drug Industry" (Ph.D. diss., Emory University, 1973), 75.

23. *Administered Prices in the Drug Industry. Hearings before the United States Senate Committee on the Judiciary, Subcommittee on Antitrust and Monopoly, 1959–1961* (Washington, D.C.: Government Printing Office, 1959–1961); McFadyen, "Estes Kefauver and the Drug Industry"; Richard Harris, *The Real Voice* (New York: Macmillan Company, 1964).

24. Ibid.

25. Eugene Beesley, "The Fourth Dimension in our Future," in *PMA Year Book, 1961–1962* (Washington, D.C.: PMA, 1962), 135–39.

26. *FDC Reports*, 16 December 1957, 7–10.

27. Ibid., 19 May 1958, 22.

28. Ibid., 18 June 1956, 13–16.

29. Ibid., 17 March 1958, 1–4.

30. Smith served as editor of the AMA's journal from 1949 to 1959.

31. "Testimony of Austin Smith," *Administered Prices: Drugs: General (PMA)*, 23 February 1960, 10618. McFadyen, "Estes Kefauver and the Drug Industry," 82.

32. John T. Connor, "1959: The Year the Public Comes to Call," presented at the Drug, Chemical and Allied Trade Section of the New York Board of Trade, New York City, 29 January 1959, Merck Archives.

33. *FDC Reports*, 2 November 1959, 3.

34. Bert C. Goss, "The Drug Industry's Public Relations," in *PMA Year Book, 1960–1961* (Washington, D.C.: PMA, 1961), 51.

35. Dominique A. Tobbell, "'Who's Winning the Human Race?' Cold War as Pharmaceutical Political Strategy," *Journal of the History of Medicine and Allied Sciences* 64(4) (2009): 429–73; Fones-Wolf, *Selling Free Enterprise*.

36. *Pharmaceutical Industry Advertising Program*, Box 67, NW Ayers Advertising Agency Collection, National Museum of American History.
37. Harry J. Loynd, "Address of the Chairman of the Board," in *PMA Year Book, 1961–1962* (Washington, D.C.: PMA, 1962), 3–9.
38. William Kloepfer, "Report of the Director of Public Information," in *PMA Year Book, 1961–1962* (Washington, D.C.: PMA, 1962), 81–83.
39. G. Fred Roll, "Report of the Public Relations Section," in *PMA Year Book, 1961–1962* (Washington, D.C.: PMA, 1962), 75–76.
40. John F. Modrall, "Comments," in *PMA Year Book, 1962–1963* (Washington, D.C.: PMA, 1963), 98–101.
41. Austin Smith, "Remarks of Austin Smith, M.D.," *PMA Year Book, 1959–1960* (Washington, D.C.: PMA, 1960), 39.
42. John H. Talbott, "Editorial: New Drive for Compulsory Health Insurance," *Journal of the American Medical Association* 172(4) (1960): 344–45.
43. Leonard W. Larson, "Mutual Problems of the AMA and PMA," in *PMA Year Book, 1962–1963* (Washington, D.C.: PMA, 1963), 346.
44. *FDC Reports*, 3 July 1961, 19.
45. "Testimony of Eugene N. Beesley," 8 December 1961, reprinted in *Drug Industry Antitrust Act. Hearings before the Antitrust Subcommittee of the Committee on the Judiciary House of Representatives*, 24 May 1962, 696.
46. McFadyen, "Estes Kefauver and the Drug Industry," 197–98.
47. "Testimony of Eugene N. Beesley"; Daniel P. Carpenter and Dominique A. Tobbell, "Bioequivalence: The Regulatory Career of a Pharmaceutical Concept," *Bulletin of the History of Medicine* 85(1) (2011): 93–131.
48. "Statement of Dr. Philip Hench," *Drug Industry Antitrust Act. Hearings before the Antitrust Subcommittee of the Committee on the Judiciary House of Representatives*, 24 May 1962, 516.
49. McFadyen, "Estes Kefauver and the Drug Industry"; Harris, *The Real Voice*; Arthur A. Daemmrich, "A Tale of Two Experts: Thalidomide and Political Engagement in the United States and West Germany," *Social History of Medicine* 15(1) (2002): 137–58.
50. Lizabeth Cohen, *A Consumers' Republic: The Politics of Mass Consumption in Postwar American* (Cambridge, Mass.: Harvard University Press, 2003).
51. Connor, "State of the Company"; "John T. Connor: An Interview Conducted by Leon Gortler, May 1, 1989," 37–38, Merck Archives.
52. Connor, "Government and Industry Relationships"; John Swann, "Sure Cure: Public Policy on Drug Efficacy before 1962," in *The Inside Story of Medicines*, ed. Gregory J. Higby and Elaine C. Stroud (Madison, Wis.: American Institute for the History of Pharmacy, 1997), 223–61; Daniel P. Carpenter, *Reputation and Power: Organizational Image and Pharmaceutical Regulation at the FDA* (Princeton, N.J.: Princeton University Press, 2010), 118–227.
53. Connor, "Government and Industry Relationships."
54. Connor, "State of the Company."
55. Connor, "Government and Industry Relationships."
56. Louis Lasagna, "Gripemanship: A Positive Approach," in *PMA Year Book, 1959–60* (Washington, D.C.: PMA, 1960), 69–70.
57. Harry F. Dowling, "Statement before Subcommittee on Antitrust and Monopoly," 14 September 1960, 7–11, Box 3, Harry F. Dowling Papers, National Library of Medicine.
58. Lowell T. Coggeshall to Senate Subcommittee on Drug Safety, 19 June 1964, Folder: Coggeshall Senate Hearing June 19, 1964, CDS, National Academies of Science Archives.
59. Dominique A. Tobbell, "Allied against Reform: Pharmaceutical Industry—Academic Physician Relations, 1945–1970," *Bulletin of the History of Medicine* 82(4) (2008): 878–912.
60. David J. Rothman, *Strangers at the Bedside: A History of How Law and Bioethics Transformed Medical Decision Making* (New York: Basic Books, 1991), pp. 51–69, 85–100; Federal Register, 30 August 1966, 31(168): 11415.
61. Chester S. Keefer to William Middleton, 6 November 1966, Box 28, William Middleton Papers, National Library of Medicine (hereinafter Middleton Papers).
62. R. Keith Cannan to James Goddard, 10 November 1966, Box 28, Middleton Papers.

63. Federal Register, 11 March 1967, 48: 3994–95. Duke C. Trexler to DRB, "Memorandum: Proposed Patient Consent Regulation of FDA," 14 March 1967, Box 28, Middleton Papers.
64. For another example of the cooperative role of academic physicians, drug firms, and the FDA in constructing drug regulations, see Harry M. Marks, "Making Risks Visible: The Science and Politics of Adverse Drug Reactions," in *Ways of Regulating: Therapeutic Agents between Plants, Shops and Consulting Rooms*, ed. Jean Paul Gaudillière and Volker Hess (Berlin: Max-Planck-Institute, 2009), 105–22.
65. PMA, *Drugs Anonymous?* (Washington, D.C.: PMA, 1967); "Drug Industry Seeks to Defeat Senator Nelson," *Congressional Record*, 1968, 114, pt. 21: 27950–51; Tobbell, "Allied against Reform."
66. Hill and Knowlton Press Release, "William Kloepfer, Jr., Joins Tobacco Institute as Vice President—Public Relations," 23 October 1967, Legacy Tobacco Documents Library at <http://legacy.library.ucsf.edu/tid/lap90c00/pdf?search=%22hill%20knowlton%20press%20release%201967%20kloepfer%22> (accessed 18 July 2010); "For Senator Clements' Report at Spring Meeting," Legacy Tobacco Documents Library at <http://legacy.library.ucsf.edu/tid/qbt92f00/pdf?search=%22senator%20clements%20report%20spring%22> (accessed 18 July 2010).
67. "Staff notes for the Communications Committee," The Tobacco Institute, 17 August 1970. Legacy Tobacco Documents Library at <http://legacy.library.ucsf.edu/tid/bet76b00/pdf?search=%22pharmaceutical%20stress%22> (accessed 16 July 2010); Mark P. Petticrew and Kelley Lee, "The 'Father of Stress' meets 'Big Tobacco': Hans Selye and the Tobacco Industry," *American Journal of Public Health* 101(3) (2011): 411–18.
68. Barbara Brown to William W. Shinn, 27 July 1977, Legacy Tobacco Documents Library at <http://legacy.library.ucsf.edu/tid/wjl21c00/pdf?search=%22william%20w%20shinn%20july%2027%201977%22> (accessed 18 May 2011).
69. Sheldon C. Sommers, "In Defense of Cigarettes," *American Druggist*, 7 September 1970, 83–89.

7

Games of Chance

Jim Crow's Entrepreneurs Bet on "Negro" Law and Order

N. D. B. CONNOLLY

In October 1951, a black man shot and killed a white police officer in the dirt alley of a Southern city, and nothing happened. The gunman never fled the scene. Local whites formed no lynch mob. White cops carried out no reprisals. In short order, the black gunman simply went back to work. This sequence of events, while certainly exceptional during any point in American history, might well seem inconceivable during the Age of Jim Crow. Yet it represented a moment that newspapers and city officials throughout the South used to mark a remarkable and still largely overlooked shift in the culture of Southern governance and enterprise.

The white officer died at the hands of a "Negro patrolman," an entirely new instrument of urban reform, created through an alliance of black and white business owners to help clean up Jim Crow's underworld. Caught in front of a known haunt for illegal gambling and "Colored" prostitution, the white cop was shot while in plainclothes, off duty, and as he reached for his pistol, allegedly refusing to identify himself in deference to a Negro in uniform. The story made national news only three weeks after the fact, and, even then, reporters buried it at the end of an article about Southern white law enforcement officials who were meeting at Miami Beach for an international convention of police chiefs. Neither officers' name appeared in the news, and reports conflicted as to whether the shooting actually happened in Atlanta or Miami. What newspapers seemed to stress most was the ability of white authorities to exonerate the black shooter, and the high praise that Southern police chiefs heaped on Negro officers while at the Miami convention weeks later.[1]

Miami was more than just the site for some historic endorsement of black law and order. It was where a small collection of black entrepreneurs and church leaders, in response to local vice and international gambling rings, played their own political game of chance. Black Miamians helped propel a "Negro officers for Negroes" movement that bore profound implications for questions of both racial justice and economic growth within Southern cities and, from there, out over the consumer economies of the United States and the Caribbean. In September 1944, Miami was where the Deep South's first five African American cops swore-in, and where white city officials, in 1950, would appoint Lawson Thomas, the region's first black judge since Reconstruction. By the time of the 1951 shooting, there were nearly four hundred black police patrolling neighborhoods throughout the urban South; Miami led the nation with forty-one Negro patrolmen.

With most American Negroes having lived, since the late nineteenth century, in the general absence of state protection, the "Negroes officers for Negroes" movement galvanized African Americans in cities as varied as Louisville, New Orleans, Atlanta, and Jackson, Mississippi. In the broadest possible terms, African Americans sought the appointment of black cops in order to gain greater access to the benevolent and putative power of the state. Such power, in the words of one black business owner from Miami, would "gradually build [Negroes] into more loyal, capable and self-respecting citizens."[2] Negro cops, in the eyes of some, would serve as shock troops for the black bourgeoisie, enforcing the economic, social, and sexual norms that seemingly typified "good order" and prosperity. Certainly, much of what was at issue was moral, as attested by the involvement of religious leaders and churches in the push for black cops. But just as plainly, as one African American lounge owner explained, "Good order means good business. We want good business."[3] Black cops provided, in part, a face for such business, becoming, for many, the face of a modernizing South.

As business in the twentieth-century South went, so went the nation. The economic modernization of Dixie transformed the entire United States, and followed what Bruce Schulman outlined as the South's evolution "from Cotton Belt to Sunbelt."[4] This process included expansive industrialization across the region and billions of dollars in federal highway projects and other government spending that converted poor rural countrysides and scattered, slum-ridden cities into a collection of sprawling and profitable metropolitan economies. In recent years, several scholars have explored the mass development of suburban real estate in the South and the resulting national electoral realignments to heighten further the centrality of the region in reshaping America over the last half of the twentieth-century.[5] Yet one of the most critical components to the South's economic revival—black law enforcement and its links to entrepreneurship—remains absent from most general accounts about the fate of business in the new, New South.

Black officers, for one, affirmed discourses of crime prevention that were essential to how white business interests governed Southern states at mid-century. In 1949, for instance, U.S. Senator George Smathers pointed to the hiring of black cops as proof that the South need not be burdened with civil rights oversight, such as troublesome "anti-business" regulations from the Fair Employment Practices Committee. The troubles black officers had in battling vice trades likewise served the rhetorical needs of Southern conservatives who, in their stated attacks on organized crime and the so-called "racketeer menace," lobbied to weaken and maintain restrictions on organized labor during the 1950s.[6] The ability of Southern whites, in direct consultation with black entrepreneurs, to appoint black patrolmen at all also helped solidify the authority of propertied African Americans, the preferred population with whom white elites continued to negotiate the South's fragile racial peace through the direct action campaigns of the 1960s. Even more than actual crime, the perception of lawlessness in the South shaped the course of investment and dictated the outcomes of political contests.

This proved no less true in how black officers impacted perceptions of the South as a whole, especially in the decade immediately following World War II. For many white entrepreneurs and potential tourists, particularly from the North, black officers affirmed at least three things about the modern South and indeed the country: (1) the possible fitness of African Americans for full citizenship, (2) that Negro communities could be cleaned up and made safe for tourism and other forms of "clean" enterprise, and (3) that Southern cities in general were ready to modernize their vice-ridden downtowns, their brutal racial regimes, and their seemingly colonial, largely agrarian economies. These were points not lost on blacks from the Caribbean and the urban North as well. Often pointing to the existence of black cops, many nonwhite visitors found great appeal in traveling to warm Southern cities that seemingly promised some measure of freedom from "Old South" indignities. And through much of the postwar period, in fact, white business people and boosters considered increased Negro tourism essential to their economic designs.

"The Negro's" relationship to law enforcement also inflected a national debate about how city governments policed the line between legitimate and declaredly illegitimate forms of capitalism. Whether understood as a "Debtor Nation" or a "Consumer's Republic," twentieth-century America was just as surely a country built with capital from illegal gambling, slum profiteering, unlawful land expropriation, feudal forms of child labor, and other dubious business practices exercised through the language of race and often abetted by government agents.[7] These were not moments of "corruption," a term that connotes an apparent aberration within an otherwise just social order, but rather "collusion," typical of how the public and private sector routinely worked together to shape both growth liberalism and racial conservatism, both the New Deal and Jim Crow.

In city after city, black law enforcement troubled earlier forms of collusion in the marketplace and helped inspire new ones. Through simply focusing on Miami, one can see how Negro cops mediated bitter contests between competing entrepreneurial interests—Negro property owners and professionals, white chamber-of-commerce types, and illegal gambling outfits operating everywhere between Harlem and Havana. Rarely if ever meeting face to face, these interests preferred to battle through street-level proxies—beat cops, low-level pushers, and the like. And each had a vested interest in maximizing their access to tourist dollars, in appropriating the powers of law enforcement, and in controlling money made from poor and working people on the streets of black enclaves. In this way, the story of black officers in Miami also serves as a story about the business of civil rights in a modernizing America.

The Great Depression came early to South Florida when a massive hurricane burst the region's real estate bubble in 1926. Birthed in a fever of land speculation, Miami, Miami Beach, and a host of newly incorporated cities turned to other forms of gambling, such as horseracing and hundreds of loosely regulated "off track" games at fixed odds (i.e., craps, roulette). At the behest of local law enforcement, segregated black communities served as designated vice zones for flesh trades and unregulated games of chance.[8] By 1931, the State of Florida legislature attempted to improve Miami's reputation and spur legitimate investment and tourism back into the region by expanding the availability of jai alai and horse and dog track betting.[9]

Miami, in the words of New York Congressman Fiorello LaGuardia, had already been "the leakiest spot in the nation" during Prohibition.[10] And with the repeal of the national alcohol ban in 1933, Miami served only as a greater conduit of vice between the United States and the Caribbean. Much of the smuggling networks used for bootlegging remained in place to accommodate new, international circuits of vice. Indeed, many of these networks expanded across the South as white gangsters from New York and Chicago muscled in to squeeze number-running outfits and "whites only" hotels and other small businesses receiving federal assistance during the recovery. Northern white migrants running protection rackets in Durham, North Carolina, for example, skimmed off pay raises mandated for Negro bellhops under the National Recovery Act.[11]

Throughout the 1930s, various organized crime outfits in several Southern cities built a kind of shadow state from bought-off beat cops, sheriffs, and judges. The owner of Miami Beach's Roney Plaza Hotel complained that newly arrived gangsters and police corruption made it "intolerable to operate a hotel."[12] He elected to pay Miami's sheriff $4,000 to help finance officers who would otherwise take bribes. Bribery became such a common feature of everyday Southern police work that cops regularly worked as bodyguards for underworld couriers, and often extorted hotel owners and small-time vice peddlers for personal gain.[13]

In the reformist spirit of the New Deal, candidates running for city government in Miami and Miami Beach challenged the notion that Greater Miami needed its sketchy reputation to attract tourists and buoy the local economy.

"Every decent man and woman in this city," stumped one city commissioner in 1935, "should make up their minds to . . . drive out of Miami, once and for all, this bunch of gangsters and hoodlums that are destroying the economic structure and the good name of [our city]."[14] The 1930s, however, was not a time to stump against the evils of Jim Crow, even as police corruption went hand in hand with racial terrorism, and as vice trades remained enabled by substandard black housing and employment discrimination.

From the perspective of African Americans, extortion and negligence were as integral to Jim Crow Era policing as excessive force. Miami's early police officers showed no aversion to shooting fleeing or unarmed blacks, sometimes in the back, for they knew the city's judges would exonerate them.[15] White cops would also regularly extort money from Negro and poor white gamblers, threatening arrest or beatings if the accused failed to offer a handsome enough bribe.[16] Like most white cops, Miami's police chief during much of the 1930s and 1940s, H. Leslie Quigg, was an open member of the Ku Klux Klan. He demonstrated no aversion to singling-out blacks for special "interrogation" sessions. These included beating the soles of Negroes' bare feet with copper-bound rulers or torturing black "suspects" with makeshift electrical devices, including live wires applied to the genitals.[17]

In addition to these brutalities, Miami's Central Negro District remained the most sparsely policed neighborhood in South Florida. With a population of some 40,000, the city's black downtown was only patrolled by two white officers. Quigg swore to never hire Negro officers or to increase the police presence in the neighborhood, despite repeated cries from black leaders and their white allies. Seeing firsthand the life-and-death costs of poor policing, Miami's wealthiest black mortician, Kelsey Pharr contended, "Decent people of the community fear for their lives."[18]

To many observers, black Miami's crime problem was not relegated to the streets; it was a problem of white paternalism in the courts as well. For even when cops made arrests, "white judges," explained the minister and storeowner John Culmer, "are inclined toward leniency because they feel Negroes are irresponsible." "I believe," Culmer continued, "our people have taken advantage of that."[19] "Frankly, I *was* a little more lenient," admitted Cecil Curry, a white municipal judge. He added, "You are not going to stop [black Miamians] from fighting, craps, cards, and the like. . . . I took into consideration that they were uneducated and have to shift for themselves from a very early age."[20] Curry's leniency included sentencing anyone convicted of killing a black person to only twelve months in county jail. By contrast, if a Negro even attempted to rob a white man, the mandatory sentence was five years in state prison.[21]

It was certainly true that employment discrimination forced many Negroes to resort to gambling, prostitution, or theft as a means of blunting the edge of poverty and property-based racism.[22] But to the chagrin of many propertied blacks, vice rings that seemed to lift Italians, Jews, and other ethnic whites into the American mainstream seemed only to grind up blacks in a cycle of violence, sexual exploitation, and attendant myths about Negro inferiority.[23] Such asymmetries inspired a tough on crime attitude among many African Americans. "There should be some hangings or electrocutions," remarked the head of Miami's largest black Baptist Church. "Life is too cheap in our section of the city."[24]

The earliest African American calls for reforms in law enforcement came as part of a wider and surprisingly effective plea within local communities for whites to recognize black business owners' *community* authority as successful entrepreneurs, their *economic* authority as landholders, and their *political* authority as taxpayers.[25] Especially after the abolition of the poll tax in 1938, black business owners across the South began applying pressure on municipal governments to better realize the "equal" in "separate but equal." Inspired, in part, by the influence and powerful white alliances enjoyed by some of the country's wealthiest African American Southerners—such as the Spaulding family of Durham, North Carolina, or Mississippi's T. R. M. Howard—black urban professionals and property owners in Atlanta, New Orleans, and other New South cities attempted to cobble together fragile interracial coalitions. Such coalitions relied on two related notions: (1) that those who paid property taxes, regardless of skin color, stood entitled to certain benefits, and (2) that second-class benefits for Negroes were better than no benefits at all. The increasingly common belief that one could build a better segregation fueled what historian Morton Sosna called "separate-but-equal liberalism." This represented a kind of market collusion, in that negotiations were often done in secret. And in Miami, as in the rest of Dixie, such negotiations occurred in direct proportion to African American voting strength, the ability of black capital to subsidize community organizing, and the ability of Negro business owners to acquire powerful white friends.[26]

Widely known as "the Mayor of Black Miami," the dentist Ira Davis helped direct the course of separate-but-equal liberalism in South Florida. Apart from having married into one of the city's wealthiest landlording black families, Davis held several important posts, including positions in the Miami Housing Authority and the American Legion. During the height of antiblack discrimination within New Deal Era housing programs, Davis was the only African American in at least three counties secure a mortgage backed by the Federal Housing Administration. To quote author and friend Zora Neale Hurston, Davis was also one of U.S. Senator George Smathers's "right hand men."[27] Smathers likewise counted Davis among his "good friends," and, by the senator's own admission, Smathers looked to Davis repeatedly as a source of "ammunition" against political rivals or unwanted federal interventions.[28]

As one of his community activities, Davis headed the Adelphia Club, an organization with analogues in other Southern cities, and one through which Miami's black business community pursued various equalization efforts. The Adelphia Club kept two full-time community organizers on payroll, and club members, claiming to have control over the Negro bloc vote, threatened to tip key elections if white politicians rebuffed what they considered to be reasonable demands. About the Adelphia Club and the black patrolmen they eventually helped appoint, staffers for Senator Claude Pepper remarked in 1949, "In [Miami's] Negro community, a group of businessmen have perfected . . . political organization."[29]

The Adelphia Club had a sister organization in the Friendship Garden Civic Club, a group for black Miami's most elite women of property, under the direction of the nurse and minster's wife Annie Coleman. Both clubs proved particularly adept at crystallizing into political arguments discontent expressed on the streets and in the saloons of Miami's Central Negro District. At weekly luncheon meetings, Coleman and Davis's groups also allowed black business activists to hammer out bitter disagreements and crucial compromises in private before bringing "The Negro's" concerns before the city commission, influential white women's groups, or the Greater Miami Chamber of Commerce.[30] Through the late 1930s and early 1940s, both groups engaged in the hard political work of getting "Colored Only" seating and bathrooms built into the Orange Bowl, establishing a "Colored Only" Beach, opening "Negro Days" on the city golf course, and securing "Colored Only" housing projects from the Public Housing Administration.[31]

One cannot account for the success of the "Negro officer for Negroes" movement absent these practices of interracial backroom politicking among the South's urban entrepreneurs. In the summer of 1944, Miami city officials "promoted" Police Chief Quigg to the Dade County Commission, clearing the way for the appointment of black officers. They then asked Ira Davis to screen personally the first five patrolmen. Fearing white backlash, the men trained in secret, and for the unit's first five years, Davis agreed to let the patrolmen use his outpatient dental clinic as their police substation. The patrolmen carried guns and badges, worked the same number of hours as whites and, remarkably, earned the same wages. Their jurisdiction remained restricted to the agreed upon borders of the Central Negro District and nearby black enclaves, however. Most significantly, white city officials prohibited black cops from arresting whites who crossed into black Miami to frequent vice businesses and nightclubs, a condition white officials had imposed on black officers throughout the South. Unless in immediate physical danger (as in the October 1951 incident), Negro patrolmen had to detain white offenders and call white officers to take the alleged perpetrator into formal police custody.[32]

The new cops embodied all the contradictions and self-congratulations of the South's separate-but-equal governing model. On the day the first five patrolmen took their oath, hundreds of children, men, and women gathered to see the event, with many marching behind the cops as they walked their first official beat. The visible reality of respectable Negroes in uniform seemed to place black Miami, in the words of one local businesswoman, "on the threshold of a new era." One young onlooker who attended the swearing-in ceremony remembered, "They were like our saviors."[33] It soon became evident, however, that these men, like white cops, were not above illegal search and seizure or a little excessive force. Nor did every Negro in Miami welcome or even respect colored patrolmen's newly bestowed authority.[34] It was not uncommon for a traffic stop or a moment of questioning between black patrolmen and a citizen to turn into some form of physical violence.[35] "Just ask for an ID," recalled one officer, "and you'd have to fight."[36]

In the midst of this racial modernization in law enforcement, organized crime rings were undergoing their own evolution and making their own impact on both the workings of illegal gambling and Miamians' day-to-day perception of crime. According to federal investigators, Chicago mobsters who once worked for Al Capone took over South Florida's $26 million a year horseracing business in 1946.[37] Lawmakers in the South and West also believed that the passage of the Taft-Hartley Act in 1947, which weakened traditional union strongholds, drove labor racketeers from the Northeast and Midwest into the seedier sides of vacation economies in Las Vegas, Havana, and Miami.[38] New York's Frank Costello and Meyer Lansky had allegedly taken over much of Cuba's expanding hotel and casino economy during this period as well. They bought off enough officials in Miami and Havana to control conventional gaming and two lucrative underground games: *bolita*, a street-level game of chance located mostly in Miami's Central Negro District, and *cuba*, named for the Cuban National Lottery on which it was based.[39]

Almost corporate in structure, South Florida's numbers rackets used bribery and international connections to make *bolita* and *cuba* sophisticated and, at times, dizzyingly complex enterprises. Game managers sold tickets in bars, on street corners, and by mail "Up North" by way of newspaper ads in the black press.[40] Sellers also reached white northerners on vacation by employing white waitresses working at strip bars and black porters and domestics working in white hotels.[41] In Havana, National Lottery administrators within Fulgencio Batista's government, paid for by Lucky Luciano, ensured that numbers played heavily in stateside games never hit. Meyer Lansky covered most of the payouts to high-ranking officers and politicians around Miami.[42] Game administrators also ensured different locations were used for the "bankers" who underwrote the games, the largely female workforce that added up the receipts, and the protection money that would go to beat cops or their superiors. Cops tended to get their cut at street level through extortion or via the underground payroll system running through higher-ranked officers.[43]

Relying mostly on nickel or dime bets, Miami's illegal lotteries represented the biggest underground moneymaker to precede the cocaine boom of the 1980s. Between 1945 and the late 1950s, *bolita* remained a steady $3 million to $4 million annual trade in the city of Miami. Across Dade County, *bolita* did $10 million in business, which, in 1946, was nearly four times Miami's entire public safety budget and matched two-thirds of all the money spent on the city's commercial construction boom.[44] As during the Depression, Negro neighborhoods housed most street-level activity, and small, family-owned white hotels or proprietorships continued to be besieged by police corruption and mob influence in order to facilitate the "managerial" side of the enterprise.

The experiment of using black patrolmen ran up against this international ring of vice, and, to the surprise of many, Negro patrolmen seemed to be winning, making national news while doing it. In their first year, Miami's black cops made over four thousand arrests, generating over $56,000 in fines for Miami's city coffers. The violent crime rate in the Central Negro District dropped by almost 50%.[45] That first year also saw Miami's Negro patrolmen, as a group, outpace Miami's white "morals squad" in terms of overall arrests. After a particularly productive weekend in which black law enforcement arrested nine *bolita* operatives (to white officers' one), Miami's police chief issued a radical new orientation for the entire force in which he publicly demanded white officers police as efficiently as their black counterparts.[46] Black cops had become so effective that, just two years after their arrival, city attorneys noticed "an organized campaign on the part of *bolita* operators to dispense with the Negro police force."[47]

The successes of Miami's law enforcement experiment echoed across the South after the U.S. Supreme Court's ruling in *Smith v. Allwright* (1944), which further empowered the urban Negro vote by outlawing the all-white primary. In short order, black business activists in Norfolk, Virginia (1945); Atlanta, Georgia (1947); and Memphis, Tennessee (1948) led the charge for patrolmen of their own.[48] Miami's black officers seemed to prove that black "law and order," in the words of the *Atlanta Daily World*, would help "the Negro . . . to emancipate himself from being a sucker to white racket operators."[49] In the subsequent anti-*bolita* campaigns sweeping through Southern cities, African Americans found, if not an end to Jim Crow, new reason to hope.

When white city officials in Miami appointed attorney Lawson Thomas as the New South's first black judge in 1950 many assigned to him similar hope. As with black patrolmen, though, Thomas fell subject to several limitations on his symbolic and actual authority. Miami city officials denied Thomas the power to hear cases involving whites and made him convene court without a bench and without wearing robes.[50] Moreover, Thomas could not hear any cases beyond misdemeanor offenses or violations of municipal ordinances. Corruption charges, gangland hits, and other felonies plaguing the Central Negro District remained beyond his jurisdiction. These limitations, in the eyes of some, made Thomas only "half a judge," or in the words of one Northern newspaper, "Judge Jim Crow."[51] Still, Thomas appreciated his new post as "a tool [that] gives us a measure of self-government within the bounds of segregation."[52]

Greater "self-government" meant expanding the material authority that black property owners held over their poorer counterparts. In very direct terms, Lawson Thomas—an Adelphia Club member—became the legal arm of black entrepreneurs. He helped Miami's black business community tether their own aims to white officialdom's broader pro-growth "morality" campaigns against gambling and strip joints, "lewd and indecent literature," white supremacist hate groups, and homosexual entertainment.[53] Racial terrorism, vice, burlesque shows, and gay entertainment were all at one time or another integral to Miami's popularity and growth, particularly during the city's Depression years. But each of these came under direct fire once the military and then private industry began dumping millions in "clean" capital into South Florida's hotels and travel infrastructure during and after World War II.[54]

Local newspapers, hotel owners, and chamber-of-commerce types looked the other way as police officers ramped up urban "reform" with crackdowns on suspected homosexuals, Ku Klux Klan members, gamblers, and the poor. (The dead white officer that opened this essay fell under this sweep.) In the Central Negro District, Negro patrolmen rounded up "female impersonators," women engaged in "unnatural relationships," and black men discovered in "compromising positions." The officers brought these "offenders" before Judge Thomas to share the Negro court's docket with petty thugs and *bolita* street peddlers.[55]

Nationally, news of black Miami's law enforcement successes dovetailed with the existing visibility of city's notable Negroes in the society pages of the *Chicago Defender, Baltimore Afro-American,* and other black newspapers. And locally, the positive press that black cops generated affirmed the common good that could come from protecting black taxpayer rights, justifying further collaborations between black business and white boosters. Even Leslie Quigg—the brutal Klan-police-chief-turned-city-commissioner—had no problem approving the use of city funds to advertise black Miami tourism in "National Negro Magazines [*sic*]." "The Negroes," as Quigg's words appear in city commission minutes, are "taxed just like everybody else for these publicity funds and they should be entitled to some benefit from them."[56] As a point of security and publicity, city officials made sure Miami's black police force made a conspicuous and honored appearance at almost every promotional event. By the early 1950s, Ira Davis, Annie Coleman, Lawson Thomas, and others among the city's black upper crust began to serve as pro-Miami boosters in their own right. They traveled the country bearing official invitations addressed from Miami's mayor to African American organizations that might consider "The Magic City" for their next religious, professional, or fraternal convention. One white banker with connections to the mayor went so far as to let black churchmen know which hotels were behind on their mortgage payments and, thus, in financial need of Negro business.[57]

The new collaborative climate around tourism allowed the start of desegregation in Greater Miami to actually precede the *Brown* decision, beginning in the region's hotels. Starting with cash-strapped hotels during the recession of 1953, and only increasing in the years that followed, larger and larger interracial or all-black conventions pushed the color bar further from view.[58] In 1956, members of the African Methodist Episcopal Church spent an estimated $2 million during their two-week convention in Miami. The event prompted more than thirty white hotels to accept Negro guests for the first time.[59] By the early 1950s, some 300,000 colored vacationers had begun traveling to Florida every year, and local white hoteliers and restaurateurs could not help but notice—and accommodate—the many "dark gentlemen from . . . the islands" and so-called "rich Negroes" from Chicago and elsewhere spending their money in Miami.[60] Recognizing a certain self-interest among the city's newly tolerant white entrepreneurs, one contributor to the *Pittsburgh Courier* quipped in 1953, "Miami is tightly jim crow [*sic*], except when it comes to taking colored folks money."[61]

To be sure, for much of the 1950s and 1960s, integrating most of South Florida's leisure amenities remained an uphill battle. It was fought on a hotel-by-hotel, season-by-season basis.[62] Nevertheless, the apparent profitability of measured desegregation and the seeming reduction of crime in the Central Negro District lured a wave of legitimate white capital and progressive white racial sentiment into black Miami. An altogether new class of entrepreneur—the white owner of the "Negro hotel"—led a growing chorus of white businessmen who claimed to find upstanding business and clean profits within black communities. Said Harry Markowitz, who owned over a hundred apartments in the Central Negro District, "The Negro tourist and convention delegate spends a billion dollars a year in the United States. That's a tremendous business which we've barely tapped."[63] In 1955, Markowitz and his wife Florence opened the Hampton House—a high-end leisure destination complete with air-conditioning, an in-ground swimming pool, maître d' service, and valet parking.[64] New black hotels, in the words of one white developer, represented a realization of civil rights and a signal reminder to all of what "the patient determination of free people with integrity of purpose" could accomplish.[65] Throughout the 1950s, headlines about "Raids Smash[ing] Miami Gaming Joints" ran concurrently with ones about new "Million-Dollar Negro Hotel[s]."[66]

Miami's interracial war on crime cut another way, however. It helped buttress a general position among white Southern politicians that Dixie stood for localism over federal intervention, property rights over socialism, and law and order and elite negotiations over "disruptive" direct action. In his travels, U.S. Senator George Smathers made sure to quote Miami's black judge, who apparently believed the Fair Employment Practices Commission, "if enacted, would set back one hundred years the progress the Negro has made in the U.S."[67] Not an opponent to fair employment in the abstract, Thomas's "moderate" position on the race question, in his own words, stood on making "local government our . . . avenue of attack."[68] As late as 1956—the dawn of direct action campaigns— Thomas was among several Adelphia Club members urging Miami's blacks to "1) Join no boycott movement. 2) Obey state laws regarding segregation until they are changed. 3) Support all legal moves by Negro organizations to end segregation."[69] Anything else, by Thomas's estimation, would only alienate white entrepreneurs from the Negro's cause.

Part of that cause included black entrepreneurs, patrolmen, and religious leaders calling for ongoing grand jury investigations of the *bolita* trade. In 1960, city attorneys produced the first hard evidence that *bolita* operatives were employed as high as the Miami offices of the Internal Revenue Service and the Dade County State's Attorney. Black officers complained that censure from white superiors frustrated their moves against *bolita* sellers. Eventually city officials discovered agents of organized crime so deeply embedded in Miami's all-white detective corps that the city commission nearly abolished the entire detective program.[70]

The ensuing "zero tolerance" policy hardly ended South Florida's vice trades; well into the 1990s *bolita* was a $15 million a year business. The move did, however, lead to the firing of scores of government employees and "top brass" in the police department. Some white officers saw the effort as a plot by the NAACP to "get Negro officers promoted to high rank in the department."[71] It, therefore, surprised many when Miami's anti-vice campaign to led to the ouster of Judge Lawson Thomas. In 1962, Lawson's wife, Eugenia, was charged with murder, allegedly calling a bloody shotgun hit on a "*bolita* house" that killed two people. Likely framed by the judge's political enemies, Mrs. Thomas, after her husband's tireless representation, was eventually acquitted. Nevertheless, the episode proved too embarrassing for Lawson and the city, forcing him to resign.[72] Poor blacks and crooked white officers, it seemed, would not be the only casualties of pro-growth law and order.

Within the history of black law and order lies a history of black business that has undeniably shaped modern "progressivism" and "conservatism," and yet remains largely absent from scholarly genealogies of both. Historically, beyond even the more dramatic theater of popular civil rights history, black attorneys, ministers, and other entrepreneurs have wielded a widely ignored causal power. To be sure, at no point in America's past has black business represented more than 3% of all business or even secured 0.5% of American businesses' total annual profits.[73] And yet, black entrepreneurs' strategic and creative commitment to capitalism—despite and often through the mechanisms of white supremacy, such as Jim Crow policing—ensured black business people influence disproportionate to their numbers.[74] Whether speaking from the pulpit, through civic associations, or in private meetings with well-connected whites, black entrepreneurs used decidedly pro-business arguments to stake their vision of civil rights on consensus issues like taxpayers' rights, crime control, and the integrity of private property. In so doing, they started the South and the country down an important, if deeply compromised, path toward racial reform and economic transformation.

Regarding the historical ties between business and civil rights, in particular, entrepreneurs are generally assumed to have played a progressive role only after the *Brown* decision, and then only by following the lead of grassroots organizers and the federal government.[75] But when historians resist the dual temptation to conflate "civil rights" with desegregation and "business" with *white* business, it becomes clear that, at least a full decade before *Brown*, black entrepreneurs helped co-author America's so-called "centrist" position on race—the pro-business template now undergirding everything from corporate support of affirmative action and the establishment of interracial, Sunbelt "growth regimes" to the proliferation of suburbia and, of course, the expansion of America's law enforcement apparatus. Indeed, contrary to common characterizations of white conservatism or anti-leftist backlash, "law and order" politics did not undo the black freedom struggle. For better, and often for worse, they were central to it.

Notes

In addition to the editors and contributors to this volume, the author wishes to thank Shani Mott, Sarah Phillips, Kevin Kruse, Louis Galambos, Matt Lassiter, Tara Bynum, Rabia Belt, Lester Spence, Andrew Kahrl, Davarian Baldwin, and Brett Gadsden for their insights on this essay.

1. "Police Chiefs Praise Their Negro Cops," *New York Amsterdam News*, 10 November 1951, 1M; "Dixie Chiefs Laud Negro Policemen," *Miami Herald*, 2 November 1951, 2B; "Negro Policemen On Duty in Southern Cities Performing Excellent Job, Chiefs Declare," *Times-News* (Hendersonville, N.C.), 5 November 1951, 5.

2. Dade County Planning Council, "Twenty-Year Plan for Dade County" (1936), quotation in National Urban League, *A Review of Economic and Cultural Problems in Dade County, Florida as They Relate to Conditions in the Negro Population* (New York: National Urban League, 1943), 27–28, 31.

3. "What Leading Miamians Are Saying. . . " from "A Welcome to Our Negro Policemen by the Citizens of Miami, September 17 [1944]," Law Enforcement (Police) City of Miami Box, Black Archives History and Research Foundation of South Florida, Miami, Fla. (hereinafter BA).

4. Bruce J. Schulman, *From Cotton Belt to Sunbelt: Federal Policy, Economic Development, and the Transformation of the South, 1838–1980* (Durham, N.C.: Duke University Press, 1994).

5. See, for instance, Matthew D. Lassiter, *The Silent Majority: Suburban Politics in the Sunbelt South* (Princeton, N.J.: Princeton University Press, 2007); Kevin M. Kruse, *White Flight: Atlanta and the Making of Modern Conservatism* (Princeton, N.J.: Princeton University Press, 2007); and Michelle Nickerson and Darren Dochuk, eds., *Sunbelt Rising: The Politics of Space, Place, and Region* (Philadelphia: University of Pennsylvania Press, 2011).

6. David Witwer, "The Racketeer Menace and Antiunionism in the Mid-Twentieth Century US," *International Labor and Working Class History* 74 (Fall 2008): 124–47, 129.

7. Louis Hyman, *Debtor Nation: The History of America in Red Ink* (Princeton, N.J.: Princeton University Press, 2010); Lizabeth Cohen, *A Consumer's Republic: The Politics of Mass Consumption in Postwar America* (New York: Alfred A. Knopf, 2003). On the utility of racism for American economic growth, see Neil Foley, *The White Scourge: Mexicans, Blacks, and Poor Whites in Texas Cotton Culture* (Los Angeles and Berkeley: University of California Press, 1999); James D. Anderson, *The Education of Blacks in the South, 1860–1935* (Chapel Hill: University of North Carolina Press, 1988); and David M. P. Freund, *Colored Property: State Policy and White Racial Politics in Suburban America* (Chicago: University of Chicago Press, 2007).

8. "Dan Hardie Backed up Tough Talk," *Miami News*, 10 August 1985, 4C; Marvin Dunn, *Black Miami in the Twentieth Century* (Gainesville: University of Florida Press, 1997), 70. For the consequences of this practice in bigger cities like Chicago and Detroit, see Davarian L. Baldwin, *Chicago's New Negroes: Modernity, the Great Migration, and Black Urban Life* (Chapel Hill: University of North Carolina Press, 2007), 26, and Victoria W. Wolcott, *Remaking Respectability: African American Women in Interwar Detroit* (Chapel Hill: University of North Carolina Press, 2001).

9. The legislature opened these games to pari-mutuel, or "pool," betting, which increased possible payouts for players with each added participant. Gerald Posner, *Miami Babylon: Crime, Wealth, and Power: A Dispatch from the Beach* (New York: Simon and Schuster, 2009), 47.

10. Posner, *Miami Babylon*, 38.

11. Walter B. Weare, *Black Business in the New South: A Social History of the North Carolina Mutual Life Insurance Company* (Urbana and Champaign: University of Illinois Press, 1973), 220.

12. "Dan Hardie Acts as Own Witness in Sholtz Hearing," *Palm Beach Post*, 9 November 1933, 1.

13. Correspondence from R. H. Johnson to the NAACP, 8 January 1929, "Administrative File, Police Brutality, 1937–1939," part 8, series A, reel 14, frame 569, Papers of the NAACP (microfilm); John A. Diaz, "Trap White Cops in Extortion Plot," *Pittsburgh Courier*, 21 May 1949, 1.

14. "Miami's New Deal: The People's Candidates . . . Gardner, Chartrand and Bridges," 19 March 1935, Manuscript Box 8, Everest George Sewell Papers, Historical Association of Southern Florida, Miami, Fla. (hereinafter HASF).

15. Correspondence from R. H. Johnson to the NAACP, 8 January 1929, "Administrative File, Police Brutality, 1937–1939," part 8, series A, reel 14, frame 569, Papers of the NAACP.

16. Diaz, "Trap White Cops in Extortion Plot," 1.

17. Dunn, *Black Miami in the Twentieth Century*, 117–24, 133–39; see also Paul S. George, "Colored Town: Miami's Black Community, 1896–1930," *Florida Historical Quarterly* 56(4) (April 1978): 432–47.

18. "'Life Too Cheap' Say Race Leaders," *Atlanta Daily World*, 24 November 1943, 4.

19. "Dixie's First Negro Judge Lauds His Own Appointment," *New York Amsterdam News*, 29 April 1950, 2.

20. Arthur Chapman, "The History of the Black Police Force and Court in the City of Miami" (Ph.D. diss., University of Miami, 1986), 122.

21. "Murder Again!" *Miami Times*, 20 November 1948, 4.

22. For great social histories of numbers rackets in the urban North, for instance, see Wolcott, *Remaking Respectability*, and Baldwin, *Chicago's New Negroes*.

23. See Daniel Bell, "Crime as an American Way of Life," *Antioch Review* 50(1/2), 50th Anniversary Issue (Winter/Spring 1992): 109–30; and Khalil Gibran Muhammad, *The Condemnation of Blackness: Race, Crime, and the Making of Modern America* (Cambridge, Mass.: Harvard University Press, 2010).

24. "Fla. Community Asks Stiff Penalty in Race Murders," *Chicago Defender*, 13 November 1943, 7.

25. "Miami Shows the Way to Negro America; Reaps Great Benefit from Ballot Use," *Pittsburgh Courier*, 22 June 1940, 24.

26. Morton Sosna, *In Search of the Silent South: Southern Liberals and the Race Issue* (New York: Columbia University Press, 1977), 19. On equalization, see Kimberly Johnson, *Reforming Jim Crow: Southern Politics and State in the Age before Brown* (Oxford: Oxford University Press, 2010).

27. Zora Neale Hurston, "A Negro's Point of View about NAACP and Political Activity," *Orlando Sentinel*, 17 July 1952.

28. Correspondence from George Smathers to Ira Davis, 20 July 1954, "Political—1950 Campaign—misc." Folder, Box 319, George A. Smathers Papers, Special Collections, George A. Smathers Libraries, Gainesville, Fla. (hereinafter UF).

29. Memorandum from George Weaver to Jack Kroll, 24 June 1949, Folder 11 "Negro Organizations," Box 37, Series 204A, Record Group 200, The Mildred and Claude Pepper Library, Florida State University, Tallahassee, Fla.

30. Stanley Ivern Sweeting, "Night Life in Miami," *The Crisis*, March 1942, 97; "The King of Clubs of Greater Miami," in "Documentary Journal" Folder, Collective Personalities Box, BA.

31. Office of the Miami City Clerk, 18 December 1946, *Resolutions and Minutes of the City Commission, 1921–1986*, Box 33, State Archives of Florida, Tallahassee, Fla. (hereinafter SAF).

32. "First Negro Police," Law Enforcement Box, Annie M. Coleman Collection, BA; Dorothy J. Fields, "Ann Coleman," Personalities-Collective Folder, Local Politics and Elected Officials Box, BA; "Patrolman (Negro) City of Miami," *Miami Times*, 6 November 1948, 9; Chapman, "The History of the Black Police Force," 233.

33. "Foreword" and "What Leading Miamians are Saying . . . " in "A Welcome to Our Negro Policemen by the Citizens of Miami," 17 September 1944, Law Enforcement (Police) City of Miami Collection, BA.

34. "Patrolman Dismissed by Nelson," *Miami News*, 9 November 1944, 1B; "Bolita Protection Told," *Miami News*, 16 February 1960, 6A.

35. "Officer Beat Them, Two Say," *Miami Herald*, 10 October 1951, 16A.

36. Edward Kimble quotation in Jacob Bernstein, "Black in Blue," *Miami New Times*, 13 November 1997 <http://www.miaminewtimes.com/1997-11-13/news/black-in-blue/>;, (accessed 1 July 2010).

37. "The Gambling Industry," *Changing Times: The Kiplinger Magazine*, March 1951, 39.

38. Bell, "Crime as an American Way of Life," 113.

39. "The Gambling Industry," *Changing Times: The Kiplinger Magazine*, March 1951, 39; Joaquin Pelayo, "The Wheels Spin in Havana," *Chicago Defender*, 25 May 1940, 13; T. J. English, *Havana Nocturne: How the Mob Owned Cuba . . . and Then Lost It to the Revolution* (New York: Harper, 2008), 56, 64, 154.

40. "Swinging the News," *Chicago Defender*, 21 January 1950, 21.

41. "Porter Found Selling Bolita at Beach Hotel," *Miami Times*, 5 February 1949, 1; Office of the Miami City Clerk, *Resolutions and Minutes of the City Commission, 1921–1986*, 28 January 1958, Box 50, SAF; "Dade Grand Jury System Background" (2), 4 (1964), "Dade County Grand Jury" Folder, Box 6, Don Shoemaker Papers, University of North Carolina Special Collections, Chapel Hill, N.C. (hereinafter UNC).

42. English, *Havana Nocturne*, 56.

43. Circuit Court of the Eleventh Judicial Circuit of Florida in and for the County of Dade, "Bolita," *Final Report of the Grand Jury*, 10 May 1960, 7.

44. "Dade Grand Jury System Background" (2), 14, Shoemaker Papers, UNC; "Nelson Declares War in Gambling and Lawlessness," *Miami News*, 24 September 1945, 1B; Corre-

spondence from Roosevelt C. Houser to George E. Holt, 18 March 1958, 1, "Dade County 1958" Folder, Box 62, Governor LeRoy Collins Papers, Administrative Correspondence, Series 776B, Record Group 102, SAF; City of Miami, *Metropolitan Miami Florida: Fifty Years of Progress* (1946), 25, 51.

45. "Police Bag 3,545 Law Violators in 6 Months of 1947," *Atlanta Daily World*, 26 February 1948.

46. "Nelson Declares War in Gambling and Lawlessness," *Miami News*, 24 September 1945, 1B.

47. "Bolita Ring Called Threat to Miami Negro Policemen," *Miami Herald*, 4 July 1946, B1.

48. *Smith v. Allwright*, 321 U.S. 649 (1944); "Justice for All; Miami's March Toward Equality Started in 1944," *Miami Herald*, 1 February 1994, 1B; Earl Lewis, *In Their Own Interests: Race, Class, and Power in Twentieth-Century Norfolk, Virginia* (Berkeley and Los Angeles: University of California Press, 1991), 197.

49. "Stop Being a Sucker," *Atlanta Daily World*, 27 October 1951, 6.

50. "Courier Records Top 1950 Events in Pictures, Stories," *Pittsburgh Courier*, 30 December 1950, 20.

51. "Townsend Visits a Different Kind of Court in Miami, Fla.," *Chicago Defender*, 2 February 1952, 11; Chapman, "The History of the Black Police Force," 125.

52. Ernesto Longa, "Lawson Edward Thomas and Miami's Negro Municipal Court," *St. Thomas Law Review* 18 (2005): 125–38, quote on 128.

53. Office of the Miami City Clerk, *Resolutions and Minutes of the City Commission, 1921–1986*, 15 October 1952, Box 42, SAF; Fred Fejes, "Murder, Perversion, and Moral Panic: The 1954 Media Campaign against Miami's Homosexuals and the Discourse of Sexual Betterment," *Journal of the History of Sexuality* 9(3) (July 2000): 305–47.

54. Gary M. Mormino, "Midas Returns: Miami Goes to War, 1941–1945," *Tequesta* 57 (1997): 5–51.

55. Longa, "Lawson Edward Thomas," 132.

56. City of Miami Resolutions, "Resolutions 25992–26025 11/4/1953," Box 43, RG 800000 Series L 2, SAF.

57. Jim Howe, "Rev. Edward T. Graham Used Cunning to Help Integrate Beach Hotels," *Miami Times*, 6 October–12 October 2004, 4A.

58. "Miami Beach Hotels Welcome NEA Negro Delegates," *Pittsburgh Courier*, 11 July 1953, 19; "Miracle in Miami Beach," *Pittsburgh Courier*, 26 September 1953, 8.

59. "Assembled in Miami," *Atlanta Daily World*, 10 April 1956, 1; "$2 Million Spent by AMEs in Miami," *Pittsburgh Courier*, 26 May 1956, A47.

60. "Evidence Taken before the Citizen's Committee of the City of Miami, State of Florida on Tuesday, August 25, 1953, at 12:45 o'clock P.M., room 221 of Shoreland Building, Miami, Florida," 193, City of Miami Resolutions, Box 43, SAF.

61. "Rogers Says," *Pittsburgh Courier*, 21 February 1953, 8.

62. "No Fla. Law Found for Hotel Bias," *Atlanta Daily World*, 5 May 1956, 1.

63. "Dade NAACP Puts Shoe on Other Foot," *Miami News*, 4 March 1962, 12A.

64. "Million-Dollar Negro Hotel is Planned in Fla.," *Atlanta Daily World*, 4 October 1953, 1; "Past Glory Fades into History," *Sun-Sentinel*, 18 February 2001, 1A.

65. "Report on 'The Colonnades': Proposed Recreation and Convention Center, Virginia Key, Miami, Florida" (Miami, Fla., 1961), 5.

66. "Raids Smash Miami Gaming Joints in Half-Mile Amusement District," *Chicago Defender (National edition) (1921–1967)*, 14 February 1953, 5.

67. "Speech Material FEPC," "General Information Concerning FEPC 1950, 52–53" Folder, Box 302, George A. Smathers Papers, UF.

68. "Judge Tells Students: Strike at Local Level," *Chicago Defender*, 11 November 1950, 11.

69. "Negro Citizens' League Board Counsels Against Bus Boycott," *Miami News*, 14 June 1956, 8B.

70. "Police Protected Racket Charged by Miami Officers," *Atlanta Daily World*, 13 February 1960, 1; "Says Negro Cops Hit Florida Racket," *Chicago Defender*, 15 February 1960, A3; Office of the Miami City Clerk, *Resolutions and Minutes of the City Commission, 1921–1986*, 5 July 1955, Box 46, SAF.

71. "2 More Tell of Bolita," *Miami News*, 16 February 1960, 1A.

72. "Ex-Judge Wins Acquittal for Wife in Murder," *Jet*, 31 May 1962, 54.

73. Leonard S. Coleman, Jr., and Stephan Carter Cook, "The Failures of Minority Capitalism: The Edapco Case," *Phylon* 37(1) (1st Qtr., 1976): 44–58, 44.

74. Juliet E. K. Walker, *The History of Black Business in America: Capitalism, Race, and Entrepreneurship* (New York: Simon and Schuster MacMillan, 1998); Weare, *Black Business in the New South*.

75. See, for instance, William H. Chafe, *Civilities and Civil Rights: Greensboro, North Carolina and the Black Struggle for Freedom* (New York: Oxford University Press, 1980), and Elizabeth Jacoway and Davis R. Colburn, *Southern Businessmen and Desegregation* (Baton Rouge: Louisiana State University Press, 1982).

8

The End of Public Power

The Politics of Place and the Postwar Electric Utility Industry

ANDREW NEEDHAM

"Sure I'm a taxpayer," said Gene Mason, "who isn't?" According to the December 1962 issue of *Spark and Flame*, the newsletter of Arizona Public Service Company (APS), the suburban Phoenix auto shop owner paid annual property taxes of $110, income taxes of $600, and $22 to license and register his car. Paying those taxes, Mason insisted, was part of being a "proud American. . . I believe in paying my fair share, even if my taxes go up." *Spark and Flame* suggested, however, that Mason's tax burden was far from equitable. The electric utility's newsletter contended that taxes in metropolitan Phoenix were high because its public competitor, the Salt River Project (SRP), paid no property taxes. While APS paid taxes of $765,866 on its power plant in Tempe, SRP enjoyed a complete tax exemption on its $45 million Agua Fria plant. *Spark and Flame* calculated that local schools would receive almost $200,000 more in funding, and Gene Mason's taxes "would drop sharply," if SRP paid "its fair share." On its final page, *Spark and Flame* painted the public utility as a bad citizen, harming all other citizens of the Valley of the Sun. "Isn't it time," the newsletter asked, "the Salt River Project paid its fair share of taxes *just like the rest of us?*"[1]

The language of *Spark and Flame* seems familiar. Decrying the inefficiencies and excesses of the public sector, "taxpayer politics" have formed a key aspect of political history since the 1970s. Taxpayer politics came to national attention through three intertwined political phenomena during that decade. First, suburban "tax revolts" became significant political movements, challenging rising property taxes and constraining public sector expansion. Second, cities across the nation descended into fiscal crisis, with blame falling widely on welfare programs and public employee unions. And, as many essays in this volume demonstrate, businessmen became more engaged in national politics, casting themselves as allies of individual taxpayers while promulgating a gospel of free enterprise.[2]

While the rhetoric of *Spark and Flame* fits well within current accounts of rise of taxpayer politics, its timing does not. The newsletter appeared more than a decade before the passage of California's Proposition 13. APS's formulation of taxpayers also differed from later portraits that emphasized grassroots groups of homeowners. Instead, the utility evoked a broad alliance of taxpayers, individual and corporate, opposed to government overreach. As APS's newsletter claimed, "We both must pay for businesses such as the Salt River Power District who do not shoulder their fair share of the tax burden."[3] These differences did not mean APS's campaign failed to find an audience. Repeated in mailings, in radio ads, and in the pages of the local newspapers, such rhetoric eventually led to passage of a 1963 bill that compelled SRP to make "voluntary" payments to the state in lieu of taxes. APS's taxpayer-oriented campaign brought about, in effect, the end of state policies granting preference to public power.

The conflict between SRP and APS, and between public and private utilities more generally in Arizona, holds important lessons about the relationship between business and politics on the local level. First, the private sector's role in the emergence of "taxpayer politics" needs broader examination over the entire postwar era. The case of postwar Phoenix suggests that local businesses appealed to taxpayer identities as an effective tool against public sector competition and, more generally, the legacies of the New Deal long before tax revolts of the 1970s brought them to national prominence. Second, business's political campaigns must be understood in space and place, as well as time. APS possessed the ability to utilize taxpayer politics because of the company's prominent role in campaigns that transformed Phoenix spatially by attracting industry and manufacturing to the city. These efforts also created new places within metropolitan Phoenix. In subdivisions built on former farm fields, Phoenicians made places where calls for limited property taxes trumped arguments for the state support of public power, arguments that had gained state sanction only twenty years earlier.[4] Finally, APS's struggle with SRP highlights the ways in which the politics of metropolitan growth and the actions of business executives created new notions of corporate citizenship. Its role in promotional efforts that transformed Phoenix's economy and its campaign in support of the city's taxpayers allowed APS to claim that, true to its name, it provided broad service to the public while also contributing to local tax coffers.

The formation of the Salt River Project spurred Phoenix's growth early in the twentieth century. In 1903, landowners outside the small city of Phoenix formed the Salt River Water Users' Association (WUA), the antecedent to the Salt River

Project. For the previous generation, the river's irregular flow had plagued Phoenix's farmers, alternately desiccating and flooding their lands. The 1902 Reclamation Act provided a solution. Mortgaging their lands and incorporating as the WUA, the Salt River Valley's farmers financed the construction of Roosevelt Dam, 70 miles upstream from Phoenix. The dam regulated the river, and the WUA provided water to its members' 250,000 acres of farmland. With the dam's completion, valley agriculture boomed. No longer vulnerable to drought and flood, farmers growing cotton, citrus, winter vegetables, and even rice, profited from the high commodity prices that accompanied World War I. With the field's new productivity, the Water Users' Association expanded operations rapidly in the 1910s and 1920s, building three additional dams and new irrigation works.[5]

Like Roosevelt Dam, the dams begun in the 1910s and 1920s served multiple purposes. They not only provided flood control and water storage. They also transformed the energy of falling water into electricity. The sale of electricity to local mines and private utilities helped defray the cost of expansion, largely covering interest payments during the 1920s, with water charges paying principle on the farmers' indebtedness. Electrical generation benefited the farmers in other ways. By 1930, 80% of the Salt River Valley's farmers had access to electricity, far beyond the 25% of farmers nationwide.[6] With electric power, farmers could pump groundwater, allowing further expansion, along with operating myriad labor-saving devices. The WUA's electrical operations remained primitive. As late as 1946, electrical customers received power at a 25-cycle frequency, causing lights to flicker and requiring specialized electric appliances. As south Phoenix resident Ruth Stanley remembered, "When we moved out here, it was only 25-cycle, you know. . . . And oh, it was such a nuisance. . . . We had to replace all our . . . motors."[7]

The WUA was not alone in the Salt River Valley. Arizona Public Service's predecessor, the Central Arizona Light and Power Company (CALAPCO), served the valley's small cities. According to the terms of a 1928 agreement negotiated with the WUA, CALAPCO served all customers within the city limits of Phoenix, Tempe, and three other small towns, while the WUA provided water and power to 250,000 acres of agricultural land. Those cities' small size left CALAPCO's service area quite small. Phoenix occupied only 9.6 square miles as of 1930, and most of the valley's land fell under the authority of the WUA. This arrangement proved cost-effective for the private utility, requiring few expensive line extensions to rural users whom private utilities believed made poor customers.[8]

Like most investor-owned utilities in the 1920s, CALAPCO was a subsidiary of a holding company. North American Light and Power owned controlling shares in CALAPCO and seventy-nine other private electrical companies scattered around the nation.[9] Directed by Wall Street investment firms, such holding companies controlled 85% of the nation's electrical power by 1928. This structure limited the expansion of electrical service in Phoenix, as holding companies with-held capital funding for utilities that possessed potential for rapid expansion.[10] Phoenix's economy, dominated by agriculture and winter tourism, seemed to have little potential for rapid growth.[11]

Nevertheless, beginning in the late 1920s, CALAPCO gained an increasing share of the local electricity market. The farm crisis of the 1920s hit local farmers hard. As commodity prices fell, farmers struggled to make water payments, and the WUA relied on revenue from electrical sales to both support operations and to service debt, leaving little ability to expand electrical operations. With its growth essentially stalled by the farm crisis, CALAPCO sold the WUA increasing amounts of power, leaving the public utility with increasing levels of debt.

Even as CALAPCO came to dominate electrical supply in Phoenix, the New Deal began to change the balance of power between public and private electric companies. Reformers had long believed that democratizing electricity's distribution and increasing domestic use would produce both social moderniza-tion and regional development. New Deal policies combined these aims with efforts to provide public competition for private companies. The Tennessee Valley Authority, Bonneville Power Authority, and Rural Electrification Agency gave far-reaching power to new public agencies, enabling the construction of public works and permitting the condemnation and capture of private electrical infrastructure. Such policies also reflected Franklin Roosevelt's disdain for the "power trust." Campaigning for the presidency, Roosevelt charged holding com-panies with cheating customers and manipulating the nation's capital markets. The New Deal thus sparked the resurgence of public power, languishing since the 1910s. Between 1932 and 1937, sixty new municipal power systems and 741 electrical cooperatives were created while eighteen states, including Arizona, authorized the creation of public utility districts.[12]

The New Deal's support for public power brought two key changes to Phoe-nix. First, it led the Arizona legislature to change the WUA's political standing. Fearing that increasing payments to CALAPCO would hamper the utility's ability to deliver water, the legislature sought to isolate the provision of water from the distribution of electricity to limit the WUA's debt service. In 1937, the legislature split the WUA into two municipal districts, the Salt River Project Agricultural Improvement District and the Salt River Power District. Although these districts became collectively known as the Salt River Project, they had dif-ferent missions. The Agricultural Improvement District would supply water to valley farms, and the Power District would generate and distribute electricity. Electrical proceeds would continue, however, to underwrite the costs of irriga-tion. The new districts were classified as municipal subdivisions of the state, allowed to refinance debt through tax-exempt municipal bonds. As a munici-pality, SRP's properties—irrigation ditches, electrical transmission lines, and power plants—were exempt from taxation. By "municipalizing" project lands and granting the capacity to offer tax-free bonds, the state legislature freed SRP from interest payments that had stymied expansion. While the Power District was free to construct its own sources of electrical generation, it also retained priority rights to power generated at federally sponsored projects.[13]

Such projects created the second change in SRP's operations. The construction of new dams on the Colorado River represented the New Deal's use of public works to spur both immediate recovery and regional economic development. While the construction of Boulder (Hoover), Parker, and Davis Dams employed capital and labor stilled by Depression, their generating capacity could meet almost all of the electrical demand of southern California and Arizona in 1940. Public agencies, including SRP, possessed preference rights to purchase electricity generated at the dams, electricity New Dealers hoped would serve as a "yardstick" for electrical rates.[14] At the dedication of Boulder Dam in 1935, Franklin Roosevelt articulated the broader philosophy that linked these projects: "To employ workers and materials when private employment has failed is to translate into great national possessions the energy that otherwise would be wasted. Boulder Dam is a splendid symbol of that principle. The mighty waters of the Colorado were running unused to the sea. Today we translate them into a great national possession." By treating capital, labor, and nature as "national possessions" managed in the public interest, federal support for public power would spur both immediate recovery and long-term growth.[15]

Many in Phoenix embraced the promise of public power. Soon after completion of Boulder Dam, a newly formed group, the Boulder Dam Power Transmission Association, began advocating the construction of power lines to carry the dam's electricity to central Arizona. Boldly declaring, "ELECTRIC ENERGY IS AS NECESSARY AS WATER AND AIR FOR THE EXISTANCE OF MODERN ECONOMIC LIFE," the Transmission Association portrayed the dam's power as enabling the region's economic modernization. The dam's power would allow farmers to tap deep aquifers, bringing additional acreage under development. It would also attract manufacturing, diversifying the valley's economy. Finally, the Transmission Association touted Boulder Dam's potential to support SRP. As the Association's newsletter stated, "The Central Arizona Light & Power Co. is consistently forging ahead in the power business as the Water Users [*sic*] Association is being forced into a secondary position." Securing power from Boulder Dam would allow SRP to "bring about the re-establishment of the Water Users as the dominating factor in the power business in Central Arizona, a position which it once held."[16]

Such beliefs reflected the view among many in Phoenix that SRP was vital to local economic development. Controlled by valley landowners, SRP represented local interests, understood local conditions, and had a history of spurring

local development, unlike CALAPCO, whose policies were determined by a dis-
tant holding company. Empowering SRP also promised to help Arizona claim its
rights to the Colorado River's water and electrical resources, preventing California
from claiming the entire river as many Arizonans feared.[17] Despite these arguments, a coalition of conservative "Pinto" Democrats and Republicans blocked
the appropriations necessary to build power lines bringing Boulder Dam's electricity to Phoenix. The perception that CALAPCO had underwritten the opposition exacerbated mistrust of private utilities among many in Phoenix. As one
Phoenician stated, the failed passage "shows Central Light has little interest for
the area and its future."[18]

The onset of World War II made the legislative defeat a temporary setback.
With Phoenix a military training and manufacturing center, the Bureau of Reclamation rushed to complete transmission lines connecting Phoenix with Parker
Dam. During the war, both SRP and CALAPCO used this power, as federal authorities suspended preference policies for the duration. The reinstitution of
preference policies after the war, however, gave SRP first claim on hydropower
from Colorado River dams. Following the war, the public utility undertook an
extensive reconstruction program, replacing its obsolete 25-cycle system with
the standard 60-cycle system to meet the needs of an increasingly residential
consumer base. No longer would SRP customers have to purchase specialized
appliances or suffer flickering lights.[19] One element of the valley's electrical business remained unchanged at the conclusion of the war. The two utilities continued to serve customers who lived in very different landscapes. SRP provided
most of its power to the valley's irrigated farms. CALAPCO served consumers
within Phoenix itself. With the postwar growth of Phoenix, however, those
geographies would change as well.

Phoenix boomed in the years following World War II. Attracting defense
industries, workers, retirees, and other migrants, the city's population increased
from 65,000 in 1940 to almost 600,000 by 1970. As with other Sunbelt cities,
Phoenix's growth was a political project. As Elizabeth Shermer details elsewhere
in this volume, the city's business elite gained control of local government and
transformed the structure of local government to attract manufacturing capital.
As she explains, boosters pursued cuts in taxes directed at business and
manufacturing that reflected the consensus of a broader cadre of industrial location strategists. These growth strategies were markedly successful in Phoenix.
Where manufacturing accounted for less than $5 million of Phoenix's annual
revenue in 1940, it had displaced agriculture and tourism by 1960 to become the
most lucrative sector of the local economy, bringing in over $600 million in an-
nual revenue.

Arizona Public Service aided and abetted this growth. In 1945, a number of
Phoenix businessmen gained control of CALAPCO after the breakup of North

American Light and Power under the terms of the Public Utility Holding Company Act (PUHCA) of 1935. The New Deal's main strike against the power trust, PUHCA broke apart holding companies serving "no demonstrably useful and necessary purpose." In the law's implementation, geographical continuity became the primary criteria for evaluating holding companies; henceforth, utilities would be required to operate within a single state or a single, contiguous area. The act also forbid agents of Wall Street firms from occupying seats on utilities' boards of directors. Both elements of the law, then, aimed at connecting private companies to local communities as a means of stemming the industry's abusive practices.[20] To satisfy these regulations, investment banks sought out local businessmen to serve as directors of the independent subsidiaries. In 1945, the SEC directed the break up of North American Power and Light. George Woods, the president of the investment bank managing the divestiture, approached a group of Phoenix businessmen organized by lawyer Frank Snell. Woods indicated that Snell had found a group of "good people . . . interested in bringing back management of Central Arizona Light and Power to Phoenix" and offered the group a fifty cent discount on stock price in exchange for serving on CALAPCO's board. The subsequent stock offering indicated that having "good people" in management was important, as the investment bank raised its offer price by a quarter point after Snell accepted.[21]

In a state like Arizona with a small business community, PUHCA's stress on local control led to the consolidation of private utilities. After its sale, CALAPCO sought to expand its customer base by purchasing Northern Arizona Light and Power Company. Snell was also invited to join Arizona Edison's board of directors, along with four other members of CALAPCO's board. When the southern Arizona utility faced financial difficulties in 1951, the overlapping boards agreed to merge the companies, forming Arizona Public Service in 1952.[22]

The new utility emphasized its local ties. Its annual report stressed that its board of "business people who have spent a large or greater part of their lives in Arizona" stood ready to introduce industries to Phoenix and Arizona. "Familiar with the areas in which they live . . . and acquainted personally with many customers," the report explained, "the company's directors know the problems and opportunities of all segments of the state's economy." With businesses "becoming increasingly aware that there is plenty of room in Arizona for industries that want to grow and prosper with the west," the utility touted the state as "a frontier with a future."[23]

APS quickly became a vital cog in Phoenix's growth machine. The company employed several of the scouts recruiting industries to Phoenix. Many board members and executives were active in Phoenix's Chamber of Commerce, with APS president Walter Lucking serving a term as chairman in the mid-1950s.

Frank Snell, the utility's primary attorney, was one of Phoenix's key boosters, a man able, one Phoenician remembered, to make local policy "over lunch at the Arizona Club."[24] In addition to participating in the Chamber's industrial re-cruitment campaigns, APS produced its own promotional material. Its bro-chure, *Industry Views of Phoenix's Valley of the Sun*, profiled high-tech industries that had moved to Phoenix, detailing the opportunities for growth that they enjoyed. So that the point was not lost, the first page of the brochure announced, "Industry, Energy, and Progress," and conveyed APS's promise that "no matter what form it may take, Public Service pledges to provide adequate supplies of ENERGY—economically—to meet the future requirements of Arizona's dynamic progress."[25]

Attracting new residents and industries was not only important to Phoenix's economy, it was central to APS's business strategy. In the early 1950s, APS began utilizing "build and grow," a development strategy for electrical utilities pio-neered by Samuel Insull in the 1920s. The strategy called for utilities to build new power plants in advance of existing electrical demand. With generation and transmission technology steadily improving until the late 1960s, new plants reduced production costs while creating increased economies of scale. As gener-ating costs decreased, utilities lowered rates, which in turn spurred greater con-sumption. In theory, "build and grow" thus led to a downward price spiral and rising utility profits.[26]

During the 1950s, APS built three new generating plants to replace aging infrastructure. At the same time, the company sought to increase demand. APS partnered with homebuilders to sponsor model "all-electric" homes, featuring refrigerated air conditioning, as well as a full range of appliances, in the annual Phoenix home show. APS backed efforts to increase domestic consumption with advertising campaigns featuring Reddy Kilowatt, the cartoon mascot of investor-owned utilities, emphasizing the benefits of inexpensive electricity. One ad from 1953 boasted: "No other family servant will do so much for so little! For only a nickel, Reddy will do five loads of laundry, vacuum the house for a month, do the dishes for two days or provide five full evenings of radio en-tertainment." Two years later, the utility rewarded the homebuilder who pro-moted "the utmost in modern electric living" at the annual Phoenix home show with a two-week, all expenses paid trip to Hawai'i.[27] Such promotional efforts reflected an industry-wide faith in utilities' ability to increase demand. Industry journals featured articles entitled "Sell or Die!" and "Sell—and Sell—and Sell," and one company president told an industry audience in 1964, "The most impor-tant elements that determine our loads are not those that happen, but those that we project—that we invent—in the broad sense of the term 'invention.' You have control over such loads: you invent them, and then you can make plans for the best manner of meeting them."[28]

The combination of "build and grow" and rapid suburbanization raised new conflicts between the utilities. The 1928 territorial agreement between CALAPCO and SRP limited APS's service area to the valley's cities, granting SRP rights to the 250,000 acres that constituted the original lands of the Water Users' Association. In 1928, this agreement had recognized the clear borders between the valley's agricultural and urban development. By the early 1950s, these borders proved less distinct. Much of Phoenix's new industrial and residential development occurred in SRP's service area. As with Levittown's potato fields, the former citrus and cotton fields north of the Grand Canal proved an ideal location for subdivisions, manufacturing plants, and commercial strips.[29] Unincorporated farmland also became city property as the City of Phoenix annexed many new developments. Between 1950 and 1960, Phoenix grew from 17 to almost 150 square miles.[30] Nearby cities such as Tempe, Scottsdale, and Peoria also annexed SRP territory. These annexations created overlapping jurisdictions between SRP and the valley's cities, blurring the lines between suburb and farm.

Who held the right to provide electrical service in these newly annexed lands? APS lawyers contended that the utility's service area had expanded in concert with the city. SRP countered that its borders remained unchanged regardless of annexation. This territorial dispute held important consequences for both utilities. Absent these customers, APS executives feared generation would far exceed demand, leaving the utility short of revenue. SRP shared similar concerns. In the early 1950s, the public utility pursued its own version of build and grow, building new natural-gas fired power plants in Tempe and Peoria and running its own advertisements in the *Arizona Republic* promoting the domestic use of electricity.[31] For a time in the early 1950s, northwest Phoenix became somewhat of an electrical no-man's-land. Both utilities rushed to connect new subdivisions to their systems. With competition threatening to entangle the two utilities' service areas, the utilities reached a new agreement in the summer of 1955. SRP agreed to refrain from expanding beyond the Project's original 250,000 acres and allowed APS to serve areas of northern Scottsdale and Peoria. It retained, however, service in the vast majority of the Project land annexed by the city. The utilities also agreed to new interconnections between their power plants, defraying some concerns about oversupply.[32]

The agreement ratified SRP's dual nature as both a supplier of irrigation water to the valley's irrigated farmers and an electrical utility serving suburban consumers. The effects of this transition can be seen in the rapid change in SRP's business between 1949 and 1964. In 1949, SRP supplied power to 17,391 residential and 1,068 industrial and commercial customers. Almost half of its electrical sales (349,985 out of 716,104 kilowatt hours) went to the 743 irrigated farms it served. Over the next fifteen years, the number of residential, commercial, and industrial customers served by SRP increased dramatically, rising to

109,823 residential and 10,977 industrial and commercial customers, while the number of irrigated farms receiving SRP electricity actually fell by more than half to 360. By 1964, irrigation-related sales had dropped to 14% of SRP's business.[33] Residential and industrial sales increasingly subsidized water costs. As early as 1952, revenue from the sale of electricity allowed SRP to reduce agricultural water charges.[34]

The changes to SRP's customer base during the immediate postwar years suggest the origins of the new conflicts between public and private power in Phoenix. Previously, SRP and APS/CALAPCO had served very different customers. Founded to serve the valley's farms, SRP retained its association with agriculture into the early postwar years. CALAPCO and APS had supplied most city dwellers. As farm fields became subdivisions and as ranch homes lined irrigation canals, however, the utilities began to serve similar populations. Territorial lines that had once delineated the borders between city and country now became a series of seemingly arbitrary lines within metropolitan Phoenix. Neighbors living on the opposite sides of Phoenix's 8th Avenue, or Tempe's Weber Road, paid their electric bills to different companies. As APS attorney Frank Snell later suggested, this situation posed a danger to SRP's agricultural customers. "Farmland became urban, it became houses. . . . And the result is that they have what? . . . Maybe 2/3 less farm land than 25 years ago, and that, someday, will be a problem. . . . I'm gonna wonder how long the rate payers are gonna let farmers be subsidized."[35]

Conflict over suburban customers also sparked APS's campaign to challenge the benefits SRP received as a public utility. CALAPCO and APS had avoided the attacks on public power that characterized much of the private utility industry. In one such attack, Raymond Moley, a Roosevelt advisor who split with the New Deal over its power policy, wrote that subsidy for public power inevitably led to a situation where "private property is absorbed, and the springs of free expression and education are polluted by government propaganda." APS, however, deferred to the broad support for subsidizing irrigation water in the arid Salt River Valley.[36] Executives from the companies were also personally acquainted, with many participating in the Phoenix Chamber of Commerce. After the 1955 agreement, however, APS's approach changed. In 1956, APS began an ongoing campaign to challenge the "unfair" advantages that SRP received. Buoyed by support from Eugene Pulliam, the conservative publisher of the *Arizona Republic*, APS began posing SRP's electrical business as "a first step toward socialism." Following Moley's lead, *Republic* editorials posed public power as the first step toward the death private enterprise itself. As one editorial contended, "If you study these matters, you'll see that government ownership of utilities is only the beginning; government ownership of all national industries is the aim."[37]

The most hyperbolic use of such rhetoric appeared in a November 1958 advertisement in the *Arizona Republic*. Readers turning to page ten found a boy staring glumly at a Bible, a key, a pencil, and a ballot. "Half of the world is trying to destroy these four symbols and what they stand for. Even in this country there are people who threaten our freedoms," the copy read. Going on, the ad pointed at public power as a dangerous step "down the road to socialism." It went on to warn, "If socialism comes to America this way—step by step," the ad concluded, "you'll never have a chance to vote for or against it. By that time, government will control your job, your independence, your thinking. Then you'll have precious little freedom to pass on to your children."[38]

What accounts for this change in APS's stance toward SRP? Partially, the utility's use of the rhetoric of anticommunism reflected the changing tone of the city's political culture in the 1950s. With Pulliam's purchase of both the *Arizona Republic* and *Phoenix Gazette* in 1946, the editorial pages of both papers issued forth attacks on centralized government and paeans to private enterprise on a daily basis. Pulliam's papers represented the key element of support for the Charter Government Committee, a Chamber-backed political slating committee that dominated local government throughout the era by running on platforms of "business-friendly" local government. The arrival of defense industry migrants also helped to deepen a political environment friendly to anticommunism.[39]

Most important for APS executives, however, was resentment over what they viewed as the unfair advantages enjoyed by SRP. These beliefs trumped the personal relationships forged in Phoenix's growth politics. Troubled by APS's attacks, R. J. McMullin, SRP's general manager, wrote to his counterpart Walter Lucking that the utilities shared "men of good will" and "friends apart from our present dispute." Playing on their shared membership in Phoenix's Chamber of Commerce, McMullin suggested negotiation to reach a "mutually beneficial solution." "Personalities and ideologies must be laid aside," McMullin wrote, "and we must sit down together with an honest and dedicated determination to achieve results."[40] Lucking rejected McMullin's proposal out of hand. "No arrangements, agreements or understandings between our Boards can eliminate the real danger of public power being substituted for private enterprise in this state," Lucking wrote. "The real problem is due to the fact that there are substantial economic inequalities between the operations of the two organizations which cannot be corrected or rectified solely by respect, cooperation, and trust."[41] Whatever the ties between the two boards, the different treatment of the two utilities created an irresolvable dispute in Lucking's view.

In one sense, Lucking had a point. By the late 1950s, SRP and APS shared similar customers and business models. Both were building new power plants and extending their businesses significantly. APS, however, had seen its growth slow in the late 1950s. While the private utility had increased its sales of electricity by

21% and 23% in 1955 and 1956, respectively, the recession of the late 1950s slowed its sales growth to 0.5% in 1957 and 5% in 1958, while SRP's sales grew by 21% and 13% in those same years as growth in former agricultural land continued.[42] Given this climate, APS's tax bill, upwards of $6 million by the late 1950s, rankled its officials. With the utilities offering almost identical prices for electricity, those taxes represented lost revenue and, to APS executives, blatant favoritism. That the two utilities' prices remained almost identical, despite APS's decrease in sales was, however, the point of the New Deal's support for public power. Tax exemptions were a means, along with preference rights to purchase low cost power from federal projects, to regulate the price of electricity. With electrical prices measured by the "yardstick" of public power, consumers would not be subject to rapid price changes and the benefits of electricity could be broadly enjoyed.[43]

SRP remained difficult to attack for reasons apart from general arguments in favor of public power. Despite the opposition of the Pulliam papers, many Arizonans from across the political spectrum remained supportive of SRP. Indeed, in 1961, Barry Goldwater presented a glowing tribute to SRP in the *Los Angeles Times*. The utility, Goldwater wrote, exemplified the appropriate relationship between local initiative and federal assistance. Emphasizing its local control, Goldwater contended that SRP symbolized "the proper kind of partnership between a free people and their government . . . with local interests solving their own problems in co-operation with the federal government." Goldwater's column emphasized the utility's central role in "making the desert bloom." While Goldwater remained neutral on the tax issue, his column encapsulated SRP's public relations efforts, writing that the utility "has been tremendously successful and we locals do take pride in the accomplishment of our valley."[44]

Goldwater's column reflected a lifetime spent in arid Phoenix, where water remained central to state politics. It also likely reflected his relationship with Steven Shadegg, manager of and main speechwriter for Goldwater's Senate campaigns in 1952 and 1958. Hired by SRP in 1959 to craft political strategy, Shadegg advised the utility to take the offensive, demonstrating the advantages that SRP provided to suburban consumers. As he wrote in a memo to Rod McMullin, "Isn't competition the American way of life? Doesn't competition always result in public benefit? If the public gains by competition in every other form of business, why isn't competition a healthy thing in the utility business in Central Arizona?" Indeed, one radio script penned by Shadegg stated, "This healthy competition provided by the Salt River Project prevents the people of Central Arizona from being dominated by a monopoly and assures the power users in both territories the benefit of low-cost competitive rates." Where SRP had previously downplayed its competition with APS, Shadegg advised SRP to "take credit for what we are accused of and build on the point that we lead the way in low rates. . . . The public will soon stop thinking competition is unfair when they understand the benefit to them—in low power rates."[45] While he did not suggest that SRP should evoke the New Deal in making the case for public power, Shadegg told the company to embrace its underlying logic.

And Shadegg's advice did point to a critical weakness in APS's case against SRP. The public may have believed that SRP enjoyed competitive advantages over APS. Pulliam's editorials likely convinced many local readers, especially new residents unfamiliar with the history of water control, that those advantages were unfair. Indeed, Rod McMullin lamented in one letter that "monopoly is a forgotten word" in the public debate.[46] APS, however, provided little explanation of the negative effects of public power. By contrast, SRP pointed to direct benefits to consumers—lower electric rates—while suggesting its power operations kept water flowing to the valley.

In 1962, however, APS turned to a strategy that posed SRP as taking advantage of Phoenix's homeowners. That year, SRP cut electricity rates by 15%, a result of new economies of scale created by the completion of Agua Fria Powerplant, creating a price differential between the utilities. APS posed SRP's rate reduction, however, as harmful to taxpayers and the larger communities in which they lived. While SRP executives argued the cuts resulted from efficient management and business acumen, APS claimed that rates were cut on the backs of taxpayers. As one editorial reprinted in APS's management newsletter argued, "The Salt River Power District recently reduced rates to a level considerably lower than Arizona Public Service. . . . This gave the impression customers were being charged exhorbitant [sic] rates," overlooking "the fact that the private firms were paying millions in taxes to school districts, and city, county, and state governments."[47] Frank Snell recalled, "We found that there were others who were quite upset, such as school districts. A school district would have one of our power plants in and be rich; another would have just as big a plant in from the Project and didn't get a dime."[48] While SRP might provide low rates, APS increasingly suggested the utility's tax exemptions harmed the broader community.

APS's advertisements made such arguments directly. "Another Day, Another $20,000 Working for You," announced one ad showing the utility's checks to city and county treasurers. APS, the ad boasted, had paid over $7 million in state and local taxes in 1961 alone. "This money is at work right now, a benefit to all Arizonans. The Salt River Power District pays *none* of these taxes on its electrical system, thus adding to the tax burden of every citizen of Arizona." Another ad pictured a teacher and student, explaining that APS paid almost $4 million toward local schools in 1961. Other ads showing bombers and missiles reminded readers that APS's taxes went to support the local aerospace industry. APS also publicized that its tax payments offset those of local residents, explaining that tax payments made by Ocotillo Power Plant reduced the school tax burden of

Tempe residents by almost $100 per year and adding that taxes would be reduced another $32.12 if SRP made similar payments. "YOU ARE AFFECTED BY THESE TAXES!" APS material proclaimed, "They let you and me pay their taxes for them."[49]

APS's 1962 campaign transformed the company's case into a populist crusade on behalf of taxpayers, homeowners, and school parents, targeting the key components of suburban political identity.[50] Unlike earlier campaigns, in which APS had been a party wronged in disputes between competing businesses, its 1962 campaign used a new language of corporate citizenship. This discourse used tax payment to create new connections between APS and homeowners. At the same time, it colored SRP's tax exemptions as a mark of civic irresponsibility. APS suggested SRP shirked its duty to fund roads, schools, and the nation's defense, betraying principles of suburban citizenship while driving suburban tax bills even higher.[51]

APS also worked to undermine the political capital SRP gained from providing water to both valley farmers and to Phoenix residents.[52] Continually referring to "the Salt River Power District" rather than "the Salt River Project," APS sought to separate the provision of water from the generation of power. While SRP insisted power sales funded its ability to supply water, APS officials argued that SRP had become primarily an electric utility and pointed out that 84% of its electricity went to "general utility customers in the same manner as APS."[53] As Walter Lucking stated in a letter to the *Arizona Republic*, "No one questions the tax exempt status of SRPD's electrical operation that are connected with irrigation. . . . But in these days of increased taxes on individuals and businesses alike, every taxpayer must seek out all possible additional tax revenue sources to help him carry the mounting tax burden." SRP, Lucking suggested, was little more than a tax evader. "No one should be fooled into believing that tax exemptions for water development should be carried over to normal, profitable business ventures."[54] Pulliam put the matter more directly: "We part company with those who use water development as a springboard for free-loading tax-free electrical operations that *do not serve agriculture*."[55] Some local residents even began questioning the wisdom of subsidizing agricultural irrigation. One winter resident of Phoenix wrote, "So far as this helps a handful of big farmers, we can see no merit in the 'cheap water' claims."[56] While APS officials never went that far—subsidizing irrigation remained a "laudable venture" in Lucking's words—it succeeded tying SRP's tax exemptions to beliefs that suburban homeowners carried excessive tax burdens.[57]

The 1963 legislative session demonstrated the effectiveness of APS's campaign. Governor Paul Fannin's opening remarks called for the taxation of SRP. Shadegg's account of the ensuing legislative session recounted that "the intensity of the issue was near fever pitch." With newspapers around the state "flooded" with letters demanding the Project be taxed, "the entire controversy," Shadegg reported, "was charged with emotion and marked by oversimplification. Our position depended on reason and patience in order to be explained, but the clamor of the Project's antagonists would not permit any rational analysis of the problem."[58]

On 28 February, Fannin appointed a committee to determine a means of taxing SRP. The committee, however, discovered that eliminating the exemptions was not as simple as it may have appeared. At its first hearing, SRP officials presented letters from Moody's, Standard and Poor's, and other municipal bond brokers. Those letters warned that taxing the utility would damage the credit rating of not only SRP, but every public entity in Arizona seeking bonded investment. As the president of Wainwright and Ramsey stated, "Any attempt by State legislators to impose added taxation on public bodies would be expected to bring into focus swift adverse reaction. . . . Many of the largest buyers of municipal bonds would not even consider a bond of an Arizona community." Faced with the letters, the committee quickly rejected the direct taxation of SRP.[59]

The bond agencies did, however, suggest a compromise. A Standard and Poor's analyst wrote that "many projects make a substantial payment 'in lieu of taxes' to the communities in which they operate." While such payments would increase rates and "make your customers unhappy," he wrote that the bond market "largely ignores the payments. . . . where these payments are junior to debt service."[60] The governor's committee presented these "in lieu" payments as the solution to the issue. Its report recommended that SRP make "voluntary" payments, in the amount of $11,245,000 over a five-year period, an amount approximating the taxes SRP would pay on its non-irrigation properties. The report characterized the payments as SRP's moral and ethical duty "to help relieve the heavy tax burdens" on Arizona taxpayers. Faced with unanimous committee approval, SRP mounted no opposition to the report. On 3 April, Fannin called a special session that passed legislation providing for "voluntary contributions by irrigation districts, power districts, electrical districts or agricultural improvement districts to the state and its political subdivisions to be used by the state and its political subdivisions as other revenue provided by taxation is used."[61]

While Shadegg portrayed the legislation as a "practical compromise," it represented a sea change in the state's official position toward SRP and public power more generally. Not long before, SRP had been regarded as perhaps the key institution underwriting the state's growth. In regulating the waters of the Salt River and supplying the valley's farmers, and in distributing much of Arizona's electric power from the Colorado River dams, SRP had connected Phoenix with Arizona's resource-rich hinterland and fueled the city's growth. The proclamation calling the special legislative session, however, portrayed SRP as failing to pay its "fair share of the cost of government." Despite the bond houses' warnings, it also envisioned direct taxation of publicly owned utilities, arguing "should any

district fail to make voluntary payments in accordance with the formula proposed, the State should, despite all legal implications and serious hazards therein,
undertake to impose an in lieu tax.. . . "[62] Above all, the proclamation signaled
changed attitudes in the state about the relationships between public power and
public service. Twenty years earlier, the state legislature had granted tax exemptions to public power districts to allow competition with private electrical companies. By 1963, a majority of state legislators, and much of the public, perceived
those tax exemptions as harming the state's taxpayers.

This change over time reveals two important issues in the historical relationship between business and politics. First, it reveals the withering effect that suburban "taxpayer" politics had upon the consumer politics of the New Deal. SRP
had drawn material support from New Deal policies that maintained public
competition protected consumers. As of the late 1950s, it had effectively used
the logic of those policies to counter attacks from APS. By the early 1960s, however, SRP no longer evoked consumer protection as a rationale for its tax-exempt
status. Instead, it stressed its mission of providing water in an arid climate. That
SRP abandoned consumer-based arguments suggests, in part, its executives' understanding of their company as primarily a water provider. Indeed, SRP officials
argued that conflict with APS would prevent the state from realizing the long
held dream of bringing Colorado River water to central Arizona.[63]

More importantly, SRP abandoned its consumerist rhetoric because of the
changing character of Phoenix. In the wake of the special legislative session, Steven Shadegg conducted a survey for SRP. His report argued that SRP suffered
from "The Problem of Image." Shadegg found that "most of the people living
within the Salt River Project have no real understanding of the Project." Homeowners, especially, perceived SRP as "just another electrical utility," or, even
worse, "a farmers' co-op operated to make cheap agricultural water available to a
handful of wealthy agriculturalists." While Shadegg advocated a number of strategies to improve SRP's image—a television series about Phoenix's history, a new
slogan, "Arizona grows where the water flows"—he argued that the real issue lay
in the transformation of the Salt River Valley since 1945. "The rush of new residents . . . the fantastic expansion of the urban areas" had changed Phoenix into a
place where homeowners concerns, and not those of farmers, held the balance
of power. Foremost among the concerns of those homeowners, Shadegg's report
discovered, was "excessive taxation for public services." These concerns over taxation called the public sector into question. The expanses of suburban homes
built in the formerly agricultural lands surrounding Phoenix, homes built
through New Deal housing policies, proved to be the places where the New Deal
logic of an empowered public sector that would curb the abuses of private utilities lost its public support. It was in those places that new notions of corporate
citizenship found purchase.

In the politics of the electrical business in postwar Phoenix, APS executives portrayed the utility as an overburdened taxpayer, articulating the same beliefs that Phoenix's homeowners articulated to Shadegg. Acceptance of the idea that corporations were citizens represented a dramatic political change since the 1930s in Phoenix and in the nation. During the New Deal, Franklin Roosevelt had attacked the "power trust" for fleecing consumers "out of millions of dollars." By endangering economic security, unrestrained, unregulated corporations such as electrical holding companies, Roosevelt argued, endangered citizenship itself. New Deal policies had broken those holding companies apart, tying the resulting component companies to specific places as a means to limit their power. Those policies had an unintended consequence, however. In creating new connections between private electrical companies and local communities, they produced the conditions whereby those companies could attack the public entities that the New Deal empowered. The local orientation of companies such as APS gained new valence as they worked to draw new business and capital to Phoenix and Arizona. As Governor Paul Fannin proclaimed in his message to the special legislative session in 1963, "The role of the investor-owned utilities in the free enterprise economy of our state is invaluable. We can point with pride to these corporate citizens."[64]

Fannin's emphasis on APS's role in the state's economy points to the new centrality of place to the utility's business and its politics. In its promotional activities, APS helped draw not abstract capital to Phoenix, but individual companies and people. These people made places for themselves by orienting themselves to their new surroundings spatially, socially, and also politically. There, migrants created their own places, "organized worlds of meaning" in the geographer Yi-Tu Fuan's description, within which "taxpayer" identities helped make sense of their local experience.[65] APS executives used such identities to create a shared experience of place. As APS executives emphasized, the company contributed broadly to its community through tax payments, much as did the city's suburban homeowners. It helped to create a new identity for the region as a modern center, as "a frontier with a future" growing through individual initiative and embrace of free enterprise. Place making lay at the heart of both the company's business and its politics. The story of Phoenix's electric utilities signals the need for historians of business and politics to orient businesses within their geographic context. Only by appreciating business's actions in the production of space and place can historians fully account for its political influence on the local level.

Notes

1. "Shadowed by SRPD Plant, Peoria Man Pays Fair Share," *Spark and Flame* [employee newsletter of Arizona Public Service Company] (December 1962), FM MSS #53, Stephen Shadegg Collection (hereinafter SSC), Arizona Historical Foundation, Tempe, Ariz. The

Shadegg Collection at AHF is currently being processed; notes will therefore provide only titles and dates. Notice of newsletter's distribution to customers from Walter Lucking to Arizona Public Service Customers, undated, SSC.

2. For "taxpayer politics" in the 1970s, see Matthew Lassiter, *The Silent Majority: Suburban Politics in the Sunbelt South* (Princeton, N.J.: Princeton University Press, 2005); Mike Davis, *City of Quartz: Excavating the Future in Los Angeles* (New York: Verso, 1990), 115–217; and Robert Self, "Prelude to the Tax Revolt," in *The New Suburban History*, ed. Kevin Kruse and Thomas Sugrue (Chicago: University of Chicago Press, 2006), 144–60. For public employee unions and fiscal crisis in the 1970s, see Joseph McCartin, "Turnabout Years," in *Rightward Bound: Making America Conservative in the 1970s*, ed. Bruce Schulman and Julian Zelizer (Cambridge, Mass.: Harvard University Press, 2008). For the political engagement of business as class in the 1970s, see the chapter by Benjamin Waterhouse in this volume, and Kimberly Phillips-Fein, *Invisible Hands: The Making of the Conservative Movement from the New Deal to Reagan*, (New York: W. W. Norton, 2009).

3. Various articles, *Spark and Flame* (December 1962).

4. I intentionally distinguish here between space, as the geographic scale transformed by processes of historical change, and place, the social worlds that people construct in space. On the transformation of space, see Henri Lefebvre, *The Production of Space*, trans. Donald Nicholson-Smith (Cambridge: Blackwell, 1991); and David Harvey, *Justice, Nature, and the Geography of Difference* (Cambridge: Blackwell, 1996). For the creation of place, see Dolores Hayden, *The Power of Place: Urban Landscapes as Public History* (Cambridge, Mass.: MIT Press, 1995); and Matthew Klingle, *Emerald City: An Environmental History of Seattle* (New Haven, Conn.: Yale University Press, 2007).

5. Karen Smith, *The Magnificent Experiment: Building the Salt River Reclamation Project* (Tucson: University of Arizona Press, 1986).

6. Leah Glaser, *Electrifying the Rural American West: Stories of People, Power, and Place* (Lincoln: University of Nebraska Press, 2010).

7. Thyrle and Ruth Stapley Oral History, 30 September 1978, Phoenix History Project (hereinafter PHP), Arizona Historical Society, Tempe, Ariz.

8. Shelly Dudley, Senior Historical Analyst, Salt River Project, personal correspondence with author, 5 January 2010.

9. *North American Co. v. Securities and Exchange Com'n*, 327 U.S. 686 (1946).

10. Richard Rudolph and Scott Ridley, *Power Struggle: The Hundred Year War over Electricity* (New York: HarperCollins, 1986), 57–68.

11. Glaser, *Electrifying the Rural American West*.

12. On ideas of electrical reform, see Ronald Tobey, *Technology as Freedom: The New Deal and the Electrical Modernization of the American Home* (Berkeley: University of California Press, 1996), 40–61; and Rudolph and Ridley, *Power Struggle*, 69–84.

13. Stephen Shadegg, *Century One* (Phoenix: Salt River Project, 1969), 28.

14. "Preference policies," put in place in 1934, gave public agencies first claim on this power with any remaining power sold to privately owned utilities. The 1930 agreement over the distribution of Boulder Dam's power required utilities, rather than the Bureau of Reclamation, to build their own power lines. Norris Hundley, *The Great Thirst: Californians and Water, 1790–1990* (Berkeley: University of California Press, 1993), 219–27.

15. "President's Talk at Boulder Dam," *New York Times*, 1 October 1935, 2.

16. The Boulder Dam Power Transmission Association of Arizona, "Boulder Dam Power for Arizona," 1, Bureau of Reclamation Project Files, Hoover Dam, Box 42, RG 75, National Archives and Records Administration, Denver, Colo.

17. The 1922 Colorado River Compact had divided the river's water between the seven states that bordered the Colorado. The compact granted Arizona rights to 2.8 million acre-feet of the river's water. These rights would go unfulfilled until the authorization of the Central Arizona Project in 1968. The Boulder Canyon Act granted Arizona rights to 18% of the electricity generated at Boulder Dam. Hundley, *The Great Thirst*, 203–20.

18. The legislation was blocked by budget-conscious conservative Democrats that dominated the state assembly. Advocates of the legislation widely blamed CALAPCO for influencing legislators. "Boulder Power Blocked," *Arizona Republic*, 26 February 1939, 1.

19. Shadegg, *Century One*, 31.
20. Rudolph and Ridley, *Power Struggle*, 57–68.
21. Frank Snell, *Arizona Bar Foundation Oral History Project: Arizona Legal History*, 20 June 1989, 31–36, Arizona Historical Society.
22. Ibid., 34–38.
23. Arizona Public Service, *Annual Report 1952*, 2, 5.
24. G. Wesley Johnson, "Directing Elites: Catalysts for Social Change," in *Phoenix in the Twentieth Century*, ed. G. Wesley Johnson (Norman: University of Oklahoma Press, 1993), 25.
25. Arizona Public Service Company, *Industry Views* (Phoenix: Arizona Public Service Company, 1956).
26. Thomas Hughes, "The Electrification of America: The Systems Builders," *Technology and Culture* 20 (1979): 124–61.
27. APS Ad, "Electricity Is a Family Affair," *Arizona Republic*, 16 February 1953, 22. For APS contest, see "Confidential to Members," 18 March 1955, 1955 Scrapbook, "Page 12–31" Folder, Box 2, Homebuilders Association of Central Arizona Records 1953–87, AHS, Tempe.
28. Both article titles and quote taken from Richard Hirsch, *Technology and Transformation in the American Electric Utility Industry* (New York: Cambridge University Press, 1989), 52–53.
29. Peter Siskind, "Fractured Suburbias: Exploring Land Use Liberalism in the 1960s and 1970s," paper presented at "The Diverse Suburb" conference, Hofstra University, 23 October 2009.
30. For Phoenix's annexation policies in the 1950s, see Carol Heim, "Border Wars: Tax Revenue, Annexation, and Urban Growth in Phoenix," University of Massachusetts Political Economy Research Institute, Working Paper Series, Number 112, July 2006, 8–9. Available at <http://works.bepress.com/carol_heim/2>.
31. Author's correspondence with Shelley Dudley. Stephen Shadegg, "Background behind the Tax Controversy," (1963?), 3, SSC. For one example of such an advertisement, see Salt River Project, "An Electric Dryer Beats the Sun," *Arizona Republic*, 2 February 1955, sect. 5, p. 2.
32. Author's correspondence with Shelley Dudley, 31 May 2011.
33. SRP customer and sales drawn from United States, Federal Power Commission (hereinafter FPC), *Statistics of Electrical Utilities in the United States, Publicly Owned* (Washington, D.C.: FPC, 1949–61).
34. Shadegg, *Century One*, 34.
35. Frank Snell Oral History, interview by G. Wesley Johnson, 7 December 1978, PHP. A map of the respective utilities' service areas can be found at <http://www.srpnet.com/about/pdfx/ElectricServiceAreaMap.pdf>.
36. Raymond Moley, *How to Keep Our Liberty: A Program for Political Action* (New York, 1952), 126.
37. "Only the Beginning," *Arizona Republic*, 12 May 1958, 6.
38. Arizona Public Service, "Which of These Will You Give Away," *Arizona Republic*, 26 November 1958, 10.
39. For the politics of the Sunbelt defense industry, see Lisa McGirr, *Suburban Warriors: The Origins of the New American Right* (Princeton, N.J.: Princeton University Press, 2002).
40. R. J. McMullin, General Manager, Salt River Project, to Walter Lucking, President, Arizona Public Service Company, 3 May 1962, SSC.
41. Lucking to McMullin, 22 May 1962, SSC.
42. FPC, *Statistics of Electrical Utilities in the United States, Classes A and B, Privately Owned* (Washington, D.C.: FPC, 1955–60); FPC, *Statistics of Electrical Utilities . . . Publicly Owned*, 1955–60.
43. Electric rates taken from FPC, *Federal Power Commission Electric Rate Survey* (Washington, D.C.: FPC, 1945–65).
44. Barry Goldwater, "A Good Reclamation Project," *Los Angeles Times*, 18 April 1961, B4. Shadegg, "Background behind the Tax Controversy," 7.
45. Stephen Shadegg to Rod McMullin, 14 April 1959, SSC.

46. Rod McMullin to V. I. Corbell, 15 May 1962, SSC.
47. William Epler, "Should Pay Taxes," *Brewery Gulch Gazette* (Bisbee, Ariz.). Reprinted in *Supervisor: Newsletter for Management, Arizona Public Service Company,* 26 November 1962, SSC.
48. Frank Snell Oral History, PHP.
49. "Another Day, Another $20,000 Working for You," "The Dollars and Sense of Education," "Taxes in Action," facsimile of advertisements placed in Arizona newspapers "to inform the people of Arizona," 1962?, SSC.
50. Lassiter, *Silent Majority,* 4.
51. Arizona Public Service Co., Press Release, "The Arizona Tax Story" and "Taxes—Questions and Answers," 1962?, SSC.
52. Since 1951, SRP had provided the city's drinking water. Michael Logan, *Desert Cities* (Pittsburgh: University of Pittsburgh Press, 2006), 144.
53. "Only a Tax Collector?" *Arizona Republic,* date unknown, SSC.
54. Walter Lucking, "Arizona Public Service Co. President Clarifies Tax Issue," date unclear, response to letter of 21 December 1962, SSC.
55. "No Longer Valid," *Arizona Republic,* 18 December 1962, 6.
56. R. G. Wiggenhorn, letter to editor, *Arizona Republic,* 21 December 1962, 7.
57. Lucking, "Arizona Public Service Co. President Clarifies Tax Issue."
58. "Background behind the Tax Controversy," 3–6.
59. Towsend Wainwright, President, Wainwright and Ramsey, to V. I. Corbell, 11 January 1963. SSC.
60. W. H. Tyler, editor, bond investments, Standard & Poor's Corp., to V. I. Corbell, 9 February 1959, SSC.
61. Paul Fannin, "Proclamation Calling a Special Session of the Twenty-Sixth Legislature of the State of Arizona," 3 April 1963, Folder 38, Box 181, Personal and Political Papers of Senator Barry M. Goldwater (hereinafter BMG), AHF.
62. Ibid.
63. As SRP President Victor Corbell wrote to Governor Paul Fannin a month before the special legislative session, "It is vital that we achieve unity here at home if our efforts to secure this project so necessary for our continued prosperity are to be realized . . . The continuation of this public, political dispute jeopardizes the Central Arizona Project." V. I. Corbell to Fannin, 26 February 1963, Folder 38, Box 181, BMG.
64. Fannin, "Message to the 26th Arizona Legislature," 3 April 1963, Folder 38, Box 181, BMG.
65. Yi-Tu Fuan, *Space and Place: The Perspective of Experience* (Minneapolis: University of Minnesota Press, 1977, 2001), 174.

9

Supermarkets, Free Markets, and the Problem of Buyer Power in the Postwar United States

SHANE HAMILTON

Buying in bulk is an omnipresent feature of contemporary capitalism. Shoppers rely on box stores, discount warehouses, and online e-tailers to stock up on enormous quantities of everything from paper towels to frozen fish sticks. The deals that consumers expect to find in the aisles of Sam's Club, Wal-Mart Supercenter, Target, and Costco are in turn largely a product of the bulk buying practices of those giant retailers. Through their sheer dominance in consumer goods sales, large-scale retailers are empowered to make ruthless demands on suppliers to drive down prices, establish product specifications, and dictate exactly when goods will arrive on store shelves. As historian Nelson Lichtenstein has convincingly argued, big-box retailers occupy the "commanding heights" of the contemporary global economy; they "make the markets, set the prices, and determine the worldwide distribution of labor" in order to satisfy the demands of price-conscious shoppers and keep their profits in line with stockholder expectations.[1]

The fearsome power of retailers to command and control global supply chains, which developed over the course of the six decades following the end of World War II, has never been confronted with effective policy action. This is surely not a preordained product of modern American political culture. A deep and abiding mistrust of big business, including large retailers, permeated all points of the political spectrum for much of the twentieth century. When U.S. retailers first began to consolidate their purchasing power in the first third of the twentieth century, a widespread hue and cry over the "chain store menace" led to significant government action in the 1920s and 1930s, culminating in passage of the anti-chain Robinson-Patman Act in 1936. The ability of big businesses to use volume buying strategies to dictate market conditions—which economists termed "monopsony power"—aroused significant concerns among producers and consumers long after New Deal attacks on big business, contrary to the notion popularized by historian Richard Hofstadter that postwar prosperity made concentrated economic power a matter of little popular concern.[2] Particularly with the proliferation of the supermarkets that came to anchor the nation's food system from the 1950s to the 1970s, public concern over concentrated buying power repeatedly registered on the political radar as a threat to the hallowed American ideals of free markets, family farms, small businesses, and sovereign consumers.

Such critiques carried the potential for a dramatic reshaping of American political discourse in the postwar era. The problem of concentrated buyer power in the farm and food economy opened up multiple opportunities for urban consumers and rural producers to unite in a broad critique of postwar American capitalism. Populist in nature rather than strictly liberal or conservative, eruptions of anti-chain sentiment belied the notion of a "consensus" approach to economic policy. At no point after the end of World War II, however, did neopopulist attacks on corporate power translate into effectual policy. One might surmise that buyer power never became an actionable political problem in the postwar period because of the rise of modern conservatism, with its conjoining of antistatist politics with the pro–big business agenda of the modern Republican Party. Or perhaps the shallowness of antitrust politics was due to the rise of a depoliticized "consumers' republic," with apathetic consumers demanding ever-lower prices from ever-larger retailers no matter the broader social or economic costs. The effective erasure of buyer power as a political problem by the end of the 1970s, however, was not due to rising conservatism or apolitical consumerism, nor even to the collusion of conservative politicians with big business lobbyists. Instead, the lack of action on concentrated buyer power in postwar America was due to outmoded antitrust policy tools operating in an economic context in which interested social groups faced significant barriers to effective political mobilization. Despite the shift from a production-driven to a distribution-driven economy during this period, public concern over concentrated economic power remained embedded in a nineteenth-century framework that drove a wedge between the political and economic interests of producers and consumers. In the case of supermarkets, that wedge prevented rural farm producers from uniting with suburban consumers to contest the increased economic power of retailers, thus contributing to a deepening political divide between "red state" populism and "blue state" liberalism that marked late-twentieth-century political culture. Ill-equipped to apprehend the long-term impact of concentrated buyer power on both food producers and consumers, neither ordinary citizens, organized interest groups, nor congressional leaders were able to translate fickle populist anger into lasting liberal policies in an economy undergoing fundamental transformations.

In her 1933 classic *The Economics of Imperfect Competition*, Cambridge economist Joan Robinson coined a new word. *Monopsony* henceforth described a market in which a single buyer exercised great power over many sellers, in distinction to the more familiar *monopoly* (connoting buyers beholden to a single seller).[3] Institutional economists thereafter relied on Robinson's neologism to describe the ways in which concentrated buying power could distort the marketplace. In its simplest and most common form, monopsony power poses a problem when a single firm is able to gain more favorable prices from suppliers (say, food processors or farm cooperatives) than smaller buyers are able to obtain. Such discriminatory pricing structures can limit competition and threaten the economic viability of wholesale or retail firms that may be highly efficient businesses despite their lack of market share. Monopsony theoretically poses the greatest threat to the broader social welfare when it is paired with monopoly power on the selling side of an uncompetitive market, thus allowing a single firm to squeeze its suppliers without passing cost savings to consumers. Less obvious are the long-term potential harms of concentrated buyer power, in which the dominance of a single buyer reduces the incentives for producers to innovate, drives some producers out of business entirely, or prevents new businesses from entering the market. In such situations, the choice of products available to consumers becomes limited in the long run even if prices remain steady. Furthermore, in contrast to monopoly power, concentrated buyer power can constrict the competitive viability of entire supply chains even if the largest single buyer maintains a relatively small market share.[4]

Even before the term's coinage and theoretical elaboration, the political problem of monopsony power ranked high in U.S. debates over the "chain store menace" in the 1920s and early 1930s. Grocers such as Kroger and the Great Atlantic & Pacific Tea Company (A&P) perfected chain retailing by the 1920s. Using centralized buying facilities to lower the transaction costs of purchasing, chain stores challenged the livelihoods of food manufacturers, wholesale distributors, and "mom and pop" corner stores. State legislatures responded between 1927 and 1939, with twenty-seven states imposing punitive taxes on chain stores. Unsatisfied, wholesale grocers in 1935 petitioned Congress for a national clampdown on chains. Aided by Senator Joseph Robinson of Arkansas and Texas Congressman Wright Patman, wholesale grocers achieved passage of the 1936 Robinson-Patman Act. Immediately hailed as the "Magna Carta of Small Business," the Robinson-Patman Act instituted a complex array of mechanisms intended to prevent large-scale retailers from using their buying power to gain advantages over smaller retailers and wholesalers. The new law marked the high tide of pre–World War II antimonopsony politics. At a time when many Americans

assumed the predations of big business were responsible for the economic collapse of the 1930s, opponents of chain stores drew on the long tradition of populist antitrust sentiment in the United States to drum up antichain hostility.[5]

The advent of a new business form—the supermarket—marked one response
to the widespread antimonopsony sentiments of the interwar period. The first
supermarkets were not chains. Instead, most of the early supermarkets, such as
King Kullen in Queens, New York, were free-standing retailers who relied on
self-service and high-volume sales at low margins to move stock out the door.
Much like Filene's Bargain Basement, which in 1909 revolutionized clothing retailing by automatically discounting unsold items, early supermarkets achieved
reputations as "price wreckers" by selling at razor-thin margins. Unlike chain
grocers, which limited the range of offerings to minimize operating costs, supermarkets displayed a dazzling array of perishable foods, dry goods, and consumer
services under one enormous roof. The supermarket business model proved so
successful by the mid-1930s that chains such as A&P, which at first resisted the
"price-wrecker" approach, began fusing their centralized buying practices with
the one-stop self-service approach of the supers. Chains including A&P, Kroger,
Safeway, Piggly Wiggly, Grand Union, and others flourished in the late 1930s by
converting small stores into larger supermarkets. Politically, however, the
merging of monopsonistic buying practices with volume-focused mass marketing brought on a renewed round of attacks, including an unsuccessful effort
by Wright Patman to institute a federal antichain tax in 1940 and a Justice Department antitrust lawsuit initiated against A&P in 1944 (not fully resolved until
1954). In general, however, antimonopsony concerns subsided during World
War II, as independent grocers prospered under wartime conditions. Shoppers
relied on corner proprietors for access to rationed items such as meat and sugar
and, with money to spend in wartime, proved willing to pay for the higher levels
of personal service offered by independent stores.[6]

Within a decade of the war's end, however, the supermarket was firmly
ensconced in American consumer culture. The 3 January 1955 cover of *Life* magazine celebrated American abundance—indeed, "mass luxury"—by depicting a
child sandwiched into a shopping cart overflowing with canned hams, plastic-
wrapped produce, and other prepackaged convenience foods. Supermarket
owners positioned themselves as "consumers' agents," at the beck and call of the
middle-class "Consumer Queen" whose power of the purse was exalted as the
main driver of the postwar economy. General Foods Corporation, which since
its founding in 1929 had focused on advertising its wares to wholesale buyers
rather than to retail consumers, shifted its focus in 1953, sensing that self-serve
supermarkets had given "Mrs. Housewife" more power over purchasing
decisions than the male wholesale buyers who controlled pre-supermarket food
procurement. American supermarkets were even more than "consumers' agents,"

however, according to their most fervent promoters. They were material embodiments of the will of the people. John A. Logan, chairman of the National Association of Food Chains, announced in October 1958 that self-service food retailing was "a form of economic democracy." Max Mandell Zimmerman, founder of the Super Market Institute, explained in 1955 that "the Super Market operator has revolutionized the housewife's shopping habits by creating a new shopping atmosphere for America, in which 'sight-and-touch' buying and freedom of choice prevail."[7]

Yet even amidst such celebratory rhetoric certain organized interest groups drew attention to the potential restraint of competition in a food economy dominated by large buyers. The National Association of Retail Grocers, a trade organization representing the independent grocers and small chains most likely to suffer from the growth of chain supermarkets, published a study in 1959 declaring that the rapid proliferation of large supermarkets entailed a "cold war" in the American consumer market that threatened to stamp out free enterprise. Pointing out that the four-year period between 1954 and 1958 witnessed 160 mergers and acquisitions within the retail grocery trade, the Retail Grocers raised the specter of a handful of large-scale retailers controlling the entire nation's food supply, from farm to processing plant. By 1958, chain stores accounted for 43% of the nation's retail food sales. Large chains such as Safeway, Kroger, and National Tea consolidated their purchasing power by erecting regional warehouses and buying directly from farm cooperatives and food processors. Smaller chains and independents likewise drew on centralized buying power, driving down transaction costs by joining "voluntary associations" and "cooperative buying" organizations such as the Independent Grocers' Association (IGA), Red and White, and Clover Farm. By pooling their purchases with other retailers, members of these "voluntary associations" could rival the large-scale buying power of national chains, meaning that monopsony rather than monopoly was quickly becoming the defining feature of supermarket capitalism.[8]

It was monopoly, however, not monopsony, that grabbed headlines in the Truman and Eisenhower years. The 1950s witnessed numerous efforts by key Democratic legislators—particularly Senator Estes Kefauver (D-TN), Representative Emanuel Celler (D-NY), Senator Hubert H. Humphrey (D-MN), Senator William Proxmire (D-WI), and Representative Wright Patman (D-TX)—to revise and extend antitrust law to address the concentration of economic power in fields ranging from steel manufacturing to broadcast media. Emanuel Celler opened a House hearing on antitrust in May 1955 declaring that "new forces transmuting the economy" raised an essential question about the nature of American capitalism in the postwar world: "How can free competitive enterprise best coexist with the H-bomb, new vaccines, the wonder drugs, electronics, univacs, automation, supermarkets, bank consolidations, giant

multiproduct conglomerates, and discount houses?" Wisconsin Senator William Proxmire declared in 1958 that price-fixing "fair trade" legislation was
necessary to protect "the independent proprietors, the free enterprise businessmen" who were "the backbone of American economic democracy." Lik-
ening "mom and pop" grocers to family farmers, Proxmire further proclaimed
that "the family [retail] business offers an ideal moral climate for the development of the invaluable qualities of character and morality."[9] Much like late-
nineteenth-century rhetoric attacking railroads, meatpackers, and Standard Oil
as "octopuses" crushing small businessmen in their tentacled grips, the antimonopoly rhetoric of the 1950s and 1960s raised fears of an economy run not on
the basis of free-market competition but on cold-blooded noncompetitive efficiency. Several key antimonopoly bills were enacted during the administrations
of both Truman and Eisenhower. The 1950 Celler-Kefauver Act and Public Law
135 both significantly boosted the power of federal antitrust enforcers. Despite
the importance of these extensions of antitrust law, however, all were aimed
solely at restricting monopoly power, not monopsony power.[10]

The fact that 1950s antitrust rhetoric was framed in the same terms as nineteenth-century producerist attacks on octopus-like "trusts" stymied the efforts
of antimonopsonists. Such rhetoric rang hollow for consumers increasingly
accustomed to the prosperity of an economy anchored by giant vertically integrated corporations. Antimonopsonists nonetheless attempted to secure new
legislation in the 1950s, fearing that concentration in the distribution industry posed an ongoing threat to small business enterprise. The most sustained
effort was spearheaded by Wright Patman, a Texas Democrat who defined his
midcentury political career as a champion of small businessmen. The Supreme
Court spurred Patman into action with its 1951 decision in *Standard Oil Co. v.
Federal Trade Commission*, which effectively gutted the Robinson-Patman
Act.[11] Patman introduced bills to bolster the act in 1956, 1957, and yet again
in 1959. A wide range of organized interest groups lobbied on behalf of Patman's efforts, including independent grocers, food brokers, produce dealers,
farm cooperatives, the Farmers Union, and the United Auto Workers. Henry
Bison of the National Association of Retail Grocers testified before the Senate
Committee on the Judiciary that Patman's bill was essential to "protect our
competitive system," which was under attack by the large-scale buyer who,
under *Standard Oil*, was granted the "freedom to do anything he wants, providing he does so in good faith." The National Farmers Union concurred,
declaring that if the farmer "has to deal with giant monopolies either in buying
or selling, he perforce becomes an economic slave." The free market, according to these antimonopsonists, could not be free if small businessmen, lacking
bargaining power, were subject to the unregulated power of volume-buying
retailer-distributors.[12]

Patman would never secure passage of his amendment, and to this day Robinson-Patman remains largely unenforced, gathering dust in the statute books. The problems with Robinson-Patman were legion. For one, the act is notoriously complex. According to a recent survey of major federal statutes, the act is the most incomprehensible as measured by the Flesch-Kincaid readability test—requiring forty-three years of formal schooling to grasp its meaning.[13] More broadly, the act reflects a nineteenth-century understanding of how concentrated economic power might pose a problem for a capitalist economy. Small businesses were upheld as the moral backbone of the nation, while "trusts" were the product of nefarious backroom deals hatched by robber barons. Price discrimination came to be the key measure of such presumed immorality under Robinson-Patman. Speaking on the House floor in March 1956, for instance, Patman declared that "the national chain buyers coerce small suppliers into granting them discriminatory favors," an act which Patman claimed was almost solely responsible for "destruction of small businesses of all kinds and a centralization of business into the hands of a few corporate giants."[14] By implying a disjuncture between the interests of small businesses and those of the consuming masses, such outmoded antitrust sentiments offered no clear remedy for the constraints to producer viability and consumer choice presented by concentrated buyer power. Such moralistic, producerist language hatched in an era of monopoly capitalism could not serve to mobilize public support for new legislation in an increasingly distribution-driven economy. Antitrust enforcers in the Department of Justice or the Federal Trade Commission could, of course, continue to take action under the auspices of the Robinson-Patman Act, but enforcement was limited to highly technical and judicially constrained actions in the realm of price discrimination. Enforcement of the Robinson-Patman Act in the postwar period was thus unlikely to resonate with the daily experiences of consumers in the marketplace, even if consumers happened to be well-schooled enough in complex antitrust law to understand why the actions might be beneficial in the long run.

Proponents of supermarkets, conversely, could readily defend economic concentration in the food system by highlighting its benefits to consumers. The Chamber of Commerce of the United States took the lead in undermining the producerist language of antitrust in the 1950s, suggesting that nineteenth-century approaches to antitrust were irrational in a consumer-driven economy. A 1957 article in the Chamber's organ *Economic Intelligence*, for instance, maintained that economic concentration only mattered from a public policy standpoint when consumers lost the power of choice. Quoting economist Joseph Schumpeter, the author declared that any other approach to antitrust was a "vindictive" abuse of government power. Chamber of Commerce representative Hoyt P. Steele informed Congress in 1955 that postwar economic concentration was solely a product of businesses competing to deliver what consumers wanted—low prices and more choices. Nobody could deny that a modern supermarket delivered a greater array of products at lower prices than mom and pop ever could. In fact, one of the few consumerist critiques of the supermarket to gain any political traction in the 1950s and early 1960s was the declaration that supermarkets offered too much choice. As Marya Mannes, a writer for *New Yorker* magazine, testified before Congress in 1961, the modern supermarket was "the greatest exercise in planned confusion since the bazaars of Samarkand," stuffed to the gills with so many products that shoppers needed "a slide rule and an M.I.T. graduate [to] figure out what we're buying."[15]

Not until the mid-1960s, during Lyndon Johnson's presidency, did the problem of monopsony again become an issue of broad public concern. With consumer food prices rising steadily in the decade even as farm prices declined, the situation was ripe for a politicized attack on the growing power of supermarkets in the nation's food economy. The main vehicle for this effort was the National Commission on Food Marketing, established by Congress in 1964 in response to a request from President Johnson. Johnson was in turn influenced by his Secretary of Agriculture, Orville Freeman, who sent him a series of March 1964 memos outlining the economic challenges faced by America's farmers. Despite high productivity, farmers were losing money and getting angry about it. The culprit, implied Freeman, was the modern supermarket: "The food retailer, once the tail end of the food marketing chain, is rapidly becoming the dominant influence in the food industry." Johnson, clearly hoping to use the issue to gain farm-country support for his 1964 presidential bid, announced at his Texas ranch on 28 March that Congress should establish a commission to investigate the nation's food system. Monopsony was not as high on Johnson's agenda as civil rights—which Johnson declared to be his "first big job" at the same press conference—but the attractions of arousing populist antimonopoly sentiment in southern, western, and Midwestern farm country seemed a safe bet in an election year, especially if the issue could be pitched as a matter of great concern for both rural constituents and urban consumers.[16]

Congress immediately set to work to establish the National Commission on Food Marketing. Hearings revealed widespread public support, with every major farm organization, retailer association, labor union, and consumer group supporting the proposed Commission with varying degrees of enthusiasm. Orville Freeman set the tone for the hearings, declaring that something about the modern food system reeked of conspiracy, as if supermarket operators treated the farm economy as a coin toss governed by the rule, "Heads I win, and tails you lose." Jack C. Toole, a cattle rancher from Shelby, Montana, used rather more colorful language: "There is more cattle rustling going on behind the meat counters of this country's chainstores than ever went on on the rangelands of the West." Kenneth B. Naden of the National Council of Farmer Cooperatives worried that continuing consolidation of retail purchasing power would ultimately make many farmers into "contract producers rather than flexible and independent business firms." The support of organized labor raised the hopes of Democrats seeking to unite the often opposed interests of angry farm folks and urban consumers. Ralph Helstein of the United Packinghouse, Food, and Allied Workers union, for instance, attacked supermarkets for driving up consumer prices and for squeezing meatpackers to lay off workers, cut wages, and close plants. Far from upholding supermarkets as a form of "economic democracy," such antimonopsonists declared giant retail stores a growing menace to the economic and political interests of farmers, workers, and consumers.[17]

After two years of intensive study, the National Commission on Food Marketing delivered to the public an enormous pile of literature that landed with a quiet thud. The main report published in 1966, *Food from Farmer to Consumer*, ran 203 pages. Ten densely worded technical supplements consumed thousands more pages. Even if the language had been simpler, the Commission's political recommendations were framed too ambiguously to be of use for policy makers. Orville Freeman ruefully noted the report was "not a blueprint for legislation," as it conveyed the overall impression that "the food marketing system is generally competitive and basically sound." In marked contrast to 1920s and 1930s attacks on the "chain store menace," the Commission's 1966 report heralded no important policy action.[18]

Despite the innocuous language in the main report, the National Commission on Food Marketing's technical studies blatantly confirmed the suspicions of rural antimonopsonists. The technical study on food retailing, for instance, noted that large retailers exercised tremendous power on the buying end of the food chain. It included the damning claim that supermarkets' buying power was more important for maintaining their steadily high profits than were efficiencies in retailing. "[Chain store supermarkets'] expense rates (labor, et cetera) are often higher [than independent grocers']," the study announced, "and they appear to lack the vigor of local companies run by owner-managers." Conversely, the Commission noted that independent retailers were able to remain profitable despite their lack of consolidated buying power because they outperformed chains in sales efficiency. For Angus McDonald of the Farmers Union, such statements verified his organization's claim that farmers and consumers were suffering from a structural imbalance in the food system. In his reading of the report, low farm prices and high retail prices were clearly the result of undeserved economic control in the hands of inefficient supermarkets. From McDonald's standpoint, sheer market power, rather than economic efficiency, accounted for the dominance of supermarkets in the postwar food economy. Sharing these thoughts with the Department of Agriculture, however, led

McDonald to be labeled "pretty far out in left field" by Orville Freeman, who decided not to push for new antitrust legislation or regulatory authority in response to the Commission's findings.[19]

Once again the issue of monopsony power, despite its potential left-populist appeal—an appeal intentionally cultivated by the Johnson administration—failed to mobilize significant political action. This failure was clearly not due to widespread apathy about big business. The mid-1960s marked, in many ways, a high tide of antimonopoly sentiment and enforcement. The Supreme Court's 1966 decision in *U.S. v. Von's Grocery* effectively empowered antitrust regulators to prevent retail mergers solely to preserve small business for small business's sake, rather than for competition's sake. An emboldened Federal Trade Commission declared in 1966 and 1967 a series of sweeping prohibitions on supermarket mergers, first halting the National Tea chain from pursuing mergers for a period of ten years, then announcing all mergers in the supermarket field suspect. But as had been the case during the 1950s, such actions focused exclusively on the problem of monopoly. Efforts to halt mergers in food retailing had little impact on the consolidated buying power that supermarkets used to bolster their profit margins.[20]

In fact, the relatively strong antimonopoly enforcement of the 1960s encouraged supermarket chains to capture more, not less, buyer power. For both independent and chain stores, the FTC's prohibition on horizontal mergers at the retail end encouraged firms to seek even greater economies of scale on the purchasing end. By the early 1970s, a mad rush was underway in the food retailing business to expand the size of stores and distribution centers, rather than buying out competitors and thus face antitrust action. Kroger, which had seen its profits and market share decline in the 1960s, hatched a plan in 1971 to build 200 "superstores" by the end of 1973. One commentator noted in 1979, at the end of Kroger's expansion campaign, that the new superstores were "as big as the Ritz, with aisles so large they almost demand roadmaps." According to Kroger CEO Lyle Everingham, the giant stores were intended to pull as much volume as possible from the company's warehousing operations to gain higher returns on equity. The strategy was successful for Kroger. By the end of the decade the company had risen to prominence as the nation's second-largest food chain behind Safeway in volume of sales, with higher returns on equity than the California-based chain. As had been the case since the passage of the 1890 Sherman Act, strong antitrust enforcement often led to unintended consequences, encouraging the largest businesses to expand their existing operations while smaller businesses were prevented from buying out competitors.[21]

Decades of consolidation in food retailing came under the most widespread attack since the New Deal during the 1970s. The counterculture spurred one important critique of the marketing machinery of the modern food system. Consumers fed up with what they saw in the modern supermarket—"plastic" produce, hormone-laden meats, and pesticide-laced farm products processed into quasi-nutritional convenience foods—turned to nonprofit cooperatives that sourced their products from small organic farms. Somewhere between 5,000 and 10,000 such food coops opened between 1969 and 1979, as food activists sought an end run around the monopsonistic supermarket by erecting an alternative food distribution network. Many college-town coops thrived, although many more found that without supermarket-style buying power, prices remained too high to attract or retain enough consumers. Food coopera-tives made little dent in the market share of larger chains, but their existence suggested a structural critique of monopsony power. Rather than singling out supposedly nefarious big businesses for colluding to control markets, counter-cultural cooperative buyers attacked the entire food system as a machine geared to maximize profits while restricting consumer choice. Significant support for this critique came with the 1970 publication of Jennifer Cross's *The Supermar-ket Trap*, a muckraking critique of the food system as "too big, too monopo-listic, inefficient, and shot through with profiteering at all levels."[22]

Even in the mainstream food economy, wildly gyrating food prices in the early 1970s compelled consumers to loudly protest what suddenly appeared to be a very unfree market. A complex set of global events in 1972 and 1973—in-cluding droughts in Eurasia, a dip in the number of American livestock, and the U.S. dollar's devaluation—sent food prices skyrocketing. Housewives across the country angrily boycotted supermarkets and demanded the Nixon administra-tion institute retail price controls. Attempting to deflect consumer ire away from Washington, in April 1972 President Nixon pointed the finger at the ambiguous "middleman." Secretary of Agriculture Earl Butz likewise blamed "the truckers, marketeers, packagers and retailers who operate between the American farmer and the American consumer." Such rhetoric inflamed consumer suspicions that supermarkets were unfairly jacking up prices; as one woman wrote to Nixon in April 1973, "It's getting to the point where you want to scream when you get to the meat counter!" Another consumer informed Earl Butz that she was "tired of 'chain stores' which I consider a monopoly," and demanded the Secretary of Agriculture explain not only why prices were so high but "why chickens so often taste as if they have been fed on fish." A northern New Jersey organization of concerned consumers, calling itself "Until Prices Drop," sent 3,700 signed peti-tions to Butz to protest "being asked to shoulder a greater tax and price burden while big business and the already wealthy do not bear their fair share."[23] The situation highlighted a growing sense among consumers that the Nixon admin-istration was unwilling to confront what appeared to be a severe failure of the free market. If supermarkets and their agribusiness suppliers were so efficient, these protestors demanded, why were chickens that tasted like fish—and all other items on supermarket shelves—so expensive?

Rural agitators seized on the consumer-driven uproar of the early 1970s to draw renewed attention to the problem of monopsony. While consumers faced sticker shock at the supermarket checkout, farmers protested that their incomes were not keeping pace with rising retail prices. No figure protested more emphatically than Texas barnstormer Jim Hightower. In his 1975 book *Eat Your Heart Out*, Hightower pitchforked food conglomerates for using consolidated buying power to drive family farmers out of business, force chickens to be factory-produced like Greyhound buses ("and the buses may taste better," he quipped), and derive profits from market power rather than efficiency. Deriding the notion that bigger was better in the food business, Hightower declared that small enterprises—from family farms to "mom and pop" grocers—were in fact more efficient than agribusinesses, but could not attain reasonable profits without the market power bestowed by sheer size. Cattlemen in the nation's heartland took such critiques to heart in 1975 when they filed a series of antitrust lawsuits seeking treble damages against the nation's largest supermarket chains, accusing A&P, Kroger, Safeway, and others of a monopsonistic conspiracy to drive down farm livestock prices while raising retail beef prices.[24]

The furor of both consumers and farmers led Congress to hold a series of hearings from 1974 to 1976 to root out the culprits behind the food mess. Senator William Proxmire, co-chairing with Wright Patman a joint committee to investigate supermarket prices, asked Safeway president William S. Mitchell point-blank if "the enormous buying power of the chains" quashed competition in the food system. Mitchell retorted that there was no "enormous buying power of chains," noting that his firm's buyers competed with many other buyers in the food marketplace—voluntary associations, other chain stores, food coops, hotels. Such explanations proved unsatisfactory to politicians under pressure from constituents, including conservatives representing rural states. Republican Senator Henry Bellmon of Oklahoma, for instance, noted that while wheat prices were collapsing in his home state in 1974 the price of cereal had increased 22%. "The market system cannot work," Bellmon declared in a point-blank critique of monopsony power, "if the distribution side does not pass on lower prices paid to [farm] producers." Consumer representatives, meanwhile, grew exasperated with political grandstanding. Carol Tucker Foreman of the Consumer Federation of America pilloried the House Judiciary Committee for calling on her organization to testify more than seven times in 1975 and 1976 "without seeing any apparent progress toward the resolution of this problem. . . . We march up the Hill and down again, but the crisis at the supermarket checkout counter persists." While consumer groups, the Farmers Union, and other antimonopsonists called upon Congress to push for antitrust enforcement in the food industry, representatives of the Department of Agriculture, food processors, the Farm Bureau, and supermarkets responded with *non sequitur* calls to rein in organized labor. Facing such an impasse, congressional leaders were relieved when food prices stabilized in 1976 and 1977, temporarily shelving the issue.[25]

The economic crisis of 1979, however, brought the matter of food prices and supermarket monopsony power once again to the political forefront. Rampant inflation, particularly in fuel and food prices, was coupled with a summertime trucker insurrection that briefly threatened food supplies in major supermarket chains.[26] Consumer and farm organizations once again lambasted the consolidation of economic power on the distribution end of the food chain. By this point, however, conservative opponents of antitrust regulatory action were better prepared to nip the uprising in the bud. First, the influence of Chicago School legal theorists such as Richard Posner and Robert Bork had persuaded many in the field that antitrust regulation should be wielded only when concentration led to quantifiable price distortions. Monopsonistic concentration has always been notoriously difficult to measure, and even where monopsony clearly existed it was nearly impossible to prove it was responsible for specific price distortions.[27] Second, by 1979 conservatives had collectively centered on the notion that the primary drivers of inflation were New Deal regulations, government fiscal policy, and the demands of organized labor. In hearings on food prices before the House Budget Committee, for instance, Thomas Carroll of the Grocery Manufacturers of America claimed that "egregious Government spending" was the primary cause of inflation. Carroll and other like-minded witnesses called for two clear-cut solutions to the food price crisis: systematic deregulation of the entire economy and implementation of the UPC bar code scanner to eliminate unionized jobs in the food sector.[28] Third, the notion that deregulation could stanch inflation was a centerpiece of the Carter administration's approach to the economic crunch of the late 1970s. Fervid deregulator and "inflation czar" Alfred E. Kahn informed the House Agriculture Committee in April 1979 that spiking food prices were due to trucking regulations, agricultural price supports, and high consumer demand. Kahn thus suggested that rollbacks of government regulations and the unfettered workings of the free market would be the most direct routes to lower prices. Antitrust investigations, Kahn admitted, might help assuage the concerns of noneconomists, but noted that populist calls for investigation of big business had "about the same incisiveness as a clarion call to motherhood."[29]

By the start of the 1980s, then, the potential for monopsony to serve as a rallying point for left-leaning populists on either end of the modern food chain was almost nil. Confronted with weak policy tools—the dead-letter Robinson-Patman Act, an underfunded and underpowered Federal Trade Commission—antimonopsonists also faced significant challenges in creating a coherent, enduring political movement in a food economy anchored by concentrated buyers. Consumer anger was focused on short-term food price swings, which were not easily attributed solely to monopsony power, and that anger quickly dissipated when prices stabilized. Farm producers, on the other hand, fretted about the long-term implications of having limited choices in the marketplace for their produce. Most consumers gave little thought to the long-term strictures on choice that could arise from a monopsonistic food economy in which farmers were forced to adapt to supermarkets' demands for uniform, high-volume, low-price production. The National Farmers Union struggled to deliver that message to consumers and Congress, but its membership by the end of the 1970s stood at approximately 300,000, while the more conservative Farm Bureau, with a membership of three million, effectively dictated the discourse on farm and food policy. Conservatives, furthermore, were able to deploy a positive vocabulary of "free markets" and had the powerful tool of deregulation to position themselves as champions of the consumer's cause.

Antitrust agitation of any stripe consequently lost all momentum in the Reagan era. Antitrust enforcement essentially halted in the 1980s, and the food industry was a primary nontarget. The House Judiciary Committee met in 1988 to survey the impacts on the food sector, with Chairman Peter Rodino (D-NJ) noting that less than 7% of food industry mergers were challenged by the FTC or the Department of Justice between 1981 and 1984, compared to a rate of 24% in the 1960s and 1970s. And in any case, supermarket profit margins dropped substantially in the 1980s from their peaks of the early 1960s and mid-to-late 1970s, making them unlikely targets for consumer ire over concentrated economic power.[30]

Even as supermarket profits withered in the deregulated economy of the Reagan era, a new food giant emerged by the 1990s to upend the entire industry. To a far greater extent than any of its competitors, Wal-Mart based its rapid rise to retail dominance on monopsony power, largely because it had to. From its founding in the early 1960s through the 1980s, the firm focused its attention on rural consumers. Faced with the logistical challenge of supplying relatively small, geographically dispersed stores, the company was forced to wring inefficiencies out of its supply chain. Hence Sam Walton's decision in the late 1970s to erect a network of sophisticated distribution centers—cavernous buildings in which suppliers' bulk lots were disassembled, repackaged, and moved with utmost haste in smaller truckload parcels to decentralized stores. These rural distribution centers served as the leading edge of Wal-Mart's invasion of the nation's suburbs by the 1990s, with each distribution center accompanied by 150 new stores to keep goods pumping through the system at full throttle. Wal-Mart furthermore used the UPC bar code, first deployed in the early 1970s, to coerce suppliers into providing exactly what Wal-Mart wanted, when it wanted it, where it wanted it.[31] By the end of the 1990s, the company indisputably occupied the food business throne. Between 1996 and 2001, the number of Wal-Mart's Supercenters (which combine food supermarketing with general merchandise sales) grew by 20% per year. Food marketing expert Jean Kinsey, delivering the 2001 presidential address to the American Agricultural Economics Association, declared Wal-Mart the leader of a "new food economy," in which "independent producers and marketing firms" had been replaced by "a set of integrated and highly managed supply chains."[32]

Contemporary voices have expressed deep concern over Wal-Mart's monopsonistic approach to food distribution. Consumers who rued the industrialization of the food chain for environmental, health, or agrarian reasons turned in droves to organic foods in the early twenty-first century, while "locavores" helped reinvigorate local farmers' markets long thought obsolete. Many consumers were guided in this mistrust of supermarket-driven agribusiness by Michael Pollan's best-selling 2005 book *The Omnivore's Dilemma*. Yet while many affluent consumers voted with their feet in the marketplace by shopping at retailers presumed less problematic than Wal-Mart, no organized consumer group has addressed monopsony as a problem of structural market imbalance in need of political redress. Meanwhile, farm producers facing the real possibility of becoming contract producers for integrated retailer-distributors have few options for political action. Testifying before Congress in 2003, University of Wisconsin-Madison law professor Peter Carstensen flatly declared that antitrust enforcers failed "to understand the differences between monopsonistic power issues and the more familiar [problem of monopoly]." Farmers in particular faced unsympathetic antitrust regulators, and so were forced to turn to the courts to pursue antimonopsony claims. Even if farmers won such suits, Carstensen noted, they tended to "focus more on specific private concerns and less on the broad public interest in ensuring open and fair markets." Still, signs of a possible revival of monopsony as an issue of actionable public concern emerged in spring 2010, when President Barack Obama's chief antitrust enforcer Christine Varney co-hosted with Secretary of Agriculture Tom Vilsack the first of five workshops on economic concentration in the food industry. With monopsonistic conditions in the farm and food economy supposedly at the center of Varney's agenda to revivify antitrust after thirty years of inaction, rural populists have applauded the move. Few expect, however, that any significant policies will be implemented, and the meetings seem to have gained little attention outside of farm country.[33]

Monopsony is an ugly and generally unfamiliar word, yet the economic world it describes is precisely the one in which postwar Americans lived. The concentrated buying power of large retailers came to shape most consumers' day-to-day shopping choices and mapped out the rules of economic engagement for the producers of the goods that ended up on store shelves. The fact that monopsony power raised legitimate economic concerns for both consumers and producers, and for firms large and small on opposite ends of supply chains, endowed the issue with a remarkable populist potential to disrupt the political impasse between liberal and conservative, red- and blue-state worldviews. Between the end of World War II and the 1970s, in fact, the problem of monopsony repeatedly offered opportunities for urban consumers and rural producers to unite around a structural critique of postwar American capitalism. Yet the political discourse of economic concentration in the modern United States has consistently centered on *monopoly*. The problem of concentrated buying power, despite being a matter of long-term economic concern, has only occasionally and briefly made for interesting political bedfellowships, generally during short-term economic disruptions. Concentrated buying power thus remains a problem that many can recognize but few can name, let alone apprehend.

Notes

1. Nelson Lichtenstein, *The Retail Revolution: How Wal-Mart Created a Brave New World of Business* (New York: Metropolitan Books, 2009), 1.
2. Richard Hofstadter, "What Happened to the Antitrust Movement?" in *The Paranoid Style in American Politics, and Other Essays* (New York: Knopf, 1965), 188–237.
3. Robert J. Thornton, "How Joan Robinson and B. L. Hallward Named Monopsony," *Journal of Economic Perspectives* 18 (Spring 2004): 257–61.
4. A comprehensive and clear summary of the economic theory of monopsony power is Roger Clarke et al., *Buyer Power and Competition in European Food Retailing* (Northampton, Mass.: Edward Elgar, 2002), 2–26.
5. Jonathan J. Bean, *Beyond the Broker State: Federal Policies toward Small Business, 1936–1961* (Chapel Hill: University of North Carolina Press, 1996), 17–36; Richard S. Tedlow, *New and Improved: The Story of Mass Marketing in America* (New York: Basic Books, 1990), 214–26; Carl G. Ryant, "The South and the Movement against Chain Stores," *Journal of Southern History* 39 (May 1973): 207–22; Joseph Palamountain, *The Politics of Distribution* (Cambridge, Mass.: Harvard University Press, 1955).
6. Tedlow, *New and Improved*, 226–35; Meg Jacobs, *Pocketbook Politics: Economic Citizenship in Twentieth-Century America* (Princeton: Princeton University Press, 2005), 15–30; House Committee on Ways and Means, *Excise Tax on Retail Stores, Vol. 1, Hearing*, 76th Cong., 3d sess., 27–30 March, 1–5, 8–11 April 1940; Joel B. Dirlam and Alfred E. Kahn, "Antitrust Law and the Big Buyer: Another Look at the A & P Case," *Journal of Political Economy* 60 (April 1952): 118–32; Roland Marchand, "Suspended in Time: Mom-and-Pop Groceries, Chain Stores, and National Advertising during the World War II Interlude," in *Produce and Conserve, Share and Play Square: The Grocer and the Consumer on the Home-Front Battlefield during World War II*, ed. Barbara McLean Ward (Hanover, N.H.: University Press of New England, 1994), 117–39.
7. General Foods Corporation, *Annual Report*, 1953, 5; John A. Logan, "Modern Food Distribution," *Vital Speeches of the Day*, 15 November 1958, 85; Max Mandell Zimmerman, *The Super Market: A Revolution in Distribution* (New York: McGraw-Hill, 1955), 322. A trenchant critique of the gendered assumptions of male supermarket managers that they were empowering the "Consumer Queen" is Tracey A. Deutsch, *Building a Housewife's Paradise: Gender, Politics, and American Grocery Stores in the Twentieth Century* (Chapel Hill: University of North Carolina Press, 2010).
8. National Association of Retail Grocers, *The Merger Movement in Retail Food Distribution, 1955–1958* (Chicago: National Association of Retail Grocers, 1959), 3; Rom J. Markin, *The Supermarket: An Analysis of Growth, Development, and Change*, rev. ed. (Pullman: Washington

State University Press, 1968), 27; Willard F. Mueller and Leon Garoian, *Changes in the Market Structure of Grocery Retailing* (Madison: University of Wisconsin Press, 1961), 20, 22; Markin, *The Supermarket*, 29, 34; Paul D. Converse, "Twenty-Five Years of Wholesaling: A Revolution in Food Wholesaling," *Journal of Marketing* (1957): 40–53; Daniel I. Padberg, *The Economics of Food Retailing* (Ithaca, N.Y.: Food Distribution Program, 1969), 19.

9. House Committee on the Judiciary, *Current Antitrust Problems, Part 1, Hearings*, 84th Cong., 1st sess., 10–13, 16–18 May 1955, 3; Senate Committee on Interstate and Foreign Commerce, *Fair Trade, Hearing*, 85th Cong., 2d sess., 21, 22 July 1958, 5.

10. Bean, *Beyond the Broker State*, 51, 59; House Select Committee on Small Business, *Congress and the Monopoly Problem: Fifty-Six Years of Antitrust Development, 1900–1956*, 84th Cong., 1st sess., 1957, H. Doc. 240, 333.

11. The decision allowed a firm to mount a complete (as opposed to partial) legal defense against Robinson-Patman enforcement by declaring that apparent price discriminations were a product of a "good faith" effort to meet competitors' prices.

12. House Committee on the Judiciary, *To Amend Sections 2 and 3 of the Clayton Act, Hearings*, 84th Cong., 2d sess., 18–20, 26 April 1956, 10; Senate Committee on the Judiciary, *To Amend Section 2 of the Clayton Act, Part 2, Hearings*, 85th Cong., 1st sess., 27–29 March, 2–5 April 1957, 971, 1008. On Patman, see Nancy Beck Young, *Wright Patman: Populism, Liberalism, and the American Dream* (Dallas, Tex.: Southern Methodist University Press, 2000).

13. David S. Law and David T. Zaring, "Law versus Ideology: The Supreme Court and the Use of Legislative History," *William and Mary Law Review* 51 (2010): 1699.

14. *Congressional Record*, 84th Cong., 2d sess., 26 March 1956, 102, pt. 4: 5602.

15. "Industrial Concentration and Monopoly Power," *Economic Intelligence*, August 1957, 1–2, Box 4, Series II, Chamber of Commerce of the United States Records, Hagley Museum and Library Archives, Wilmington, Del.; House Committee on the Judiciary, *Current Antitrust Problems, Part 2, Hearings*, 84th Cong., 1st sess., 23–25 May, 6 June 1955, 1655; Mannes quoted in John J. Lindsay, "The Giant Non-Economy Size," *Nation*, 9 December 1961, 472.

16. Orville L. Freeman to Lyndon B. Johnson, 2 March 1964, Folder 17, Box 4259, RG 16, Records of the Secretary of Agriculture, Entry 17, General Correspondence (hereinafter NARA RG16, E17), National Archives II, College Park, Md.; Orville L. Freeman to Lyndon B. Johnson, 24 March 1964, ibid; Lyndon B. Johnson, "The President's News Conference at the LBJ Ranch," 28 March 1964, in *Public Papers of the Presidents of the United States* (Washington, D.C.: GPO, 1964), 428, 430.

17. Senate Committee on Commerce, *Study of Food Marketing, Part 2, Hearing*, 88th Cong., 2d sess., 8, 13, 16, 22, 23, 29, 30 April 1964, 183, 247, 224, 259, 261.

18. Orville L. Freeman to Charles L. Schultze, 14 November 1966, Folder 24, Box 4458, NARA RG 16, E17; Senate Committee on Agriculture, *National Commission on Food Marketing, Hearing*, 94th Cong., 2d sess., 23, 25 June 1976, 41.

19. National Commission on Food Marketing, *Organization and Competition in Food Retailing* (Washington, D.C.: GPO, 1966), 333, 334; Angus McDonald, "The National Commission on Food Marketing: Legislative Analysis Memorandum #1–66," 21 June 1966, 2, Folder 24, Box 4458, NARA RG 16, E17; Orville L. Freeman to DeVier Pierson, September 15, 1967, Folder 3, Box 4632, NARA RG 16, E17.

20. Richard J. Archer, "Techniques of Litigating Government Merger Cases Conglomerates and Other Modern Merger Movements: Acquisitions under Antitrust Attack," *Business Lawyer* 25 (January 1970): 723–34; Louis M. Kohlmeier, "Acquisitions by National Tea Barred for 10 Years in a Broad FTC Ruling," *Wall Street Journal*, 16 March 1966, 3; "Food Buyers and Sellers," *New Republic*, 28 January 1967, 9.

21. Markin, *Supermarket*, 1, 19; Walter J. Salmon, Robert D. Buzzell, and Stanton G. Cort, *The Super-Store: Strategic Implications for the Seventies* (New York: Family Circle, 1972), 11; "Shifting Gears," *Forbes*, 1 November 1972, 29; "Big Marketplace, Big Stores," *Forbes*, 10 December 1979, 101.

22. Warren J. Belasco, *Appetite for Change: How the Counterculture Took on the Food Industry*, 2d ed. (Ithaca, N.Y.: Cornell University Press, 2007), 33, 37, 87–93; Jennifer Cross, *The Supermarket Trap: The Consumer and the Food Industry*, rev. ed. (Bloomington: Indiana University Press, 1976), 118.

23. Isadore Barmash, "President Scores Biggest Industry," *New York Times*, 9 April 1972, F1, 4; Earl L. Butz, "The Farmer as the Good Guy," *New York Times*, 15 April 1972, 31; Deborah Plys to Richard M. Nixon, 5 April 1973, Folder 3, Box 5689, NARA RG 16, E17; Helen Malasig to Earl Butz, 4 February 1973, ibid., Folder 1; Virginia Harris and Fern Krauss to Earl Butz, 18 April 1973, ibid., Folder 3. On the broader context of post–World War II consumer protests, see Lawrence B. Glickman, *Buying Power: A History of Consumer Activism in America* (Chicago: University of Chicago Press, 2009), 255–310.

24. Jim Hightower, *Eat Your Heart Out: Food Profiteering in America* (New York: Vintage Books, 1975), 158–60, 180, quote on 117; "Cattle Feeders Sue Store Chains," *Wall Street Journal*, 3 December 1975, 18. The cases not settled out of court were ultimately dismissed by a federal judge: "U.S. Judge Dismisses 12 Suits by Cattlemen against Food Chains," *Wall Street Journal*, 14 December 1977, 16.

25. Joint Economic Committee, *Food Chain Pricing Activities, Hearing*, 93d Cong., 2d sess., 9, 12, 16, 17 December 1974, 164; Senate Committee on Agriculture, *Food Market Structure and Marketing Costs, Hearing*, 94th Cong., 1st sess., 27, 28 February, 3 March 1975, 4–5; House Committee on the Judiciary, *Food Industry Antitrust Report Act, Hearing*, 94th Cong., 2d sess, 4, 6 February, 17 March 1976, 33; Senate Committee on Agriculture, *National Food Marketing Commission, Hearing*, 94th Cong., 2d sess., 23, 25 June 1976, passim.

26. Shane Hamilton, *Trucking Country: The Road to America's Wal-Mart Economy* (Princeton, N.J.: Princeton University Press, 2008), 223–24.

27. Richard A. Posner, "The Chicago School of Antitrust Analysis," *University of Chicago Law Review* 127 (April 1979): 925–48; Charles F. Hyde and Jeffrey M. Perloff, "Can Monopsony Power be Estimated?" *American Journal of Agricultural Economics* 76 (December 1994): 1151–55.

28. House Committee on the Budget, *Food Inflation, Vol. 5, Hearing*, 96th Cong., 1st sess., 9 July 1979, 51, 53, 54, 102, 104.

29. Eduardo Canedo, "The Origins of Neoliberalism: Jimmy Carter and the Ideology of Deregulation," presentation at the Policy History Conference, Charlottesville, Va., 4 June 2006; House Committee on Agriculture, *Review of Administration's Efforts to Deal with Food Price Inflation, Hearing*, 96th Cong., 1st sess., 4 April 1979, 10–36, 14, 16.

30. House Committee on the Judiciary, *Mergers and Concentration: The Food Industries, Hearings*, 100th Cong., 1st sess., 11 May 1988, 1; Edward W. McLaughlin and Gerard F. Hawkes, "Twenty Years of Change in the Structure, Costs, and Financial Performance of Food Chains," *Agribusiness* 2 (Spring 1986): 115–16.

31. Lichtenstein, *The Retail Revolution*, 35–43.

32. Jean Kinsey, "The New Food Economy: Consumers, Farms, Pharms, and Science," *American Journal of Agricultural Economics* 83 (December 2001): 1122–23, 1113.

33. Senate Committee on the Judiciary, *Monopsony Issues in Agriculture: Buying Power of Processors in Our Nation's Agricultural Markets, Hearings*, 108th Cong., 1st sess., 30 October 2003; Christopher Leonard, "Federal Regulators Launch Probe of Big Agriculture," *Associated Press*, 8 March 2010; Christine A. Varney, "Vigorous Antitrust Enforcement in this Challenging Era," address before the Center for American Progress, 11 May 2009: available at <http://www.justice.gov/atr/public/speeches/245777.pdf>.

10

Rethinking the Postwar Corporation

Management, Monopolies, and Markets

LOUIS HYMAN

While postwar American politicians juxtaposed the free markets of the U.S. economy to the centrally planned economies of the USSR, John Kenneth Galbraith, the celebrated postwar economist and intellectual, argued in 1967 that "we have an economic system which, whatever its formal ideological billing, is in substantial part a planned economy."[1] For his main evidence, Galbraith pointed to the operations of the five hundred largest industrial corporations that produced two-thirds of this planned-but-capitalist economy's manufactured goods. Despite free market ideology, these corporations carefully avoided market-based relationships. Managers, capital, and supply chains were all internalized rather than contracted. Through planning, Galbraith argued, corporations "minimize[d] or [got] rid of market influences" and it was this private planning by corporations, often bigger than many of the world's governments, that defined postwar American capitalism.[2]

In Galbraith's model, big businesses—planned and inefficient—had to be big because they had to contain all the functions that they would not trust to the market. His critique of planning compared the American to the Soviet economy, where the planned economy underpinned a repressive society. Yet in the United States, the main bugbear of the misuse of economic power had always centered on monopoly, not planning. In a convoluted way, the fall of this American planned economy twenty years before the fall of the Soviet one partially resulted from the postwar attempt to restrain what was seen as a new form of monopoly, the conglomerate. While either the government or the market could have disciplined the growth of conglomerates, only the markets had any meaningful effect, despite vocal objections by regulators. This gnarly history reveals the complex transformation underway as the postwar corporation became the corporation of today.

The conglomerate was a new form of the corporation that rose in importance during the postwar period emerging from the defense economy, the rising stock market, and the strict antimonopoly laws of the period. It was not a monopoly but shared the monopoly's ability to inspire a fear of economic concentration. Neither horizontally nor vertically integrated, the conglomerate corporation was a hodgepodge of different industries. In only a few years, conglomerators like Charles "Tex" Thornton of Litton Industries and James Ling of LTV assembled companies among the largest in the United States. Investors admired the "synergies" made possible by the triumph of these men who claimed that they could manage anything.[3] At the height of the infatuation with conglomerates in 1965, *Time* magazine reported that it was the "hard-driving Litton management" that boosted the value of Thornton's acquisitions, and Litton was seen as the best place for young executives to learn the most innovative management techniques.[4] Lammot du Pont Copeland, president of Du Pont, jested that "running a conglomerate is a job for management geniuses, not for ordinary mortals like us at Du Pont."[5] A mystique about their management underpinned their rising values, yet it was mergers and acquisitions that enabled most conglomerate growth.

The real source of most conglomerate "value" emerged instead from financial chicanery predicated on a rising stock market that enabled aggressive mergers and acquisitions. While most postwar firms relied on retained earnings, conglomerates creatively borrowed from capital markets to finance their expansion. By 1969, these stock market darlings disappeared, as a suddenly bearish market undid their complicated financial schemes.[6] The financial practices of the conglomerates in the 1960s inaugurated an era of financial daring more closely associated with the 1980s. While the names of many conglomerates were forgotten, their financial methods were not, and it was partially through their example that finance took a new hold on American business.

Yet the conglomerate, at the same time, came in the 1970s to represent the worst excesses of the bloated postwar corporation. The largest conglomerates of the mid-1960s, like LTV, fell apart by the mid-1970s, or, like General Electric, so totally reorganized themselves as to be celebrated as harbingers of a new kind of corporation. The new lean corporations of the post-1970s period found their intellectual and managerial roots, curiously, in the sprawling conglomerates of the postwar period. Without the failure of the conglomerate, the explanations of "how a firm should operate" that guided the post-1970s capitalism would not have been possible. Conglomerates provided the perfect narrative through which a generation of management consultants could buttress their theories of corporate organization and, in the process, help justify and implement a new form of the American corporation. In the critique of the conglomerate, a new set of financial and organizational ideas became dominant and reshaped the way business experts understood the relationship between monopolies, markets, and the corporation. Every assumption about the corporation was rethought.

Americans have a long history of opposing monopolies, believing that through the power of market concentration a company could dominate an industry and thereby price gouge consumers, undermine small businesses, and subvert the political process. Antitrust laws, beginning with the Sherman Anti-Trust Act of 1890, sought to defend small business against the power of these large monopolies. While the specific ways in which monopolies consolidated and used their power might have been theoretically rigorous, popular reasoning has held that if a corporation seemed powerful, the only explanation was that it was too big. U.S. Steel, as the classic example, could buy out its competition and then set steel prices for the country, to its own advantage.[7] Bigness was sufficient, in many quarters, to prove insidiousness.

Postwar conglomerates, similar in size to monopolies, elicited the same level of anti-bigness resentment, yet unlike monopolies, they lacked the market power to set prices. Conglomerates contain interests in wildly dissimilar businesses. While U.S. Steel owned wire, structural, and many other forms of steel manufacturing, LTV at its apex in 1968 produced golf balls, rental cars, missiles, electronics, and packaged meat. Unlike a monopoly, which dominates a market, a conglomerate usually does not. While the advantages of price-setting are obvious, the advantages of a string of unrelated business units are not. Size does not always create pricing power.

Why the conglomerate arose to prominence in the postwar period has been debated.[8] One argument holds that conglomerates arose from the windfall tax provisions of World War II. Profitable corporations looked for companies to buy with losses and reduce their taxes, rather than give their windfall profits to the U.S. government. For example, Textron, began as a textile company but through its acquisitions eventually became a diversified conglomerate. Textron enjoyed exemption from federal taxes until 1964 from these "tax carry-forward" losses.[9] While the argument for a tax-based origin of conglomerates makes sense, the evidence points us toward other explanations. Even the FTC in its 1948 investigation seeking out these new conglomerates could only find one in the entire country, despite an enormous rise in mergers during and after World War II.[10] Conglomerates like Textron initially bought and sold other companies in a desperate search for ways to avoid their tax bills. What pushed the explosion of conglomerates, long after the war ended, was the combination of increasingly strict enforcement of antitrust law, a rising defense economy, and a renewed interest in financial innovation unseen since the Crash of 1929. The passage of the Celler-Kefauver Anti-Merger Act reaffirmed the importance of antitrust law in the United States, and between 1950 and 1967, the federal government launched 801 antimerger cases.[11] Conflating mergers,

monopolies, and a classic American fear of the effect of economic power on politics, the Tennessee Democratic Senator Estes Kefauver declared that "through monopolistic mergers the people are losing power to direct their own economic
welfare. When they lose the power to direct their economic welfare, they also lose
the means to direct their political future."[12]

While the editors of *Fortune* magazine bristled under what they saw as government's attack on bigness, the largest corporations, which were frequently oli-
gopolies, went overlooked as the government focused on small horizontal
acquisitions in the same industry such as manufacturing and mining.[13] These
cases accounted, however, for only 4% of the total acquisitions in mining and
manufacturing in the period.[14] Acquirers needed to be wary, but could still buy
companies that they wanted. Although the Celler-Kefauver Act gave the government the power to regulate conglomerate mergers, there still needed to be proof
that the merger would lessen competition.

By buying companies in unrelated industries, conglomerates did not come
under the purview of the antimonopoly law, despite becoming bigger. The rapid
expansion of conglomerates brought suspicion. Americans, long accustomed to
equating size with concentration, did not know what to make of these mega-
corporations that were not monopolies.

The justification for these conglomerates, for those who ran and invested in
them, was an abiding American faith in scientific management and in progress.
Postwar Americans returned to school in droves on the G.I. bill. Professional
management schools turned out more MBAs than ever before in American history. The prewar shopclerk-turned-CEO increasingly became the MBA-turned-
CEO. Through management science, redundancies could be eliminated and
economies of scale leveraged, it was believed, to turn any business profitable.[15]
Conglomerators used this belief in management to justify their acquisitions. An
undervalued company just needed better leadership. For the conglomerate these
acquisitions hedged the risk of progress. In the space age, buying one's way into
high-tech industries like aerospace and electronics offset the risk that some older
industries would suddenly wink out of existence. Textron's 1956 annual report
had only one sentence only its cover: "stability through diversification."[16]Its
pages extolled the virtues of its investments in aluminum, radar antennae, and
titanium fasteners, as well as its textile factories. Conglomerators claimed they
were managers of risk, not monopolists of price.

For all the excitement surrounding the management expertise of the conglomerators, the reality was far less mundane than improving operations. Conglomerates relied on corporate finance for profits, not improved operational management. Since conglomerates kept acquisitions independent and were usually in
unrelated industries, the "synergies" could only come from the relatively small
expenses of corporate overhead. Management science, as an ideology, legitimated

conglomerates' acquisitions, but in reality, while management was trusted to smooth over acquisitions, the profits came from clever corporate finance.

Rupert Thompson, the head of Textron in the late 1960s, explained that conglomerates worked better than regular corporations because they could put money "wherever it worked most efficiently."[17] Cash from all the Textron divisions went to a Textron bank account, where Textron management determined how to reallocate the cash across its many enterprises.[18] A profitable, but slowly growing company would not receive as much cash as a fast-growing but cash-short division.[19] For instance, when Textron purchased Homelite, a manufacturer of chainsaws, pumps, and generators, in 1955, Homelite used Textron's greater access to capital to overcome a cash shortage in its operations and build two new factories.[20] Homelite profits trebled, yet expansion was tempered. Every division needed to achieve 25% profit on Textron's invested capital, or face restructuring or sale. By 1963, the original textile division that had given Textron its name could no longer meet this bar and was unceremoniously sold.[21] Conglomerators saw companies as assets to be bought and sold, managed if necessary (and easily since it was a learnable science), not as a life's work. Save for a few exceptions, the actual management of these companies was nothing exceptional. Profit growth came from leveraging debt into more acquisition, not through increased productivity.

Reliance on finance began with the acquisition. Litton Industries, a conglomerate run by Harvard MBA Charles "Tex" Thornton, relied on the rising stock market of the late 1950s and early 1960s to amass a sprawling empire of companies, ranging from small electronics manufacturers to colossal shipyards. Through the services of the investment bank Lehman Brothers, Thornton arranged stock swaps between his conglomerate, Litton Industries, and the acquired company.[22] Stockholders believed in the aura of the conglomerate and its management expertise such that when a conglomerate exchanged stock with an acquired company, the value of that company's stock (now a part of the conglomerate) rose. In effect, acquired companies could trade their stock to a conglomerate for a premium, and then the conglomerate would in turn realize an additional premium from the stock market that expected the conglomerate to raise efficiency at the company. These acquisitions, done through investment banks, required no cash. Without an exchange of cash, according to the tax code, no taxes had to be paid on the increased value of the stock.[23] When the conglomerates sold off portions of those companies, however, they received real cash. The trade-off between the paper value of stocks and the real value of cash made conglomeration possible. As the stock rose, this practice enabled conglomerates to acquire boundlessly.[24]

Possibly more than any other man, James Ling's rise and fall exemplified the workings of the postwar conglomerate. Like many other major conglomerators, he started out with a small business in the defense- and oil-fueled economy of the Sunbelt, but through a discovery of corporate finance, he quickly transformed it into a massive conglomerate. As his contracting company grew in the 1950s, he realized that his tax rate as a sole proprietorship was taxed at 91% like personal income while the highest corporate tax rate was 52%.[25] Incorporating, and initially selling his company's stock door-to-door, the small-time Ling eventually made connections with New York investment bankers White, Weld & Co., who began to issue debt on his behalf.[26] Ling repeatedly bought and sold companies by issuing debt. Using that cash to purchase a company, he would then issue cheaper, long-term debt against the assets of this new company to retire the old debt. In this way he turned debt into defense companies, just as the federal government's contracts remade the Sunbelt into the center of the defense economy.[27] Operational improvements were incidental to the reshuffling of debt and equity. In many ways, Ling's focus on finance presaged the "financialization" associated with the 1970s and 1980s. Before the leveraged-buyout became a household term, James Ling pioneered the practice of using debt to construct an empire.

By 1962, Ling's ambitions had outstripped those of White, Weld & Co., and he decamped to the more sophisticated investment bank Lehman Brothers, who also supported Litton Industries with their debt issues. With Lehman behind him, he extended his conglomerate to buy the Dallas aerospace company Chance Vought, which manufactured planes for the navy, and named his company, Ling-Temco-Vought (LTV). Focusing on the financial rather than the managerial, Ling restructured his stocks, exchanging higher-dividend preferred stock for the lower-dividend common stock. Despite slightly declining earnings, the number of shares decreased by a third, so that the earnings per share—a key measure of a company's value—went up.

While this should not have affected the market value of the company, stock analysts on Wall Street simply saw a jump in the earnings per share of the company. Ling had fooled Wall Street, which only whetted his appetite. In 1964, he audaciously split LTV into three separately traded public corporations, whose stocks were owned by LTV, now simply a holding company. Nothing in the earnings or operations of its multiple divisions had changed, yet when the stocks of these three companies were sold, the market value increased nearly five times.[28] Over a further series of acquisitions and stock maneuvers, Ling became seen as a financial genius. Each additional conquest further cemented his reputation and the increasing value of LTV became a self-fulfilling prophecy, allowing him to carry out his financial plans on an unprecedented scale.

In April 1968, James Ling thought he had it all figured out. His backers at Lehman Brothers, and then Goldman Sachs as well, had arranged a complicated plan to sell various stocks, bonds, and options of his subsidiaries as integrated "units" onto the market.[29] With this cash, he could buy all the stock he needed to expand his empire. From electronics to meat to steel, LTV would span the entire U.S. economy. By 1969, Ling had gone from a Texas electrical contracting company with $3,000 in assets to the twenty-fifth largest company in the Fortune 500, bigger even than Lockheed, where he had, so long ago, taken a second, night-time job during World War II.[30] Ling's triumphs strained his finances to the breaking point, but he continued to trust that he would be able to spin-off portions of his acquisitions to settle his debts as he had so many times before.

Ling was master of a new world, but he was not alone. By the late 1960s, conglomerates like LTV had become a dominant new form of the corporation. By 1967, 150 mergers happened each month, 70% of these by conglomerates— a 25% rise over the previous year's national record.[31] Gulf & Western, Litton, and ITT dominated headlines with their rapid sales growth, achieving gross revenues in 1966 of $1 billion, $1.2 billion, and $2.1 billion, respectively.[32] With the rising percentage of conglomerate mergers and their rising importance in the economy, the Justice Department, under both Presidents Lyndon Johnson and Richard Nixon, began to take greater notice.

In 1968, the FTC announced that because of "growing concern" that conglomerates could "substantially lessen competition," closer investigations would begin.[33] The government investigations could not have come at a worse time for the conglomerates. For the first time, a major conglomerate, Litton, reported a decline in revenues, which compelled many analysts to "wonder," as the *New York Times* reported, "if the interchangeability of management skills from one industry to another truly exists."[34] Rather than miracles of management, perhaps conglomerates were only "paper pyramids" of finance. Tactical moves like LTV's splitting into separate companies undermined the "synergy" argument that justified the conglomerate.[35] If Ling expected the three companies to succeed independently, then what had been the value of the conglomerate's management synergies?

The pressure of the government, as well as the dawning realization that these conglomerates did nothing to increase the underlying value of their business units, caused a sharp downturn in stock prices.[36] SEC chairman Hamer Budge told *Time* magazine that "conglomerate financing offer[ed] only 'an illusion of security' . . . [with only] apparent improvements."[37] Complex accounting, not managerial genius, artificially improved the bottom line of these companies in a way that "many investors do not have the knowledge or patience to interpret."[38] With the end of the 1960s bull market, stocks could no longer be swapped between companies for a premium, and the merger movement was brought to an end. For Ling, the sudden shift meant that no one bought the strange "units" from Lehman or Goldman, and he found himself short on cash. A fire sale of his assets ensued, and as he sold into a declining market, LTV—and the mystique of James Ling—unraveled. In 1969, LTV operating profits fell 90 percent.[39]

Why have we understood that the financialization of the economy began in the 1970s and not with James Ling and the conglomerates? By 1969, James Ling stood out so much that the Johnson administration launched an investigation into the complicated dealings that he and a few others undertook. Once revealed, the financial schemes of the conglomerates were denounced as aberrations within the 1960s economy, worthy of government and investors' suspicion. Wall Street analysts and the wider public came to see the rapid growth of these conglomerates and their rising earnings per share as accounting fictions dangerous to capitalism.[40] By 1970, the Justice Department's antitrust chief, Richard McLaren, told Congress that anticonglomerate laws were no longer needed because the stock market had done what no law could: devalued their business model. The threat of antitrust action by the Justice Department against five major conglomerates including LTV, coupled with the stock downturn, was enough to end the merger movement.[41]

By the end of the 1960s, public suspicions of these big conglomerates, whether monopolies or not, had been aroused and their stocks began to fall much faster than even the now bearish market.[42] Between the Justice Department and the press, investors had their choice of worrying if the government would split up the conglomerates, or even worse, if conglomerates were nothing more than hype, whose growth in profits had come from acquisitions and accounting, not increased productivity.[43] The real danger of conglomerates might not have been power, but weakness. The size of these companies might have fundamentally undermined the productivity and value of American business.

At the beginning of the 1970s, the stock market and American business began to reconsider what they thought they knew about the American corporation and the conglomerate in particular. Rather than just a clever way to use retained earnings and evade taxes, so much of the conglomerate growth was achieved through borrowed money. If the rise of the conglomerate had brought many corporations under the control of those who privileged finance above production, the demise of the conglomerates did not restore operations to the center of the economy.

While the 1960s conglomerates only feigned the reorganization of the corporation, management consulting firms offered an explanation for the conglomerates' failure and a plan to truly remake the corporation. These consultants helped disseminate a view of the corporation as a portfolio of investments rather than a unified operation. General Electric (GE) was the most important example of a conglomerate that made the transition from the 1960s to 1970s, exemplifying how postwar corporations transformed under the direction of management consultants.

Management consultants who began as efficiency experts in the 1930s started to take on the more strategic role of helping CEOs decide which parts of their businesses should be kept and which should be divested in the wake of the conglomerate frenzy.[44] Bruce Henderson, a consultant and engineer who had founded Boston Consulting Group (BCG) in 1962, emerged in the 1970s as one of the strongest voices of the new portfolio view of corporations. Conglomerates had been criticized for providing nothing but capital, but Henderson saw investment as the core value proposition of the corporate structure. The corporation's business units were nothing more than investments.

This simple idea was revolutionary because it considered the corporation not as independent businesses operated by a manager, but as the singular portfolio of an investor. The CEO would treat each unit like a separate investment, with its cash reallocated, not by where the cash was created, but by where it would earn the greatest return. Henderson believed that a successful company "behaved as an investor, not as an operator."[45] In what came to became known as the BCG Growth Matrix, created in 1968 and first published in a 1970 essay entitled "The Product Portfolio," Henderson redefined basic corporate strategy by combining growth and cash into one easy-to-understand schema. Imagine a 2 by 2 matrix, with growth on the vertical axis from low to high, and cash generation on the horizontal axis, from high to low.[46] Where the growth is low and the cash flow is high sits the now commonplace term "cash cow." For Henderson, the cash cow was a mature company that had a large share of the market and generated lots of cash, but whose market was not growing.[47] Henderson's key idea was that the cash generated by this "cow" should not be reinvested in itself. Without growth, the return on that additional investment would be less than that invested in fast-growing units. Instead capital should be reinvested in businesses that could grow, at the top of the matrix. Henderson's jargon classifications for these two kinds of companies—"stars" (the high-growth, high-cash creating companies just above the cash cows) and the "problem children" (the high-growth, low-cash creating companies just below the cash cows—mattered less than the new ways of viewing them.

Rather than treating good management as simply "profitable," Henderson believed good management was at root good capital investment, a belief that necessarily shifted resources away from the mature firms that employed most Americans to new service-oriented firms like those in finance. For the corporation, Henderson's view demanded that even profitable units should be divested when their capital could be better employed elsewhere. A diversified conglomerate, in this view, could have a distinct advantage over single-purpose companies; the advantage derived not just from being in different sectors, but from operating concerns in different stages of the business lifecycle. Postwar conglomerates had reduced risk, but they did not increase profitability, because postwar CEOs had not conceived of their collections of companies as an investment portfolio.

The strategic brilliance of many conglomerates' industrial subsidiaries dimmed when viewed through Henderson's matrix. Many of the companies neither grew nor generated cash. These "dogs" needed to be sold off or shut down since they served no role in a successful portfolio. Cash could not be invested in them profitably and they produced no cash to invest elsewhere. Henderson's matrix fostered and reflected a new mindset about the corporate organization in the 1970s that turned away from conglomerates to more narrowly defined firms. As corporations that had grown through conglomerate acquisitions in the 1960s began to consider the importance of all these business units, Henderson's matrix, and other similar ideas, came to the fore to describe a new leaner corporation.

Fred Borch, the president of General Electric from 1963 to 1972, radically reorganized and diversified GE by embracing and then turning away from the conglomerate model. Although his predecessor Ralph Cordiner, 1950 to 1963, was a vocal proponent of the idea that "a great manager could manage anything," under his tenure GE remained focused on electrical products developed inside the company, abhorring acquisitions.[48] Having risen through the GE ranks, including some time in the GE internal consulting practice, Borch completely believed that GE possessed the managerial talent to make it in any industry.[49] If Cordiner believed that "the growth curve of the use of electricity" was the best predictor of GE's future, Borch envisaged growing in new directions, beyond electrical goods.[50] In this regard, his belief in universal management fit completely with the legitimating ideology of conglomerates, and like those conglomerates Borch set out to expand GE beyond its traditional limits, including by acquisition.

Unlike the other conglomerates, General Electric had enough internal capital to create entire industries from scratch. Relying on an internal committee called the Growth Council, Borch targeted nine new markets both in products (nuclear energy, computers, commercial jet engines, polymer chemicals) and services (entertainment, community development and housing, personal and financial services, medical services and products, education) that were completely outside GE's traditional focus.[51] Thanks to its retained earnings and credit rating, GE could easily finance diversification both internally and through acquisition, without the need for many conglomerates' financial creativity.

The Growth Council and Borch overestimated GE's managerial ability to get many of these ventures off the ground, from misunderstanding the basic economics of an industry to spending millions on insignificant acquisitions. Without capital constraints, GE investments lacked discipline. The success of these enterprises ran from colossal failure, like computers and entertainment, to wild success, like aerospace, medicine, and financial services. While the successes would set a new direction for General Electric, the profusion of products encumbered GE as it had other conglomerates. Complexity overcame performance. Capital was invested with an eye to growth, not to profit. By 1966, despite $3 billion in revenue growth, GE profits had not increased at all.[52] Five of the nine initiatives proposed by the board of growth had, moreover, failed.[53]

In 1970, about the same time as the rest of America began to lose its faith in conglomerates, Borch realized that General Electric could not and should not produce everything. The turning point came when Borch and one of his head financial executives, Reginald Jones, considered buying Honeywell, a competitor to IBM, in an effort to consolidate its computer products. Instead of buying Honeywell, Jones ended up selling GE's mainframe business, profitably and shrewdly exiting an industry in which it had no competitive advantage. Selling, rather than buying, was a complete cultural reversal of the growth-centered history of GE and set an important new precedent.[54] Borch had realized, at this point, that the unstructured growth of the postwar period needed to come to an end. Neither returning entirely to its old business, nor embracing all that was new, Borch recognized his errors and set GE on a new, leaner path. While other conglomerates fell apart, GE reinvented itself with a little outside help from management consultants.

Bringing in outside consultants from BCG, McKinsey & Company, Arthur D. Little, and other firms in 1971, GE developed a new strategic portfolio outlook similar to that extolled by Bruce Henderson.[55] Following Henderson's thinking, all the consulting firms produced customized matrices that emphasized returns, not just growth. Borch did not think a 2 x 2 matrix with just two variables could capture the complexity of GE's operations, so McKinsey offered them a 3 x 3 matrix instead, which weighed many factors but in the end looked very similar to the BCG matrix.[56]

Borch and GE management reoriented the company away from growth for growth's sake. Instead of capital being seen as unlimited, a GE strategist from that time said that managers had to "imagine that they were making a presentation to an investment bank to get funds."[57] Capital scarcity, as well as talent scarcity, made GE focus on these "resources be[ing] allocated to the best businesses."[58] Under this new rubric, Borch consolidated departments into "strategic business units" that could be classified through such a matrix.

Henderson's insights, if not precisely his model, helped set GE in a new strategic direction that was followed by his successors Reginald Jones and ultimately Jack Welch. Borch's profit-less diversification had been transformed into a profitable portfolio. Through the Jones and Welch regimes, the dogs were sold off and the cash cows were harvested for reinvestment in the stars, which turned out to be largely outside GE's original field of electrical goods in medical devices and especially financial services. By 1979, nearly half of Fortune 500 companies were using portfolio planning techniques, conceived by Henderson and enacted by General Electric, to manage their business units.[59] General Electric through

conglomeration and divestment had transformed from a manufacturing company into what was to become a financial services company.

Henderson's successor Jack Welch may have taken credit for GE's increased
profitability, but what we think of as Welch's ideas were already works in
progress. Even his famous strategic rule—if GE could not be one or two in a
market it should exit the market—reflected the ideas that had begun with one
young academic in the late 1970s, Michael Porter. Porter had received his economics Ph.D. from Harvard in 1973 as corporations began to shift away from
the postwar conglomerate model. Consultants and corporate strategists were
trying to figure out how to answer Henderson's question of whether a business
unit should be owned or divested. While it was clear that cash should go to
stars, it was less clear if an unsuccessful business could be turned around or if it
was inevitably going to lose money. In 1979, Michael Porter, having witnessing
the fall of diversified conglomerates, offered a new answer in his concept of the
"Five Forces Model" that turned old divisions between monopolies and markets on their heads. In his model, all successful corporations were narrowly
focused monopolies.

In the Five Forces Model, Porter synthesized competition and monopoly
into one framework, allowing both to happen at once, and expanded the notion
of competition from markets to supply chains. While traditional corporate strategists had considered rival companies the sole source of competition, Porter
reframed competition more broadly within the microeconomic question of
"capturing surplus" that was at the center of the definition of a monopoly. What
Porter implied was that successful companies could not just wrest surplus from
their competition, but had to do so from their suppliers and from their consumers as well. Porter's key insight was that the firm, at the center of the competition, is competing not only with other companies but with suppliers and
customers as well. While firm rivalry still mattered, so too did the pressures from
the "bargaining power of suppliers," the "threat of substitute products or services," the "bargaining power of customers," and the "threat of new entrants."[60]
These other four forces counted just as much as the competition.

The Five Forces Model enabled Porter's later notion of the "value chain."
Companies, in his view, always occupied specific locations on a supply chain,
from raw materials to final products. At each link in the chain, value was added,
but who got that value depended on a balance of market power, that is, on how
close the firm was to a pure monopoly. Companies that did not have a clear sense
of their location on the supply chain, such as sprawling conglomerates, risked
their investors' capital. The vast majority of acquisitions, often in the name of
conglomeration, by large corporations in the 1960s ended up being resold. Porter later found that by the 1980s General Electric had divested 78 percent of its
acquisitions made before 1975.[61]

Conglomerates were not monopolies, but in analyzing their fall, consultants and strategists, like Porter, formulated a new way of thinking about the corporation that demanded they become more like monopolies. If in competitive markets profits were impossible, then the only answer was to make sure one's business was not in a competitive market. As Porter described, competitive markets offer the "worst prospect for long-run profitability."[62]

What value did the conglomerate add that an investor could not duplicate in the market? If management expertise could be had through consultants, the only value that a conglomerate added would have been the ability to reinvest cash without losing it to taxes. Arguably, paying out capital to investors through dividends, which the government taxed both as corporate profits and as investor profits, destroyed the available pool of capital.[63] Porter's evidence showed that reinvestment in core businesses might be a good idea, but allowing companies to act as investors—acquiring companies in unrelated fields—only eroded shareholder value.[64] CEOs made bad choices and paid too much. Porter argued that diversification as an end-in-itself offered little value to the buyer. The investor model of corporate portfolios held true, but only as a way to manage internal growth or limited strategic acquisitions in related industries, not to acquire anything that appeared profitable.

With Henderson's model, the internal relationships of business units began to look less like parts of one company than many firms in a closed market. Some of the functions of those units could be carried out more cheaply, it turned out, in the actual market. Porter extended Henderson's thinking, arguing that business units whose products were in competitive markets should be divested because above-average returns were impossible. If the global wheat market was efficient and reliable, a bread company should not buy wheat farms, it should buy wheat. With this new viewpoint, whether or not a company should integrate vertically depended on the surplus to be captured not the reliability of supply. In an efficient market with reliable delivery connections, like those of trucking and containers during the 1960s and 1970s, supply had become more reliable.[65] If Galbraith's postwar corporation sought to minimize exposure to supply risk, Porter offered a way to strategically consider a company's relationship within a supply chain and to profitably manage it. Once a corporation was seen as a collection of companies, it was only a short step to just replacing one of those internal companies with an external company. Outsourcing was the rational solution for any product or service that could be found in a competitive market.

Good corporate strategy meant outsourcing to the market everything that the firm could not monopolize. Only by focusing on a company's core strengths where there were natural barriers to entry—where the company had a monopoly—could above-average returns to capital be realized. Capital could be freed from non-monopolistic activities and reallocated. The internalization that Galbraith critiqued would have to end. After Porter explained his "Five Forces," controlling the supply chain did not matter as much as controlling its most monopolistic positions. Markets and monopolies went hand-in-hand for this new era of corporate strategies. The monopoly/market either/or of the postwar period had ended.

In 1983, with a Harvard professorship and new synthesis of how this new economy worked, Porter co-founded The Monitor Group, a strategic management consulting firm. Books, teaching, and consulting converged as a framework for disseminating Porter's ideas of the corporation. The view of the proper organization of the corporation was now a far cry from the conglomerate of the postwar period. While few consulting companies were necessary for the operation of the postwar economy, after the 1970s, management consulting companies would grow and proliferate to provide managerial talent for corporations from outside their own ranks. Management was a service like any other and outsourced to the market. New lean corporations could spread quickly through the American and the global economy, pushing operations outside of themselves and relying on the market for managerial talent, financial capital, and anything else that they could not monopolize in the value chain.[66]

After the end of the postwar era, Americans forgot that there was a difference between profit and prosperity. The "good jobs" that all those bloated, planned corporations made possible became harder and harder to find. The patriotic pride that Ralph Cordiner could feel in the 1950s at being the head of an "American manufacturing company ... devoted first to serving the United States" had been replaced by the rising profitability of finance. What Jack Welch offered instead was a financial services company that trimmed the number of U.S. employees from 285,000 in 1980 to 168,000 in 1998 and closing 43% of all manufacturing plants.[67] These investments in the GE portfolio were the most efficient, according to the 3 x 3 matrix.

Conglomerates may have been denounced for their bigness out of a fear of market power, but in their descent they fostered a new mentality that demanded all successful firms become monopolies, at least at specific points on the value chain. The ideal corporation was now a narrow monopoly—not a sprawling empire—that relied on the market for as many goods and services as possible. This corporation reoriented itself to the market in ways that Galbraith could not have imagined only a few years earlier. His erudition built on a lifetime of scholarship and government service could provide little insight into the economy after the postwar moment ended. Through Henderson's and Porter's theories, firms could now strictly delimit their boundaries. In the 1970s and 1980s, the successful corporation's boundaries, shocked by the experience of the conglomerates' fall and the intellectual revolution of consultants became more self-consciously focused.

The sprawl of the postwar conglomerate would disappear but Ling's aberrant financial methods, so repellant to Americans of the 1960s, would be almost normal to Americans of the 1980s, who would endlessly celebrate the debt traders and M&A experts of Wall Street. While the conglomerates fell apart in 1969, Lehman Brothers and other New York investment banks remembered their lessons in creative finance. Conglomerates like Litton and LTV may have emerged out of the postwar defense economy in the Sunbelt, but their financing came out of New York. Finance had returned. While 1968 has been noted for its many world historical events, the downfall of James Ling and his role in shaping that post-1968 world have been largely forgotten. The merger and acquisition methods that Ling pioneered in his rise to power became essential lessons of finance, even as Ling himself fell from grace and was forgotten. Although in 1969 SEC chairman Hamer Budge "applaud[ed] such conservatism ... [as shaped the financial practices] of us who are old enough to have lived through the Depression," that generation's grip on power was waning and the younger generation's memory was short.[68] Legitimated by the ideas and practices unleashed in the formation and the destruction of the postwar conglomerate, a new American corporation arose that amalgamated monopoly and market.

Notes

1. John Kenneth Galbraith, *The New Industrial State*, First Sentry Printing (Boston: Houghton Mifflin Company, 1969), 6.
2. Ibid., 26.
3. Harvey Segal, "The Urge to Merge: The Time of the Conglomerates," *New York Times*, 27 October 1968, SM32.
4. "Corporations: Into the $1 Billion Club," *Time*, 20 August 1965.
5. Barton Biggs, "Day of Reckoning," *Barron's*, 3 April 1967, 3.
6. "Corporate Scapegoats? Washington is More to Blame for Mergers than Wall Street," *Barron's*, 17 March 1969, 1.
7. For the best history of U.S. Steel, see Kenneth Warren, *Big Steel: The First Century of the United States Steel Corporation 1901–2001* (Pittsburgh: University of Pittsburgh, 2001).
8. Robert Sobel, *Age of Giant Corporations: A Microeconomic History of American Business, 1914–1970* (Westport, Conn.: Greenwood Press, 1972), 195.
9. Ralph Winter, "Miscellany Corp.," *Wall Street Journal*, 31 January 1967, 1.
10. Willard Mueller, "The Celler-Kefauver Act: The First 27 Years," Committee Print, Subcommittee on Monopolies and Commercial Law, Committee on the Judiciary, House, Congress, 95th Cong., 2d sess., December 1978, 7; Sobel, *Age of Giant Corporations*, 196.
11. Congress, House, Committee on Judiciary, "The Celler-Kefauver Act: Sixteen Years of Enforcement," 16 October 1967, 3. Willard F. Mueller wrote the report while he was the director of the Bureau of Economics at the Federal Trade Commission.
12. Senator Carey Estes Kefauver, *Congressional Record*, 96: 16452, quoted in Congress, House, Committee on the Judiciary, "Investigation of Conglomerate Corporations," Part 7, serial no 91–23, 91st Cong., 2d sess., 3.

13. Max Ways, "Anti-trust in an Era of Radical Change," *Fortune*, March 1966, 128–31.
14. "Sixteen Years of Enforcement," 4.
15. Segal, "The Urge to Merge," 142.
16. Textron, *Annual Report*, 1956.
17. Winter, "Miscellany Corp.," 1.
18. Ibid.
19. Ibid.
20. Ibid.
21. Ibid.
22. Sobel, *Age of Giant Corporations*, 199. This example of conglomerate financing is drawn from Sobel's work.
23. Terry Robards, "FTC to Study Rights to be a Conglomerate," *New York Times*, 14 July 1968, F1.
24. Lee Burton, "The Merger Surge," *Wall Street Journal*, 19 September 1967, 1.
25. James Tanner, "Road to Riches," *Wall Street Journal*, 16 May 1960, 1.
26. James Tanner, "Ling's Empire," *Wall Street Journal*, 18 August 1967; Sobel, *Rise and Fall*, 81.
27. For more on the relationship between the South and the defense industry, what Bruce Schulman calls Fortress Dixie, see Bruce Schulman, *From Cottonbelt to Sunbelt: Federal Policy, Economic Development, and the Transformation of the South, 1938–1980* (New York: Oxford University Press, 1991).
28. Sobel, *Rise and Fall*, 92.
29. Ibid., 97.
30. Fortune 500 archive, <http://money.cnn.com/magazines/fortune/fortune500_archive/full/1969/> (accessed 10 April 2010).
31. "Corporations: Double the Profits, Double the Pride," 8 September 1967; David Jones, "F.T.C. will Study Major Mergers in Mixed Fields," *New York Times*, 9 July 1968, 59.
32. "Corporations: Double the Profits."
33. Jones, "F.T.C.," 1.
34. John Abele, "Conglomerate Mergers Get Spotlight," *New York Times*, 10 July 1968, 51.
35. Segal, "The Urge to Merge," 142.
36. "Business: The Conglomerates' War to Reshape Industry," *Time*, 7 March 1969.
37. Ibid.
38. "Business: Cooking the Books to Fatten the Profits," *Time*, 11 April 1969; Charles Stabler, "The Conglomerates," *Wall Street Journal*, 5 August 1968, 1; "Memories of the Roaring Twenties," *Wall Street Journal*, 28 February 1969.
39. "Corporations: Ling Sticks with Steel" *Time*, 2 March 1970.
40. "Business: The Conglomerates' War."
41. "Corporations: Ling Sticks with Steel."
42. John Abele, "Market Place: Analysts View Conglomerates," 26 August 1969, *New York Times*, 54.
43. Sobel, *Age of Giant Corporations*, 208.
44. For the origins of management consulting, see Christopher McKenna, *The World's Newest Profession: Management Consulting in the Twentieth Century* (New York: Cambridge University Press, 2006).
45. Henderson, "The Corporate Portfolio," 204.
46. The curious inversion of the axes has been maintained by writers on management strategy despite running counter to how all other graphs are made.
47. Bruce Henderson, "The Anatomy of the Cash Cow," in *Perspectives on Strategy from the Boston Consulting Group*, ed. Carl Stern and George Stalk (New York: John Wiley & Sons, 1998), 200.
48. William Rothschild, *The Secret to GE's Success* (New York: McGraw Hill, 2007), 102; Rothschild was corporate strategist with General Electric, where he worked from the 1950s to the 1980s; Ralph Cordiner, *New Frontiers for Professional Managers*, McKinsey Foundation Lecture Series (New York: McGraw-Hill, 1957), 29.
49. Rothschild, *The Secret*, 157.
50. Cordiner, *New Frontiers* 11.

51. Rothschild, *The Secret*, 129.
52. Ibid., 151.
53. Ibid., 153.
54. Ibid.
55. Ibid., 159.
56. Pankaj Ghemawat, "Competition and Business Strategy in Historical Perspective," *Business History Review* (Spring 2002): 46.
57. Rothschild, *The Secret*, 163.
58. Ibid.
59. Ghemawat, "Competition and Business Strategy," 49.
60. Michael Porter, "How Competitive Forces Shape Strategy," *Harvard Business Review* (March–April 1979): 137.
61. Michael Porter, "From Competitive Advantage to Corporate Strategy," *Harvard Business Review* (May–June 1987): 48.
62. Porter, "How Competitive Forces Shape Strategy," 137.
63. Henderson, "The Corporate Portfolio," 204.
64. Porter, "From Competitive Advantage," 48.
65. For more on postwar trucking, see Shane Hamilton, *Trucking Country: The Road to America's Wal-Mart Economy* (Princeton, N.J.: Princeton University Press, 2008); on the shipping container, see Marc Levinson, *The Box: How The Shipping Container Made the World Smaller and the World Economy Bigger* (Princeton, N.J.: Princeton University Press, 2006).
66. Michael Porter even wrote one of his early well-known articles on globalization and corporate strategy. Michael Porter, "How Global Companies Win Out," *Harvard Business Review* (September–October 1982): 98–108.
67. Thomas O'Boyle, *At Any Cost: Jack Welch, General Electric, and the Pursuit of Profit* (New York: Vintage Books, 1999), 33.
68. "Memories of the Roaring Twenties," 10.

11

The Politics of Environmental Regulation

Business–Government Relations in the 1970s and Beyond

MEG JACOBS

On 11 January 1970, the *New York Times* ran a story entitled, "Industrialists Get Word: Environment." "The message of 1969 for industry sounded loud and clear. 'Environment' is the new watchword," the article explained. "Its impact promises to be tremendous—to some extent in terms of dollars, but also in terms of procedures and philosophies." In this new era, the story reported, citizens would have a powerful influence over business, with a new set of regulatory rights: they could prevent the opening of new plants, require factories to comply with expensive pollution regulations, and force corporations to pay millions of dollars to clean up messes they had already made. Anyone had a legal right to take these actions on the grounds that business was contaminating the environment or, even more shocking to industry, that executives were making choices that were aesthetically unpleasing. From writing environmental legislation to overseeing its administration to taking business to court for noncompliance, citizens could subject industry to an extensive new regulatory regime. "What started as perennial complaints of women's clubs and the Izaak Walton League [an outdoors organization] about dirty water has suddenly assumed the shape of an economic revolution whose ultimate dimensions still are indeterminate," reported the *Times*. As one businessman put it, "We should start preparing right now for a no-growth economy."[1]

This was not simply business hysteria or media hype. Ten days earlier, on New Year's Day, 1970, Richard Nixon signed a historic piece of legislation, the National Environmental Policy Act (NEPA). This legislation ushered in a new era of business regulation, the Environmental Era, one at least as momentous as the Progressive and New Deal Eras. To a far greater extent than in the previous eras, this moment of regulation subjected business to an ongoing contestation, in Congress, the courts, and administrative agencies, between ordinary citizens and the nation's businesses. Between 1969 and 1977, Congress passed eighteen major pieces of legislation to regulate conservation and pollution. Although little noticed at the time of its signing, the inclusion of environmental impact statements in the NEPA, which committed the government to assessing the environmental risk of any federal action and considering policy alternatives, opened the door to a permanent and ongoing review of government policy. Even in periods of conservative rule, the very nature of this regulatory regime, with its broad statutory basis, its inclusion of counterchecks to business power, and its reliance on the courts as a form of enforcement, made it enduring.

The 1970s have generally been seen as an era of deregulation, beginning with Richard Nixon's pro-business orientation. Along with tax cuts and budget reductions, deregulation gained support as part of a more general antigovernment attitude that became central to conservative thought and policy. Yet it was precisely the persistence and, in many ways, the intensification of liberal reform in the 1970s that gave conservatives a ready target to attack.[2] Indeed, the expansion of regulation on business between 1970 and 1976, when Republicans controlled the White House, was as great, if not greater, than what had occurred in previous periods like the Progressive Era or New Deal. The conservative appeal to get "government off our backs" gained traction only in a world of growing regulation.

The most dramatic expansion took place with environmental regulation, which resulted in continued contestation between business groups and the regulatory state.[3] In the first stage of modern business regulation, inaugurated with the Interstate Commerce Act of 1887, Congress set up independent commissions to regulate business practices. The New Deal, which led to the second stage, saw an explosion of business regulation. In addition to creating regulatory commissions as the previous era had, New Dealers sought to create organized interests to offset business power. In 1935, Congress passed a sweeping piece of business regulation, the National Labor Relations Act, which in many ways typified the second stage of business regulation. This measure, and the creation of organized labor as an effective interest group, was at the heart of what John Kenneth Galbraith later identified as a postwar pluralistic system of countervailing powers.

With the third phase, ushered in largely by the National Environmental Policy Act, Congress further expanded the institutional powers that could check business influence. In this stage, citizens, as public interest groups, had rights to compel business regulation, and they could turn to the federal courts as an effective arena to carry out policy and fight regulatory battles. Precisely because the statutory design of the Environmental Era included checks on business power by citizens and extended regulation from agencies to the courts, this phase has proved the most far-reaching and enduring, the least subject to business capture or rollback. To be sure, the story is not one of environmentalists' triumphing over the interests of business. But thirty years later, the fights between business groups and the regulatory state persist.

Creating a New Regulatory Regime, 1970

The 1970s approach to the environment marked a significant departure from the past. Since the Progressive Era, conservationists, with the help of the Department of the Interior, had managed federal land and natural resources. Starting with Gifford Pinchot in the Forest Service, conservationists promoted the interest of business in development against the public desire to preserve natural beauty. Preceding the Environmental Era, business interests had prevailed, especially those in the oil, gas, mining, and timber industries. Before reapportionment in the 1960s, these extractive regions had disproportionate representation in Congress, and the seniority and committee system reinforced the strength of Southern Democrats, where oil and natural gas interests were strongest. For years, liberals fought unsuccessfully to remove the oil depletion allowance, a tax break that subsidized the industry. Even when President Johnson signed the Wilderness Act of 1964, this historic measure, in the absence of a fully mobilized environmental movement, had to accommodate business interests. The measure protected national lands, but it also granted mining rights.[4]

The modern environmentalism of the 1970s sprang forth from several forces. As Samuel Hays has argued, the spread of this new social movement reflected a postwar shift from the politics of production to the politics of consumption. As Americans became more affluent, their goals changed from achieving a basic standard of living to assuring a good quality of life. Beginning with concern over radiation fallout from atomic testing, the public was aware of the dangers of postwar technology. As suburban homeowners, they came to confront the perils of the toxicity in their everyday lives. As Adam Rome has shown, homeowners had to confront the problems of overflowing septic tanks, detergents in their drinking water, and exposure to other contaminants. What they gained in new homeownership with modern conveniences, they also sacrificed in open space, frequent flooding, and other detrimental side effects from rapid land development. When Rachel Carson published her best-selling book *Silent Spring* in 1962, there was already a receptive audience eager to hear more about the dangers of modern living. From Carson, the public learned about the threats of pesticides in the food chain. Unlike earlier environmental efforts to preserve remote places of natural beauty, Carson focused her attention on everyday suburban life.[5]

The dramatic popular outrage in response to the Santa Barbara oil spill on 29 January 1969, when 200,000 gallons of crude oil covered an 800 square-mile radius, reflected an emerging environmental consciousness. A new ecological perspective informed this mindset. Barry Commoner, one of the founders of ecology, captured this perspective best in his view that "everything is connected to everything else." No longer were beauty and health the primary concerns, now what was at stake was the very survival of the Earth as humans had known it. In *Look* magazine, journalist David Perlman articulated this view of the Earth as a fragile finite system, best captured in the 1969 photograph of Planet Earth from space. "As human population increases and technology improves, man in his ecological blindness is suicidally attacking the foundation of life itself." It had taken two million years for the population to reach one billion in 1800, 130 years to reach 2 billion, 30 years for 3 billion, and just 14 years between 1960 and 1974 to reach 4 billion. That growth and technological progress resulted in what Commoner called "ecological backlash."[6] The environmental movement came to question the very legitimacy of economic growth, and as a result, this new ecological perspective posed a fundamental ideological challenge to the values of corporate America.

That ecological perspective received increasing attention, even among Nixon administration officials. At the April 1969 Centennial of the American Museum of Natural History, Under Secretary of the Interior Russell E. Train espoused an apocalyptic view. "If environmental deterioration is permitted to continue and increase at present rates, [man] wouldn't stand a snowball's chance in hell [of surviving]." Senator Ted Stevens of Alaska, a critic, expressed surprise for what seemed like a radical shift in popular attitudes toward the environment. "Suddenly out of the woodwork come thousands of people talking about ecology." In the fall of 1969, *New York Times* editor Robert Bendiner confirmed that the concern with ecology was more than a fad. "Call it conservation, the environment, ecological balance, or what you will, it is a cause more permanent, more far-reaching, than any issue of the era—Vietnam and Black Power included."[7] Another *Times* editorial summed up what was a stake: "Fight for Survival." "Sacrifice will be required and so will large-scale expenditure of governmental funds. . . . But the price of evasion will be self-annihilation."[8]

Environmentalism had more appeal in certain areas of the country than in others. As Samuel Hays has explained, areas with a long history of urbanization were more likely to share environmental values. According to public opinion polls, citizens in New England, New York, New Jersey, Florida, Michigan, Wisconsin, Minnesota, and three Pacific Coast states expressed the deepest interest. These regions were more urbanized, and increasingly suburbanized, with information and service-based industries, all of which attracted residents with higher degrees of education. It was in these regions where citizens cared the most about quality of life issues. Those areas where the primary influence was rural and raw-material extracting—Oklahoma, Texas, Louisiana, New Mexico, Arizona, Utah, and Nevada—exhibited substantially less interest in the issue of environmental degradation.[9]

Within Congress, environmentalism gained support, especially among Democrats. Senator Henry Jackson and Senator Edmund Muskie, two powerful Democrats who were considering a run for the presidency in 1972, led the charge. Each authored a bill to call for the creation of an executive body charged with protecting the environment. In 1969, Congress passed the National Environmental Policy Act, a measure stronger than what either had pushed for. The bill created the Council on Environmental Quality (CEQ) and also required the government to conduct a thorough study of the environmental impact of proposed programs. These detailed environmental impact statements had to include policy alternatives and had to undergo public scrutiny before the CEQ could approve the action. Inclusion of this requirement assured ongoing conflict between supporters and opponents of the environmental viewpoint.

The act gave the federal government the authority to regulate the environmental impact of corporations on an economy-wide basis through expensive mandates on states and compliance costs for businesses. A sweeping piece of legislation, the measure posed a fundamental challenge to private property, markets, and states rights. As it stated,

> The purposes of this Act are: To declare a national policy which will encourage productive and enjoyable harmony between man and his environment; to promote efforts which will prevent or eliminate damage to the environment and biosphere and stimulate the health and welfare of man; to enrich the understanding of the ecological systems and natural resources important to the Nation; and to establish a Council on Environmental Quality.[10]

The Council on Environmental Quality would give the president expert advice on environmental matters. Under section 102c, the CEQ was charged with reviewing Environmental Impact Statements, which were now required for any project receiving federal funding.

On 1 January 1970, Richard Nixon signed the National Environmental Policy Act of 1969. Once it was clear that the measure would pass with strong support, Nixon sought to co-opt this new political force. As he contemplated the 1970 midterm elections and his bid for reelection in 1972, Nixon warmed to the issue. He had won the 1968 election with only a slim electoral majority, and he was looking to improve on those returns. The president also hoped that a demonstrated concern for the environment would offset some of the tumult over the

Vietnam War and make him more appealing as a moderate candidate. To heighten the drama, Nixon signed the bill on New Year's Day, symbolically ushering in the start of a new environmental decade. Seeking the opportunity to get out ahead on the issue and thwart the political opposition, Nixon staffed, legitimized, and institutionalized this new environmental policy impulse. For starters, he appointed Russell Train, the undersecretary of the Interior and a committed environmentalist, to head the CEQ.

In his 1970 State of the Union address three weeks later, President Nixon affirmed his commitment to the environment. "The great question of the seventies is, shall we surrender to our surroundings, or shall we make our peace with nature and begin to make reparations for the damage we have done to our air, to our land, and to our water?" These were bold questions from a Republican president. Laying down the gauntlet, the president articulated a grand vision. "We can no longer afford to consider air and water common property, free to be abused by anyone without regard to the consequences. Instead, we should begin now to treat them as scarce resources, which we are no more free to contaminate than we are free to throw garbage into our neighbor's yard." To clean up the country, the federal government would play an active role. "Clean air, clean water, open spaces—these should once again be the birthright of every American. If we act now, they can be."[11]

Who would enforce this new environmental commitment? Activists kept up constant pressure on the nation's political leaders. Along with the help of Senator Gaylord Nelson, 24-year-old Denis Hayes spearheaded an effort to stage a national Earth Day in the spring of 1970. Hayes set up Environmental Action as a coordinating committee to develop plans for demonstrations across the country. Teach-ins started in January, the first at Northwestern University, where between 8,000 to 10,000 students and faculty members participated. Barry Commoner addressed the audience as "fellow survivors," and he, along with other critics, described Nixon's budget requests in his State of the Union address as laughable, too small by a factor of ten.[12] Speakers dismissed Nixon's efforts as nothing more than a way to outmaneuver them. "President Nixon seems to think that the environment issue is a good thing to quiet down the campuses and patch up the country," said Andy Garling, one of the student leaders coordinating Earth Day.[13]

The group planned a fantastic event, with nearly 20 million people participating in the first Earth Day on 22 April 1970. After Earth Day, Environmental Action continued to mobilize support and put pressure both on corporations and on government. At the state level, activists also sought to influence the implementation of environmental laws. In Michigan, a law professor named Joseph Sax authored a bill to give individual citizens the right to go to court in search of relief and damages for environmental harm.

By the summer of 1970, the White House knew environmentalism was growing stronger, even within Nixon's own administration. The President's Council on Environmental Quality issued its first report, identifying 1970 as a "turning point, a year when the quality of life has become more than just a phrase; environment and pollution have become everyday words; and ecology has become almost a religion to some of the young."[14] Secretary of the Interior Walter Hickel told the nation's leading oilmen, "The right to produce is not the right to pollute."[15] In recognition of this new social force, the Small Business Administration announced the removal of smoke from the smokestack on its governmental seal.[16]

To administer new environmental regulations, in July 1970 Nixon created the Environmental Protection Agency (EPA). The Agency came at the suggestion of Roy Ash, whom the president had charged with streamlining the bureaucracy. It was therefore surprising when Ash, who was seen as the businessman's representative within the administration, suggested the creation of a new agency, and one with such sweeping authority. In a memo to Nixon, he explained that the existing agencies were fundamentally inadequate to address this "environmental crisis" because of the interrelated nature of pollution and the developmental perspective of the existing cabinets. "Our National Government is neither structured nor oriented to sustain a well-articulated attack on the practices which debase the air we breathe, the water we drink and the land that grows our food," Ash wrote. "Indeed, the present departmental structure for dealing with environmental protection defies effective and concerted action."[17]

The new agency would regulate businesses across the economy, establish mandates for the states, and impose compliance costs. Unlike the Federal Trade Commission, which was an independent regulatory body, the EPA would be an executive agency and therefore its administrator would serve at the president's discretion rather than serve a fixed term. Its functions included research, setting national standards, and enforcing pollution controls. Other departments would transfer their regulation of smog, water pollution, industrial waste, sewage, radiation, and pesticides to EPA. EPA would also oversee environmental impact statements. It opened its doors for business on 2 December 1970, with William Ruckleshaus, the 38-year-old assistant attorney general, as its first administrator.

Five days later, Ruckelshaus attracted wide media attention when he delivered the keynote address to the second International Clean Air Congress. EPA, he said, was starting with "no obligation to promote commerce or agriculture." He would not be beholden to industry. Instead, he promised to enforce "reasonable standards of air quality," and he saw himself as the government spokesman for the "development of an environmental ethic" among businessmen and citizens. On 11 December, Ruckelshaus announced his first offensive. He would give the mayor of three cities with known water pollution problems, Cleveland (where the river had gone up in flames), Detroit, and Atlanta, six months to come into compliance or he would bring a suit against them. Years later, he would earn the name "The Enforcer" after the Dirty Harry character in the popular Clint Eastwood movies.[18]

The year 1970 ended with the passage of the Clean Air Act, which set national air quality standards, as well as statutory deadlines for compliance. The act took aim not only at factories and power plants but also at automobiles, which were the biggest source of pollution. The law required a 90% reduction in emission levels by 1975.

In his second environmental message, in January 1971, Nixon requested fourteen pieces of new legislation. The president called for the need to regulate water pollution, strip mining, ocean dumping, toxic waste, and noise. He asked for legislation to tax sulfur in fossil fuels and lead in gasoline. He also asked Congress to grant citizens the right to sue in court for clean water. The inclusion of citizen participation in the structure of administrative policymaking had little precedent and posed a fundamental change in administrative law. The EPA even supplied funds to groups like Environmental Action for citizen education and to legal groups for their fees in court cases. Indeed the Supreme Court ratified that participation through a series of cases, ruling that environmental organizations had "standing" against noncompliant businesses and lax administrators.

Institutionalizing a Movement, 1971–1980

Businessmen understood the threat of this new regulatory world, fearing the impact of compliance costs and restrictions on their industries. Farmers opposed pesticide controls, manufacturers resisted emission standards, as did the auto and power industries, while extractive businesses fought against public land measures. More generally, business leaders and conservatives argued that environmental regulations would lead to job loss and stymie economic growth. Trying to strengthen their image and public reputation, the five industries that polluted the most—electric utilities, steel, oil, paper, and chemicals—took out half of all the 1970 advertisements in leading magazines like *Time*, *Newsweek*, and *Business Week*.[19]

The 1970 elections, in which Democrats made advances over Republicans, changed the political calculus on the environmental question for the White House. Despite Nixon's attempts to seize the initiative on the environmental issue, he had trouble fully making it his own, especially given the divisions within his own party. As he contemplated the 1972 presidential race, he had to balance his support of environmental measures to appeal to moderate voters against his need to retain backing from business and the right. The institutionalization of environmental policy and its fleet of White House spokesmen gave the very real impression of an administration that was taking the lead on implementation of new laws and policies. Once empowered, they could not be fully contained and at times their initiatives proved politically expedient. Nixon therefore found himself contending not only with environmentalists outside of his party but also within his own administration.

On the day that Nixon presented his ambitious 1971 legislative package to Congress, the National Industrial Pollution Council, a group of leading industrialists convened by the Commerce Department, attended a reception at the White House. While they pledged to help clean up the environment, they would not, they told Nixon, be made the "scapegoats" in the campaign for clean air and water. In their first report, they distanced themselves from the "extreme position" of environmentalists. "The view that no material should be permitted to be released into the environment unless it can be shown to be harmless to man and his environment could be likened to a requirement of proof of innocence by the accused rather than proof of guilt by the accuser." Nixon attempted to assuage them. "This Administration, I can assure you, is not here to beat industry over the head."[20]

But if Nixon soothed them, the EPA's William Ruckleshaus gave them cause for concern in his address later that day. "Industries and businesses that must operate in the market place of free choice know that they must change, they must adapt, they must accommodate to changes in public attitudes or they will surely die."[21] Politics, it now seemed, was defined by what the *New York Times* described as a "conflict between those who see man as masters of the earth, free to mine its topsoil or befoul the water or darken the sky if economic necessity requires such action, and those who see man as the earth's guests with the responsibilities and good manners of a guest."[22]

In August 1971, the Committee on Environmental Quality proposed an ambitious program to achieve the standards set out in existing regulations, calculating its cost at roughly $105 billion over six years. Whereas the government would pay for two-thirds of water pollution costs through sewage treatment plants, private industry would pay for air pollution, which would amount to almost $24 billion.[23] Russell Train, the head of CEQ, said the total expenditure would be less than 1% of the gross national product and far less than the costs of pollution itself in terms of adverse health and other damages.

The compliance proposal triggered a firestorm from the nation's businessmen and its congressional critics. General Motors chairman James Roche denounced the "instant ecologists, the new consumerists and other professional critics of private business." "The search for scapegoats," he told a New York crowd of leading executives, "leads away from personal responsibility and into self-excuses."[24] The chairman of Mobil Oil, Rawleigh Warner, Jr., warned its stockholders that the country would face an energy crisis unless environmental regulations were eased, especially the restrictions on offshore drilling.[25] The National Industrial Pollution Control Council insisted that the public's concern with the environment would result in government policies, "which are incompatible with the economic health of our society." Urging a "go slow" approach, Maurice Stans, Secretary of Commerce, warned that compliance costs might "throw thousands of people out of work" and result in "whole communities to be run through the economic wringer." "We have just about reached the end of the line as far as spending large sums for pollution control is concerned," lamented Lewis Foy, president of Bethlehem Steel.[26] "This business of yelling 'ecology' every time we get ready for a new project has got to stop," argued a leading conservative, Senator James Eastland of Mississippi.[27] Meanwhile, David Rockefeller, the head of Chase Manhattan Bank, argued that business ought to take up the mantle of reform "to prevent the unwise adoption of extreme and emotional remedies." If they did not, then the day would come when corporations would have to complete "social audits" to demonstrate their social responsibility.[28]

Nixon played a delicate balancing act. In 1971, he worried about the threat of Senator Edmund Muskie, who seemed like he would be the front-runner for the 1972 Democratic nomination and was one of Capitol Hill's most vociferous environmental advocates. Activists groups that had organized Earth Day were turning to campaign politics. Environmental Action launched its "Dirty Dozen" list, naming the twelve legislators in the House and Senate with the worst voting records on the environment.[29] At the same time, Nixon did not want to alienate his business support. Upon transmitting the 1971 CEQ report to Congress, he urged the country's lawmakers to approach the issue "with a strong sense of realism." As the business community had done, Nixon injected the issue of cost. "How clean is clean enough can only be answered in terms of how much we are willing to pay and how soon we seek success." In even more stark terms, verging on rebuke, if not reversal of his support of the movement, Nixon said, "It is simplistic to seek ecological perfection at the cost of bankrupting the very taxpaying enterprises which must pay for the social advantages the nation seeks."[30] A month before the 1972 election, he vetoed the Clean Water Act, which proposed to require industry to apply for permits to pollute the nation's water supply.

Congress easily overrode Nixon's veto. The act won broad support across party and regional lines because the federal funding for water sewage treatment plants functioned as traditional pork barrel public works spending. Most politicians were happy to receive federal money that would create jobs for their constituents and also clean up their water.[31] Indeed, since 1970, the only environmental budget requests that Nixon had made that required congressional authorization were for water sewage treatment plants. The act called for an even greater increase of federal money, and Nixon vetoed it on the grounds that it would be too expensive. Nixon had a comfortable lead in the polls and a month later defeated Democratic candidate George McGovern in a landslide election.

Nixon supporters hoped this 1972 victory would set the stage for a more conservative approach to governance, including on the environment. In the eyes of its opponents, the EPA had gone too far and had to be reined in. In 1973, as one congressional critic put it, "Lest we be accused of crying 'Wolf,' consider the surprising consequences, unimagined and unintended by the Congress which passed it, of the court interpretation and bureaucratic administration of the National Environmental Policy Act."[32] Carl Bagge, president of the National Coal Association expressed ongoing surprise at how much environmentalists had achieved. "Politically, the consumer movement, the environmental ethic and the drive to participatory democracy," said Bagge, "are all pushing regulatory agencies to adopt policies that were considered irrelevant a few years ago."[33] Critics derided environmentalists as radical extremists who nevertheless had amassed substantial power. Neoconservative Irving Kristol described them as "basically suspicious of, and hostile to, the market precisely because the market is so vulgarly democratic—one dollar, one vote. . . . The 'new class' . . . wishes to see its ideals as more effectual than the market is likely to be."[34]

The power of a small number of public interest groups to influence the administrative politics of environmental regulation aroused particular concern. Environmentalists had formed groups such as the Environmental Defense Fund, the Natural Resources Defense Council, and the Sierra Legal Defense Fund, which brought citizen lawsuits against noncompliant corporations and administrators who did not enforce environmental laws. Citizen groups could conduct their own testing in order to get government agencies to act and could file lawsuits to require offenders to assume responsibility. Citizen lawsuits brought under federal environmental laws were small in number, but generated much media attention. They could prevent industry from locating in a particular region on grounds of health hazards.

These public interest groups argued for a new ecological view of property, successfully challenging the rights of private property over environmental claims. The 1972 *Just v. Marinette County* decision by the Wisconsin Supreme Court ruled in favor of the state, under the Shoreland Protection Act, to prevent owners of property from filling in wetlands for development. The Court explained, "An owner of the land has no absolute and unlimited right to change the essential natural character of his land so as to use it for a purpose for which it was unsuited in its natural state and which injures the rights of others." As a result, the Court sided with the right of a state to regulate the environment for the public good over the rights of private property owners.[35] The Clean Air Act, the Clean Water Act, the Endangered Species Act, and others gave the federal government the power to regulate land use, and these judicial rulings suggested a liberal application of the law.

After 1972, businessmen and their conservative allies initiated a coordinated counteroffensive, focusing on the exorbitant cost of compliance, especially for small businessmen. As the economy stalled, arguments about the economic impact gained traction, especially as states and localities implemented new regulations. In New Jersey, environmental activists sponsored a bill, based on the 1970 Michigan law, to allow citizens to sue environmental polluters for damages in state courts. The Chamber of Commerce opposed the measure on the grounds that it would force businesses to leave the state. "This is legally a ghastly way to go about it," said James O'Brien, a lawyer from the Chamber at the state Senate hearings. "I think this measure will serve to retard the improvement of the environment." A New Jersey industrialist argued that "if the state's environmental laws were fully enforced, industry and transportation would grind to a halt."[36] In 1974, the Chamber of Commerce spearheaded a grassroots campaign to challenge the infringement of public rights on private land use. In a 1974 mailing to local affiliates, the Chamber asked, "What if the government declares it in the public interest to 'preserve open space' and says you may continue to own your land, but you may not build anything on it?" The pamphlet warned, "Believe it or not, there are 'experts' in Washington advocating such policies."[37]

Environmentalists consistently refuted the charge that pollution control caused factories to shut down. Professor Sax, author of the Michigan law, denied the charges of capital flight from the state and a loss of jobs. The only factories that might find environmental laws challenging, he contended, were marginal facilities that relied on outmoded production and were likely close because they were technologically obsolete. By the end of 1974, fewer than one hundred plants had closed because of environmental regulations, with the loss of 12,000 jobs. In comparison, environmental control led to the creation of a million new jobs in water treatment plants, solid waste management, mass transit, and other fields.[38]

In Congress, environmentalism remained strong, even as high levels of inflation, slowing productivity, job loss, and the Arab oil embargo of 1973–74, in which Americans to worry about the price of environmental protection. The oil crisis also triggered concerns over energy conservation and fuel efficiency. The result, in 1975, was a bill to mandate vehicle fuel economy standards to be met by 1985.

The auto industry, other business interests, and conservatives, including former California governor Ronald Reagan, hated this measure as a form of regulatory excess that would decimate Detroit. Reagan was contemplating a challenge to President Gerald Ford, who he thought had been too willing to accommodate new social forces like environmentalism. In an attempt to retain business support and forestall Reagan's challenge in the Republican primary, President Ford told an assembly of conservative small businessmen, "We must free the business community from regulatory bondage so it can produce." "I say to the businesses represented here today, I hear your cries of anguish and desperation. I will not let you suffocate."[39] Yet, to the ire of businessmen and conservatives, on 22 December 1975, Ford signed the Energy Policy and Conservation Act, which created CAFE standards for the auto industry.

When Jimmy Carter won the presidency in 1976, he, too, sought to balance the costs of environmental regulation against the political strength of this movement. As a small businessman from the South, Carter was a moderate Democrat who was more sympathetic to market-based solutions for the nation's problems than were the northern liberals in his party. Seeing inflation as the biggest threat to the country, Carter pushed hard for fiscal austerity, even as millions of Americans were losing their jobs. Although not as conservative as his Republican opponents, Carter shared a belief that government regulation had become too burdensome to the economy. He sympathized with the need for more cost-benefit analysis in designing regulations and he favored flexibility about implementation. So, for example, under his watch, the EPA adopted the "bubble concept" enabling firms to increase pollution from one source if they reduced it from another, as long as the total amount adhered to the clean air requirements.[40]

Yet Carter was also a committed environmentalist. He believed in the need to protect the environment, as well as the health and safety of citizens. He also sought to strengthen his middle-class suburban support, believing that the Democratic Party had outgrown its traditional New Deal working-class base, and in that way environmentalism served his political purposes. In 1977, Carter signed a strip-mining bill, the Surface Mining Control and Reclamation Act, to reduce the harmful effects of extraction, especially in eastern coal regions. The act required public permitting and imposed the cost of reporting on firms. The measure gave automatic standing to citizen groups during the implementation and enforcement process. Carter also signed Clean Air Act Amendments, which imposed strict performance standards and deadlines for cleanup and mandated the installation of scrubbers in old plants.

Carter pushed hard for energy conservation and the development of alternative energies. He was reacting in part to the second oil shock, which occurred in the summer of 1979 in the wake of the Iranian Revolution, when instability in the Middle East led to a decline in oil exports. But Carter also supported conservation as a matter of conviction, expressed most forcefully in what became known as his malaise speech. In July 1979, as Americans lined up at the pump, with gas supplies in short supply, Carter told them the solution was simply to use less. "In a nation that was proud of hard work, strong families, close-knit communities, and our faith in God, too many of us now tend to worship self-indulgence and consumption," the president said. That was unfortunate, the president preached. "We've learned that piling up material goods cannot fill the emptiness of lives which have no confidence or purpose." The path to moral regeneration, and to energy independence, was to cut back substantially. At the same time, Carter successfully introduced legislation to commit the government to funding the development of alternative energies, including solar power, setting a goal of meeting 20% of the country's energy needs from renewable sources by the year 2000.

As the economy continued to stagnate in the late 1970s, the business community pushed the cost-benefit argument for deregulation to the fore. Conservatives funded their own legal groups, like the Mountain States Legal Fund founded in 1976 by Joseph Coors, and think tanks to denounce what they saw as command-control regulation. The American Enterprise Institute launched the magazine *Regulation* to promote the view that government imposed costly regulations on business. In 1976, Murray Weidenbaum and Robert DeFina wrote a report for the American Enterprise Institute calculating the costs of regulation, reporting an annual cost of over $8 billion for environment and energy related regulations. The Business Roundtable conducted a similar study, reporting that the cost of pollution controls for the largest forty-eight U.S. corporations was roughly $2 billion. According to this study, EPA imposed higher compliance costs than any other social regulatory agency.[41]

By 1980, as the election approached, conservatives accelerated their attack on environmental regulation as a threat to economic growth. On Earth Day 1980, the tenth anniversary of the first celebration, the business-oriented National Coalition for Growth announced, "Our national wealth isn't limited by our natural resources. If growth has any limits at all, it's our personal resources—our drive, our dedication and our desire to lead better, more fulfilling lives."[42] "The environmentalists tried to move a little too far and too fast and did not have a proper concern for some of the trade-offs," said Richard Lesher, president of the U.S. Chamber of Commerce, reflecting on the first decade of regulation. "As I look ahead, what we have to do is balance environmental needs with energy needs, inflation and other national priorities. We have to go back and clean up the laws—get the extremes out of them."[43]

In the 1980 election, Ronald Reagan scored a decisive defeat over Jimmy Carter. Along with his fierce anticommunism, Reagan was committed to scaling back the federal government, a bold vision that stood in contrast to Carter's tepid mixture of market-oriented deregulation and continued government-led initiatives. The group of environmental advisers Reagan assembled charted a plan for regulatory rollback. They said that environmental programs had to be evaluated based on their economic impact and on what they claimed was a sounder scientific basis. Days after Reagan's victory, David Stockman, a conservative Republican legislator, said, "There should be a fundamental revision of all the environmental laws of the 1970s, including the Clean Air and Water Acts, the Toxic Substance Act, and the Resource Control and Recovery Act."[44] As a representative from Michigan, Stockman also sought a revision in automobile emission standards. His deregulation agenda reflected more than the interests of his constituents; for Stockman, and for a whole generation of conservatives, Reagan's election promised the possibility of an ideological and political challenge to the entire regulatory regime constructed in the last decade.

Change would be hard to accomplish. Before leaving office, Carter signed two historic environmental measures, which reflected and symbolized the strength of this new regulatory regime. The Alaska National Interest Lands Act set aside 104 million acres for preservation under federal protection. The Superfund bill required responsible parties to clean up toxic waste dumps or reimburse the government for performing the clean up. The act specifically encouraged citizen groups to conduct their own testing, file lawsuits, and implement cleanup plans. The EPA found support from a vibrant and emerging community of public interest activists, and even as the Republican Party drew in larger numbers of supporters, including in the South and West, environmentalism remained politically popular.[45] Indeed, in 1980, two-thirds of the public was concerned about the environment, even as support fell among the nation's leaders to just one-third.[46] As Denis Hayes, who had organized the first Earth Day and, in 1980, directed the Solar Energy Research Institute, explained, "The environmental movement is institutionalized."[47]

Losing Battles, Winning the War, 1981–2010

The staying power of environmental regulations became clear in the 1980s. Under Reagan, the White House laid out a far-reaching conservative agenda, which favored business interests. With the help of ideologically committed bureaucrats and congressional allies, they pushed forward on deregulation, on the fight against inflation, and on tax and budget cuts. Liberals lost ground on many fronts, including tax cuts and the defeat of labor.

Reagan made clear that he did not share the values of environmentalists and even saw them as illegitimate. He drew strength from the South and the West, where the oil and gas industry, along with utilities, mineral, timber, and livestock interests, sought to rollback environmental regulations on natural resources and fossil fuels. He capitalized on the so-called sagebrush rebellion, in the mountain states, where western businessmen sought to transfer land back to the states where then it could be sold for development. Southern extractive regions shifted from Carter to the GOP, where they received more support from a new president who was known for saying things like, "Trees cause more pollution than automobiles do."

For Secretary of the Interior, Reagan appointed James Watt, former director of the Mountain States Legal Foundation, which received financing from business corporations to defend their interests against federal public land holdings. For head of the EPA, he selected Anne Gorsuch of Colorado, who was known for wearing fur coats, smoking two packs of cigarettes a day, and driving a car that got bad gas mileage.[48] Both Watt and Gorsuch set out to dismantle the regulations of the previous decade. As Watt put it, he would change "several hundred" regulations so completely that no one "would ever change them back because he won't have the determination that I do."[49] Their efforts worked in tandem with the cabinet-level Task Force on Regulatory Relief, a presidential commission that sought to overturn or delay implementation of hundreds of regulations. C. Boydon Gray, the chief counsel of the Task Force, told an audience at the U.S. Chamber of Commerce, "If you go to the agency [EPA] first, don't be too pessimistic if they can't solve your problem there. If they don't, that's what the Task Force is for."[50] This kind of end run would prove unnecessary. After a short time in office, Gorsuch bragged that she cut the thickness of the book of clean water regulations from six inches down to half an inch.[51]

With the help of David Stockman, whom Reagan appointed as director of the Office of Management and Budget, these bureaucrats sought to gut environmental regulations through budget cuts. As a congressman, Stockman had made it clear that he did not think pollution was a real threat. EPA's budget for pollution control dropped 46% and its staff declined by 40%.[52] The amount allocated for research was cut in half.[53] Stockman also cut the budgets of the Office of Surface Mining and the Occupational Safety and Health Administration, which would translate into lax enforcement of regulations.[54] Even though Reaganites opposed the centralization of power, they preferred to have strong administrators set the tone and policy for regulation, especially in cases where the states set more rigorous standards. Watt and Gorsuch made it clear what rules their staff should and should not enforce. As one EPA official explained in an interview, "The entire organization is suffering from a paralysis from the top down."[55]

Still, public interest groups could take them to court for failure to enforce regulations. As Jeremy Rabkin, a conservative critic put it, the courts functioned as "full managing partners in the administrative state."[56] To rein in this threat, the Department of Justice, under Edwin Meese, approved of efforts to challenge standing for environmental groups to sue in courts.[57] Meese also oversaw the appointments of judges to the U.S. Supreme Court, Federal Circuit Court of Appeals, and U.S. Court of Federal Claims, who would deliver rulings less sympathetic to public interest groups.

Bureaucratic warfare could only go so far. Business interests and their conservative allies slowed enforcement on emissions, waste, and acid rain. In practice business groups had more resources for the politics of implementation.[58] But they did not eliminate any regulatory programs, and their influence could be easily offset. So, for example, environmentalists joined with organized labor to stave off an attack on the enforcement of occupational health and safety.[59]

By 1983, these conservative attacks on environmental regulation triggered a countermobilization. Membership in environmental groups and funding for them grew. Between 1981 and 1985, environmentalist groups filed 35 lawsuits against the Environmental Protection Agency, the Department of Energy, and the Nuclear Regulatory Commission for nonenforcement. Public scandal forced both Watt and Gorsuch to resign, in Gorsuch's case for mismanagement of the Superfund. Congress restored EPA's budget to its 1980 levels.

In the 1984 election, environmentalists made their presence felt in one-third of the congressional races, as well as in state-level contests.[60] In states like Colorado, the sagebrush rebellion was losing out to those who saw recreation, outdoors, and the environment as important to the regional economy and way of life. Colorado Senator Gary Hart, a supporter of the environment, ran in the 1984 Democratic presidential primary, and in 1986, his junior colleague from Colorado, Democrat Timothy Wirth, emerged as a leading environmentalist in the Senate. Many moderate Senate Republicans also supported environmental programs. Under pressure, Reagan signed wilderness bills adding more acreage to federal holdings in the forty-eight continental states than had any of his predecessors.[61]

In 1990, Reagan's successor, George H. W. Bush signed the Clean Air Act Amendment, a bipartisan effort authored by Senator Wirth and Republican Senator John Heinz (R-PA). This bill pioneered the use of "cap and trade" as a way to control emissions through market-based incentives. This system set a national cap for sulfur dioxide and gave every plant its own pollution allowance, which firms could trade. As a result, the act created new markets for private businesses that could supply low-sulfur coal or cheap scrubbers to reduce sulfur-dioxide emissions.[62] After living through the uncertainty of Reagan's administrative approach, many businessmen, especially large corporations, preferred clear statutory guidelines.

The Right was furious with Bush for signing the measure. To appease his conservative base and win support from business, Bush changed his tune. In 1991, Vice President Quayle chaired the Council on Competitiveness, which sought to weaken environmental regulations. In 1992, Bush denounced Al Gore as "Ozone Man," and, in the Pacific Northwest, where logging interests conflicted with environmentalists' concerns over endangered species, Bush said, "It's time to make people more important than owls."[63]

By the end of the Reagan-Bush era, however, 75% of Americans thought of themselves as environmentalists. Participation in environmental groups and grassroots organizations had more than doubled.[64] In the end it was Bill Clinton and Al Gore, not George Bush, who would occupy the White House. Under Gore's leadership, the issue of global warming gained national prominence.

Conservatives came to understand that they needed an alternative approach to counter the strength of this regulatory regime. In the 1990s, they developed their own public interest movement. Groups like the Federalist Society trained and educated a cohort of legal scholars who took on the environmental movement on ideological grounds. They argued that exorbitant regulatory costs and restrictive rules stifled economic growth. Beyond that, they insisted that only the market could effectively combat problems like pollution and environmental degradation. By presenting alternative ideas about the public good and meaningful discussions about costs and trade-offs, they were able to attract lawyers, pose important challenges, and ultimately make some progress.[65]

The 1994 elections returned Congress to Republican control and gave environmental opponents an opportunity to undo the legislative gains of the previous decades. With a large number of freshmen Republicans from the West, they espoused a strong defense of property rights. A Heritage Foundation policy analyst, John Shanahan, explained, "The freshman class and a fair number of the sophomore class are fairly hard core about the idea that the federal government has encroached on their lives. The idea that drives this movement is to dismantle the environmental laws."[66] In passing the Unfunded Mandates Act of 1995, they succeeded in limiting the federal government's authority to impose mandates on state and local governments, requiring legislators to vote that the cost was worth the benefit. They also blocked global warming legislation.

But without a legislative rollback, conservative gains could be reversed. During the George W. Bush years, business and their conservative allies once again fought bureaucratic wars, this time rewriting rules in a quieter fashion. They also reduced funding for EPA, which massively cut back on civil and criminal suits against violators. In contrast, the Bureau of Land Management received 50% more funding and in turn the agency more than tripled the number of drilling permits for oil and gas.[67] The EPA, under Bush, blocked California and sixteen other states from adopting tougher automobile emission standards than the national standard. When Barack Obama took office, the EPA reversed that decision. While the Bush years slowed advances of environmental regulation, they failed to dismantle environmental laws and overturn this regulatory regime.[68]

The Endurance of the Environmental Era

Why have environmental regulations endured and even expanded? Here the comparison with labor rights, which grew out of the New Deal Era of regulation, is instructive. In each case, new laws took power away from businessmen to

decide how to manage and run their businesses, and this triggered a countermobilization by industry. That reaction weakened labor but did not stop environmentalism from growing. The New Deal regime legitimized and depended on
the power of organized labor, which proved both a strength and weakness. In the
middle decades of the twentieth century, the labor movement was powerful and
robust. But its power was confined to certain industries, concentrated in certain
regions of the country. In many parts, the National Labor Relations Act was rendered toothless at the state level by right to work laws. As union power continued to decline, so, too, would the New Deal regulatory regime.

The strength of environmental regulation came from institutionalizing broad
citizen participation. By being involved in every part of the regulatory process,
from mobilizing at the grassroots to investigating compliance to bringing lawsuits against lax administrators, citizens sustained and expanded this regulatory
regime. In contrast to the situation with labor, states strengthened environmental laws. Unable to rewrite the statutory laws for environmental regulation, conservatives could score temporary victories in thwarting regulations. But they
failed to eliminate the power of EPA to regulate business or even permanently
tame it. Thus, regardless of who holds power in the White House, the environmental regulation of business has endured.

Notes

1. Gladwin Hill, "Industrialist Get Word: Environment," New York Times, 11 January 1970,
   471.
2. See, for example, David Vogel, Fluctuating Fortunes: The Political Power of Business in America
   (New York: Basic Books, 1989) and Hugh Davis Graham, Civil Rights and the Presidency:
   Race and Gender in American Politics, 1960–1972 (New York: Oxford University Press,
   1992).
3. For an overview, see Samuel P. Hays, Beauty, Health, and Permanence: Environmental Politics
   in the United States, 1955–1985 (New York: Cambridge University Press, 1987).
4. Marc Allen Eisner, "Environmental Policy from the New Deal to the Great Society: The
   Lagged Emergence of an Ideological Dividing Line," in Conservatism and American Political
   Development, ed. Brian J. Glenn and Steven M. Teles (New York: Oxford University Press,
   2009), 21–52.
5. Adam Rome, The Bulldozer in the Countryside: Suburban Sprawl and the Rise of American
   Environmentalism (New York: Cambridge University Press, 2001).
6. Karen R. Merrill, The Oil Crisis of 1973–1974: A Brief History with Documents (Boston:
   Bedford/St Martin's, 2007), 92.
7. Jack Lewis, "The Birth of EPA," EPA Journal, November 1985, <http://www.epa.gov/his-
   tory/topics/epa/15c.html>.
8. "Fight for Survival," New York Times, 4 January 1970, 152.
9. Samuel P. Hays, A History of Environmental Politics since 1945 (Pittsburgh, Pa.: University of
   Pittsburgh Press, 2000), 25–26.
10. The National Environmental Policy Act of 1969.
11. Annual Message to the Congress on the State of the Union, Richard M. Nixon, Public
    Papers of the President, 22 January 1970.

12. "8000 Jam 1st Teach-In, Cheer Critics of Gov't," *Environmental Action*, 21 January 1970.
13. David Bird, "Pollution Fight Gains in Colleges Here," *New York Times*, 23 February 1970, 1, 25.
14. Rome, *Bulldozer in the Countryside*, 221.
15. "Pollution Code Urged by Hickel," *New York Times*, 18 July 1970, 11.
16. "Agency Seal Joins Clean-Air Fight," *New York Times*, 10 July 1970, 56.
17. Ash Council Memo, Executive Office of the President, President's Advisory Council on Executive Organization, Memorandum for the President, Subject: Federal Organization for Environmental Protection, 29 April 1970. <http://www.epa.gov/history/org/origins/ash.html>.
18. Lewis, "The Birth of EPA."
19. Gladwin Hill, "Many Environment Ads Held 'Blatantly' False," *New York Times*, 5 November 1971, 59.
20. James M. Naughton, "Speaks to Businessmen," *New York Times*, 11 February 1971, 1, 80.
21. "Nixon Gets the 'Message' But Path Is Not Easy," *New York Times*, 14 February 1971, E2.
22. "The Environmental Conflict," *New York Times*, 14 February 1971, E10.
23. E. W. Kenworthy, "Pollution Panel Foresees Gains," *New York Times*, 7 August 1971, 1, 11.
24. Brendan Jones, "G.M. Chief Scores Business Critics," *New York Times*, 11 March 1971, 55.
25. "Mobil Oil Assesses Ecology Impact," *New York Times*, 19 May 1971, 65.
26. Gladwin Hill, "Cost of Cleanup," *New York Times*, 4 June 1972, F1, 10.
27. "Bonanzas Come First," *New York Times*, 19 November 1971, 46.
28. David Rockefeller, "A 'Social Audit,'" *New York Times*, 1 May 1972, 33.
29. According to Samuel Hays, 60–70% of those who appeared on the list would lose at the polls. Hays, *Beauty, Health, and Permanence*, 463.
30. E. W. Kenworthy, "Pollution Panel Foresees Gains," *New York Times*, 7 August 1971, 1, 11.
31. Paul Charles Milazzo, *Unlikely Environmentalists: Congress and Clean Water, 1945–1972* (Lawrence: University of Kansas Press, 2006).
32. Rome, *Bulldozer in the Countryside*, 249.
33. Richard A. Harris and Sidney M. Milkis, *The Politics of Regulatory Change: A Tale of Two Agencies*, 2d ed. (New York: Oxford University Press, 1996), 9.
34. Ibid., 55.
35. Rome, *Bulldozer in the Countryside*, 235.
36. Walter H. Waggoner, "Industry Assails Bill to Let Individuals Sue Polluters," *New York Times*, 31 March 1973, 76.
37. Rome, *Bulldozer in the Countryside*, 246.
38. "Cost of Environment," *New York Times*, 7 October 1975, 34.
39. James Naughton, "President Vows He Will Reduce Industry Curbs," *New York Times*, 18 June 1975, 85.
40. A. O. Sulzberger, Jr., "New Air Pollution Policy to Give Industry Flexibility on U.S. Rules," *New York Times*, 4 December 1979, A1.
41. Richard A. Harris, "Environmental Policy from the Great Society to 1980: A Coalition Comes Unglued," in *Conservatism and American Political Development*, ed. Brian J. Glenn and Steven M. Teles (New York: Oxford University Press, 2009), 127.
42. Hays, *Beauty, Health, and Permanence*, 413.
43. Philip Shabecoff, "Earth Day '80 Dawns Tomorrow Amid Reflection and Plans for a New Decade," *New York Times*, 21 April 1980, A16.
44. Philip Shabecoff, "Reagan Group Seeks Shift in Pollution Law," *New York Times*, 14 November 1980, A18.
45. Hays, *Beauty, Health, and Permanence*, 429.
46. Ibid., 60.
47. Shabecoff, "Earth Day '80 Dawns Tomorrow," A16.
48. "Anne Gorsuch Burford, 62, Dies; Reagan EPA Director," *Washington Post*, 22 July 2004, B6.
49. Hays, *Beauty, Health, and Permanence*, 495.
50. Harris and Milkis, *Politics of Regulatory Change*, 256.
51. "Anne Gorsuch Burford, 62, Dies," B06.

52. Judith A. Layzer, "Environmental Policy from 1980 to 2008: The Politics of Prevention," in *Conservatism and American Political Development*, ed. Brian J. Glenn and Steven M. Teles (New York: Oxford University Press, 2009), 232.

53. Harris and Milkis, *Politics of Regulatory Change*, 256.

54. Hays, *Beauty, Health, and Permanence*, 504.

55. Harris and Milkis, *Politics of Regulatory Change*, 254.

56. Jeremy Rabkin, "The Judiciary in the Administrative State," *The Public Interest* 71 (Spring 1983): 62–84.

57. Harris and Milkis, *Politics of Regulatory Change*, 272–73.

58. Hays, *History of Environmental Politics*, 130, 135; Hays, *Beauty, Health, and Permanence*, 287–328.

59. Hays, *Beauty, Health, and Permanence*, 188.

60. Ibid., 505.

61. Ibid., 507.

62. Ibid., 130.

63. Layzer, "Environmental Policy from 1980 to 2008," 236.

64. Ibid.

65. Steven M. Teles, *The Rise of the Conservative Legal Movement: The Battle for Control of the Law* (Princeton, N.J.: Princeton University Press, 2008).

66. Layzer, "Environmental Policy from 1980 to 2008," 239.

67. Ibid., 246.

68. Meg Jacobs, "Wreaking Havoc From Within: The Energy Policy of George W. Bush in Historical Perspective," in Julian E. Zelizer, *The George W. Bush Presidency: A First Historical Assessment* (Princeton, N.J.: Princeton University Press, 2011), 138–68.

12

The Corporate Mobilization against Liberal Reform

Big Business Day, 1980

BENJAMIN WATERHOUSE

I can see it now. Ralph Nader, after consulting with the Paul M.
Warburg Professor of Economics emeritus at Harvard [John Kenneth
Galbraith] on the AT&T telephone, mobilizes his forces. They arrive in
Washington on Boeing planes flown by UAL or AA or EAL and pro-
ceed to their ITT hotel via a GM taxi running on Exxon gasoline. They
then prepare press releases for Time and Newsweek, and preen and
prance to get in front of the ABC and CBS cameras. The day is climaxed
by an appearance of Ralph Nader on an NBC talk show sponsored by
IBM, at which he explains the evils of big business.
Herbert Stein, "Let's Hold a 'No Business Day,'"
—*Wall Street Journal*, 7 January 1980

In Boston's Copley Square, two corporate executives were hanged in effigy as
10,000 construction workers marched to protest a lack of jobs, high interest rates,
and nonunion construction companies. In Michigan, "Citizens' Lobby" staged a
mock trial of Hooker Chemical Company for polluting the Love Canal neighborhood in Niagara Falls, New York. In Hollywood, Standard Oil Company of
California took home top honors—a live pig—at the "Cornelius Vanderbilt 'Public
Be Damned' Bad Business Awards." The charge? Windfall profits in the midst of a
crippling energy crisis. And in the nation's capital, a "Corporate Hall of Shame" in
Union Station publicly indicted eleven major corporations for corruption, pollution, and greed. In more than a hundred communities nationwide, a vast coalition
of consumer, environmental, labor, religious, and civil rights groups protested bad
behavior at America's biggest firms. "Stop Crime in the Suites!" they cried—office
suites, that is. It was Thursday, April 17, 1980, and it was Big Business Day.[1]

The brainchild of consumer advocates Ralph Nader and Mark Green, Big Business Day was a nationwide public protest to raise awareness of the threats that large companies posed to democracy, justice, and economic welfare. It was also an effort to re-energize the disparate mass of liberal reform groups known collectively as the "public interest movement," which had fallen into disarray amid the economic "malaise" of the late 1970s. Its organizers hoped to set a policy agenda for the future. "Just as the 1950s scrutinized the labor movement and the 1970s big government," a labor leader argued, "this 'Day' will mark the 1980s as the decade to correct the abuses of big business."[2] Echoing their Progressive Era forebears, Big Business Day's proponents blamed unchecked corporate power for myriad social woes and hoped that a day of public activism would spark a legislative movement to regulate and restrain large corporations.

Despite its sponsors' high hopes, however, Big Business Day failed to achieve its major goals. As a media event, it was little noted and not long remembered. Unlike its organizational inspiration, the first "Earth Day" in 1970, the event neither excited the public nor became a regular occurrence. (In the early 2000s, the group "Citizen Works" resurrected the idea of "Big Business Day" to protest the Bush administration's links to oil and defense companies, but that "Day" similarly failed to catch on. Earth Day, by contrast, has been an annually recognized event since the 1970s.) Given the political and economic climate in which Big Business Day occurred, its failure to grab headlines is perhaps unsurprising. In April 1980, the Iran hostage crisis entered its fifth month, the price of gasoline topped one dollar per gallon, inflation was more than 14%, and the prime interest rate for loans approached 20%. Politically, the nation was focused on hotly contested presidential primaries in both parties. A week before Big Business Day, George H. W. Bush famously lampooned Ronald Reagan's "voodoo economics," and Edward Kennedy waged a divisive campaign to wrest the presidency from Jimmy Carter. Clearly, it was a bad time to refocus Americans' attention on the perils of corporate corruption.[3]

Big Business Day's inability to make a media splash was merely the symptom of a larger failure. For the reform groups who devoted months to fundraising, planning, and grassroots mobilizing, the "Day" was supposed to bring new life to what had recently been a powerful set of interests. Instead, it became a potent symbol of their declining political influence. In the decade after he published his exposé of the automobile industry, *Unsafe at Any Speed,* in 1965, Ralph Nader built a powerful consumer advocacy operation that fundamentally recast consumer product safety law. Environmentalists also notched major wins in those years, as Meg Jacobs explains in this volume, setting emissions standards and regulating land use. Organized labor shaped federal regulatory policy as well, especially through the creation of the Occupational Safety and Health Administration in 1970. Armed with lobbyists, lawyers, media specialists, and grassroots organizing techniques, this broad-based "public interest movement" was one of the most powerful forces in American politics, spearheading a tidal wave of regulation between the 1960s and the mid-1970s.[4]

During the Carter administration, however, that legislative juggernaut came to a halt. The central strategies from the early years—the mass demonstrations and consciousness-raising activities at the heart of Big Business Day—were ineffective by 1980. Although these "middle-class reform groups," as social scientists call them, played a greater role in the United States than in other democratic nations, after the late 1970s they were largely relegated to litigating existing laws and regulations through the courts. Their days of exciting public attention and enacting new policy were over.[5]

Big Business Day 1980 was emblematic of a larger shift in American politics. During the 1970s, progressive reformers who sought to limit the social, economic, and environmental power of business lost political clout. At the same time, conservative defenders of what they called "free enterprise" experienced a political resurgence. Conservative policy institutes like Heritage and Cato blossomed, and business groups raised unprecedented funds for political campaigns. "New Right" politicians combined a militaristic foreign policy, a traditionalist social vision, and a libertarian economic outlook. Corporations and business associations directed tremendous resources into "economic education" programs in the United States and abroad, touting the virtues of free trade and free competition, as well as the economic inefficiencies of labor unions and government regulation.[6]

At the same time, a cadre of corporate executives, business associations, and small business owners engineered a revolution in lobbying practices, organizing in new ways to promote business-friendly policies both in the halls of Congress and in public debate. This mobilization by business leaders relied on many of the same strategies that the public interest movement had pioneered, including media shaping and widespread organizing on the local level. Big Business Day showed business's political mobilization in action. In a poignant irony, the public interest movement's campaign to fight corporate bigness was thwarted in large part by the very object of its animus—politically powerful business people. Led by national employers' associations, corporate leaders united to undermine the event organizationally, mute its media impact, and reframe its central message, taking full rhetorical advantage of the country's economic woes. Their tactics grew from a decade-long campaign, and their successes in April 1980 reflected their lasting influence on political culture.

The capitalist class has always played a vital role in American public life and business complaints about government intervention are as old as the Republic. Nonetheless, between the 1930s and the 1960s, overt political organizing among individual companies and business associations was relatively muted and narrowly focused. During the New Deal, anti-Roosevelt executives led by the heads of DuPont formed the short-lived American Liberty League to oppose Social Security and the National Labor Relations Act.[7] During the postwar "consensus" years, advisory boards like the Business Council and the Committee for Economic Development accepted and accommodated the central tenets of Keynesianism, regulation, and the pursuit of managed growth.[8] Although business groups like the National Association of Manufacturers (NAM) maintained a conservative assault on New Deal labor policies and played a vital role in limiting unionization, particularly through the Taft-Hartley Act of 1947, they largely resided at the periphery of American politics.[9] Large corporations retained small staffs of paid lobbyists—known as "Washington Representatives"—who worked on firm-specific issues, but the collective influence of business was slight.

During the 1960s, however, certain business leaders began to urge a more proactive, organized, and unified approach to politics. In 1963, five former directors of NAM formed the Business-Industry Political Action Committee (BIPAC), the country's first corporate political action committee (PAC). Although campaign finance law barred corporations from giving to political campaigns and PACs themselves did not receive official legislative recognition until 1974, BIPAC coordinated and centralized campaign donations from individuals who supported "business-friendly" candidates, helping to fund important conservative victories in the 1966 midterm elections.[10] Like the American Medical Association, which had created the first nonunion PAC in 1961 (labor PACs had existed since the 1940s), BIPAC was motivated by efforts within the Kennedy administration to strengthen regulations on pharmaceutical companies and the medical profession, as Dominique Tobbell explains in this volume.[11]

Political activity also stirred in the 1960s as changes in global capitalism influenced old titans of American industrial production. Price inflation rose ominously in mid-decade, due to Vietnam War spending and rising labor costs, especially in heavily unionized sectors like construction and manufacturing. Higher costs, combined with notably greater competition from German and Japanese firms, created a crisis of profitability among many large-scale American manufacturers. In 1965, General Electric Vice President Virgil Day organized the Labor Law Study Committee, a group of about sixty companies represented by their industrial relations executives, and labor lawyers, in response to efforts by organized labor to overturn section 14b, the "right to work" provision of Taft-Hartley. Four years later, retired U.S. Steel chairman Roger Blough assembled a national network of industrial corporations united by their worries over inflation in the construction industry. Blough's group, the Construction Users' Anti-Inflation Roundtable, merged with the Labor Law Study Committee in 1972 to form the Business Roundtable.[12] By the mid-1970s, the Business Roundtable, a consortium of chief executive officers from approximately 150 of the country's largest (mostly industrial) firms, had revolutionized business lobbying by using CEOs themselves to influence policy makers.

The nation's oldest and largest employers' associations—NAM and the U.S. Chamber of Commerce—also increased their lobbying and public outreach efforts by enacting major structural and strategic reforms. Founded in 1895, NAM had a historic commitment to fighting labor power, but by the early 1970s it broadened its scope to lobby on regulatory, tax, and foreign trade policy. In 1973, NAM relocated its headquarters from New York to Washington, as its president explained, to keep "in touch with the rapidly changing scene on the Hill."[13] To improve its lobbying, NAM launched a Public Affairs Committee to centrally coordinate seven field branches, informing members about upcoming votes and organizing phone and mail barrages to Congress.[14] The U.S. Chamber of Commerce, created at the request of President Taft in 1912 to provide the unified voice of the entire business community to policy makers, was larger than the NAM and historically took on a broader set of issues. It leaders likewise expanded the group's reach in the early 1970s, overhauling its organizational structure and creating a series of affiliated organizations to encourage business people to participate in politics at the local level.[15]

The mobilization of groups like the Business Roundtable, NAM, and the Chamber emerged when growing economic fears joined with acute cultural anxieties and a sense of legislative impotence. By the late 1960s, a refrain—not brand new, but increasingly fevered—echoed through boardrooms, convention halls, and golf courses across America: a powerful current of anti-business sentiment posed an existential threat to the entire business system and, by extension, the survival of freedom itself. In 1971, soon-to-be Supreme Court Justice Lewis Powell captured the essence of this widespread alarm in a confidential memorandum, ominously titled "Attack on American Free Enterprise System," that he drafted at the request of a friend at the U.S. Chamber of Commerce. Powell both encapsulated the existential threat that business faced and proposed an organizational solution—by banding together through organizations like the Chamber of Commerce, business leaders should proactively confront and refute the powerful "anti-business" sentiment that so permeated American society.[16] The memo's most immediate effect was to prompt the Chamber to restructure and expand its lobbying activities. More broadly, it encouraged business leaders from across the country to join in an effort to resurrect the good name of free enterprise.

Both privately and publicly, corporate leaders bemoaned Americans' evident loss of faith in business. Although 55% of Americans had expressed "a great deal of confidence" in the leaders of major companies in the mid-1960s, only 28% did so by the early 1970s. (In the aftermath of Watergate and the fierce recession of 1975, the number fell to 15, and never again reached anywhere near its 1960s' high.)[17] As Powell explained and countless business leaders repeated, the public's distrust of business led to a rash of new restrictions on business in the form of consumer, environmental, and workplace regulations. The creation of the Environmental Protection Agency (EPA) and the Occupational Safety and Health Administration (OSHA) in 1970 seemed to institutionalize anti-business sentiment. The continued success of "social regulations"—so called because they monitored firms' behavior as social actors—helped unite otherwise disparate business interests. Unlike "economic regulations," which controlled competition to the benefit of some firms over others, social regulations applied across industries and created added costs for all affected companies (though not to the same degree). The rise of social regulations thus united business people by defining a common enemy: the increasingly powerful activists within the public interest movement.

Many American business leaders felt economically uncertain, culturally degraded, and legislatively out-foxed in the early 1970s, and their anxieties birthed a powerful commitment to reasserting their voice in the political system. Looking back during the Carter administration, one lobbyist reflected that "[f]ifteen years ago, the businessman was told that politics is dirty, you shouldn't get involved. Now they know if you want to have a say, you've got to get in the pit."[18] And indeed, by the end of the 1970s, business's concerted effort to "get in the pit" had yielded undeniable results and *Business Week* heralded the arrival of "a potent new business lobby" led by NAM, the Chamber, and the Business Roundtable.[19] Following minor successes limiting certain types of strikes and expansions to antitrust law, an ad hoc coalition of business groups dominated by the three major employers' associations played vital roles in the defeat of two major pieces of liberal reform legislation in 1977 and 1978.[20] The first, a paramount priority for Ralph Nader's consumer organizations since 1969, would have created a Consumer Protection Agency to centralize and coordinate consumer safety regulations and institutionalize the voice of consumerism within the federal government. The second was a massive push by organized labor to expand the size and enforcement power of the National Labor Relations Board and to facilitate unionization. Both bills fell ignominiously to defeat at the hands of what congressional insiders called an unprecedented corporate lobbying campaign.

Corporate lobbying, particularly by the chief executives at the Business Roundtable, also shaped policy by successfully pulling President Carter to the center on a number of issues, especially in the first half of his term. Carter had campaigned as a populist, but once elected he actively sought the counsel of industrial leaders, including prominent Democrats on the Roundtable like

DuPont's Irving Shapiro and Alcoa's John Harper, often to the chagrin of progressives on his staff.[21] Corporate leaders urged the president to place a higher emphasis on inflation than unemployment and lobbied him to accept provisions that watered down (beyond recognition, in the view of many liberals) the full-employment provisions of the Humphrey-Hawkins Act of 1978. Within the fight against inflation, moreover, Carter adhered to business's admonitions against mandatory wage-price controls, which Nixon had implemented in 1971. Instead, he imposed voluntary controls before quickly abandoning them in favor of monetary contraction.[22]

Despite such victories, however, the "crisis of confidence" that had vexed business leaders in the early 1970s was not fully expunged by the end of the decade. Although they were better organized and better funded, the heads of business organizations still worried deeply that anti-business public sentiment threatened to create onerous regulations, taxes, and other restrictions on profitability. Although liberals, Keynesians, and Jimmy Carter himself clearly bore the brunt of the public's sour mood, economic "malaise" also translated into anger at business in general and large corporations in particular.[23] Business lobbyists' victories over the labor and consumer bills had been quite narrow, and executives worried that a slight change in the political breeze could bring them to ruin. As public interest figures like Ralph Nader continued to draw large crowds and media attention and an avowed liberal like Edward Kennedy ran an increasingly credible campaign to unseat and replace Jimmy Carter, business leaders in 1980 still took the dire warnings of the Powell memorandum to heart.

Even though corporate leaders saw their mobilization as precarious and fraught, liberal reformers greeted the rising strength of the business lobby with extreme alarm. For members of the public interest movement, business's political successes in the late 1970s were nothing short of devastating. "This Congress is a wholly owned subsidiary" of business, Ralph Nader declared when the House voted down the Consumer Protection Agency in February 1978.[24] When the labor law reform bill fell to a business-backed filibuster in the Senate shortly thereafter, the liberal outcry grew even louder. Denouncing business opposition to the bill as "the most vicious, unfair attack upon the labor movement in more than 30 years," United Auto Workers President Douglas Fraser publicly resigned from the Labor–Management Group, established by the Nixon administration to facilitate dialogue and harmony between business and labor leaders.[25] Reeling from the bitter defeats and furious over the role conservative business groups had played, Mark Green, a former "Nader raider" and head of the public interest group Congress Watch, began to plot a counterattack against business's political juggernaut. Green's strategy eventually coalesced into Big Business Day 1980, whose specific aim was not only to raise awareness of corruption and malfeasance at large firms, but to protest corporate power and kick-start legislative activities to reign in Big Business.[26]

Green quickly attracted support from a wide variety of public interest organizations, all of whom hoped that Big Business Day would recapture the momentum for liberal reform. Many were veterans of the social struggles of the 1960s and early 1970s, when the public interest movement had coalesced around an infrastructure of research centers, law firms, and grassroots organizations. Ideological heirs to the Progressives of the early twentieth century, public interest activists were predominantly white and middle class, especially young professionals (like lawyers and doctors) who disdained the "organization man" aura of modern business. Unlike traditional New Deal Democrats, including working-class labor leaders, public interest activists had a populist aversion to bigness of any type, including "big government," which they believed was too susceptible to corruption or capture. They were less interested in using the power of the state to promote economic growth than in devolving political power through procedural reforms that made both the state and the market more accountable to the public.[27]

Amid a stagnating national economy and the divisive racial and class politics of the post-1960s civil rights movement, a schism emerged within liberalism, pitting working-class, labor-oriented Democrats against middle-class (sometimes called "New Class," "New Politics," or "New Left") liberal reformers.[28] The so-called "crisis of liberalism" had splintered the reform movement, whose organizational integrity also suffered as the protest movements of the late 1960s waned with the end of the war in Vietnam. After the tremendous success of Earth Day in 1970, for example, activists had attempted other national "Days" around such specific issues as hunger, solar energy, and energy conservation (World Food Day 1975, Sun Day 1978, and Big Oil Day 1979), none of which matched Earth Day's grassroots support or media draw.

To take a stand against Big Business, Mark Green hoped to reunite the fractured base of reform-minded activists and revive the spirit of public demonstration and legislative activism that had been so effective in the 1960s. With a seed grant of $15,000 from the New York-based Stern Foundation, supplemented with money from Nader-affiliated groups, Green assembled a diverse coalition of religious and civil rights groups, environmental and consumer organizations, academics, journalists, and several self-styled "progressive" unions.[29] Reflecting both the class schism within liberalism and the political power of business leaders, AFL-CIO president Lane Kirkland declined to participate because, according to Ralph Nader, DuPont's CEO Irving Shapiro threatened that doing so would compromise ongoing labor–management negotiations.[30]

In the fall of 1979, this coalition organized in earnest, mobilizing grassroots support for protests, rallies, and demonstrations, and articulating a specific legislative program. The political cornerstone of Big Business Day would be the "Corporate Democracy Act," a far-reaching piece of legislation that reflected Ralph Nader's long-standing call for federal corporate chartering. Under the proposed law, companies with more than 5,000 employees would be required to reserve seats on their boards of directors for consumer and worker representatives. This proposal to alter the structure of large companies in the name of democracy and transparency reflected the public interest movement's theory of the firm, itself a vestige of the nineteenth century. For reformers like Nader and Green, corporations were fully *public* institutions accountable for the greater good, not sacrosanct private entities bound only to the dictates of their shareholders.[31]

The Corporate Democracy Act was symbolic, promoted to make a statement about corporate social responsibility and set an agenda for future legislation, rather than to pass immediately. The public performance of Big Business Day, however, was designed to have a more immediate effect by calling public attention to the ill effects of large corporations on American society. Big Business Day's potential to enflame public distrust of the business community was not lost on business leaders, whose anxieties over their public approval remained acute. In January 1980, the executive directors of the U.S. Chamber of Commerce learned of Big Business Day through their public relations specialist Karna Small. Small, a former business journalist who appreciated the importance of positive press to the Chamber's lobbying, reported that Green had recruited such luminaries of the Left as John Kenneth Galbraith, Arthur Schlesinger, Jr., and Cesar Chavez. "[T]here are a lot of heavyweights involved in this project to castigate corporate America," she warned. "I'm sure the media coverage will be substantial on this one."[32]

The Chamber sprang into action, mobilizing the pan-business networks that had recently been so successful with Congress. A taskforce that included the leaders of NAM, the Business Roundtable, and the American Petroleum Institute collected intelligence on participants and specific events and communicated its findings to trade associations, specific firms, and municipal chambers of commerce. Working quietly so as not to create undue publicity or confirm conspiracy theories about corporate collusion, the Chamber-led taskforce shared this information with state and local business groups, preparing them for what to expect on April 17 and laying out a broad strategy to mute the event's effect.

Members of the Chamber's taskforce saw this countermobilization as a welcome opportunity for local business people "to refute some of the false premises" and "provide the public with the real facts" about business. Its mailings urged business owners to "buy space in newspapers" and "meet with opinion leaders in the community, with editorial writers and other media officials, with school and other educational leaders." The taskforce also produced debate primers to help business people prepare for the "false or exaggerated charges" that protestors would "hurl" ("business is greedy; its profits are 'obscene'; business 'buys' power in Congress") by providing pro-business talking points: American companies created an "average of 2.5 million new jobs each year," gave "nearly $1.5 billion in philanthropy," and invested in clean air and water and workplace safety.[33]

Part of this public education strategy involved deliberately redefining the terms of debate over Big Business Day. Although public interest activists frequently claimed that their target was only the largest and least democratic institutions, and that they were not opposed to business in general, business leaders drew no such distinctions. Echoing conservatives' long tradition of vilifying liberalism as anticapitalist, the Chamber taskforce declared that the public interest movement was "clearly calling for the transformation of U.S. private enterprise into a government-controlled and socialist system." Moreover, despite efforts "to project the idea that [their] target is only *big business*," the groups behind Big Business Day favored "*anti-business* legislation that small business people should be as concerned about as those serving large companies" (italics added). To stress the political stakes, the taskforce deliberately rechristened the event "Anti-Business Day" in all its correspondence.[34]

The linguistic sleight of hand that recast "Big Business Day" as "Anti-Business Day" obfuscated the critique of size and recast the debate between defenders and foes of business itself. This strategy was effective organizationally, as well as rhetorically, for it allowed the Chamber-led coalition to notch a very tangible triumph in the weeks leading up to April 17: the overwhelming nonparticipation of small business owners in Big Business Day. In March 1980, Michael Schippani—a labor organizer enlisted by Green and Nader to coordinate the national campaign—worked to recruit small business owners, whom he called "an essential constituency," by invoking a sense of solidarity among small companies, consumers, and workers, joined in opposition to the corrupting power of large corporations. Small firms suffered, Schippani wrote, while their large competitors received tax credits and government subsidies, but the policies Big Business Day promoted would help the little guy. The Corporate Democracy Act would only apply to the very largest corporations, thus making small ones more competitive, and the public shaming of corporations for pollution, price gouging, and antiunion tactics likewise held small firms innocent.[35]

Employers' associations, of course, saw the matter quite differently. The Chamber of Commerce and NAM rose to newfound prominence in the 1970s by defending their small-business constituents (the majority of their members) against liberal regulatory and tax policies that, they argued, imposed unfair costs and stifled entrepreneurship. In an article that the Chamber distributed with its Big Business Day materials, the organization lauded small business as part of

America's "natural heritage" and reassured small business owners that their interests were deeply entwined with those of large firms and the economy in general.[36] Preaching pan-business unity, the Chamber called for solidarity between small and large firms, quite the opposite of Schippani's message.

The structure of business's countermobilization ensured that those arguments reached their intended audience. When a copy of Schippani's plea to small business reached the Chamber of Commerce, the taskforce quickly sent word through its networks that "'Anti-Business Day' and its legislative manifesto can be detrimental to all American companies, regardless of size."[37] Observing correctly that the public interest movement aimed to "drive a wedge in the business community between big and small companies," the taskforce declared that "every small business should declare its strong opposition to the objectives of Big Business Day and its sponsors."[38] The result was striking. According to organizers, Schippani's letter led to virtually no participation among small business owners or their representative associations. Business unity had triumphed.

Residual cultural insecurity and fears of enflaming anti-business sentiment compelled employers' associations to maintain a low profile as they mobilized against Big Business Day. Economic conservatives from outside the business world were unconcerned about public relations or alienating consumers and thus felt freer to attack the event more vehemently and openly. Hallmarks of New Right commentary, including *Human Events* and *National Review*, inveighed against the "professional leftists" behind the event.[39] The think tank Heritage Foundation assembled a coalition of economists and business professors and declared that April 17 would be "Growth Day," a day to *celebrate* business. This "National Coalition for Growth" openly attacked public interest activists as cultural elitists who favored quality-of-life issues for the upper-middle class at the expense of economic prosperity. Framing public interest reform as elitist carried a special salience during the deep and worsening economic recession of 1980 and reflected the New Right's broader strategy of painting liberals as indifferent to "regular people."[40]

The Chamber of Commerce publicized "Growth Day" to its members but declined to officially sponsor it, worried that doing so would perpetuate an image of a Big Business assault on Big Business Day. Several large corporations, however, ignored the Chamber's PR-based warning. Mobil, for example, purchased a full-page advertisement in the *New York Times* to promote Growth Day as "Something to Celebrate."[41] More confrontationally, defense conglomerate United Technologies used an ad in *Harper's* to denounce "anti-business bigots" and list its many social contributions: "making products, providing jobs, meeting payroll, paying taxes."[42] United Technologies' combativeness reflected an approach to political activism closer to non-business conservative organizations than to the supremely cautious employers' associations.

Despite their different strategies and varying levels of concern for how the public viewed "the business community," employers' associations and their ideological fellow-travelers in think tanks and editorial boards were united on the important issue: the need to distort the public interest movement's actual critique into an assault on business in general. Pro-business conservatives were simply not speaking the same language as public interest activists, and the two camps held vastly divergent understandings of economics, power, and rights. Since meaningful debate was impossible, each side competed for the elusive middle by making the other side look unappealing, and the battle-ground was the media.

April 17 turned out to be a nice day for a protest, with mostly sunny skies and temperatures in the 50s in major East Coast cities.[43] The Big Business Day planners successfully united dozens of organizations in events across more than one hundred communities. It is impossible to know exactly how many people participated in the teach-ins, demonstrations, rallies, and marches that day; the vast number of affiliated groups meant that no single organization kept permanent records. The total numbers were not as important to the coalition as the hopes that the diverse spirit of reformist activism had found a collective outlet for its outrage over corporate power.[44]

Although Big Business Day events played out across the country, the headline events occurred in Washington, D.C. In the Cannon Office Building next to the Capitol, more than 300 people gathered to hear speeches by Ralph Nader and other famous activists, as well as dramatic testimonials by "victims of corporate abuse." Congressmen Ben Rosenthal (D-NY) and John Conyers (D-MI), two longtime allies on consumer and civil rights issues, introduced the Corporate Democracy Act to limit the power of boards of directors and promised to create "shadow boards of directors" to monitor large corporations and launch lawsuits when necessary.[45] Later, activists convened at the National Visitor Center in Union Station, where a "Corporate Hall of Shame" singled out major petroleum, chemical, finance, and pharmaceutical companies for various offenses.[46] After a press tour and speeches by Mark Green, socialist Michael Harrington, and Esther Peterson—Jimmy Carter's special assistant for consumer affairs and the event's only direct link to the White House—the day capped off with a reception at the Rayburn Office Building.[47]

Meanwhile, conservative business leaders fought message with message, movement with movement. To mark "Growth Day," Heritage hosted a break-fast gathering whose keynote speaker praised the capitalist system as "the finest wealth-generating tool in the world."[48] To spotlight business's message and attract media attention, the Chamber of Commerce bedecked its marble headquarters on LaFayette Square with giant American flags and 70-foot-tall, red-white-and-blue banners. Gallantly streaming in the spring air, the flags proclaimed the great social benefits of "America's 15 million businesses"—jobs, benefits, consumer products, and philanthropy. To make sure journalists noticed, a Chamber employee worked through the crowd at Nader's morning rally and pointed it out. "Come and take a look at our banner," he said. "It's big enough so Jimmy Carter can read it if he looks out the White House windows."[49]

The Chamber's flags and the "Growth Day" breakfast were small gestures that belied the substantial planning, media manipulation, and message shaping by united business leaders who genuinely feared that Big Business Day could become another Earth Day. The clearest evidence of their success came in the mainstream news coverage. Headlines in national dailies like the *Washington Post*, the *Los Angeles Times*, and the *New York Times* stressed both "critics and defenders" of business and provided (often derisive and humorous) comments from business leaders to balance quotes from Green or Nader. Invoking a phrase coined by an executive at Mobil, *Time* magazine dubbed the event "demonstration by press release" and summed up the nation's collective reaction as "a fairly large yawn."[50] Despite business leaders' widespread worry about an anti-business media circus, Big Business Day clearly failed to make a major splash.

Public interest activists viewed the event as a mixed bag. Although conservatives and organized business leaders claimed a major public relations victory by taming the allegedly "liberal press," liberal reformers viewed the media landscape in exactly the opposite terms: since large corporations controlled the major news outlets, they reasoned, any publicity was a triumph for their movement! At the very least, some claimed, the "Day" had kept public pressure on corporations to be more socially responsible. Victor Kamber, then a staffer at the AFL-CIO's Department of Building Trades, believes the event rejuvenated progressivism within certain unions and encouraged future activism and mobilization. Kamber points to the success of the building trades union winning a union contract to construct a Toyota plant in Kentucky several years later as a positive legacy of Big Business Day.[51]

Other participants and long-time advocates for public interest causes look back on Big Business Day 1980 more pessimistically. With declining public appeal, demonstrated by lackluster media coverage, activists could not raise funds for a follow-up event. In the months that followed, the "shadow boards" released a report to little fanfare, Mark Green left Congress Watch for New York politics, and the Corporate Democracy Act died in committee. In the fall of 1980, slightly more than half of American voters elected Ronald Reagan, an avowed antiliberal who preached the virtues of individualism and freedom. Although Reagan was not the first choice of most business leaders, who worried that he was too beholden to religious voters and were suspicious of his fiscal policies, they appreciated his overt faith in unfettered markets and unregulated enterprise. Putting Big

Business Day in context, Ralph Nader has argued that it really marked "the last gasp of the ascending consumer" and the "breakthrough of the later stage of the corporate state."[52]

Whether Big Business Day's failure truly augured the arrival of "the corporate state" is a contested historical problem. Scholars argue whether Reagan really "undid" the New Deal or whether his "Revolution" had a greater effect on discourse and political culture than on actual policy.[53] The story of Big Business Day clearly illustrates, however, that the coordinated rhetorical assault by well-funded business associations created vital discursive space that helped conservative politicians. The tactics that the Chamber of Commerce and its allies employed in the early months of 1980 were honed during a long campaign that conservative business leaders, economists, and think tanks waged throughout the 1970s. Lobbying both Congress and the public with increasing sophistication and success, pro-business conservatives shifted the debates away from business practices and toward high-minded ideas about free markets. The pro-capitalist, pro-growth, and antielitist message on display during the mobilization against Big Business Day helped marginalize progressive reform in the 1970s and 1980s, and constitutes a central element of conservative politics today.

Notes

1. Chris Black and Timothy Dwyer, "They Marched for Jobs," *Boston Globe*, 18 April 1980; Martin Baron, "Did Miss Piggie Break into Big Biz in Role of Oscar?" *Los Angeles Times*, 18 April 1980.

2. William Wynn quoted in "Landrum-Griffin for big business?: Labor–Consumer Coalition Plan to Expose Corporate Crimes," enclosed with Karna Small to Richard Lesher et al., 29 January 1980, Box 10, Records of the U.S. Chamber of Commerce, Hagley Museum, Wilmington, Del. (hereinafter USCOC).

3. *Economic Report of the President* (Washington, D.C.: United States Government Printing Office, 1981); Robert Shogan, "Bush Accuses Reagan of 'Economic Madness,'" *Los Angeles Times*, 11 April 1980.

4. Lizabeth Cohen, *A Consumers' Republic: The Politics of Mass Consumption in Postwar America* (New York: Vintage Books, 2003), 347–63.

5. Jeffrey Berry, *The Interest Group Society*, 4th ed. (New York: Pearson, 2007); Michael McCann, *Taking Reform Seriously: Perspectives on Public Interest Liberalism* (Ithaca, N.Y.: Cornell University Press, 1986); David Vogel, "Government–Industry Relations in the United States: An Overview," in *Comparative Government–Industry Relations: Western Europe, the United States, and Japan*, ed. Stephen Wilks and Maurice Wright (Oxford: Clarendon Press, 1987), 91–116.

6. Alice O'Connor, "Financing the Counterrevolution," in *Rightward Bound: Making America Conservative in the 1970s*, ed. Bruce Schulman and Julian Zelizer (Cambridge, Mass.: Harvard University Press, 2008), 148–68; Bethany Moreton, *To Serve God and Wal-Mart: The Making of Christian Free Enterprise* (Cambridge, Mass.: Harvard University Press, 2009).

7. Kim Phillips-Fein, *Invisible Hands: The Making of the Conservative Movement from the New Deal to Reagan* (New York: W. W. Norton, 2009), 3–22.

8. Robert Collins, *The Business Response to Keynes, 1929–1964* (New York: Columbia University Press, 1981).

9. Elizabeth Fones-Wolf, *Selling Free Enterprise: The Business Assault on Labor and Liberalism, 1945–1960* (Urbana: University of Illinois Press, 1994); David Vogel, *Fluctuating Fortunes: The Political Power of Business in America* (New York: Basic Books, 1989).

10. Julian Zelizer, *On Capitol Hill: The Struggle to Reform Congress and Its Consequences, 1948–2000* (Cambridge: Cambridge University Press, 2004), 113.

11. Author telephone interview with Bernadette Budde, Senior Vice President, BIPAC, 7 April 2011.

12. "Construction Users Roundtable, Labor Law Study Committee Join Forces as the Business Roundtable—For Responsible Labor–Management Relations," *Business Roundtable Report*, No. 72–12, 28 November 1972.

13. E. Douglas Kenna, "Industry's Priorities for America's Progress," 79th Congress of American Industry, 6 December 1974, Box 200, Records of the National Association of Manufacturers, Hagley Museum, Wilmington, Del. (hereinafter NAM).

14. David B. Meeker, "New Perspectives for Business Leadership," 4 February 1975, Box 200, NAM.

15. "Seventy-five Years of Achievement, 1912–1987," U.S. Chamber of Commerce (Washington, D.C.), 1987, Series III, Box 9, USCOC; Thomas J. Donohue, "Chamber Development," presentation to the Board of Directors of the Chamber of Commerce of the United States, 23 June 1978, Series I, Box 1d, USCOC; Cathie Jo Martin, "Sectional Parties, Divided Business," *Studies in American Political Development*, 20 (Fall 2006): 160–84.

16. Lewis Powell to Eugene Sydnor, "Confidential Memorandum: Attack on American Free Enterprise System," 23 August 1971, Series 2, Box 28, USCOC.

17. "Confidence in Leaders of Ten Institutions, 1966–1984," Box 132, Robert M. Teeter Papers, Gerald Ford Library, Ann Arbor, Mich.

18. Albert Abrahams, chief lobbyist for the National Association of Realtors, quoted in "The Swarming Lobbyists," *Time*, 7 August 1978.

19. "A Potent New Business Lobby," *Business Week*, 22 May 1978.

20. Rudolph A. Pyatt, Jr., "Business Profile: A Foe's Views of Pickets Bill," *Washington Star*, 28 March 1977, Box 200, NAM; Eileen Shanahan, "Antitrust Bill Stopped by a Business Lobby," *New York Times*, 16 November 1975.

21. Esther Peterson to Stu Eizenstat, 9 June 1978, "The President's Meeting with the Business Roundtable, June 15, 1978 at 11 a.m.," Domestic Policy Staff—Eizenstat Papers, Box 157, File Business Round Table / Business International Roundtable, Jimmy Carter Presidential Library, Atlanta, Georgia.

22. Judith Stein, *Pivotal Decade: How the United States Traded Factories for Finance in the Seventies* (New Haven, Conn.: Yale University Press, 2010), 190–92; Benjamin Waterhouse, "A Lobby for Capital: Organized Business and the Pursuit of Pro-Market Politics, 1967–1986" (Ph.D. diss., Harvard University, 2009).

23. Seymour Martin Lipset and William Schneider, *The Confidence Gap: Business, Labor, and Government in the Public Mind* (Baltimore: Johns Hopkins University Press, 1983).

24. "A Winning Streak for Business," *Business Week*, 27 February 1978.

25. Jefferson Cowie, "Notes and Documents: 'A One-Sided Class War': Rethinking Doug Fraser's 1978 Resignation from the Labor–Management Group," *Labor History* 44(3) (2003): 307–14.

26. Merrill Brown, "Big Business Day: The Voice of the 'Stakeholder' Is Rising," *Washington Post*, 14 April 1980.

27. Michael McCann, "Public Interest Liberalism and the Modern Regulatory State," *Polity* 21(2) (Winter 1988): 373–400; David Vogel, "The Public-Interest Movement and the American Reform Tradition," *Political Science Quarterly* 95(4) (Winter 1980–81): 607–27.

28. See Stein, *Pivotal Decade*.

29. "Organizational Affiliations of Big Business Day Advisors and Directors," Box 10, USCOC; Author interview with Victor Kamber, 18 February 2010; William T. Poole, "The Corporate Democracy Act and Big Business Day: Rhetoric vs. Reality," Heritage Foundation, *Backgrounder #113*, 11 March 1980, available at <http://www.heritage.org/Research/Reports/1980/03/The-Corporate-Democracy-Act-and-Big-Business-Day-Rhetoric-and-Reality> (accessed 1 April 2010).

30. Ralph Nader, "A Growing Movement: International Labor Rights," 17 August 1999, available at *The Nader Page*, <http://www.nader.org/interest/081799.html> (accessed 1 April 2010).

31. Jules Bernstein, Mark Green, Vic Kamber, and Alice Tepper Marlin, "Conceptual Draft of the Corporate Democracy Act," in *The Big Business Reader: On Corporate America*, ed. Mark Green et al. (New York: Pilgrim Press, 1991), 500–511.

32. Karna Small to Richard Lesher, 29 January 1980.

33. Richard Breault to Washington Corporate Representatives, 25 January 1980, Box 10, USCOC; "Background Information on Anti-Business Day, April 17, 1980," Box 10, USCOC.

34. "Background Information on Anti-Business Day."

35. Michael Schippani to Friend, 6 March 1980, Box 10, USCOC.

36. "American Business is Small Business," unidentified article enclosed in "Background Information on Anti-Business Day."

37. "Background Information on Anti-Business Day."

38. Richard Breault to Members of the Chamber of Commerce, 9 April 1980, Box 10, USCOC.

39. "April 17 'Big Business Day' Professional Leftists Gang Up on Free Enterprise," *Human Events*; Kevin Lynch, "On the Left," *National Review*, 4 April 1980.

40. "Growth Day 1980: We Have Something Good to Say about America," Display Ad, *New York Times*, 2 April 1980, A12; John Howes, "Big Business Day," *Heritage in the News*, Spring 1980, Box 10, USCOC.

41. Mobil, "Something to Celebrate," Display Ad, *New York Times*, 17 April 1980, A27.

42. United Technologies, "Anti-Business Day," *Harper's* (April 1980): 1559.

43. Weather 1, *Washington Post*, 17 April 1980, C2.

44. "150 Cities to Hold Big Business Day Events," 10 April 1980, Press Release, Box 10, USCOC.

45. Robert A. Rosenblatt, "Critics and Defenders Turn Out for Big Business Day," *Los Angeles Times*, 18 April 1980; Merrill Brown, "Coalition Attacks Big Business," *Washington Post*, 18 April 1980.

46. The eleven companies were: Citicorp, Eli Lilly, Castle and Cooke, Occidental Petroleum, DuPont, U.S. Steel, American Electric Power, Winn-Dixie, Grumman, Exxon, and Fluor. Some accusations were explicit, such as the charge that U.S. Steel closed plants without giving advance notice to workers; others were more vague, such as Exxon's indictment, in Mark Green's words, "just for being Exxon" and DuPont's lobbying. (CEO Irving Shapiro also ran the Business Roundtable.) See Judith Miller, "Nader-Led Drive Aims at Business," *New York Times*, 10 April 1980.

47. "Big Business Day Convention Program, April 17, 1980," brochure in possession of the author. The author would like to thank John Richard and Ralph Nader of the Center for Study of Responsive Law in Washington, D.C., for supplying a copy of the program.

48. A. O. Sulzberger, Jr., "Critics and Proponents Mark Role of Business," *New York Times*, 18 April 1980.

49. Rosenblatt, "Critics and Defenders."

50. "Business: Nader's Antibusiness Bust," *Time*, 28 April 1980.

51. Kenneth B. Nobles, "Toyota Agrees on Union Workers to Construct Plant in Kentucky," *New York Times*, 28 November 1986. Kamber interview with author, 18 February 2010.

52. Ralph Nader, personal correspondence with author, 13 December 2009.

53. See Sean Wilentz, *The Age of Reagan: A History, 1974–2008* (New York: Harper Collins, 2008).

Epilogue

KIM PHILLIPS-FEIN AND JULIAN E. ZELIZER

Although the period covered by the essays in this book ends with the beginning of the first presidential administration of Ronald Reagan, many people today see the 1980s as the start of a new era of business power in politics. It was in this decade that an aggressive embrace of the private sector, a diminishing role for government regulation of the economy, and the widening chasm between rich and poor, all began to seem the most striking aspects of American capitalism. While contests remained over the political power of business, in the wake of the fall of the Soviet Union, an ideal of unregulated capitalism came to exercise a deep control on the national political imagination in a way that it had not done even at the height of the cold war.

Following the 1990s, these trends have only accelerated. The media has continually been filled with stories about how different business interests have been able to influence the regulatory agencies that remain in place and reap enormous economic benefits from tax breaks and direct subsidies. The vast expansion of the world of corporate interest groups has become a defining feature of the political landscape. With each presidential and congressional campaign, Americans learn about how wealthy donors have filled the coffers of candidates from both political parties. Today, many people assume that business power in politics is an inevitable, unavoidable part of contemporary political life—perhaps to be criticized, but nonetheless something that has been around forever and that arises naturally from the economic might of corporate America.

Yet by looking closely at business and its efforts to influence politics throughout the postwar years, the authors whose work is collected in this book demonstrate that the evident weight of business in political life today actually had to be carefully constructed over time. Even for business, wealth and social status do not automatically confer political power. This was especially true in the middle years of the twentieth century when other political forces, including organized labor, were able to expand their muscle. Business actors have thought long and carefully about how to organize to affect the government in the ways that they believe will be to their ultimate benefit. They have not been able to assume that the state is automatically theirs to operate; they have felt the need to find ways to shape it and to try to guide public opinion. They do not always agree, either. The content of business politics has changed over time and reflects many contests between regions, economic sectors, and ideological visions, even as it generally tends to be hostile to creating a state that has the power to effectively and independently challenge the authority of the private sector.

At the same time, the essays collected here show that there may be ways in which the political culture of the United States is especially hospitable to the political activities of business. The political power of business is not always (or only) a result of conscious mobilization. It arises, also, from the ways that the structure of government institutions, the nature of the democratic process, and the political ideas have shaped national debates. The broader context of American politics makes it easier for business to accomplish its political goals than many other social groups, giving business certain opportunities that are foreclosed to others.

Finally, the work gathered here suggests that understanding the power of business in politics today means looking back before 1980. Business mobilization for political ends is not new within American politics; it was an important part of the history of the postwar liberal era. As these essays show, business people were rarely pure antistatists. They sought, rather, to structure a regime that would serve what they believed were the interests of business, however they defined these. Often, they tried to insist that their interests were identical to the interests of the broader population, even as workers, consumers, civil rights activists, and environmentalists (among others) argued that what was good for business was not simply good for everyone else. The activism of business changed over time, and different business people pursued divergent courses at the same moment. The late 1940s efforts of oil evangelicals like R. G. LeTourneau, for example, coexisted with the Cleveland businessmen's grudging acceptance of antidiscrimination legislation. The labors of the businessmen around the Phoenix Chamber of Commerce to create a haven that could serve as an alternative to the New Deal took place even as the entrepreneurs of Miami sought a more effective police presence. In the 1970s, new business organizations such as the Business Roundtable were born as the pressures of the recession and the need to counter an aggressive public interest movement brought a new level of coordination to business politics. Today, the political organizing of business has become in many ways institutionalized, compared to the visceral and angry moment of the reaction against liberalism in the 1970s and the initial victories of the conservative movement. The work collected here indicates that analyzing business politics closely will yield insights into many periods throughout the postwar years, and that doing this historical work is necessary in order to understand the power of business in politics today. The nature and the content of postwar liberalism—as well as the conservative opposition to it—reflects the efforts of business people to make their perspectives felt in political life, even at moments when they were not at all sure that they would be able to succeed.

This volume is not intended to settle the many arguments and debates about how business operates in politics, to provide a complete description of the many battles and conflicts over political economy in the postwar years, or to advance a comprehensive theory for the role of business in American political life. Our goal has been both more modest and farther-reaching: to demonstrate the way that a field of archival research is opening up a new era in the study of political economy by showing the ways that analyzing the ideologies, activities, and institutions of business can transform our understanding of areas of political life that range from the tax code to evangelical Christianity, from economic regulations to the rise of law-and-order politics and beyond. Fine as it is, we anticipate that the work collected here will just be the beginning.

INDEX

Note: Material in tables is indicated by italic page numbers. Endnotes are indicated by n. after the page number.